CONCRETE DEMANDS

Between the 1950s and 1970s, Black Power coalesced as activists advocated a more oppositional approach to fighting racial oppression, emphasizing racial pride; asserting black political, cultural, and economic autonomy; and challenging white power. In *Concrete Demands,* Rhonda Y. Williams provides a rich, deeply researched history that sheds new light on this important social and political movement, and shows that the era of expansive Black Power politics that emerged in the 1960s had long roots and diverse trajectories within the 20th century.

Looking at the struggle from the grassroots level, Williams highlights the role of ordinary people as well as more famous historical actors, and demonstrates that women activists were central to Black Power. Vivid and highly readable, *Concrete Demands* is a perfect introduction to Black Power in the 20th century for anyone interested in the history of black liberation movements.

Rhonda Y. Williams is Associate Professor of History and Founder and Director of the Social Justice Institute at Case Western Reserve University. She is the author of *The Politics of Public Housing: Black Women's Struggles Against Urban Inequality,* and co-editor of *Teaching the American Civil Rights Movement: Freedom's Bittersweet Song* (Routledge).

CONCRETE DEMANDS

The Search for Black Power in the 20th Century

Rhonda Y. Williams

NEW YORK AND LONDON

First published 2015
by Routledge
711 Third Avenue, New York, NY 10017

and by Routledge
2 Park Square, Milton Park, Abingdon, Oxon OX14 4RN

Routledge is an imprint of the Taylor & Francis Group, an informa business

© 2015 Taylor & Francis

Library of Congress Cataloging-in-Publication Data
Library of Congress Cataloging in Publication Control Number:
2014027468

ISBN: 978-0-415-80142-3 (hbk)
ISBN: 978-0-415-80143-0 (pbk)
ISBN: 978-0-203-12222-8 (ebk)

Typeset in Bembo
by Apex CoVantage, LLC

CONTENTS

ACKNOWLEDGMENTS

This book, many years in the making, has gone through its own birth pangs and transformations. It began as another project—one I was supposed to complete in a couple of years—for Heather Ann Thompson's "Rethinking" series on American Social and Political Movements of the 20th Century. Time passed swiftly as I took on new responsibilities, particularly founding and directing the Social Justice Institute at Case Western Reserve University (CWRU). But even as I carved out time here and there to write, it became increasingly clear that the book Routledge signed was becoming something else. Heather and Kimberly Guinta (my awesome editor at Routledge) offered to pull the book out of the series, and let it become its own self. Throughout the entire process, they both have provided advice, cheerleading, and tremendous patience.

There were numerous witty and loving "thanks" I had imagined writing, but I now find myself in the unenviable position of having to cut, cut, cut! So forgive the primarily laundry-like list of names to follow. I appreciate all of you and, in the end, I figured you would rather I save as much of my word count for the story itself, and see less gushing praise. So here we go.

I finished *Concrete Demands* because of the people who inspired, encouraged, and hugged me—as well as this project. I want to give special thanks to David Goldberg (for sharing his research and trusting me with documents!), to Yohuru Williams (for the gazillion conversations, line edits, and Peanut Butter Crunch!), and to Megan Ritchie Jooste (by way of Heather) for her editing advice and encouraging emails.

At CWRU: graduate students Anthony Crumbley (who graduated), Michael Metsner, and Erik Miller helped with the research. Michael also helped prepare the bibliography. To Laila Haidarali, Jenifer Barclay, Shennette Garrett-Scott, and Shannen Dee Williams, all former fellows in the African American Studies

Postdoctoral Program in the College of Arts & Sciences. Numerous faculty and staff colleagues provided citations, spirit-support, victuals, or all three. They include Ken Ledford, Deepak Sarma, Joy Bostic, Pete Moore, Peter Haas, Janice Eatman Williams, Tanetta Andersson, Marilyn Sanders Mobley, Christine Ash, Latisha James, Chalana Gilliham, Allison George, Deborale Richardson Phillips, Shaii White, Misty Luminais, Kayode Omoyosi, and my dean Cyrus C. Taylor. Thalia Dorwick read the entire manuscript and shared her enthusiasm and feedback as a non-expert reader. "Mother" Krista Franklin's artistic energy moved me to create the book cover.

To the folk of "E.C." (East Cleveland) who checked on how the book and I were faring. They include many of the community researchers for the Social Justice Institute's "Voicing & Action Project": Brandon King, Michele Hill, Leslye Huff, Nancy Nolan-Jones, Lady Red Joy, Pamela Owens, LaVora Perry, Hank Smith, and Earl Williams. Also, Walter "Big Walt" Melton, Derrick Griffin, Caroline Cole, Rosey Terry, Belinda Kyle (for telling me about *The Black Power Mixtape*), Trevelle and Aiesha Harp, and Ndeda N. Letson.

I have been blessed by the generosity of a network of scholars beyond my current institution. They include Lisa Brock, Clarence Lang, Jama Lazerow, Erik McDuffie, Donna Murch, Derek Musgrove, Alondra Nelson, Karen Sotiropoulos, Robyn Spencer, Stephen Ward, and anonymous reviewers. To Peniel E. Joseph. To Ernie Allen, who shared with David Goldberg, who shared with me. To Sister Sonia Sanchez, Muhammad Ahmad, and Donald Freeman—for the stories. To Norma Freeman. To the archivists in the Washingtoniana Division of the D.C. Library who accommodated me at the last minute: John Muller and Derek Gray. To my U.S.-Australian Connection: "Coach" Dennis Harris, Cleveland Councilman Kenneth Johnson, Greg Langjhar, William Harris, Lori Urogdy Eiler, Dr. Colin Dillon, ("Dr. D"), John and Karla Brady, Trevelyn Brady, Leroy Loggins (my Baltimore homeboy who lives in Australia), Damien Bani, Paula Colby, and Michael Aird. Michael opened up his personal library to me as well as shared photos and stories about family. To my Colchester-UK Connection: Laila, John Haynes, Colin Samson, Michael Phillip, Candyce Kelshall, Dusan Radunovic, and Sanja Bahun.

To Dr. Mary Frances Berry, still my mentor and friend.

To Kevin C. Johnson and Rhonda D. Frederick. You know why.

To my nephew Darrell and niece Sherell Williams, who have both made me "A2." I love you. Now, how you gonna help make a better future, young people?

And, to My Trio, who remind me about laughing, and dancing, and smiling; listen to me go on-and-on about this and that; accept me for who I am and desire to be; and truly know my spirit and provide unconditional love: Thank you Mom and Dad—"Ginny" (Virginia L. Williams) and "Booney" (Nathaniel McAlister Williams Sr.)—and "Brotherman" (Nathaniel McAlister Williams Jr.). Because of you . . .

INTRODUCTION

I have never known a Negro in all my life who was not obsessed with black power.

—*James Baldwin (1968)*[1]

People just have to get used to that word, "Black Power."

—*Shirley Chisholm (1969)*[2]

In 1968 Amy Jacques Garvey published *Black Power in America* through United Printers Limited located on Marcus Garvey Drive in Kingston, Jamaica. The pamphlet's featured essay titled "The Source and Course of Black Power in America" began this way: "What depths of emotion a small word can evoke! Hate and love seem to take the highest rating of all. While words, by themselves, seem harmless, but combined with another they have explosive reaction." For instance, she explained, the use of the word "for" in the 40-year-old slogan "Africa for Africans" had profound implications. It challenged "European Imperialists in Africa" and served as "a hope and goal to Africa's sons and daughters all over the world." Similarly, "BLACK POWER now confronts the United States of America." She continued: "This slogan—in the minds of the whites—seems to conjure up black magic, as it strikes fear in their hearts, and even causes the Government to become concerned, as to what actions these two magic words may cause black citizens to commit."[3]

Thirty-five years later, ruminating on his own role in raising consciousness about Black Power, Kwame Ture (Stokely Carmichael) recalled the moment when he uttered "just two ordinary" words—black and power—at a June 1966 rally in Greenwood, Mississippi. Those words traversed the nation, and eventually the world, with lightning media speed. "Who could have thought it?" he observed. "I mean, two simple, clear, very commonly used English words. One an adjective, the other a noun. Basic. Nothing the least obscure or academically pretentious about them. Nothing mysterious or even slightly ambiguous either."[4]

Yet, as Amy Jacques Garvey, Stokely Carmichael, and others quickly discovered, the words black and power, while separately "harmless and inoffensive," had become "apparently incomprehensible in combination" and "entirely beyond the cognitive reach of the white national media and public."[5] Dr. Martin Luther King Jr. was among those who immediately offered an explanation for the growing public trepidation that accompanied the marriage of black to power. According to King, those two words together "give the impression that we are talking about black domination rather than black equality."[6]

The first black U.S. congresswoman, Shirley Chisholm, also offered her view. Shortly before mounting her 1972 campaign for the presidency, Chisholm reflected on the phrase in her speech at Howard University. "Everybody," she explained, "is so hysterical and panic stricken because of the adjective that precedes the word power—'black.'" She, then, offered her take: Black Power simply reflected black people's desires to control their destinies. So, that meant, "People just have to get used to that word, 'Black Power.'"[7] People also would have to get used to the word "power" in combination with many other adjectives that demanded dismantling race, ethnic, gender, and economic hierarchies and recognition of people's human rights. All of this, however, would be easier said (and arguably subverted) than done.

Jacques Garvey, Carmichael, King, and Chisholm, of course, were not the only ones trying to come to grips with the term. Lots of people had lots to say about Black Power, particularly after 1966. This did not mean, however, that they all understood it in the same way or could agree on a central definition. As Ture observed in 2003,

> Before the dust settled, this verbal combination would inspire scholarly debate, learned dissertations, hysterical denouncements from press and pulpit, and require us to write a number of explanatory essays and a book. We would discuss them on college campuses, in churches, and from all manner of public platforms and media forums; on national network television as well as local channels. Yet even today, I keep reading that "one major problem was that SNCC (or Carmichael) failed to define the term clearly."[8]

He clearly disagreed with this assessment, noting: "It sure do seem to me that I, along with a lot of the folk in SNCC, spent an entire term as chairman doing little else but defining Black Power." Where he and others ultimately "failed," he opined, was in producing "a definition that the opinion industry wanted to hear." Then, he proceeded to challenge the reigning political and historical narrative that depicted Black Power as a sinister rerouting of the black liberation struggle. With a characteristic, assertive wit, Ture stated: "But, c'mon gimme a break. We certainly did not change the entire direction of the black movement or the attitudes of black America merely by combining two simple words at a rally in Greenwood, Mississippi. That's silly and absurd, even for the American media."[9]

Amy Jacques Garvey clearly agreed. Her essay's full title—"The Source and Course of Black Power in America"—did not leave her readers guessing as to her broad goals in writing, nor did her analysis, which explicitly urged readers to consider the roots and routes of Black Power. Not surprisingly she privileged the impact of Marcus Garvey, boldly proclaiming that many of the new purveyors of Black Power "were Garvey's under-stud[ies]." She traced Black Power's genealogy as born from the rich and fertile soil of "Father and Mother Garveyites," and the aroused and angry "New Negro" to Malcolm X. She shared how Rev. King, who honored Garvey by placing a wreath at his shrine, had remarked, "He was the first man, on a mass scale, and level, to give millions of Negroes a sense of dignity and destiny."[10] She argued that white power and violence produced the political situations and oppressive conditions that fueled oppressed people's desires for national liberation. In other words, within two years of Black Power becoming a liberation slogan in 1966, Amy Jacques Garvey sought to proffer an initial history that drew attention to many decades, movements, and persons in the making. In her estimation, the specific arrival of the era of expansive Black Power politics had a history that extended back many decades into (if not before) the 20th century.

Amy Jacques Garvey's view was but one of many that sought to contextualize the movement. There were other persons, ideas, organizations, and events that seeded and inspired mid-1960s Black Power and influenced its proliferation and demise afterward. In the words of author Richard Wright, who himself published a travelogue on the independence struggles of the Gold Coast colony titled *Black Power* in 1954—a decade before Black Power became a rallying cry: "Expressions spring out of an environment, and events modify what is written by molding consciousness."[11] While Wright was talking explicitly about "Negro literature," political philosophies and struggles are also "written." Indeed, the overarching concepts and driving imperatives that emerged under the mantle of mid-1960s "Black Power"—including the phrase itself—were not wholly novel. Unarguably, the immediate politics and "social situations" of the mid-1960s contributed to the rise of Black Power. But so too did previous decades of struggles, generations of activists, philosophies, and shifting political cultures. In other words, the publicly heralded Black Power phase of the black freedom struggle has a history, progenitors, and complex pathways that expose, as I have written elsewhere, "its precursors, influences, overlaps, and coexistence with other activist traditions."[12]

A narrative synthesis for the reader versed and not so versed in this history, *Concrete Demands* seeks to chart the roots, routes, and expressions that comprise the search for Black Power politics in the 20th century. An ancestral and mapping project, it explores black people's various struggles to become self-determined, paying particular attention to the emergent streams and forerunners of the Black Power phase of the liberation struggle. It adds to a rich, nuanced, and growing body of scholarship on black freedom struggles that critically informed this narrative and to which I am indebted. These include studies on civil rights, Black Power, black nationalism and internationalism, black radicalism, and black women's struggles, including those on public housing and welfare rights.

What of this term, "Black Power"? Rooted in the broad search for empowerment for black people, "Black Power" is arguably a general and timeless goal. However, "Black Power" represents a historically contextualized set of oppositional ideologies and politics. Undergirded by race consciousness and pride, nationhood, self-determination, and sovereignty, Black Power is a politics in which black people placed less faith in white goodwill and paid more attention to the structures of power. In doing so, they demanded the authority to control decisions, as well as resources, impacting black people's lives and circumstances. While this has often meant mounting efforts to challenge if not alter regimes of oppression, it has not always resulted in (or even for some necessitated) transforming oppressive regimes.

For generations, there have always been black people who have hoped for liberty and struggled for rights and inclusion in a country that espoused it. However, the daily battles and indignities intrinsic to living in a white-controlled nation fertilized by notions of black inferiority and economic inequality also served as constant reminders of a different, murkier reality. In eras rife with nation-building, wars, and rights and liberation struggles, this murkier reality produced caution, angst, disgust, and desire—all of which gave rise to concrete demands and impassioned liberation struggles in a nation built on, and at times aggressively intent upon, maintaining racial and economic hierarchies. It fueled nationalist and radical struggles during the first half of the 20th century, as well as explicit articulations of "Negro" and Black Power between World War II and 1966. This signaled both the emergence and suppression of a robust unapologetic black politics that took center stage in the 1960s and 1970s era of expansive Black Power politics. By 1980 the zeitgeist of Black Power had publicly waned in the face of new political and economic forces.[13]

The narrative begins, in Chapter 1, in the early 20th century with a stark example of how black people experienced white power in the East St. Louis riot.[14] It occurred during an age when the United States and European nations were embroiled in wars for power, and when race and self-determination battles undergirded quests for national superiority. In this context, the East St. Louis riot of 1917 emerged as an exemplar of the profound racial anxiety and violence that reinforced the desire to preserve the United States as a nation where white people had power and black people remained powerless. While unfortunately there are numerous, diverse examples of racial antipathy that one could choose from, this particular incident of brutality provides a starting point to delineate a range of travails confronting black people, as well as introduce a rich and varied set of race-conscious and race-first political actors who expressed outrage and engaged in resistance.

There existed a continuum of concrete demands—urgent needs, things asked for, and questions raised. Those who responded held multiple, if not competing, ideologies and goals grounded in specific local and political contexts that fueled their quests for rights and power. In the early 20th century, the overlapping relationships among, for instance, Ida B. Wells, Hubert Harrison, the Garveys (including Marcus Garvey, Amy Ashwood Garvey, and Amy Jacques Garvey), and A. Philip Randolph offer just one example of how black empowerment ideas and strategies intersected. These race-conscious women and men would gain inspiration from each other, as well as part ways based on their views about the promise of U.S. liberty, their experiences with white power, and their belief in how to bring about change in the face of that power. Black people—far from a social, economic, and ideological monolith—tried to make sense of what they and others experienced every day.

By the early 1900s, white power had coalesced in the rise of Jim Crow and disfranchisement, the maturing of industrial and agricultural capital, the growth of the state and empire, and domestic and international conflicts. Black struggles for empowerment—to be self-determined people with measures of authority and respect—were always in dialogue with, though not limited in their imagination by, white power in the U.S. nation. Whether the focus was integration, separation, or expatriation, the concepts of self-determination and nationhood—either among black people or in relationship to the United States—stood at the center. In the opening decades of the 20th century, then, the political elements familiar in the era of expansive Black Power had been seeded. Race pride, militant cultural aesthetics, assertions of dignity that brooked no white counsel, black economic radicalism, self-defense, expressions of black manhood, proto-black feminism, and black nationalism and internationalism were all there. These ideas, frameworks, expressions, and strategies clashed, mingled, and merged, as did their purveyors who were influential progenitors of Black Power proliferation.

While *Concrete Demands* narrates, synthesizes, and analyzes "coming of age" and proliferation stories of Black Power, I do not claim to write a comprehensive study of the Black Power movement. There are historical actors, organizations, and campaigns that one will find underrepresented or even absent.[15] Even when engaged, they may not receive as full a treatment as some readers may seek or have come to expect. Such is the nature of narrative history.[16] An array of actors across time, space, ideology, gender, and social class are in dialogue in *Concrete Demands*. The story is as much about the changing context, roots, routes, and expressions that help us understand the popularizing of Black Power, as it is about the emergence of struggles in the Black Power era. Sometimes the historical actors and narrative undoubtedly will (and should) feel familiar and feature known incidents, campaigns, and organizations.

It is important to remember, however, that even when featuring the now "iconic" historical actors, they, too, were ordinary people—part of the masses navigating, braving, succumbing to, and battling the injustices throughout the United States and abroad at the time. They *became* iconic because their lives, voicing of issues, charisma, or courage either came to the attention of those in power, or influenced many seeking to change the status quo. This often catapulted them into the public eye—whether in their own historical time or as a result of historical investigation. But for all those who became icons, there are many more who have contributed to the struggle. We know that everyday people—those whose names are not as well known—confronted and in their own ways navigated the vitriol of white citizens and power structures. They appear as well.

Just as well-known and less celebrated people comprise *Concrete Demands,* so too do the voices of women and men who engaged in quests for power from the early 20th century through the era of expansive Black Power politics. Indeed, black women contributed in generative ways as intellectuals and mentors before 1966, alongside their roles as activists, cultural workers, and critics.[17] Black women espoused race-first, self-determination, and intersectional agendas—whether as militant rights activists, black nationalists, black radical feminists, or low-income rights and power advocates. They played vital activist roles in formal Black Power organizations and in struggles during the Black Power era. And while it almost seems trite to write, it behooves us to remember that just as within any group, black women's voices, political positions, and activism were varied. This, at times, meant that black women's activism did not *a priori* upend male privilege or patriarchy. When most edgiest, however, these race-conscious black women critiqued presumptions of race, gender, social class, and sexuality that too often reaffirmed exploitation and marginalized statuses.

This book examines intersections between the local and international, as well as traverses and links U.S. geographies, rural and urban. It does this while also spotlighting cities (those places paved in literal concrete) and the specific efforts that embody the philosophical streams and variety of struggles emerging particularly after 1966. By that time the majority of black people lived in towns and cities in the Upper South and in the North, Midwest, and West. For instance, Atlanta, Washington, D.C., Cleveland, Detroit, and New York are featured here as hubs and staging grounds for black consciousness, black electoral power, economic radicalism, and the grassroots politics of survival that raged from coast to coast.

Concrete Demands unfolds in two parts. Part One comprises the first three chapters, which examine the multiple persons, ideologies, reactions, and social situations that presaged and established the context for the eventual popular congealing and proliferation of those two words—"black" and "power"—that caused so much excitement and anxiety domestically and globally. These chapters focus on, in the words of Amy Jacques Garvey, "the sources and courses" of Black Power politics—that is, the roots and routes, as well as continuities and discontinuities, between eras and people.[18] For that most remembered historic cry in 1966 did not emerge out of nowhere on a sweltering summer day. This much Carmichael told us himself.

The seeds of Black Power were watered by individual and collective desires for racial affirmation, self-determination, and autonomy, and grew as a result of tenacious white illiberality and oppression. Moments of promise, advancement, and the potential of political and economic transformation affected black people's lives and demands. However, even then, there was a persistent underlying sense, born out by reality, that the United States as a "land of liberty" really belonged to the privileged few. These were the people who managed to wield and hold onto social, political, and economic power whether in the South or the presumed promised lands of the North, Midwest, or West.

Navigating these realities often meant that, as Richard Wright conveyed in a speech titled "The Psychological Reactions of Oppressed People" published in *White Man, Listen!* (1957), black people did a lot of "acting"—often to avoid "undue harm." These realities also revealed the persistent sense of oppression, both virulent and subdued, that ultimately produced screams from the margins. The sublimation "of aggressiveness," alongside faith in the potential of legal changes, would give way to more vocal responses against unjust treatment.[19] Witnessing how black people experienced the long and short arms of power in a racially constituted nation, in fact, is to comprehend why demands for race-first politics, consciousness, solidarity, pride, autonomy, and sovereignty continue to entrance black humanity and shape black activism.

The early 20th-century efforts for self-determination provided portents of Black Power struggles ahead. This does not mean that the 1960s' incarnations of Black Power were inevitable or predictable; only that upon examination, they had seeds in the social, political, and economic inequalities forged in the era of modern race relations and imperialism. There existed hopes that history would unfold differently. However, the squelching of these hopes for racial justice—whether as a result of outright white recalcitrance, gradualism, the recalibration of racism, or continued exclusions—would continuously feed demands for black autonomy and control.

After World War II and during the rise of the Cold War when anti-colonial, anti-imperialist, and worldwide black freedom struggles increased, the national question took on renewed vigor as it had in the first decades of the 20th century. As seen in Chapter 2, during this time, the phrases "Negro power" and "Black Power" made their initial public and print appearances courtesy of Paul Robeson and Richard Wright. However, black radical organizations and leftists such as Robeson, Wright, Claudia Jones (who wrote about black self-determination), and many others experienced censure. Nevertheless, this did not fully eliminate, even if it marginalized or suppressed, streams of black militancy, radicalism, or nationalism.

The attacks on black leftists arose at the same time that interracial, and at times anti-Communist, struggles for black rights, access, and acceptance blossomed. This is the context in which those active in rights and power struggles grew up and came of political age. Among the most recognized were Malcolm X, Frances Beal, Lorraine Hansberry, James Forman, Stokely Carmichael, Angela Davis, Max Stanford, Donald Freeman, Eldridge Cleaver, and Joanne Byron (Assata Shakur). Between the 1950s and June 1966, the ideologies, revolutionary struggles, and at times actual paths of veteran and neophyte activists crossed. As former Communist Party member and black nationalist Harold Cruse wrote in "Revolutionary Nationalism and the Afro-American" in his 1962 article in *Studies on the Left,* black people's search for power had to be rooted in the context and realities of the day or "the real conditions under which eighteen to twenty million Negroes in the United States live." Cruse captured the concrete conditions of black people when he wrote that black people consistently suffered "varying degrees from hunger, illiteracy, disease, ties to the land, urban and semi-urban slums, cultural starvation, and the psychological reactions to being ruled over by others" neither of "their kind," nor by those kindly disposed to their liberation.[20]

The years 1963 to 1966 covered in Chapter 3 emerged as a prolific period of activist upsurge and proliferation of Black Power philosophies, strategies, and networks. "Now" met "Mississippi Goddam" met *The Fire Next Time,* the March on Washington, and the Negro revolt. Distinct (but overlapping) in cultural and political expressions, each catchphrase, song, book title, event, and insurgency revealed an increasing urgency, declining patience, and unapologetic desire for black control and autonomy. New questions took precedence, including the following: Who does and who should control decision-making authority, resources, and wealth? Who should decide the terms of black living? Will the status quo ever dismantle itself?

The sentiments that emerged in 1966, then, in the rallying cry of "Black Power!" were not only firmly grounded in the experiences that punctuated black lives and freedom struggles for many decades, but also produced the particular child of the post–World War II era. Providing a longer narrative arc exposes not just the activists and organizations, but also Black Power's coming of age process with stages of development, contingencies, ruptures and continuities, *and* historical markers that help to expose a rich and nuanced story—not necessarily a lengthier story without distinctions.[21]

After June 1966 and in the midst of the substantial media and public attention given to "Black Power," the era of expansive Black Power began. Part Two of *Concrete Demands* focuses on the time period from 1966 through the mid-to-late 1970s, with each chapter providing a different yet overlapping slice of the history of Black Power politics and struggles in the Black Power era. Chapter 4 narrates the "arrival" of Black Power as a rallying cry and the issues, organizations, campaigns, and intellectual and cultural expressions that proliferated in its wake. Chapter 5 explores divergent urban Black Power struggles; Chapter 6 documents Black Power's international routes, networks, and impacts; and Chapter 7 explores the intra-racial critiques and limits of politics in the Black Power era. The post-1966 years were marked by what historians refer to as the Black Power movement, the result of generations of empowerment ideas and efforts. These efforts had to be seeded and watered, blossom and wither, cross-pollinate and grow anew until the moment when the Black Power phase of the black liberation struggle flourished in the wake of the "right" mix of people, circumstances, and quite frankly communication and media networks. This was a time when masses of people were on the move. Black people talked, wrote, theorized, and engaged in Black Power organizations and power struggles during that era. Not all of them would claim the mantle of Black Power, even as they waged battles for self-determination and different forms of control such as poor people power, women power, and community power. Yet they were all responding to changing political and economic structures of white supremacy, expressions and realities of democracy, and impositions of empire domestically and globally.

For this reason, then, *Concrete Demands* consistently seeks to call out of the shadows forms of white power structured by ideology, race, economics, and gender, as well as regimes of subjugation, violence, and control. It explores how the search for power and the cry of Black Power did not simply flip the script or mimic white power. It was much more complicated than that. While anyone could generate and espouse a language of racial dislike, having the power and apparatus to replicate a power structure to enforce inequality was entirely another matter. Whether one agrees, understands, has knowledge about, or subscribes to the philosophies, strategies and tactics, or rhetoric that sought power for black people in the 20th century, the struggles carried out under its broad umbrella and in the specific era of its proliferation emerged out of black people's racial and economic realities—the evidence of things done.

As the Chinese-American radical activist Grace Lee Boggs maintained, echoing the views of C.L.R. James, the Caribbean Marxist intellectual: With regard to struggles for power and liberation, the "ideas that matter are created by individuals in particular historical circumstances to cope with their conditions of life."[22] Black people, then, have attempted to address concrete demands, if not at times reinventing, even transforming, their lives in rural and urban communities at home and abroad. Their journeys were exhilarating and turbulent, life-inspiring and deadly, sometimes forward-looking, other times retrograde, impactful one way or the other, and by all means illuminating. It is to those Black Power journeys that grew up and waned in the 20th century, but still have no end in sight, that *Concrete Demands* now turns.

Notes

1 James Baldwin, "Black Power," in *The Cross of Redemption,* ed. Kenan, 81.
2 Shirley Chisholm, "Speech at Howard University," in *Say It Loud!,* ed. Ellis, 107–108.
3 Amy Jacques Garvey, *Black Power in America,* 4.
4 Carmichael with Thelwell, *Ready for the Revolution,* 523.
5 Ibid., 524.
6 King, *Where Do We Go From Here: Chaos or Community?* (1967), in *Testament of Hope,* ed. Washington, 574.
7 Shirley Chisholm, "Speech at Howard University."
8 Carmichael with Thelwell, 524.
9 Ibid.
10 Amy Jacques Garvey, *Black Power in America,* 7–8.

11 Wright, *White Man, Listen!*, in *Black Power: Three Books from Exile*, 747.

12 Rhonda Y. Williams, "Black Women, Urban Politics, and Engendering Black Power," in *The Black Power Movement*, ed. Joseph, 82.

13 This is not the first study to attempt linking strains of black protest, and specifically black nationalist struggles in the early 20th century, with the rise of Black Power in the mid-to-late 1960s. See Amy Jacques Garvey, *Garvey and Garveyism*; Vincent, *Black Power and the Garvey Movement*.

14 In this way, *Concrete Demands* departs from other studies that begin their exploration of the origins of the Black Power movement during or after World War II. See Joseph, *Waiting 'Til the Midnight Hour*.

15 For instance, there is a growing literature on the black campus movement. See Biondi; Bradley; Rogers; and Rojas.

16 Hopefully the bibliography will help guide readers who seek more information on a specific person or organization. This scholarship is rich and only continues to grow. For a sampling of the scholarship published in my last year of writing, see Horne, *Black Revolutionary*; Joseph, *Stokely*; Theoharis, *The Rebellious Life of Mrs. Rosa Parks*; and Plummer, *In Search of Power*. Junior scholars are crafting exciting studies that will contribute to the scholarship on Black Power and black liberation movements. Examples include Joshua Guild's study on Shirley Chisholm, Robyn C. Spencer's forthcoming book on the Black Panthers as well as her new project on the black anti-war and anti-draft movement, Sherie M. Randolph's study on Florynce Kennedy, Stephen Ward's study on James and Grace Lee Boggs, Tanisha C. Ford's research on black culture, fashion, and rights and power politics, and Anne-Marie Angelo's work on the Black Panthers in Israel, the United Kingdom, and the United States.

17 On black women nationalists and radicals, see Taylor; Gore; McDuffie; and Davies. On black women and civil rights, see Lee; Ransby; and Collier-Thomas. On black women and Black Power, see Sharon Harley, "'Chronicle of a Death Foretold': Gloria Richardson, the Cambridge Movement, and the Radical Black Activist Tradition," in *Sisters in the Struggle*, eds. Collier-Thomas and Franklin; Angela D. LeBlanc-Ernest, "'The Most Qualified Person to Handle the Job': Black Panther Party Women, 1966–1982," and Tracye Matthews, "'No One Ever Asks, What a Man's Role in the Revolution Is': Gender and the Politics of the Black Panther Party, 1966–1971," both in *The Black Panther Party [Reconsidered]*, ed. Charles E. Jones; Kimberly Springer, "Black Feminists Respond to Black Power Masculinism," Stephen Ward, "The Third World Women's Alliance: Black Feminist Radicalism and Black Power Politics," and Rhonda Y. Williams, "Black Women, Urban Politics, and Engendering Black Power," all in *The Black Power Movement*, ed. Joseph. Also see Springer, *Living for the Revolution: Sisters in the Struggle*, eds. Collier-Thomas and Franklin; and *Want to Start a Revolution?*, eds. Gore, Theoharis, and Woodard.

18 Ula Taylor references tracing the roots and routes of black modernity, as articulated by Paul Gilroy, in her examination of intellectual pan-African feminists Amy Ashwood Garvey and Amy Jacques Garvey. Taylor, "Intellectual Pan-African Feminists," in *Time Longer than Rope*, ed. Payne and Green, 177.

19 Wright, *White Man, Listen!*, 671.

20 Harold Cruse, "Revolutionary Nationalism and the Afro-American," *Studies on the Left* 2:3 (1962): 12–25.

21 There is no questioning the influence of the "long movement" frameworks on historical narratives and historiographies of the civil rights and Black Power movements. However, a strident rebuttal has warned that continuously lengthening the chronological framework of movements can result in the loss of historical specificity as well as the ability to diagnose the limits and challenges of the struggle. I refrain from "allying" my study with either tendency. One of my goals is to document resurgent and multiple streams of broad ideas and strategies that not only traverse time, but also expose

the context and direct and indirect lineages—either through persons or ideas—of the proliferation of Black Power in the 1960s and 1970s. There exist ruptures and discontinuities as well, and these speak to the particularities of time, place, and political and economic conditions. On the "long movement" framework, see, for instance, Dowd Hall; Singh; and Theoharis and Woodard's edited volume *Freedom North*. For a critique of the potential pitfalls of a "long movement" framework, see Cha-Jua and Lang.

22 Grace Lee Boggs and C.L.R. James would eventually split over ideological differences. Grace Lee Boggs, *Living for Change,* 45.

PART I
Roots & Routes

1

A MAD SOCIETY

Crucibles and Portents of Black Power

Let the world know that "we are Negroes and beautiful."

—*Amy Jacques Garvey (1926)*[1]

Black people clamored at the murderous outrage in the almost 141-year-old republic. Just days before Independence Day in 1917, one of the most violent racial conflagrations of the 20th century exploded in East St. Louis, Illinois, just across the Mississippi River from St. Louis, Missouri. A growing black migrant population in the urban South and North and the attendant contest for jobs increasingly spurred white worker resentment. During World War I, labor strife had resulted in white workers striking in cities, and white employers hiring black strikebreakers. In East St. Louis, white workers believed that the city "must remain a white man's town."[2] The specter of black competition and expressions of black autonomy, alongside black people's increase in numbers, upset the white order of things.

On July 1, armed white joyriders decided to travel through black neighborhoods and fire on black homes. Returning gunfire, black residents apparently killed two white police officers. The next day the melee amped up. White people shot, assaulted, and killed black men, women, and children. They attacked black businesses and torched black homes in Black Valley, as the "Negro" part of East St. Louis was called. On this particular occasion in 1917, in the midst of a global war that the United States had entered just three months before, black people had confronted a barrage of homegrown violence. Facing a racial scourge that spread unchecked, many black people fled elsewhere. Some stayed and fought. When it was all over, 39 black and nine white people lay dead—a travesty spurred by racial hatred and economic competition.

News traveled. While the epicenter of the incident was East St. Louis, black people's outrage issued from elsewhere in the country, thereby exposing the linked concerns of black people across geographical boundaries. "In the shadow of the awful calamity at East St. Louis," the Negro Fellowship League in Chicago quickly posted bulletins inviting people to gather in its Reading Room at 3005 State Street to pass a resolution from the "colored citizens of Chicago." The league charged public officials with "reckless indifference" and "call[ed] upon press, pulpit and moral forces to demand . . . punishment." The league's founder, Ida B. Wells-Barnett, chaired that meeting. A black anti-lynching and women's rights activist, she followed her own suggestion to take a trip to East St. Louis to gather facts about the atrocity. Immediately upon her arrival, she met numerous black women who began sharing their stories. These laundresses; mothers; widows; and wives of boiler washers, warehouse workers, graders, railroad workers, and packing house workers invited her into their burned out and looted residences where they described beatings, shootings, and people fleeing for their lives.[3]

Wells-Barnett's trip resulted in a pamphlet that provided "damning descriptions" of the melee that claimed one too many black lives.[4] *The East St. Louis Massacre: The Greatest Outrage of the Century* drew on over 50 interviews. There was Mrs. Emma Ballard, whose husband George worked for the Kansas City Railroad. The Ballards had four children and lived in "a six room house, nicely furnished" with a piano. The cries of "Come out, niggers" by the mob between midnight and 1 a.m., alongside seeing 14 men beaten and two killed, sent her and her children packing. Emma Ballard later found her husband in St. Louis, where they decided to stay. James Taylor told of seeing two black men who were coming home from work at 4:15 a.m. hung by a white mob from a telegraph pole and shot to pieces. He also told of black women being pulled off of streetcars after which "stalwart men jumped on their stomachs and finished them by tramping them to death."[5] At a time when purity, piety, and submissiveness defined the Victorian ideal of white middle-class womanhood, black women lived outside the bounds of protection.

All manner of black women and men responded to East St. Louis—from those in the working class to the middle class, to economic radicals, and nationalists. The interracial National Association for the Advancement of Colored People (NAACP) organized a mass Silent Protest Parade in New York and also published a report titled "Massacre at East St. Louis" in its *Crisis* magazine. Founded in 1909, the NAACP became a prominent civil rights organization that waged legal campaigns to contest black exclusion and fight for integration. The *Crisis* was its media arm. Its editor, sociologist and NAACP co-founder W.E.B. Du Bois, reported on East St. Louis and spoke out. Others did as well.

At the Liberty League's July Fourth rally at the Metropolitan Baptist Church in New York, the league's founder, black socialist Hubert Harrison, unveiled the first edition of *The Voice: A Newspaper for the New Negro* in which he penned an editorial about the goings-on in East St. Louis. Harrison not only called for armed self-defense—"Negroes must kill white men in defense of their lives and property"—but also argued that black people should hit whites in the "pocketbook." They should withdraw whatever money they have from local savings banks and redeposit it elsewhere. Condemning freedom U.S. style, Harrison wrote: "This nation is now at war to make the world 'safe for democracy,' but the Negro's contention in the court of public opinion is that until this nation itself is made safe for twelve million of its subjects, the Negro, at least, will refuse to believe in the democratic assertions of the country. The East St. Louis pogrom gives point to this contention."[6]

The soon-to-be leader of the largest mass black nationalist organization, Marcus Garvey, called the East St. Louis massacre "a crime against the laws of humanity," "the laws of the nation," "Nature," and "the God of all mankind."[7] Garvey co-founded the Universal Negro Improvement Association (UNIA) and African Communities Imperial League in 1914 in Jamaica with Amy Ashwood, whose parents' house often served as a base for meetings.[8] Upon immigrating to the United States, she helped Garvey build the U.S.-based UNIA as well. Appalled by the assault on black life in East St. Louis, Marcus Garvey asserted: "This is no time for fine words, but a time to lift one's voice against the savagery of a people who claim to be the dispensers of democracy."[9]

These particular black women and men, who only later became iconic leaders in the fight for black freedom, not only met and influenced each other, but also on occasion shared the same public stage as they battled white supremacy. The year before the East St. Louis pogrom, Marcus Garvey and Ida Wells-Barnett had met in Chicago, where she lived. Apparently, Wells-Barnett had "impressed" Garvey with her "determined militancy, initiative, and proven track record on the lynching problem."[10] In a 1917 article, Garvey praised her "among others, as being 'conscientious workers . . . whose fight for the uplift of the race is one of life and death.'"[11] In November 1918, not only did Wells-Barnett speak at a UNIA meeting with Garvey and trade unionist A. Philip Randolph, but the UNIA also appointed her and Randolph as delegates to the Versailles Peace Conference. The State Department, however, denied them passports.[12]

This diverse group of, at times, incongruous compatriots—integrationists, nationalists, and socialists—sought freedom for black people. Indeed, they shared a commitment to challenging white supremacy and advancing black equality and racial pride. They did not, however, always agree on how to achieve this broad purpose. In fact, how they imagined their status relative to white people in the United States and each other often led to different claims, end goals, and even fractious battles and critiques. Therein lies the portentous power embedded in the representative responses and interactions of Wells-Barnett, Du Bois, Harrison, Randolph, and Garvey. Intended to protect, liberate, advance, and fortify black people, such anti-racist struggles included black women's radical critiques against race, gender, and class oppression; liberal and nationalist demands for self-determination (whether economically, territorially, culturally, or institutionally); and tactics from civil disobedience to self-defense. These social struggles, as well as the complexity of political alliances forged, sustained, terminated, and forgotten over time, expose the overlaps as well as the range of progenitors, positions, platforms, and unresolved issues that prepared the soil for the emergence of post–World War II rights and power struggles.

The travesty of East St. Louis, and the impromptu and organized, quotidian and organizational reactions to it, spotlighted the concrete experiences of being black in the United States. Black people's hopes for an unqualified freedom in the face of tenacious white illiberality produced concrete demands. This included establishing self-reliant and autonomous black institutions and communities sometimes within and other times separate from the United States. Throughout the early to mid-20th century, white supremacist political, economic, and social relations consistently thwarted black people's desire for dignity, joy, safety, and fairness. This was so whether in East St. Louis, Chicago, New York, or in other rural and urban home-places across the nation. Such stark realities, at the very time that the United States was making the world safe for democracy, rendered questionable the nation's ability to extend justice to black people.

In the early 20th century, racial segregation, violence, and imperial expansion helped water black militancy, global anti-racism, and nationalist ideologies and struggles—all of which would have to cross-pollinate to create political and social environments that produced the era of expansive Black Power politics in the 1960s and 1970s. The philosophies and actions of race-conscious and proud black people in the early 1900s would help seed the soil.

Race-Conscious Black People

While the deadly strife of 1917 registered as an outrage, it was not as if black people at the turn of the 20th century and in the early 1900s experienced something totally new. Black communities had to consistently navigate the daily offenses, personal indignities, and systemic inequalities that followed on the heels of centuries of enslavement. After the Civil War and Reconstruction, many generations of black people devised multiple and divergent strategies to survive and experience joy and autonomy, and in the 20th century this included advancing their economic stations and fighting for freedom unqualified by race. These race-conscious intellectuals and activists made countless demands for personhood, citizenship, nationhood, and respect. As they did so, they experienced legal and extralegal terror. Violence was part of a broader cache of mundane practices and institutional behaviors that became more entrenched through modernized forms of de jure and de facto racism in the post-slavery era. Wells-Barnett's early experiences and ongoing activism poignantly and aptly convey these realities.

This daughter of enslaved parents not only reported on, but also personally suffered the wrath of, state-sanctioned inequality and mob violence. As the story goes: In 1884 the single Ida B. Wells had purchased a ticket for the first-class car, or "ladies car," on the Chesapeake and Ohio Railroad. She took her seat on the Memphis-bound train and waited for her ticket to be collected. When the white conductor reached her, he asked her to move. Wells refused, and a struggle ensued. It ended with the conductor dragging her from the ladies car to the rousing applause of white passengers—but not before she bit that conductor's hand and fought valiantly against two other white men who handled and removed her. Wells sued the railroad, and actually won a $500 settlement. The Tennessee Supreme Court, however, reversed the decision on appeal. Wells's case preceded the landmark U.S. Supreme Court case *Plessy v. Ferguson* (1896) by not quite a decade. In order to test state-mandated segregation, Homer Plessy bought a first-class ticket—that is, for travel in the white section of the train. He was arrested and, in his case, the U.S. Supreme Court upheld legalized segregation, thereby establishing the "separate but equal" clause. Efforts to redeem and exalt the nation as white began to suffocate hopes for black social and political equality that had accompanied the Thirteenth, Fourteenth, and Fifteenth amendments and Reconstruction.

The same year as the Plessy incident in 1892, Ida Wells became an exile from her home in Memphis. Already an outspoken journalist 25 years before the East St. Louis massacre, Wells had written an editorial in her newspaper, the *Free Speech*, that publicly critiqued white people for their murderous behavior, particularly the lynching of three black businessmen—Calvin McDowell, Henry Stewart, and Thomas Moss, owners of the People's Grocery. The store was a concrete incarnation of the drive to establish independent black businesses, provide needed goods to the black community, and achieve financial security while integrating into the U.S. capitalist economy. On these scores, the store did not fundamentally challenge racial segregation or the U.S. economic order—even if it sold groceries at more reasonable prices. However, it did (as had black attempts to engage in the political process) upset race relations by threatening white economic control. Unlike the masses of black people who labored primarily as agricultural and service workers, these black entrepreneurs possessed some economic means. Whites killed Moss, McDowell, and Stewart for their audacity, that is, opening a store in Memphis that competed against a white proprietor and using weaponry to defend themselves against white assault. Moss was Wells's friend, and his and his partners' deaths incensed her.

Wells's activism and strident critique of racism and its political and economic impact on black people anticipated traditions of militant civil rights activism and black feminism that influenced Black Power politics. In the early 20th century, she argued that white men deployed the oft-used excuse for lynching—charges of rape—to justify their heinous acts. After her speak-truth-to-power article, not only did white mobs run her newspaper partner out of Memphis and destroy their office, but they also threatened to kill Wells if she ever returned. Wells did not return, but neither did she halt her activism. In her pamphlets, she revealed the threadbare lies of lynching law that subjugated black manhood *and* black womanhood. She gained international renown for vociferously questioning the racial, gender, class, and political status quos.[13] As far as Wells was concerned, black women and men unquestionably deserved fair and humane treatment as U.S. citizens. If they had to use protest, the courts, the media, or even firepower to confront white power, this is what they must do.

Race-conscious politics and black militancy pervaded the early 20th century, an era that Rayford Logan referred to as the "nadir" (1875 to 1920). During these decades, white society gutted black civil and voting rights, and Jim Crow governed social and political relations. Race also shaped monopoly capitalism, labor practices, and employment opportunities (or lack thereof) whether in personal household, industrial, agricultural, or prison economies. Such racial exploitation, whether through domestic or laundress work, low wages, debt peonage or sharecropping, or convict leasing, made possible the amassing of industrial and corporate wealth in the late 19th and early 20th centuries, as well as afterward.

As a race-first socialist in the age of capitalist expansion and proletarian revolutions, Hubert Harrison vigorously challenged black people's subjugation by white supremacists, politicians, and even white economic radicals. Born in 1883 in St. Croix, Virgin Islands (which became a territorial possession of the United States in 1917), Harrison had become a quick study of mainland U.S. Jim Crow and class politics as a black laborer. He moved to New York in his late teens and began working jobs as a hotel hall boy and elevator operator. He earned his diploma through night school and worked for a short time as a postal clerk. In 1909, the same year as the founding of the NAACP, Harrison joined the Socialist Party. Five short years later, Harrison resigned (or was expelled) after growing "disgusted by the party's lack of commitment to black workers and the New York leadership's racist treatment of him."[14] Committed to an anti-racist labor struggle, Harrison aligned himself with radical organizations that addressed race and class, if not always both simultaneously. He joined the International Workers of the World (IWW) or "Wobblies," and became editor of the UNIA newspaper, the *Negro World*. While Harrison would eventually leave the Garveyite fold, in 1917 the UNIA still animated him—as it did many other black working-class people, native and immigrant to the North and South, who lived under U.S. apartheid.

The UNIA had a black nationalist approach. It desired to advance black people and their economic positions. However, the UNIA did not focus on building black worker solidarity or challenging industrial exploitation through socialism. Instead, in this age of nation-building, the UNIA built its following by regaling black working-class people with nationalistic language, symbolism, pageantry of racial pride (specifically esteeming dark-skinned black people who are often disparaged in a color-conscious world); the organization also advocated for black political autonomy and building an independent black economy. Co-created by Marcus Garvey's future wives Amy Ashwood and Amy Jacques and kept alive well into the 1960s, Garveyism and the UNIA's brand of black nationalism focused on institution-building, cultural affirmation, and self-sufficiency. It captured the imaginations and support of the laboring masses and directly influenced future generations of Black Power progenitors and acolytes.

The existence of race-conscious devotees—whether integrationist "race women" and "race men," black nationalists, or black socialists—exposed the common belief that race unjustly shaped opportunities in the United States. Such agreement, however, did not mean they concurred on how to contest white supremacy. Like for all human actors, life's circumstances and political milieu shaped the concrete demands of black activists. Born in 1887 in St. Ann's Bay, a rural town in Jamaica, Marcus Garvey became a printer's apprentice at 14 years of age and eventually a foreman, but was blacklisted from the industry after siding with workers during a 1907 strike.[15] Over the next eight years, he founded two unsuccessful newspapers, worked on a Costa Rican banana plantation, protested worker exploitation, traveled to London, and found his calling as a "race leader" after reading Booker T. Washington's *Up From Slavery*. Garvey had hoped to meet Washington, the father of Tuskegee Institute, but arrived in the United States in March 1916, four months after his death. Washington endorsed economic self-sufficiency and publicly prioritized black industry and vocation over fighting for the franchise, civil rights, and higher education. While Washington accommodated segregation publicly, he focused on amassing political power and wealth through industry, labor, and autonomous black institutions. He became a political broker through his Tuskegee machine and by serving as a racial mediator and gatekeeper until his death in 1915. White politicians looked to him for advice on appointments, and white benefactors provided him with resources.

Washington's public adherence to racial accommodation in an era of white terror and control in the South represented yet another strategy of black advancement. It, however, unnerved and galvanized other black leaders. The black nationalist Bishop Henry McNeal Turner viewed Washington's stance on race relations as a betrayal of black liberty, but not because Turner believed in the democratic promise of the United States. The perils and lessons of Reconstruction, Redemption, and new U.S. imperial ventures undermined any such faith. In fact, Turner held little hope that the United States would treat black people fairly, and proposed racial separatism and expatriation to Liberia. In doing so, Turner presaged Garvey's Back-to-Africa movement and espoused what scholar Wilson Jeremiah Moses has described as classical black nationalism with its emphases on civilizing, missionizing, and reclaiming black Africa.

Other activists like Callie House (born enslaved in 1861) would also adamantly disagree with any hint of accommodating to white supremacy. She considered the exercise of black political rights essential to assuage black suffering. For almost 20 years, since 1896, the Nashville-born Callie House (nee Guy) had fought for pensions for ex-slaves through the National Ex-Slave, Mutual Relief and Bounty Pension Association. Based in her home state of Tennessee, the association represented hundreds of thousands of black working-class and poor people in the fight to secure wages for unpaid labor under slavery and service during the Civil War.

As historian Mary Frances Berry writes, in helping to launch the first mass struggle for reparations, House paid dearly for her activism; those who antagonized the status quo often did. Herself a washerwoman, House's concrete demand—for reparations—positioned her as a target of government repression.[16] In 1916, the same year that Washington died of high blood pressure, the government indicted House on charges of supposedly circulating fraudulent notices promising pensions. She would serve a year in prison. Shortly thereafter, Marcus Garvey arrived in the United States. The East St. Louis riot had not yet taken place.

Race Nationalisms and Pan-Africanism

One among many black migrants from the South and Caribbean, Marcus Garvey, the soon-to-be premier proselytizer of black nationalism and racial separatism, settled in Harlem. This mecca of black life experienced a cultural flowering prompted in part by the rise of consumer culture and leisure made possible by industrial rationalization. Harlem was also, however, a burgeoning racial "ghetto" where waves of black migrants concentrated in an area about 50 blocks long and eight blocks wide. In fact, Harlem had single blocks where up to 7,000 people lived mostly in overcrowded apartments and furnished rooms.[17] Garvey himself had roomed with a Jamaican family when he first arrived in Harlem. Earning meager wages, some tenants held rent parties, which provided a way to have fun with friends while raising enough money to pay exorbitant rents. Economic inequality had become normal fare; so too had racial terror.

By the time of Garvey's immigration to the United States, the Ku Klux Klan (KKK) had been reborn and extended its wrath to all non-white Anglo-Saxon Protestants. The number of lynchings increased in the South, where most black people still lived. While the majority of black agricultural workers toiled on land that was not theirs, a significant number of black farms existed. By 1890 black people who sought and gained homesteads in the South after the Civil War owned about 121,000 farms and had formed a farmers' alliance and union. Two decades later, this increased to nearly 219,000 farms owned by one million black farmers covering almost 15 million acres. By 1920 black farmers owned 14 percent of all U.S. farms.[18] This brought not only measures of independence, but also racial resentment.

Legal oppression buttressed by racist cultural propaganda also proliferated during this era. To great white acclaim, D. W. Griffith had released his and the country's first full-length feature film, *Birth of a Nation,* in 1915. Based on Thomas Dixon Jr.'s *The Clansman* (1905), the film presented the Civil War as a lost cause, the removal of black people (depicted as uppity, savage, and simple-minded) from office as appropriate, and the reunification of the North and South into a white nation as a triumph. This message resonated with white espousers of racial superiority, who believed black people incapable of possessing the intellect to wield political power. It also reaffirmed racial and economic hierarchies as natural and appropriate.

President Woodrow Wilson applauded Griffith's film as an accurate depiction of history. This was not out of step with Wilson's drive for racial empire. The same year that Wilson lauded *Birth of a Nation,* he sent troops to occupy Haiti, the first Caribbean nation to gain independence from slavery through black revolt in the early 1800s. An architect of the League of Nations after World War I, Wilson advocated racial self-determination for white nations, but not people of color, who were inferior subjects in their empires. This was part of the race-based logic and character of U.S. democracy. Hubert Harrison understood this, admonishing black people not to be "silly fools" and "gird up [their] loins" for the fight against the "evils" of "lynching, disfranchisement and segregation" on U.S. soil.[19]

Even so, the propaganda of U.S. freedom lured migrants and immigrants who imagined better lives. This included Marcus Garvey. During his early years in Harlem, he met Wells, Randolph, and Harrison, and in September 1917 after the East St. Louis horror, he launched the UNIA in the United States. Then, Garvey began crisscrossing the country to recruit followers. By the late 1920s even East St. Louis would boast its own UNIA chapter.[20]

The 21-year-old Amy Jacques also immigrated to the United States from Jamaica. She would become a key theoretician and steward of Garveyism and a forgotten bridge to the post–World War II era of pan-Africanism and Black Power politics. Amy Jacques boarded the SS *Carrilo* in Kingston Harbor in 1917. Five days later, her ship debarked at Ellis Island. When she arrived in New York, she encountered a city of growing black ethnic diversity, with Caribbean immigrants meeting southern black migrants and native black city dwellers—not always on amiable terms. This diaspora of black people crossed paths on the streets, in stores, at work and play, and in the neighborhoods.

Although black migrants and immigrants' experiences varied, as black people they similarly encountered racial inequality. This included overcrowded neighborhoods—like those in Harlem—and inadequate housing, scarce or low-wage jobs (primarily domestic service for black women), marginal schools, and racial violence. These matters, which influenced black people's daily realities, expose the concrete roots of black hardships and political activism.

"New Negro" militancy grew, including among black male veterans who returned from war only to discover that their lives and well-being still meant little to most white Americans. NAACP leader and black poet James Weldon Johnson dubbed 1919 the "Red Summer"—when at least two-and-a-half dozen race riots exploded. Such white hostility, however, met black militancy. Jamaican poet Claude McKay captured this fighting spirit in his famous poem "If We Must Die": "Like men we'll face the murderous, cowardly pack, Pressed to the wall, dying, but fighting back." This same poem many decades later inspired militant civil rights and Black Power activists such as James Forman of the Student

Nonviolent Coordinating Committee (SNCC) and Assata Shakur of the Black Panther Party and Black Liberation Army.

The UNIA propagated the message of early 20th century New Negro militancy, and attracted proud race-conscious black people. This included Amy Jacques who, after hearing Marcus Garvey speak, became a diehard black nationalist town crier. This life-changing moment occurred for her on a Sunday in New York in 1919. She went to the 6,000-seat Liberty Hall on 138th Street, paid her 35-cent admission, and listened rapturously to the burly, dark-skinned man who lectured before her.[21] While it is unclear exactly what Marcus Garvey talked about that particular day, he likely shared some of the UNIA's proposed solutions to black people's second-class citizenship—all predicated on developing an "independent base of operations" and building a black nation "that will stand out signally, so that other races and nations can see, and if they will not see, then feel."[22] With attention to black unity, pride, and economic advancement, the UNIA also tapped into the powerful global desires for national wealth and racial self-determination prevalent during the initial decades of the 20th century. This meant operating independent institutions such as grocery stores, laundries, restaurants, a printing plant and newspapers, a steamship line, and even a doll company.[23]

Within three years, and only months after Amy Ashwood and Marcus Garvey divorced (they had separated after three months of marriage in early 1920), Amy Jacques had not only become "Garvey's personal secretary" and "confidante," but also his second wife, according to historian Ula Taylor.[24] This was in 1922. By this time, Ashwood had moved to England where she became a part of the émigré and native Caribbean community, supported building racial unity internationally, and advocated for the liberation of black women in the African diaspora. Taking over the mantle of Garveyism in the United States, Amy Jacques Garvey joined the ranks of thousands of black laboring women in the UNIA. Some served in leadership, others in the nurses' corps and ladies auxiliaries. She praised black women who, as intimated by Wells's protestations, were too often deemed scurrilous by white society. Amy Jacques Garvey and the UNIA believed black women deserved to be seen as feminine beings and acknowledged as nurturers of the race in the United States and internationally. Moreover, she viewed black women as "part of an international sisterhood" who, like their compatriots in India, Turkey, and Egypt, should no longer view themselves as "slaves to their husbands," but instead in "co-partnership with their men."[25] In this way, Amy Jacques Garvey questioned male dominance, but without ultimately upsetting traditional gender roles and patriarchy.[26] These complicated gender politics prefigured stances of later religious and cultural black nationalist groups, such as the Nation of Islam (NOI) and the US Organization, as well as anticipated intra-racial gender dynamics impacting black liberation struggles in the 1960s.

The UNIA and its vision of race pride and dignity galvanized black people worldwide, creating a mass power base troubling to many. As part of the Back-to-Africa movement, Garvey instructed black people to immigrate to the motherland.

Africa was for Africans. He specifically focused his attention on Liberia. He was not the first to do so. Free black people and ex-slaves had already emigrated there, and Liberia had been at the center of Turner's African dream. In fact, Turner established the International Migration Society in 1896, the same year as the formation of Callie House's ex-slave pension association.[27] Establishing an independent and separate black nation in Liberia, according to Garvey, would convey self-help, self-reliance, and "show evidence of [black people's] own ability in the art of human progress."[28] Not to do this, to leave the race "scattered," indicated "imbecility."[29] Garvey's "race nationalism" conceptualized a black Zion in Africa that challenged European imperialism and the ruling black Americo-Liberian elite—former U.S. slaves who settled there in the early to mid-1800s. However, not many U.S. black people immigrated as part of Garvey's Back-to-Africa movement. In fact, Garvey himself never visited Liberia.

Nevertheless, Garvey's provocation both excited many black people, as well as earned him the enmity of others. This included W.E.B. Du Bois, the father of pan-Africanism, who refused to forego his demand that U.S. society accept as equals its black daughters and sons. Espousing faith in the Talented Tenth, this young Du Bois believed that the educated black elite must lift up the black masses and fight for integration. Over the decades, his views changed under shifting personal, political, and economic circumstances. Ultimately, he did the very thing that he vociferously protested against: he left the United States and lived in Ghana as an expatriate. In the early 20th century, however, Du Bois had few compliments for Garvey or his popular UNIA movement.

The UNIA's First International Convention of the Negro Peoples of the World drew 25,000 conferees to Madison Square Garden.[30] There, they adopted the UNIA's "Declaration of Rights of the Negro Peoples of the World." The declaration, which helped to establish Garvey as a key global evangelizer of black nationalism (his teachings would reach to Australia), enumerated 12 complaints and 54 demands. The declaration condemned racial discrimination, white vigilantism and unfair judicial treatment, colonial subjugation, taxation and forced military obligation without representation, Jim Crow public accommodations, inferior healthcare and schools, unequal access to jobs and unfair wages, and political exclusion.[31]

After listing its grievances, the UNIA registered its concrete demands "to encourage [the black] race all over the world and to stimulate it to a higher and grander destiny." Echoing the U.S. Declaration of Independence, the UNIA declaration stated: "Be it known" that "all men are created equal and entitled to the rights of life, liberty, and the pursuit of happiness." It then called for adherence to both nationalistic and universal claims, such as black people "should not be deprived of rights and privileges common to other human beings." They should be treated with "even-handed justice before all courts of law and equity in whatever country [they] may be found." They should not suffer the "use of the term 'nigger,'" racial exclusion, or violence of any kind. They should have the rights of representation and authority in all realms of life. Exalting African history and culture, its royalty and great empires, Garvey inspired pride among thousands of ordinary black people.

A promoter of race-based enterprise, Garvey stated, "[A] beggar race can never be respected. Stop begging for jobs and create your own."[32] He joined a cadre of black women and men who invested their money in real estate, insurance companies, fraternal and financial organizations, and other black businesses such as funeral parlors, barber shops, groceries, and doctors' offices to cater to working-class black people who already experienced racial separation and exclusion in the North and South.

In the age of industrial growth, where consolidated wealth held sway and power, black entrepreneurs, or bourgeois economic nationalists, also sought economic autonomy. Washington, who influenced Garvey, inspired black entrepreneurs in the North, and also founded the mostly southern National Negro Business League in 1900. It is still in existence. Three years later, Maggie Lena Walker, who had joined the black women's mutual benefit society, the Independent Order of Saint Luke, founded the Saint Luke Penny Savings Bank in Richmond, Virginia. When Walker died in 1934, the bank was reorganized into the Consolidated Bank and Trust Company, "the oldest continuously existing black-owned and black-run bank in the country."[33] In 1905, the Louisiana-born Sarah Breedlove—known as "Madame C. J. Walker"—invented a line of black beauty and hair products and became the first black millionaire and a philanthropist. Madame C. J. Walker's daughter Lelia Walker supported Garvey.[34] A thriving "Negro Wall Street" developed in Tulsa, Oklahoma. There, black lawyers, physicians, realtors, and other professionals opened offices in the black neighborhood of Greenwood. Tragically, the alleged assault of a white woman by a black man led to the Tulsa race riot and the destruction of the thriving black epicenter in 1921. The black community would rebuild, only to fall prey to class flight and urban renewal after World War II.

While black people started schools, banks, insurance companies, and stores, they still had trouble creating enough jobs or businesses to serve black communities. The preponderance of failing businesses alone provides evidence of that. According to Theodore Vincent, at least one-half to two-thirds of black businesses listed in the 1920 census had disappeared a decade later. Of 88 banks, about half existed in 1930, with less than two handfuls holding financial resources of $500,000 or more. The stock market crash no doubt wreaked some havoc on this score. Out of 200,000 manufacturing businesses, black people owned 1,500. Overall black businesses captured only two percent of the black retail market.[35]

Even with successful establishments, black businesses did not necessarily extend wealth beyond a small middle class or deposit more money in the wallets and purses of the majority of the black masses. Poverty remained widespread. So, too, did low-wage agricultural and service work and debt-peonage and convict-leasing systems that exploited the labor of black people—nine million of whom lived in the South. Living remained a struggle. The growth of industries, corporations, wealth, and profit remained firmly in the hands of white male capitalist elites, which also meant, in fact, that most working-class whites did not fare well economically either.

In his strivings for collective economic security, Garvey did protest Gilded Age wealth accumulation, as well as the class pretensions of black people. He did not presume, though, to imagine economic systems that veered too far from a modified capitalism.[36] Some of his black American and Caribbean brethren, however, did. They espoused black economic radicalism in an age of revolution in Russia and socialist protest in the United States. Hubert Harrison, for instance, did not believe equality could be achieved in a capitalist system. Cyril Briggs, who founded with Richard B. Moore and Grace Campbell the African Blood Brotherhood (ABB) in 1919, critiqued capitalism as well as supported armed self-defense and anti-imperialist struggles in their magazine *The Crusader*. ABB members were among the first to join the Workers Party after its formation. The Workers Party eventually became the Communist Party USA (CPUSA). Black U.S.-born leaders and black socialists, A. Philip Randolph and Chandler Owen, editors of *The Messenger* (published 1917 to 1928), believed in "scientific radicalism" or exposing the unequal relationship between race, wealth, and power in order to forge interracial working-class solidarity and trade unionism.

Race-conscious politics in the age of Jim Crow were not for the fainthearted. Debates within the black community were scathing and divisive—revealing real differences in ideology and strategy. In their linking of racial and class oppression, black radicals remained committed to contesting capitalist relations. In fact, Harrison and Randolph eventually parted ways with Garvey partly for this reason.[37] Their positions on capitalist relations foreshadow similar tendencies emergent in 1960s' black leftist organizations such as the Revolutionary Action Movement, the Black Panther Party, and the League of Revolutionary Black Workers, particularly in cities where, over time, an increasing number of black people resided.

During and in the midst of the New Negro era, more than 1.5 million black people migrated to cities. Black militancy and a burgeoning black population intensified race relations in neighborhoods and at work. They also contributed to the flowering of black culture and nightlife, including dance clubs featuring blues and jazz. Black people lauded their talents and positively defined their blackness through theatrical, visual, musical, and literary productions. The East Coast manifestation of the black arts and intellectual movement, known as the "Harlem Renaissance," unfolded between 1919 and the Great Depression, and had its Midwest counterpart in 1940s' Chicago.

The New Negro (1925) captured this cultural zeitgeist—one that exposed a desire to combat black subjugation in its many forms. A Harvard University graduate and Howard University English professor, editor Alain Leroy Locke maintained in *The New Negro* that black migration, new social adjustments created by industry, and black "class differentiation" had transformed the "Negro." Black people were casting aside the "tyranny of social intimidation" and expressing a new attitude that called "for less charity but more justice."[38] Wrote Locke: "Each generation . . . will have its creed, and that of the present is the belief in the efficacy of collective effort, in race co-operation. This deep feeling of race is at present the mainspring of Negro life. It seems to be the outcome of the reaction to proscription and prejudice; an attempt, fairly successful on the whole, to convert a defensive into an offensive position, a handicap into an incentive."[39]

The same year as the publication of *The New Negro,* the Harlem Renaissance's most prolific black woman writer, Zora Neale Hurston, arrived in New York. The collection included one of her short stories, *Spunk.* Born around 1901, Hurston grew up in the all-black town of Eatonville, Florida, and attended black educational institutions including Morgan Academy (now Morgan State University) in Baltimore and Howard University in D.C. She also attended Barnard College in New York where she was the first black woman to graduate. Documenting the cultural experience and life of working-class black people in Florida and Louisiana, Hurston challenged the totalizing perception of black people as "tragically colored" and instead attended to "the positive side of the black experience."[40] Her contemporaries included Claude McKay and Langston Hughes, whose poems also appeared in *The New Negro.*

Alongside racial pride and affirmation, racially militant black art conveyed black political agendas. In June 1926, Hughes published "The Negro Artist and the Racial Mountain" in the *Nation.*[41] Born in Joplin, Missouri, just one year after Hurston, Hughes had moved to New York City in 1921. By 1924, he had begun writing for the *Crisis.* In his essay, Hughes argued that black artists had a duty "to change through the force of [their] art that old whispering 'I want to be white,' hidden in the aspirations of [their] people, to 'Why should I want to be white? I am a Negro—and beautiful!'"[42]

Just weeks later, in her July 10, 1926 essay in the *Negro World,* Amy Jacques Garvey mentioned Hughes's "splendid article," wondered whether he belonged to the UNIA, and marked him "in any event . . . as a keen student of Garveyism" in that he had "stamina enough to express its ideals." Then she echoed his message. She declared that while the race was still "in the making, and steadily moving on to nationhood and to power," "we are Negroes and beautiful."[43] The literature and writing of Hurston, Hughes, Amy Jacques Garvey, and others, as well as the cultural renaissance in black Chicago yet to come, presaged the mottos of "black and beautiful" and "black and proud" (no less complicated by color and gender consciousness), which are most remembered as part of the 1960s' cultural black revolution.[44]

In the first decades of the 20th century, ripe with an assertive black ethos that contested the inferiority of black people, Audley Moore reveled in learning about the "glories of Africa." "I never went to sleep since then, never," recalled Moore, who cut her intellectual and activist teeth as a Garveyite.[45] Born in New Iberia, Louisiana, in 1898, this woman, who became known among black militants as

"Queen Mother," was quite familiar with the hardships of the South, its racially exploitative labor regimes and its deathly practices. Her maternal grandfather was lynched and, as a young child, she witnessed another man's lynching outside her home.

Audley Moore often regaled listeners with a story about the first time she encountered Marcus Garvey. For Moore (like Amy Ashwood and Amy Jacques), it was at a public event. As Moore reported, Garvey had come to New Orleans in 1921 to give a speech, but police summarily arrested him. Police viewed Garvey as a foreigner and an enemy agitator, and the black passions he aroused as emblematic of the threat he posed to prevailing racial norms and U.S. stability. After vociferous protest, the police released him. The next day, 3,500 black lecture-goers, many of them armed, gathered at the Longshoreman's Hall (with police in attendance) to hear Garvey. Moore tells the story, which some historians suggest might be apocryphal: "[I packed] two guns—one in my bosom and one in my pocketbook. My husband had a 45."[46] Efforts by police to arrest Garvey failed when attendees drew their weapons. Unprepared, the police left, and Garvey spoke. "They knew they would have been slaughtered in that hall that night," stated Moore more than 50 years later, "because nobody was afraid to die. You've got to be prepared to lose your life in order to gain your life."[47] Black armed resistance had deep roots as a protective response. Indeed, for some black people who bore witness to quotidian white violence and state repression, armed resistance resonated as quite necessary, if not sensible.[48]

Truly moved by Garvey's message, Moore and her family seriously thought about moving to Africa. An aunt, however, dissuaded her. Closing their grocery store, Moore and her husband instead moved to Santa Monica, California, then Chicago, Illinois, and finally Harlem, New York. Racial discrimination propelled each leg of their trip. Once in Harlem, they realized escaping Jim Crow was not to be. There, as elsewhere, white-only real estate designations indicated where black people could live. In theaters, black people could not sit in the orchestra seats, but had to sit upstairs in the buzzard's roost. Jobs in stores were often off-limits, and there were no black streetcar or subway workers. Black women sold their domestic, sometimes sexual, labor on street corners. No matter where black people went in the country, racial discrimination made an appearance. The movement to secure black political and economic autonomy called Moore with a vengeance.[49]

Like other black nationalists and economic radicals, Moore took to urban corners to share her views on the racial state of affairs. Stepladder speaking provided one way to reach the black masses. Black feminist radical Vicki Garvin, who became a trade unionist, pan-Africanist, and expatriate in Ghana, first heard Audley Moore speak on 125th Street and Lenox Avenue.[50] In commandeering the corners, Audley Moore navigated women's proscribed spaces of respectability and broke into a primarily male domain of public agitation. She was a woman among mostly men—the most famous of whom, at this time, was Hubert Harrison, known as "Black Socrates." Harrison extolled to passersby the need for economic justice for black working-class people. Like Harrison, Moore became an educator in "the university of the streets" in the very neighborhoods often burdened by the ills born of neglect and exclusion.[51]

Throughout the years, Moore became an esteemed anti-racist "town crier" and "secular prophet" who rallied for her people's liberation, particularly those multiply marginalized such as prisoners and welfare-reliant mothers in the 1950s. She organized working-class women in the Harriet Tubman Association, rent strikes, and furniture move-back-ins when landlords evicted families. She also started the Universal Association of Ethiopian Women in the 1950s in New Orleans, and became mentor to a number of post–World War II Black Power progenitors and activists including Malcolm X, Max Stanford, and Stokely Carmichael.[52] Indeed, Carmichael described Moore as one of the "keepers of the flame . . . ceaselessly exhorting us to keep historical and revolutionary faith with our ancestors' long history of struggle and resistance."[53]

While the UNIA's home base was in Harlem, its philosophy found sympathetic working-class people worldwide. By 1923, 400 chapters existed in Canada, Great Britain, Africa, and Central and South America, and another 500 chapters existed in the United States, most extensively "in the rural and small-town South,"[54] where most black people lived. In 1940 more than three quarters of black people lived in the South, and almost half in rural areas, that is, until the greatest black migration in the World War II era dramatically changed the geography of race in the country.[55] Moore's home state of Louisiana had 80 UNIA chapters, the largest number in the nation.[56] Some of the UNIA chapters actually were former ex-slave pension association chapters.[57] From Callie House's pension association movement to Marcus Garvey's UNIA, Audley Moore, and Malcolm X, there existed a tree with roots and multiple branches.

As black people organized and migrated, so did their ideologies and organizations. Garveyism not only made its way to New Orleans and entranced Audley Moore, but it also trekked to Omaha, Nebraska, by way of Philadelphia with Earl Little and his wife Louise Langdon Norton. Earl Little and Louise were avid Garveyites who met in Montreal where Little had settled after leaving his first wife and their three children. Involved in UNIA activities there, Earl and Louise eventually married and dedicated themselves to the UNIA.[58] They moved to Philadelphia, where Louise gave birth to their first son Wilfred in 1920, and then relocated to Omaha a year later to start a UNIA chapter. There in Omaha, Earl Little's speechmaking in support of the UNIA had resulted in KKK harassment and the need to move his family, including his young son Malcolm (the couple's fourth child and the man history would have to reckon with as Malcolm X), to Lansing, Michigan.

The year Malcolm was born, 1925, also marked the beginning of the waning of the Garveyite movement though its legacy and most stalwart members would continue to impact black liberation campaigns in the decades to come. Deemed a "notorious Negro agitator" by assistant director of the Bureau of Investigation (the precursor to the FBI), Garvey was put under surveillance by J. Edgar Hoover, the man who decades later made it his professional and personal mission as FBI director to undermine rights and power activists who challenged U.S. racial practices. The bureau hired the first full-time black bureau agent, known as "800," to infiltrate the UNIA.[59] Eventually, the FBI jailed Garvey on federal mail fraud charges and two years later in 1927 the U.S. government deported him. That same year, Harrison, upheld as "the first militant apostle of the New Negro," died during an operation.[60] A year later, the 67-year-old Callie House died of uterine cancer.

Neither Garvey's deportation nor white intimidation more broadly could fully extinguish black people's varied and countless demands for respect, freedom, and economic and political autonomy. After all, Garvey and other black activists, such as Earl Little, were responding to white power, which was well entrenched and thriving. Continuing his UNIA lectures, it was only a short time until Little drew the wrath of the white supremacist organization, the Black Legion, which burned down the family's house in 1929. Two years later, Little lay dead alongside trolley tracks, many believed at the hands of the Legionnaires. It was a chain of events that led Malcolm's mother into a relationship with "Michigan's bedeviling welfare bureaucracy" and ultimately the state mental hospital.[61] A child who stole food to assuage his hunger and found himself living with a white foster family before being sent to a juvenile home at age 14, Malcolm would eventually move to Boston to live with his sister. This son of Garveyites would grow up with knowledge of the man who had galvanized his parents' activism and created the largest black mass-based organization in the country. Nevertheless, Malcolm Little still had to find his own way through both streets and prison to a familial and community black nationalist legacy that challenged the limited views of Africa, self, black people, white society, and his own potential and power. In this way, his journey reveals the philosophical and political continuities, as well as ruptures, in the search for race, nation, and power.

Economic Depression, Self-Determination, and Radicalism

The stock market crash of 1929 and the resulting Great Depression served as a context for economic critique and radicalism. Laissez-faire capitalism and unregulated business practices had thrust the country into severe economic instability, marking the end of the 1920s and the early 1930s as an era rife with bank failures, unemployment, dustbowls, Hoovervilles, and long breadlines. For the masses of black people, the Depression exposed the brutal and seemingly intractable poverty that already structured their lives. Almost 40 percent of black people versus 14.6 percent of white people living in cities nationwide received relief.[62] Rents, food prices and malnutrition, insurance rates, unemployment—everything increased. The activist Ella Baker and progressive journalist and Communist Party member

Marvel Cooke wrote about the "Bronx slave market" in the *Crisis* in 1935. Daily, white housewives went to these street corner marts to hire domestic servants thrown out of work by the Depression. Vicki Garvin's mother was one among many women who stood on "the slave line" in search of a job.[63] Black women, young and old, gathered as early as 8 a.m. and sometimes waited through the afternoon for an opportunity to do an hour or a day's work. Usually, they were paid between 15 and 25 cents an hour. Sometimes, however, men "offer[ed] worldly-wise girls higher bids for their time."[64]

A future friend of Garvin and fellow black Communist radical, Louise Thompson also wrote about the Bronx market. Born in Chicago in 1901, Thompson went to school at University of California Berkeley and made her way to Harlem where she connected with black artists and activists such as Garvin and Cooke.[65] She married fellow Communist Party member William Patterson, who would deliver with Paul Robeson a petition to the United Nations in 1951 charging the United States with the genocide of black people. Thompson's article appeared in the Communist Party's *Woman Today* in 1936 and described the plight of black women workers. According to historian Erik S. McDuffie, it was in "Toward a Brighter Day" that the phrase, not the concept, "triple exploitation" appeared in print for the first time. This presaged black feminist stances, critiques, and organizations such as the Third World Women's Alliance and its journal *Triple Jeopardy* in the 1970s.[66]

The New Deal followed on the heels of the Great Depression. Ushered in under President Franklin D. Roosevelt, the New Deal was a potpourri of "alphabet" programs to spur national recovery and provide relief and jobs. Passage of federal legislation required responding to and placating the fears and desires of white southerners and conservative allies in other parts of the nation who were hell bent on maintaining racial hierarchies and preserving state autonomy. Middle-class black people did receive federal government appointments, and black working-class people did access, to varying degrees, New Deal programs. Overall, however, race constrained black people's New Deal experiences.

The Social Security Act excluded domestic and agricultural workers. A significant majority of black workers fell into this category. Qualifying for state relief also proved difficult. The future garment shop union organizer Florence Rice, who lived in New York, and Mosel Brinson of Millen, Georgia, were denied relief because they refused to work for white families. Brinson wrote to the United States Department of Agriculture (USDA) in 1935: "These poor white people that lives around me wants the colored people to work for them for nothing and if you won't do that they goes down to the relief office and tell the women—'don't help the colored people, we will give them plenty of work to do, but they won't work.'" Pinkie Pilcher, who lived in Greenwood, Mississippi—the city and state that civil rights and Black Power activists targeted decades later—experienced this as well. Pilcher wrote to President Roosevelt about the Public Works and Works Progress administrations two days before Christmas in 1936: "These white women at the head of the PWA is still letting we colored women when we go to the office to be certified for work to go hunt washings," and black men, who went to WPA project sites, would continuously be sent away and told "come back tomorrow come back Monday."[67] In public works jobs, like in the private market, black people experienced employment discrimination.

The financial disaster of the 1930s also ignited nationalist and radical protests to counter ongoing and new racial exclusions. In the Black Belt South, including Mississippi, Alabama, and Louisiana, black people continued to desire to control their own land and their own labor. Land ownership had brought self-sufficiency and power, and those who stayed in the South organized to protect their property against local white politicians and landowners as well as discriminatory New Deal government policies that privileged white-owned farms.[68] In the cities, black people also formed organizations that continued to publicly counter racial discrimination as part of broader efforts to secure economic opportunities. Black women, for instance, united in housewives' leagues and organized "Don't Buy Where You Can't Work" campaigns.[69] These campaigns of racial protest and solidarity in cities across the country focused on securing employment in stores operating in black communities. Black people also continued to rally for fair treatment in government programs, as well as establish businesses to foster financial independence. This included the Lost-Found Nation of Islam (NOI) founded by Wallace D. Fard in July 1930 in Detroit, the Midwest hub of Henry Ford's automobile factories.

Espousing an "unorthodox" or "modified" version of Islam, the NOI claimed that the U.S. "Negro" was really an "Asiatic blackman," part of a group of original men who ruled from Asia.[70] NOI followers believed that white people were devils created by a mad scientist named Yacub. While the origin narrative registers as peculiar, the focus on white people's vicious treatment of black people resonated with reality. Conveying for some an acerbic and disquieting mixture of messianic millenarianism, racial pseudoscience, territorial separatism, and race-based capitalism, the NOI preached the deliverance of black people lost in the wilderness of an oppressive United States. For the NOI, race and religion served as the main epoxy of their nationalist and self-determination dream—in contrast to Garvey's African homeland.

The NOI grew under the leadership of Elijah Muhammad whom the prophet W. D. Fard endowed as the "Last Messenger." Born Elijah Poole, Muhammad grew up in poverty in Sandersville, Georgia. One of 13 children, his father was a sharecropper and his mother a domestic worker. Dropping out of school in fourth grade, Poole worked for the Southern Railroad Company and the Cherokee Brick Company.[71] He migrated to Detroit (which also would become a post-World War II hub of black radicalism) with his wife Clara. Not a year after the stock market crash, the story goes that Poole, a Garveyite, met Fard and learned of the NOI. Starting as a minister, Poole was given the name "Karriem"; he rose to Supreme Minister, and then the Messenger of Allah. In 1934, NOI moved its headquarters to Chicago, the home of the worst race riot in 1919 and also of a bustling center of black political, cultural, and economic activity.

The NOI adhered most closely to the precepts of Garvey rather than the race-based socialism of a Harrison or trade unionism of a Randolph. Indeed, Poole saw the NOI as the appropriate organization to inherit the black nationalist struggle, particularly calls for race pride, economic nationalism, and sovereignty in the form of a black-controlled territory. Moreover, the NOI established black-owned businesses, including a 140-acre farm in upstate Michigan and small groceries and restaurants.[72] In their vision of a racially separate nation, patriarchy reigned. Reaffirming the "allegedly complementary subjects [of] a masculine man and a feminine woman," the woman was the "queen of the universe" and a housewife, and the man the breadwinner.[73]

Between the mid-1930 and the early 1940s, the NOI experienced severe growth pangs. It suffered from what scholar Claude Clegg III poignantly summarized as "destructive disunity, overly competitive leadership, law enforcement harassment, and organizational penury."[74] The NOI questioned the validity of the U.S. government and devalued U.S. political participation and military service. Still a fairly small and marginal movement, the NOI gained more converts during and after World War II in inner cities and in prisons. Malcolm Little started his journey toward the NOI while in prison. Two decades later, the NOI would grow exponentially under his charismatic leadership and, like the Garvey movement, draw its membership from working-class black people, particularly those experiencing extreme social and economic marginalization.[75]

Alarmed by the rise of black nationalist politics and its own relevance, the Communist Party waged a battle for the minds of black people. They pondered the "Negro Question," and particularly expressed concern about black workers enamored by (or Communist Party members might say distracted by) race and nationhood.[76] The Sixth World Congress of the Communist International—with the convincing of Harry Haywood (nee Haywood Hall), a black U.S. veteran from World War I, former ABB member, and Communist Party member—responded to this state of affairs by issuing its "Black Belt" thesis in 1928.[77] The Black Belt thesis linked class and race by positioning southern black workers, such as coal miners and farmers, as an oppressed nation within a nation. Vladimir Lenin had argued this very point as early as 1913, stating that the denial of equality and rights meant "Negroes (and also mulattoes and Indians) . . . must be considered an oppressed nation."[78] As such they had the right to economic and national self-determination. During the years of the Popular Front (1935–1939), the rise of fascism led to a declining emphasis on socialist revolution and a rising interest in aligning with black liberal and reform organizations and the black middle class. The radical notions of a "nation within a nation" and "self-determination," however, would grow with renewed vigor after the Second World War.

Black radicals also increasingly understood their own racial oppression and self-determination struggles within the broader context and history of global struggles against imperialism. There were deep roots. In the wake of European empire-building grounded in the partitioning of Africa in 1885, pan-Africanists had called for political unity and challenged the subjugation of black people throughout the diaspora. Du Bois attended the First Pan-African Congress in London in 1900 as its secretary, and in 1919, he organized the Second Pan-African Congress. Held in Paris, the congress communicated an anti-racist global agenda. In a matter of a few decades, Du Bois joined black, race-conscious, economic radicals in the ongoing struggles to advance freedom for blacks at home and abroad.

One of those black economic radicals was Paul Robeson. Twenty-eight years after the First Pan-African Congress was held in London and the same year as the Communist Party's resolution on black self-determination, the soon-to-be renowned black actor and Communist sympathizer Robeson traveled to London to perform in the musical *Show Boat* at the Theatre Royal as well as several other concerts. This son of an escaped slave father (who had become a respected pastor) and a mother descended from free blacks (who helped found the Free African Society in Philadelphia) counted among his audience the Queen of England and the Prince of Wales. It was not Robeson's first time in London. The all-American Robeson, who grew up in segregated Princeton, New Jersey—a city he described as "spiritually located in Dixie"—had made several trips abroad simply to get more work as a concert singer and actor.[79] It was difficult for black people stateside to get jobs other than those in unskilled industrial, agricultural, or domestic service work. The Depression only worsened the odds.

England offered Robeson opportunities. Unlike previous trips, however, this time he and his wife Eslanda Goode Robeson relocated to London and began more than a decade-long journey that impacted his politics. According to Robeson, living "among the people of the British Isles and travel[ing] back and forth to many other lands" shaped his "outlook on world affairs."[80] Paul and Eslanda met British socialists, "common people," and West African students and seamen. He learned of their struggles and "discovered" African culture, as well as the reaches of the British Empire and European fascism. These encounters, alongside his visit to the Soviet Union, internationalized his politics. Robeson did not return to the United States until 1939, and when he did he vigorously spoke out against the oppression of black people and laborers.[81]

In the United States, the Communist Party had gained a measure of credibility in the black community because of its Black Belt thesis and its stand on racial justice struggles. In particular, the Communist Party's legal arm, the International Labor Defense (ILD) represented the Scottsboro Nine, nine black youths aged 13 to 21 years who were falsely accused of raping two white women in Alabama in 1931. The party's support of the young men alongside its Black Belt thesis allowed Audley Moore, at least initially, to imagine a place for black nationalists like herself in the party. She signed up in 1936 in Harlem and became the secretary of the Harlem Communist Party's office in the early 1940s. The CPUSA also supported the Alabama Sharecroppers Union, which bridged "homegrown radicalism" with the philosophy of black self-determination.[82]

By the mid-1930s, the CPUSA had rhetorically linked its anti-racist and anti-fascist agendas. This pleased black economic radicals. In particular, the CPUSA opposed the rise of Benito Mussolini and Adolf Hitler in Europe. The party stood against Mussolini's invasion of Ethiopia in 1935 that had deposed Emperor Haile Selassie (Ras Tafari), heralded as the black messiah of the Jamaican religious movement Rastafarianism. In fact, Selassie had ascended to power the same year as the adoption of the Black Belt thesis.

Through the press, mass meetings, and demonstrations, black people had expressed solidarity with Ethiopia—one of only two independent African countries. The other was Liberia.[83] Both figured in the political vision of Garveyism in Jamaica and the United States, and the attack on Ethiopia, in particular, registered as an assault on black self-determination.[84] Langston Hughes penned two poems about Ethiopia, both in September 1935. "The Call of Ethiopia" appeared in *Opportunity* magazine, and the "Ballad of Ethiopia" in the Baltimore *Afro-American* newspaper. Hughes had seen promise in communism before the invasion. He traveled to the Soviet Union and served a stint as leader of the black communist League of Struggle for Negro Rights in 1930.[85] He served on the national council of the league with Harry Haywood, Cyril Briggs, and Louise Thompson.

A young Ella Baker also protested the invasion of Ethiopia, which eventually fell to Italy—not to regain its independence for another six years. In just a couple decades, Baker would become the "mama" of SNCC and eventually be endowed with the honorific title "Fundi"—someone who passes skills from one generation to the next. The young Baker believed in black self-determination and critiqued capitalism. She believed that the Communist Party "was the most articulate group for social action"—this despite the fact that "it may not have been well organized all the time."[86] Baker was an internationalist (she worked as a reporter, for instance, for the *West Indian News*), a proponent of economic justice who exposed the exploitation of domestic workers, and a race woman. Historian Barbara Ransby describes Ella Baker as a radical democratic humanist—and this political positioning included steadfast criticism of imperialism.[87] She, however, neither became a member of the Communist Party nor embraced Garveyism. Her cautions about racial separatism would echo in the mid-to-late 1960s' debates about SNCC's transition to black consciousness, all-black projects, and Black Power.

In 1936 the leftist-inspired National Negro Congress (NNC) succeeded the League of Struggle for Negro Rights. A united front of black political, economic, and fraternal organizations, NNC focused on the economic "raw deal" that black people suffered across class and ideological lines. Its campaigns included the Domestic Workers Union in New York City in 1937, an association formed to protect black women workers who labored in private households. Black radical women spearheaded such efforts to organize black domestic workers in southern and northern cities. Among the organizers was NNC delegate Louise Thompson.[88]

The first "SNICK"—the Southern Negro Youth Conference (SNYC)—also emerged out of the NNC. Founded in 1937, SNYC held its first conference in Richmond, Virginia, and two years later moved its headquarters to Birmingham, Alabama. During its 12 years of operation, the black leftist student organization nurtured radical activists such as Esther Cooper Jackson and James Jackson and boasted 10 chapters throughout the South where the group worked to encourage black unionization and voting rights. A. Philip Randolph became the NNC's first president and continued his trade union organizing efforts through the Brotherhood of Sleeping Car Porters. He, however, would resign his presidential position in protest of an anti-war position pushed by Communist Party members and sympathizers.[89]

The Communist Party held a progressive stance on black self-determination. However, this stance existed alongside white chauvinism. Black leftists often argued that the CPUSA seemed more concerned with class, international party politics, and growing its base by appealing to white laborers. In one of the most radical of political and economic arenas, race retained its discriminatory power. Given this political reality, race-first politics remained a relevant and forceful option. During the 1940s and 1950s, while most black people never aligned with socialist or Communist Party politics, the number of black party members as well as sympathizers declined. Suppression and redbaiting accounted for some of this. Others such as black novelist and party member Richard Wright were critical of the party's racial politics. Audley Moore, who "began to assert the African American national question within the Party" in the 1940s, also grew increasingly dissatisfied with the eliding of racial issues and resigned in 1950.[90] In 1958 the CPUSA officially dropped its Black Belt thesis, arguing, "Black outmigration from the South had nullified this position."[91] However, the concept of a nation within a nation survived. So too would dreams of an actual sovereign nation in the Black Belt South among religious and cultural nationalist organizations.

Bridges to the 1940s

The massive upheavals of World War II shaped the expectations and struggles of black people nationally and internationally in the 1940s. Whether in the Gold Coast colony, Harlem, New Orleans, Chicago, or elsewhere, calls for self-governance and the urban and rural realities of black people sparked protest. The proliferation of freedom campaigns—whether the pan-African freedom charter spurred by Amy Jacques Garvey or the Pittsburgh *Courier*'s evocation of the "Double V" campaign (victory over fascism abroad and racism at home)—circulated across national boundaries.

Wartime also politicized a new generation of black people. An organization called Conscientious Objectors Against Jim Crow formed. Contesting the Selective Training and Service Act of 1940 that impressed 18- to 45-year-old men into the military, some black men refused to enlist or responded so provocatively that they were declared 4-F—mentally or morally unfit for service. Bebop musician Dizzy Gillespie and hipster Malcolm Little both let military officials believe that they just might not know which enemy to shoot—Germans who had done nothing to them or white segregationists.[92] NOI members refused to register for the draft or support the war. This often earned them five years in the penitentiary. Arrested in 1942, Elijah Muhammad served his sentence in the Federal Correction Institution in Milan, Michigan, and while there he spread word of the NOI and gained recruits.

Those black men and women who had volunteered out of a sense of mission, faith in democracy, or belief that black people could prove they were worthy of equal citizenship, like those before them in previous wars, experienced disappointment. Their experiences broadcast the U.S. dilemma. Black people suffered racial discrimination on military bases, at U.S. training centers, and even by humanitarian organizations such as the American Red Cross. The edifice of racial inequality had stood firm in the midst of a war fought for freedom, and this had a radicalizing effect. It evoked concrete demands for rights, protection, and power.

Not surprisingly, then, some black World War II and later Korean War veterans joined burgeoning rights and power struggles. This included the Deacons for Defense, which formed in Jonesboro, Louisiana, in the mid-1960s to protect local rights activists from the KKK.[93] It was also the case with Robert F. Williams, from Monroe, North Carolina, who had been dishonorably discharged from the military for contesting discrimination in 1946. After living in Detroit for about a decade, Williams returned to Monroe where he reinvigorated the local NAACP chapter. Espousing a militant integrationist ethos by 1961, Williams supported armed self-defense, eventually fled to Cuba, and subsequently became a mentor, alongside Audley Moore, Malcolm X, and others, for Black Power militants in the Revolutionary Action Movement and the Republic of New Afrika (RNA).

These wartime realities alongside the greatest black migration of the 20th century produced massive upheavals that compounded racial tensions and intensified protests. While many black people had stayed in the South and, therefore, would became the foot soldiers and "inside agitators" for black liberation struggles there, millions of other black people were on the literal move.[94] The greatest black migration occurred between the 1940s and 1960s. Four to six million black people relocated to cities in the South, North, Midwest, and West, truly transforming black Americans from a rural to an urban people. Some of these migrants earned relatively higher wages and experienced the thrill of urban nightlife in their new cities. They also were subjected to higher living costs and the pain of discrimination.

Chicago exemplified this duality. Black migrants, who became midwestern "New Negroes," flooded into the city, looking to manifest their freedom in a not quite hospitable place cast as a promised land. Even so, the growth of black neighborhoods gave rise to a vibrant black political and organizational culture—a cultural renaissance that could hold its own against the more heralded Harlem

Renaissance. Black art, theater, literature, and music flourished in the Windy City where winters were harsh, and racial politics grew increasingly taut, particularly as the black population increased competition for jobs and housing. The future author of *Black Power,* Richard Wright had lived in Chicago. He founded in 1936 the South Side Writers Group, which provided a haven for black cultural workers, a few of whom later emerged as literary elders in the 1960s' Black Arts Movement. In 1940, Wright published *Native Son,* a book that explored the grittiness of black people's lives in the "ghetto"—the rats, crowded tenement conditions, low-wage work, and violence undergirded by racial and gender tensions that made living a challenge for decades to come.[95] Out of these concrete conditions black self-help efforts as well as self-determination sentiments grew.

Residential racial discrimination expanded through the growing deployment of restrictive covenants and other local, state, and federal programs and policies. As early as 1926, the Chicago Real Estate Board had begun pushing the use of covenants by dispatching speakers to white neighborhoods to convince residents to adopt them. By the late 1920s, racially restrictive covenants, which prevented black people from occupying homes unless they lived in them as janitors, servants, or chauffeurs "in the basement or in a barn or garage in the rear," covered over 85 percent of Chicago.[96] Carl Hansberry had bought his house in one of these white neighborhoods near the University of Chicago. White residents filed a class-action lawsuit to evict Hansberry and his family from a subdivision known as South Park or Washington Park. The father of the not yet famed playwright of *A Raisin in the Sun,* Carl Hansberry was a black realtor who also worked with black civic organizations such as the NAACP and the Urban League. His brother William Leo Hansberry taught African history at Howard University, and founded the Ethiopian Research Council a year before the Italo-Ethiopian conflict.[97] Also a U.S. deputy marshal, Carl Hansberry filed a landmark lawsuit to contest racially restrictive covenants in 1937. While waging this battle, his family braved what his daughter Lorraine described as "a hellishly hostile 'white neighborhood' in which literally howling white mobs surrounded [their] house."[98]

One grade ahead of Lorraine Hansberry at Englewood High School was her childhood contemporary James Forman. He lived two blocks east of South Park on 61st and Prairie avenues in Chicago. Both of them came of age during a period of intensifying economic, anti-fascist, and legal campaigns. Forman's temperament reflected that mood. Increasingly, the personal racial insults and boundaries shaping black people's daily lives disgusted them both. A precocious nine-year-old, Forman delivered the *Chicago Defender* in 1937: "More important than the sale of the papers was my reading them and developing a sense of protest, a feeling that we as black people must fight all the way for our rights in this country."[99] Forman remembers that, at that time, white people owned and controlled all areas east of South Park. "We had to fight for every block we crossed."[100]

Lorraine, too, described being pummeled, cursed, and spat upon on her way back and forth to school. She recalled, "I also remember my desperate and courageous mother, patrolling our household all night with a loaded German luger, doggedly guarding her four children, while my father fought the respectable part of the battle in the Washington court."[101] Like Ida B. Wells-Barnett with her Winchester rifle, Audley Moore and her .45 caliber gun, and numerous other unknown and unnamed women (and men), the former schoolteacher and ward committee member Nannie Louise Perry Hansberry protected her family against aggressive white violence with her pistol. It was a life-affirming act in response to the threat of potential death. Lorraine Hansberry herself, while a committed peace activist until her premature death in 1965, believed in the necessity of armed self-defense as a tactic in the battle against oppression.

In 1943, after six years of litigation and in the same year as the Detroit riot, the U.S. Supreme Court decided in *Hansberry vs. Lee* not to uphold the Washington Park subdivision restrictive covenant. The Supreme Court, however, did not rule racial discrimination unconstitutional. Instead the court refused to support the class-action lawsuit because only 54 percent of white homeowners—not the required 95 percent—had supported the restrictive covenant. If the white homeowners had had enough support, the Hansberrys could have very likely lost their case and have been forced to move. As a result, winning the case was bittersweet. Even with the family's personal victory, restrictive covenants remained legal. Carl Hansberry died two years after the U.S. Supreme Court decision, and some 15 years later Lorraine Hansberry wrote her Broadway play set on the South Side of Chicago. *A Raisin in the Sun* (the title of which comes from Langston Hughes's poem "A Dream Deferred") rendered the emotional and physical costs of racial hatred and discrimination.[102] Wrote Hansberry: "My people are poor. And they are tired. And they are determined to live. Our Southside is a place apart: each piece of our living is a protest."[103]

Across the nation, cities and suburbs became places apart that expanded in decidedly racial ways. Restrictive covenants provided one legal tool in the residential segregation kit—at least until declared judicially unenforceable in *Shelley v. Kraemer* in 1948. Three of the court's nine judges supposedly had to recuse themselves from the case because "they lived in covenanted areas."[104] The Kraemer court decision, however, was not a panacea—not with the firm girding of white attitudes, real estate blockbusting practices, steering, and bank and government redlining. Together, these private, business, and government practices triggered white flight and racial turnover in neighborhoods thereby maintaining, while reconfiguring, segregation. In fact the 1930s into the 1940s marked the initiation of federal slum clearance, discriminatory housing mortgage practices, and urban renewal policies that not only reinforced, but also tremendously expanded racial segregation. This also triggered demands for desegregated, fair, and open access in the rental and homeownership markets. Over the next two decades, in the same eras of decolonization in Africa and Asia, northern and western U.S. cities imagined as promised lands and fashioned into second ghettos would be recast as occupied territories, urban reservations, and internal colonies.

Even with favorable rulings, most black people could not afford to buy a house. As renters, the rural and urban black poor and working class overwhelmingly depended on white landowners or landlords. This too often meant substandard residential conditions and unfair agreements—whether under labor contracts as agricultural workers residing on farms or dwelling leases as renters in cities. In both instances, the concern with dilapidated housing, exorbitant rents, and sanitation provided a foundation for the concrete demands made by activists and everyday people as they sought to at minimum improve and at best transform their daily lives.

In cities throughout the country, low-rent subsidized housing did provide affordable shelter, but only for a small percentage of those in need. It also became an abettor of downtown growth and urban redevelopment. Government officials and developers needed places to put people, mostly black and low-income, dislocated by urban projects such as office buildings, convention centers, highways, or commercial districts. With the federal government's passage of the U.S. Housing Act of 1937 and Act of 1949, public housing "projects" opened, but not in suburbs. Many white suburban residents did not want black middle-class homeowners in their communities (represented by the character of Karl Linder and the Clybourne Park Improvement Association in *A Raisin in the Sun*), let alone low-income black people living in subsidized apartments. Such vigorous resistance along with the support of white elected officials often prevented public housing from entering suburbia.

Public housing, then, became the child of cities, proliferating in New York and Philadelphia, in Cleveland and Chicago, in Baltimore and Atlanta, and in Birmingham, Alabama. No matter what region of the country, public housing traditionally opened on a Jim Crow basis. In this way, the state built racial segregation and discrimination into neighborhoods and the shallow social safety net. Despite this, and detractors' disparagement of government-subsidized housing as socialistic and therefore anti-American, low-income black (and white) residents welcomed the promise of modernization. These new apartments, for which there were long waiting lists, represented little bits of heaven, particularly for pioneer black families who had resided in tenements and squalid apartments without indoor plumbing. Amaza Spruill expressed extreme happiness when she and her husband received news that they had been accepted in Poe Homes, the first public housing complex to open in the Upper South city of Baltimore, Maryland. It was for blacks only.[105]

Despite the urban politics shaping public housing, residents made lives for themselves there. They raised families and made friends. They sponsored recreational activities, started organizations, and they also protested poor living conditions. For some future tenant and welfare rights activists such as Johnnie Tillmon, the deteriorating living conditions and disparagement they experienced as public housing tenants, alongside ongoing poverty in cities, sparked discontent and protest. Moreover, not only did Black Power activists grow up in public housing, but "the bricks" also became critical sites of organizing in the civil rights, anti-poverty, and Black Power era.

For a short time Angela Davis lived in public housing. There, as youngsters, she and her friends experienced a sense of safety. Her family moved out of public housing and into a single-family wooden house with steeples and gables and grass. In the white neighborhood where Jim Crow was still in full force, the young Angela—as had the young Lorraine and so many other anonymous black youths—would become witness to the ugliness of racial hatred. The hostility was palpable. Davis writes in her autobiography: "At the age of four I was aware that the people across the street were different—without being able to trace their alien nature to the color of their skin. What made them different from our neighbors in the projects was the frown on their faces."[106] In a very short time, white residents began to sell their houses, and the area became known as "Dynamite Hill." Angela's parents, like Lorraine's, also kept guns hidden in the house "and vigilance was constant."[107] North or South, Chicago or Birmingham, it did not matter; black people were searching for better lives and proclaiming their humanity, and they took different measures to protect themselves while doing that.

In cities, like in rural communities, black people had to confront white power. The pervasiveness of racial segregation, oppression, and white supremacy provoked black activist demands for political control. Wherever black people ended up, they experienced a mixed bag of opportunity and discrimination. This reality, alongside an increasing U.S. government aversion to leftist politics often expressed through anti-Communism, left an indelible impression on the teenage Angela Davis. Davis was the child of a black radical mother, Sallye Bell Davis, who had joined SNYC. Angela Davis recounted learning that even in "the paragon of racial concord," New York City, the FBI followed her girlfriend's father, who was a black communist, while another friend's family, which was interracial, had a hard time finding a place to stay. And on the West Coast in Los Angeles where other members of her family settled, some had success as property owners, while others experienced "such difficult straits they were living off welfare."[108]

Race also influenced access, or lack thereof, to jobs. This impacted black people's economic security, as well as shaped their ideologies, politics, and protestations in the early 1940s. Michigan resident and Colored Women Democratic Club member Lutensia Dillard sent a letter to President Roosevelt in April 1941. "We aren't getting a fair deal," she wrote. "Some of our boys are being drafted for service for our country and here we are in a free land are not aloud [sic] to work and make a living for their wives and childrens."[109] Her lament was nothing new, but their organized response was.

Months later, A. Philip Randolph was seemingly propelled by the suggestion of another "sister" who, at a mass meeting held earlier in Chicago, proposed "throw[ing] 50,000 Negroes around the White House."[110] In June 1941, indeed, Randolph threatened to organize an all-black march on the nation's capital to protest the exclusion of African Americans from federal departments and defense contracts. Imbibing the spirit of the "Double V" campaign and presaging future mass marches on D.C., Randolph demanded that black workers have access to wartime jobs. If not, black people would mount "a monster and huge demonstration at Lincoln's monument [that would] shake up white America."[111] Boasting activist roots that extended back to the era of New Negro militancy and socialist critique, Randolph saw "Negro Americans" as "a mammoth machine of mass action" who must "in this period of power politics" be ready to assert pressure on behalf of "the vital and important issues of the Negro."[112]

Black people held March on Washington meetings in numerous cities. In 1941 in Chicago James Forman remembers at the age of 12 attending mass rallies and church meetings called by Randolph.[113] On June 25, 1941, President Franklin D. Roosevelt responded; he signed into effect Executive Order 8802, which created the Federal Employment Practice Committee (FEPC) to investigate discrimination, thereby averting the march. While ultimately seeking inclusion, the March on Washington Movement (MOWM), organized in 1941, publicly displayed black people's desire for economic opportunities by calling for a blacks-only movement aimed at pressuring government officials to provide legislation protecting black citizen-workers' rights. While the doors may have been pried open a crack, fully unfettered they would not be.

Low-wage work and the lack of jobs created desperate situations and responses. Sometimes this included crime, and this threat of crime—whether real or imagined—provided the police with opportunities to monitor and, as many black residents thought, occupy their neighborhoods. Moneymaking illicit businesses and leisure pursuits and other hallmarks of informal economy undoubtedly existed in black neighborhoods. According to Forman, during the 1940s, some of his friends used marijuana (though he did not), and "the rugged life of Chicago's South Side [included] a life dominated by gang warfare and petty stealing."[114] Numbers rackets, juke joints, theft, and even drug peddling landed black men and black women in jails and prisons across the United States. Malcolm Little was one of them.

In 1946, the same year Elijah Muhammad was released from the penitentiary in Michigan, Malcolm went to Norfolk Prison Colony in Massachusetts on a burglary charge. While incarcerated, he spent a lot of time reading in the prison library. Books by black intellectuals, like Du Bois's *Souls of Black Folk,* and Carter G. Woodson's *Negro History,* and J. A. Rogers's *Sex and Race,* captured his attention, as did the revolutionary anti-slavery struggles of the enslaved Nat Turner in 1831 and white abolitionist John Brown in 1859, and "Gandhi's accounts of the struggle to drive the British out of India."[115] In prison, Malcolm also discovered the NOI. His experience portended the emergence of prisons as a key site for politicizing black working-class and poor people. After his release in August 1952, Malcolm X began his meteoric rise as a Muslim minister in the NOI.

In the early to mid-1940s, however, Malcolm Little was conked, zoot-suited, and mesmerized, not like his father by a black political firebrand, but by the pursuit of pleasure and money. In this moment, hipness, not racial militancy, ruled his days and nights. This Malcolm was not imagining an activist future—even as he joined others in avoiding the draft through a performance of mental illness. Maybe amidst war mobilization he had an inkling of the profound black diasporic political uprisings underway, but surely he never envisioned himself as a globally recognized spokesperson of black people who would have the temerity to accuse the United States of human rights violations before the United Nations.

In so many ways Hansberry's lament about "places apart" captured the daily experiences of millions of black people. Their hardships in the face of voluminous social, political, and economic oppression by individuals and the government fed desires for racial self-determination. This, alongside the winds of Cold War–era global change and the tides of local fervor that demanded rights and equality, tamped down, as well as hurried, the storms of "Negro" and "black" power revolts in the days, years, and decades ahead.

Notes

1 Amy Jacques Garvey, "I am a Negro—and Beautiful," in *Modern Black Nationalism,* ed. Van DeBurg, 58.
2 Palmer, 119.
3 Ida B. Wells-Barnett, *The East St. Louis Massacre,* 16, http://lincoln.lib.niu.edu/cgi-bin/philologic/getobject.pl?c.5065:4.lincoln.
4 Giddings, *Ida,* 563–566.
5 Wells-Barnett, *The East St. Louis Massacre,* 16, Also see Nikki Brown, who argues that the East St. Louis riot was also a watershed moment for middle-class black women who more vociferously began challenging all aspects of racial discrimination and violence. Nikki Brown, 22, 24–27.
6 Hubert Harrison, "The East St. Louis Horror," in *A Hubert Harrison Reader,* ed. Perry, 94.
7 Tabitha C. Wang, "East St. Louis Race Riot: July 2, 1917," in *The Black Past Remembered & Reclaimed: An Online Reference Guide to African American History,* ed. Quintard Taylor, www.blackpast.org/aah/east-st-louis-race-riot-july-2-1917.
8 Duncan, 43.
9 "Speech by Marcus Garvey, July 8, 1917," www.pbs.org/wgbh/amex/garvey/filmmore/ps_riots.html. Also see Tony Martin.
10 Plummer, *Rising Wind,* 15.
11 Giddings, *Ida,* 585.
12 Ibid., 590; Plummer, *Rising Wind,* 15, 18.
13 Giddings, *Ida,* 6. According to Ida Wells, at least 10,000 lynchings of mostly black people by white people occurred in the South between 1878 and 1898. See Hine and Thompson, 167.
14 Winston James, 125.
15 Christopher Alan Bracey, 56.
16 Berry, *My Face Is Black Is True.*
17 Frank Byrd, "Harlem Rent Parties," August 23, 1938, American Life Histories: Manuscripts from the Federal Writers' Project, 1936–1940, American Memory, Library of Congress, http://memory.loc.gov/cgi-bin/query/r?ammem/wpa:@field%28DOCID+@lit%28wpa221011010%29%29.
18 The homesteads were in Georgia, Florida, Alabama, Mississippi, Louisiana, and Arkansas—many of which were in what became known as the Black Belt South.

These statistics come from the history section on the PBS website: "Homecoming: Sometimes I'm Haunted by Memories of Red Dirt and Clay," and "Black Farming & Land Loss: A History," www.pbs.org/itvs/homecoming/history.html. According to the website, by 1969, black farmers only owned six million acres of land.

19 Hubert Harrison, *When Africa Awakes,* 1920 (Reprint, Baltimore: Black Classic Press, 1997), 32.
20 Lang, 19.
21 Amy Jacques Garvey, *Garvey and Garveyism,* 15.
22 Vincent, 18.
23 Van DeBurg, *Modern Black Nationalism,* 11.
24 Taylor, *The Veiled Garvey,* 1.
25 Taylor, "Intellectual Pan-African Feminists," in *Time Longer than Rope,* ed. Payne and Green, 187–188.
26 Taylor, *The Veiled Garvey,* 12. For a definition of "community feminism," see p. 2.
27 Berry, *My Face Is Black Is True,* 32.
28 Amy Jacques Garvey, *Garvey and Garveyism,* 23.
29 Ibid.
30 Tony Martin, 60; Vincent, 114.
31 Universal Negro Improvement Association, "Declaration of Rights of the Negro Peoples of the World," in *Modern Black Nationalism,* ed. Van DeBurg, 23–31.
32 Amy Jacques Garvey, *Garvey and Garveyism,* 27.
33 Consolidated Bank and Trust closed its doors in 2011. Premiere Bank took over its locations and operations. Elsa Barkley Brown, 616.
34 Vincent, 130.
35 Vincent, 53.
36 Cedric Robinson, *Black Marxism,* 214.
37 Unlike some, however, Randolph not only criticized the UNIA, but also called for Garvey's deportation.
38 Locke, 5–10.
39 Locke, 11.
40 Mary Helen Washington, "Zora Neale Hurston: A Woman in Half Shadow," in *I Love Myself When I am Laughing,* ed. Alice Walker, 17.
41 Langston Hughes, "The Negro Artist and the Racial Mountain," in *Modern Black Nationalism,* ed. Van DeBurg, 52–56.
42 Hughes, "The Negro Artist and the Racial Mountain," 55.
43 Amy Jacques Garvey, "I Am a Negro—and Beautiful."
44 Before black became beautiful, the color "brown" provided a middle ground for constructing racial identity and asserting pride. See Laila Haidarali, "Polishing Brown Diamonds: African American Women, Popular Magazines, and the Advent of Modeling in Early Postwar America," in *Unequal Sisters,* ed. Ruiz with DuBois, 535–550.
45 Queen Mother Moore, interview by E. Menelik Pinto, 1985.
46 Raymond R. Sommerville, "Queen Mother Audley Moore," in *Notable Black American Women Book II,* ed. Jean Carney Smith; "The Black Scholar Interviews: Queen Mother Moore," *Black Scholar* 4 (March–April 1973): 52. Also see Harold, 1.
47 "The Black Scholar Interviews: Queen Mother Moore," 52.
48 Akinyele Omowale Umoja defines armed resistance "as individual and collective use of force for protection, protest, or other goals of insurgent political action and in defense of human rights." Included in this category are "armed self-defense, retaliatory violence, spontaneous rebellion, guerilla warfare, armed vigilance/enforcement, and armed struggle." For more specific definitions of each, see Umoja, 7–8. On armed resistance in the black freedom struggle, also see, for instance, Emilye J. Crosby, "'This nonviolent stuff ain't no good. It'll get ya killed': Teaching about Self-Defense in the African-American Freedom Struggle," in *Teaching the Civil Rights Movement,* eds.

Armstrong, Roberson, Williams, and Holt, 159–73; Strain; Simon Wendt, "The Roots of Black Power?," in *The Black Power Movement,* ed. Joseph, 145–166.

49 Audley (Queen Mother) Moore, interview by Cheryl Gilkes Townsend, 1978, in *The Black Women Oral History Project*, ed. Hill.

50 McDuffie and Woodard, 516.

51 Watkins-Owens, 92–111.

52 Janet R. Gornall, "Audley Moore and the Politics of Black Revolutionary Motherhood," article manuscript in author's possession.

53 Carmichael also mentioned Mae Mallory and Malcolm X. See Carmichael with Thelwell, 101.

54 Taylor, *The Veiled Garvey,* 41. Quote in Hahn, 471.

55 Donna Murch, "A Campus Where Black Power Won," in *Neighborhood Rebels,* ed. Joseph, 91.

56 Rolinson, 20.

57 Berry, *My Face Is Black Is True,* 233–236.

58 Marable, *Malcolm X,* 16; McDuffie and Woodard, 512–514.

59 *Marcus Garvey: Look for Me in the Whirlwind.*

60 Winston James, 126.

61 Marable, *Malcolm X,* 33.

62 Rhonda Y. Williams, *The Politics of Public Housing,* 26.

63 McDuffie and Woodard, 517.

64 Ella Baker and Marvel Cooke, "The Slave Market," *Crisis* 42 (November 1935): 330–331.

65 Gilmore, 217. On Louise Thompson, see p. 135.

66 McDuffie, *Sojourning for Freedom,* 112.

67 Florence Rice, interview by Gerda Lerner, September 23, 1970; Mosel Brinson to United States Department of Agriculture, February 4, 1935; Pinkie Pilcher to President Roosevelt, December 23, 1936, in *Black Women in White America,* ed. Lerner, 275, 399–400, 401, respectively.

68 See Kelley, *Hammer and Hoe;* Daniel, *Dispossession.*

69 Joe William Trotter Jr., "From a Raw Deal to a New Deal? 1929–1945," in *To Make Our World Anew,* ed. Kelley and Lewis, 409–444.

70 Vincent Harding, Robin D.G. Kelley, and Earl Lewis, "We Changed the World, 1945–1970," in *To Make Our World Anew,* 477; Ula Taylor, "Elijah Muhammad's Nation of Islam: Separatism, Regendering, and a Secular Approach to Black Power after Malcolm X (1965–1975)," in *Freedom North,* eds. Theoharis and Woodard, 177–195.

71 Clegg. Also, "A Historic Look at the Most Honorable Elijah Muhammad," www.noi.org/about_the_honorable_elijah_muhammad.shtml.

72 Clegg, 99.

73 Ula Taylor, "Elijah Muhammad's Nation of Islam," 191, 195.

74 Clegg, 82.

75 The number of temples grew from 16 in 1955 to 50 in 1960. Ula Taylor, "Elijah Muhammad's Nation of Islam," 177–178.

76 For instance, black Bolsheviks had attended the Fourth Pan-African Congress in New York in 1927. While this gave a "nod to Soviet racial policy," it was still a race-first gathering. Michael O. West and William G. Martin, "Contours of the Black International," in *From Toussaint to Tupac,* ed. West, Martin, and Wilkins, 15.

77 The son of slaves, Haywood grew up in Omaha and Minneapolis but experienced the South as a black soldier. Gilmore, 62.

78 Cited in Claudia Jones, "On the Right to Self-Determination for the Negro People in the Black Belt," *Political Affairs* 25:1 (January 1946): 71.

79 Robeson, 10.

80 Robeson, 32.

81 Kelley, *Freedom Dreams,* 52. Ransby, *Eslanda.*
82 Kelley, *Hammer and Hoe,* xii; Weigand, 20–21.
83 Selassie was heralded as the black messiah of the anti-racist religious movement Rastafarianism in Garvey's Jamaica. Munro, 38. On Italo-Ethiopian War, also see Kelley, *Race Rebels;* Plummer, *Rising Wind;* and Von Eschen.
84 Michael O. West and William G. Martin, "Contours of the Black International: From Toussaint to Tupac," 14.
85 Kelley, *Freedom Dreams,* 49.
86 Ransby, *Ella Baker,* 95.
87 Ibid., 95–99.
88 McDuffie, *Sojourning for Freedom,* 115.
89 Bush, 128.
90 "Historical/Biographical Note," Audley Moore: FOIA File (United States Federal Bureau of Investigation), TAM 410, http://dlib.nyu.edu/findingaids/html/tamwag/moorea_foia_fbi.html.
91 Nikhil Pal Singh, "The Black Panthers and the 'Undeveloped Country' of the Left," in *The Black Panther Party [Reconsidered],* ed. Charles E. Jones, 77.
92 Plummer, *Rising Wind,* 74.
93 Lance Hill, *The Deacons for Defense.*
94 Mary Frances Berry, Presentation, ASALH, Jacksonville, Florida, September 2013.
95 In 1945 Horace R. Cayton and St. Clair Drake wrote *Black Metropolis* and Chicagoan Gwendolyn Brooks, who joined the South Side Writers Group, published *A Street in Bronzeville.* A sociological study and a book of poetry—they both exposed the nitty-gritty of black urban living in Bronzeville. Darlene Clark Hine, "Chicago Black Renaissance," in *Encyclopedia of Chicago,* www.encyclopedia.chicagohistory.org/pages/240.html; Davarian L. Baldwin, 121–155.
96 Allen R. Kamp, "The History Behind *Hansberry v. Lee,*" *U.C. Davis Law Review* 20 (1986–1987): 484.
97 Plummer, *Rising Wind,* 40.
98 Hansberry, 20–21.
99 Forman, *The Making of Black Revolutionaries,* 29.
100 Ibid., 21.
101 Hansberry, 20–21.
102 Joseph, *Waiting 'Til the Midnight Hour,* 4.
103 Hansberry, 45.
104 "Breaking Restrictive Covenants," in *Black Women in White America,* ed. Lerner, 410. Also see Hirsch; Sugrue, *Origins of the Urban Crisis;* and Rhonda Y. Williams, *The Politics of Public Housing.*
105 Rhonda Y. Williams, *The Politics of Public Housing,* 43.
106 Davis, 78.
107 Ibid.
108 Ibid., 85.
109 Lutensia Dillard to President Roosevelt, April 23, 1941, in *Black Women in White America,* ed. Lerner, 405.
110 William P. Jones, 1.
111 A. Philip Randolph, "Call to the March, July 1, 1941," in *Let Nobody Turn Us Around,* ed. Marable and Mullings, 309–310.
112 Ibid.
113 Forman, *The Making of Black Revolutionaries,* 30.
114 Ibid., 26, 33.
115 Malcolm X with Alex Haley, 174–176.

2
FROM "NEGRO POWER" TOWARD BLACK REVOLT

"If there is no struggle," [Frederick] Douglass taught us, "there is no progress. Power concedes nothing without a demand. It never did and it never will." So let us next discuss the struggle that still must be waged, and the Negro power that can win our demand.

— *Paul Robeson (1958)*[1]

As World War II ended, the Cold War heated up, and quests for racial justice in the United States multiplied, "Black Power" and "Negro power" made their print debuts—one as the title of a travelogue in 1954 and in a 1957 *Ebony* article, the latter in a memoir in 1958. These phrases attracted public attention and news coverage; however, neither became rallying cries nor provoked a groundswell of black activism. For sure, the reality of black subjugation spurred outrage as well as activism in the United States. Unlike in the mid-1960s, however, when the word "black" in Black Power evoked a bevy of frenzied responses, during the 1950s the word "red" and all it implied held sway. The fear of "Reds" and the perceived and real sympathies with Communism and the Soviet Union incited "scares" and nationalistic anxieties that produced political campaigns to upend, contain, and manage protest at home and abroad. Even so, the 1950s marked a noteworthy coming-out moment for Black Power and Negro power, especially when "red" met "black."

In this volatile decade, a dozen years before the phrase Black Power gained popular cache as a freedom movement slogan, the native son of Mississippi and Chicago-based author Richard Wright published *Black Power*. The book shared a black self-determination story. It was not, however, one native to the United States. Instead, it detailed the saga of the anti-colonial struggle unfolding in the British-controlled Gold Coast colony. Wright recognized that in Africa, as in the

United States, black people suffered white supremacist rule, and just an ocean away they were initiating a battle for national sovereignty. Soon, the Gold Coast colony would become independent Ghana and, in winning its liberation, a potent symbol of black political power throughout the diaspora, including in the United States.

Two years after the publication of *Black Power,* Wright published another significant book. *The Color Curtain* documented the Afro-Asian Conference in Bandung, Indonesia, in 1955. The future co-founder of the Revolutionary Action Movement (RAM), Donald Freeman remembered reading *The Color Curtain.* That was 1958—the same year that Paul Robeson published his memoir in which he explicitly discussed "Negro Power." A college student at the time, Freeman recalled the profound effect *The Color Curtain* had upon his political outlook. "I ain't been the same since" Freeman stated, continuing: "Now I had read [Wright's] novels, but that book . . . [t]hat beyond blew my mind. I was a different person from then on. It was how I learned about the Bandung world."[2]

Four years later, Freeman read Robeson's memoir *Here I Stand,* as well as learned more about the pan-African activist-intellectual Du Bois. Both of these men influenced Freeman, too. Why? They paid an "excruciatingly painful price" for their radical activist commitment. Robeson suffered ostracism, loss of employment, and surveillance. Both men had their passports revoked. Stated Freeman: "[Robeson and Du Bois] are the two African Americans that Don Freeman most appreciates in terms of their commitment to the liberation of ALL OPPRESSED peoples on the planet earth, especially African Americans." He continued, "That's my commitment. The same commitment they had. Those two people."[3]

The writings and commitments of Wright, Robeson, and Du Bois provide a window into black people's mid-20th-century power politics. Equally important, these political goings-on bring our attention to a broader spectrum of events, ideas, men *and* women activists, and organizations coalescing around black liberation during the 1950s. The Gold Coast colony, as a "place apart" in the African diaspora, stood as one symbol of the "mandate of national liberation," and the Bandung Conference ushered in a notion of Afro-Asian solidarity (whether actualized or not) that fueled a black revolutionary zeitgeist. These 1950s events, and the black militancy undergirding them, exposes a multi-pronged activist politics that continued to privilege racial self-determination and sovereignty alongside concrete demands for economic power and community control. It also augured critique and repression.

The Cold War decade of the 1950s undoubtedly betrothed political realignment, ruptures, and erasures, giving rise to a black protest culture that privileged integrating into and reforming the U.S. nation-state while simultaneously seeking to sideline if not suppress black nationalism and black radicalism. In fact, Harold Cruse lamented as early as 1964 in his article "The Roots of Black Nationalism," published in the independent, New York-based, black newsletter *Liberator,* that the younger generation of black activists did not have a deeper historical understanding of not just 10 years prior, but over 50 years of struggle and politics that created the dynamics they confronted. In Cruse's estimation, this discontinuity would make for "a-historical," "limited," and "oversimplified" understandings of American realities. Yet, in his critique also lay something else: evidence of keepers of "power" flames. These keepers forged political contexts, left legacies, and carried memories of activism past and, during their lives, some of them served as conduits of knowledge for the discontented in the 1960s.[4]

Radicalism and Power in the 1950s

The roads to Richard Wright's *Black Power* and *The Color Curtain*—and the broader realities and ethos that they captured and symbolized—actually began in the mid-1940s with familiar and new black actors, as well as shifting global politics. In this way, it is a narrative better conveyed by taking a quick trip back to that decade and, then, trekking forward again to the 1950s.

By the mid-1940s, anti-colonial struggles had arrived on the world stage. In fact, according to Cedric Robinson, "The Second World War was followed by decades of race war on a global scale," and that race war took place in the midst of an ideological Cold War.[5] The "iron curtain" fell and split the world into competing spheres of political influence controlled by white superpowers. The United States as superpower engaged in an ideological battle with its wartime ally the Soviet Union and, under these geopolitical circumstances, other nations aligned with one or the other. By 1955, however, several dozens of African and Asian colonies not only won their independence, but they increasingly resisted becoming beholden to either superpower. Instead they mounted a non-alignment movement, one that positioned them as part not of an iron curtain, but of a "color curtain" that heralded Third World solidarity.

As the Cold War heated up and decolonization flourished, so did the push for statist-based international human rights. The United Nations became the embodiment of that political move. Formed in San Francisco, the United Nations had its headquarters in New York City. Its location there not only placed it squarely within the orbit of U.S. influence, but also made it a convenient and consistent target for black radical activists seeking to publicize and secure relief from U.S. racism. W.E.B. Du Bois during his last years with the NAACP presented to the United Nations the first petition on behalf of black people in 1947. The petition's name conveyed the weightiness of its desires: "An Appeal to the World: A Statement on the Denial of Human Rights to Minorities in the Case of Citizens of Negro Descent in the United States of America and an Appeal to the United Nations for Redress." Over the next decade, other U.S. black radicals and nationalists followed a similar strategy. William Patterson presented "We Charge Genocide," which Robeson helped to write, in 1951 on behalf of the leftist Civil Rights Congress (CRC), and Audley Moore presented a petition in 1957. Black nationalist Malcolm X, who became a political being in the 1950s, too, sought an audience before the United Nations in the mid-1960s. In doing so, Malcolm X had followed in the footsteps of Paul Robeson (his "only living hero other than the Honorable Elijah Muhammad"), as well as Patterson and Moore.[6] While incarcerated, Malcolm admired Robeson's courage to criticize the U.S. state and stand against white supremacy and the Korean War. As black nationalists and leftists, they all wanted the world to know that the United States violated black people's human rights, and that its self-avowed claim as leader of the "Free World" foundered regularly on the shoals of race.

In 1946, the same year as the iron curtain's rise, but almost a decade before the color curtain heralded in Wright's book, Richard Wright left the United States where places apart were the norm. Seeking a respite from acerbic U.S. racial politics, Wright embarked upon an eight-month sojourn to Paris. In 1946 his books roused resentment with several letters sent to the FBI calling him a "nigger," "one of the biggest [sic] spreaders of race hatred there is in the world," and "a black nazi" because he critiqued race relations through his fiction, *Native Son* (1940) and *Black Boy* (1945).[7] The legend of Paris's racial tolerance, as well as its existentialist intellectual movement, lured the author away from the "Black Metropolis."[8] On his way back to the United States in early 1947, Wright stopped for a short time in London where he met the Trinidadian political activist and "father of African emancipation" George Padmore. The chair of the International African Services Bureau (IASB), which sought African independence and self-government, Padmore had taken a leadership role in organizing the Fifth Pan-African Congress.

As timing would have it, the noted "father of pan-Africanism" W.E.B. Du Bois also had begun discussing organizing a Pan-African Congress in the mid-1940s. In conceiving a proposed Fifth Pan-African Congress, Du Bois worked with Amy Jacques Garvey, a critical purveyor of black nationalism and steward of Garveyism internationally. Ironically at the height of the Garvey movement, Du Bois had dismissed its namesake as a racial chauvinist promoting wrongheaded colonization schemes. In 1944, Amy Jacques Garvey had approached Du Bois to ask for his help in preparing an African freedom charter to present to the United Nations. During these discussions Du Bois suggested holding a Fifth Pan-African Congress and asked Amy Jacques Garvey to be a co-convener. U.S. government officials, as well as members of the NAACP, however, stymied Du Bois's efforts.[9] No matter, Padmore and the IASB brought the Fifth Pan-African Congress to fruition in Manchester, England, in October 1945—the same month as the ratification of the United Nations Charter.[10]

Unlike the previous pan-African congresses, the Manchester congress privileged African intellectuals such as Nigeria's Nnamdi Azikiwe, Kenya's Jomo Kenyatta, and the Gold Coast colony's Kwame Nkrumah. These anti-colonial activists, who became African presidents and prime ministers, had received part of their education at British as well as U.S. black colleges. Lincoln (then all-male), Howard, and Fisk universities became safe intellectual spaces for progenitors of political self-determination and black independence abroad and at home.[11] This had been the case as early as the 1930s. Azikiwe attended Howard University in

1930 and graduated from Lincoln University. As president of Lincoln University, Horace Mann Bond, the father of future student activist and Georgia legislator Julian Bond, taught African nationals who would, according to historian Yohuru Williams, apply anti-racist frameworks learned in the United States to their anti-colonial struggles. These struggles, in turn, would inspire U.S. black activists.[12] For instance, Horace Mann Bond mentored Nkrumah. As a student at Lincoln, Nkrumah learned about Garvey, whose "idealized visions" of African unity and economic autonomy "were like manna from heaven"; such ideas inspired Nkrumah and influenced his pan-African political desires.[13]

At the Fifth Pan-African Congress in Manchester, Padmore introduced Du Bois as the father of pan-Africanism. Du Bois brought greetings on behalf of black Americans and then "relinquished the podium to the rapporteur for the session, [Kwame] Francis Nkrumah."[14] Amy Jacques Garvey, who almost two decades later documented the influence that Garvey's quest for "African national and racial equality" had on Nkrumah, could not afford to go to the Manchester congress.[15] Amy Ashwood Garvey, however, did attend. Already in England and participating in the IASB, she not only welcomed delegates to the opening session, but true to form, she also spoke about and challenged women's oppression.[16]

The Manchester congress marked a critical departure. As part of the black diasporic community, African political activists and intellectuals confronted the prevalent idea of gradual independence and trusteeship of African colonies. The newly formed United Nations, as well as many black American activists whose political leanings ranged from liberal to leftist, including Du Bois, had held this moderate view. African intellectuals, however, had envisioned African independence differently. Self-determination, national liberation, or "call it what you may," self-governance was a right.[17] Their demands echoed components of the 1941 Atlantic Charter, which served as the basis of the United Nations Charter. The Atlantic Charter held that nations had the right to self-government, sovereignty, and economic advancement, and could not usurp another nation without its citizens' approval. Birthed in the context of Nazi Germany's aggression, the Atlantic Charter, however, referred primarily to European nations—not its colonies. Even so, its rhetoric, as well as its Eurocentricism, likely inspired the movement for an African freedom charter and subsequent anti-colonial struggles.

When Richard Wright met George Padmore in 1947, the Manchester congress was already two years old. Its tenets of national self-determination, however, had remained politically trenchant. By this time in the Gold Coast colony, Nkrumah had already begun acting out its mandates as secretary of the United Gold Coast Convention (UGCC), a political party that sought independence from Britain. Nkrumah went to jail for the first of numerous times in 1948 in the midst of a violent disturbance that erupted in the country when police fired on local black veterans (killing three) as they protested outside the governor's castle, demanding cost-of-living increases and relief from exorbitant retail prices on imported goods. Black veterans, as in the United States, had begun demanding better from the nations that they served in wartime. By the time the protest ended, 29 people had been killed and 237 injured. As a member of the youth arm of the UGCC, Nkrumah helped organize laborers, farmers, and trade unionists, men and women, across the colony. Tired of economic exploitation, UGCC members sought "the right to control their total destiny," as well as "their ancestral homeland."[18] Within the next year, after internal organizational disagreement over whether the expansion of the vote should be accompanied by property qualifications, Nkrumah left the UGCC movement and formed the mass-based nationalist Convention People's Party (CPP), which sponsored "positive action" or Gandhian-styled nonviolent campaigns for "self-government now."

Further north on another continent, on the same side of the Atlantic Ocean, Robeson, who had met Nkrumah in London in the 1930s, traveled from England to Paris. There, in April 1949, the same year as the Chinese Revolution, Robeson attended the World Peace Conference. The night before he departed England, he met with the Coordinating Committee of Colonial Peoples in London and the president of the anti-apartheid South African Indian Congress. When he arrived in Paris, he joined a throng of 2,000 students who asked him to "say in their name that they did not want war. That is what [he] said."[19] In an unrehearsed moment, with his boisterous, deep voice resonating, Robeson said, "We in America do not forget that it is on the backs of the poor whites of Europe . . . and on the backs of millions of black people the wealth of America has been acquired. And we are resolved that it shall be distributed in an equitable manner among all of our children and we don't want any hysterical stupidity about our participating in a war against anybody no matter whom. We are determined to fight for peace. We do not wish to fight the Soviet Union."[20]

Reporting his remarks stateside, the *Associated Press* presented Robeson as a traitor, who depicted the United States as an oppressive racial regime—one that black people would not defend against the Soviet Union. Although the article ostensibly misquoted Robeson, it did communicate a reality. The United States did oppress black people. That inarguable truth, however, did not move U.S. officials, who sought to govern a nation built on racial hierarchy while finding itself embroiled in a tenacious ideological battle for global influence. Robeson's reputation and career took a beating, as did the black radical politics he represented.

By now, individuals and organizations ideologically akin to Robeson had garnered the full antipathy of black and white anti-Communists. In the United States, President Harry Truman, a democrat, established loyalty oaths for government employees. Blacklists emerged. Labor and rights organizations purged leftists. Flirtations with the Soviet Union, Communism, or leftist politics, including publicizing U.S. racism, reverberated as traitorous. Federal government officials called U.S. citizens before Congress to publicly disavow any Communist affiliation, affirm their patriotism, and testify against others suspected of subversion. Black racial liberals, who were anti-Communist, found themselves criticizing black leftists along ideological lines even when they possessed similar anti-segregationist politics. This was the case when Major League baseball player Jackie Robinson testified against Paul Robeson in government hearings. In the hyper-paranoid environment of McCarthyism and the Cold War, Robeson's outspokenness—as well as that of Hollywood stars, artists, leftists, and ordinary people, or anyone who stood against the status quo—drew the attention of the U.S. Department of State. Joseph McCarthy, a Republican senator from Wisconsin, further fueled fears of subversion. The prevailing fear of Communist infiltration in the U.S. government and society swept not only the likes of Du Bois and Robeson into the folds, but also the black radical feminist activist Claudia Jones.

Claudia Jones was born in 1915 in Trinidad—in the same year that Griffith's *Birth of a Nation* regaled white America and in the same home-place of Stokely Carmichael, a man generations her junior who nationally popularized "Black Power" as a rallying cry. Jones arrived in the United States by way of Ellis Island on February 9, 1924 on the SS *Voltaire* with her three sisters and aunt, just like Amy Jacques Garvey and many other West Indian immigrants had before her and would after her. Once in the United States, Jones and her family confronted life. Suffering the loss of her 37-year-old mother to spinal meningitis in 1933 in the midst of the Great Depression and herself languishing in a sanatorium for almost a year in 1934 fighting tuberculosis, Jones knew well the hardships of inadequate housing, poor health, and daily poverty. In 1935 she graduated high school and began working. According to biographer Carol Boyce Davies, Claudia Jones labored in sales, as well as in a laundry, factory, and millinery. Between 1935 and 1936 she organized with others in defense of the Scottsboro Boys, joined the Communist Party, and became chair of the national council of the Young Communist League. By 1942 she was in the crosshairs of the FBI. This woman, who became a leading theoretician in the CPUSA, unabashedly supported black self-determination, particularly in the Black Belt South, and called attention to the "super-exploitation" of black women workers. She wrote about it, spoke on it, and drew the enmity of the U.S. State Department because of it.[21]

In 1946, Jones published an article in the Communist Party's journal *Political Affairs*. In it, she argued that the right to black self-determination required "energetic struggle for concrete partial demands" linked to "daily needs and problems."[22] Three years later, the same year that Robeson spoke at the World Peace Conference, Jones penned "An End to the Neglect of the Problems of Negro Women," also in *Political Affairs*. With the threat of deportation hanging over her head after her first arrest in January 1948, Jones, as had Communist Party member Louise Thompson, exposed the triple oppression of black women workers. In fact, she saw them as "the most oppressed stratum."[23] On average, they earned half as much as white women. Wrote Jones: "Little wonder, then, that in Negro communities the conditions of ghetto-living—low salaries, high rents, high prices, etc.—virtually became an iron curtain hemming in the lives of Negro children and undermining their health and spirit."[24]

Bodily, economic, and state violence against black women had no geographical boundaries. Black women suffered. Claudia Jones described the case of Rosa Lee Ingram as one that especially "dramatize[d] the oppressed states of Negro woman-hood."[25] A widowed Georgia sharecropper, Ingram, with two of her 14 children, sat on death row, convicted for killing a white man who threatened to rape her in 1947.[26] Ingram protected herself, and when police arrested her, other black women protested her incarceration and unmasked state violence and systems of exploitation. As Jones wrote, "The Ingram case illustrates the landless, Jim Crow, oppressed status of the Negro family in America," as well as the "degradation of Negro women today under American bourgeois democracy moving to fascism and war."[27] She exposed the manifestations of racism, capitalism, imperialism, and sexism in the U.S. polity and, for that matter, the Communist Party itself. Her analysis not only contributed to a black feminist radical tradition, but also anticipated future critiques of state power. Jones, too, became the target of state persecution: she, like fellow West Indian Marcus Garvey, experienced arrest, prison, and deportation.[28]

Under the stewardship of Senator McCarthy, the federal government held hearings, or as many referred to them "witch-hunts," against presumed Communist subversives through the House Un-American Activities Committee (HUAC). The State Department served a deportation order on Claudia Jones in 1950 and revoked both Robeson's and Du Bois's passports, alleging that given their Communist sympathies and criticism of U.S. racial politics, allowing them to travel internationally "would be contrary to the best interests of the United States."[29] This was not a new tactic. As early as World War I, the State Department refused to issue passports to those it considered agitators. Du Bois was among the few black delegates who made it to Versailles "by ruse" or "connections to powerful whites."[30] In 1950, Congress also passed, over Truman's veto, the McCarran Internal Security Act, which required Communist organizations to register with the government. The act established a board to investigate suspected subversive organizations as well.

Black essayist and novelist James Baldwin, who had become an expatriate in Paris, returned to New York that same year "at the height of the national convulsion called McCarthyism." Having marched as a youth in a May Day parade that called for "landlords to tear the slums down," Baldwin initially knew little "about Communism," but "a lot about the slums." His statement captures one of the many ways in which the Communist Party in the 1930s made itself relevant and attracted black urban dwellers to their cause. While Baldwin, a Trotskyite at age 19, had become an anti-Communist when the United States and Soviet Union were still allies, he had harsh words for McCarthyism: "This convulsion did not surprise me, for I don't think that it was possible for Americans to surprise me anymore; but it was frightening, in many ways, and for many reasons"—not the least of which was scapegoating, anti-intellectualism, the repression of radical calls for liberation, and the flouting of human rights.[31]

In 1950, the same year that the U.S. State Department initially ordered Jones deported and stripped Du Bois and Robeson of their right to travel, Robeson's *Freedom* newspaper began circulating. The Harlem-based newspaper took its place alongside other alternative all-black independent news publications, such as *The Voice, The Messenger,* and *The Crusader.* Black radical writers and artists wrote the stories. Having moved from Chicago to New York, Lorraine Hansberry wrote articles on child labor and African anti-colonial movements. By 1952 she had become *Freedom's* associate editor.[32] Active in peace and freedom movements and a student of Du Bois, who taught African history and culture at the Jefferson School for Social Science, Hansberry resigned a year later from the newspaper to focus on her playwriting. Robeson also led with Du Bois the Council on African Affairs (CAA), an organization that supported the decolonization and national aspirations of African countries.

Black radical activists such as Hansberry, W. Alphaeus Hunton Jr., Shirley Graham, William Patterson, and Louise Thompson Patterson, who helped sustain the CAA, not only fueled the imagination of contemporary radicals, but also would cross paths with some of the next generation's black radicals, nationalists, and feminists. For instance, Hunton wrote a letter to the editor in the May 1962 *Liberator* warning black militants to beware of potential traitors in their ranks. Shirley Graham and W.E.B. Du Bois, who married, lived among and conversed with black expatriates in Ghana and China. While Frances Beal had not heard of Louise Thompson Patterson prior to founding the Third World Women's Alliance, Thompson Patterson, who articulated "triple exploitation," would work with that organization about two decades later.[33]

In the early 1950s as the young Beal came of age politically, Thompson Patterson participated in building a short-lived black feminist radical organization. Together with Beulah Richardson ("Beah Richards"), Thompson Patterson formed the Sojourners for Truth and Justice (1951–1955). Inspired by the theoretical writings of Claudia Jones, the Sojourners included Shirley Graham, Eslanda "Mrs. Paul" Robeson, Dorothy Hunton, and Frances Williams among others. Richardson had met Thompson Patterson, Paul Robeson, and Graham in the kitchen of actress and social activist Frances Williams. Langston Hughes was there too. At the time Richardson, a broke, aspiring actress, lived in Los Angeles. The city had not yet become known for the Watts uprising and Black Panther Party, and Beah Richards had not yet become famous for her role as the mother in *Guess Who's Coming to Dinner.* Shortly after meeting the Pattersons, Richards decided to move to New York and live with them. On her way cross-country to the East Coast, she stopped in Chicago where she entered a poetry contest and won $300 for her 1951 poem "A Black Woman Speaks." The prize money came in handy, paying for the last leg of her trip to the Big Apple.[34]

The Sojourners, acting in a long tradition of black women anti-lynching crusaders such as Wells-Barnett, exposed domestic terror against black women and their families and called for women globally to support their human rights causes.

For instance, they, too, rallied around the Ingram case, as did Audley Moore and Vickie Garvin, two members of the New York–based United Women's Committee to Save the Ingram Family. The Civil Rights Congress (CRC), which emerged out of an armed, anti-lynching, racial conflagration in Tennessee, initiated a campaign to publicize the Ingram case as well.[35] The Sojourners also supported the Defiance Campaign in South Africa in 1952, organized by the African National Congress (ANC) and the South African Indian Congress to protest apartheid and government repression.

The CAA, Sojourners, CRC, as well as other black leftist formations, experienced repression during the Cold War. Without a doubt, such political attacks on avowed black leftists undercut their organizations and legitimacy. In this climate, liberal demands for racial equality prevailed over radical expressions for justice. Even so, black militancy and strivings toward black self-determination not only survived as undercurrents into the next decade of mass-based protests, but would be reinvigorated, in part, by an ongoing domestic politics of containment, gradualism, and trenchant racist resistance.

In early 1952, while Wright was in Europe again, this time in London, trying to finish his existentialist novel *The Outsider* (1953), he once again sat at the kitchen table of George and Dorothy Padmore. The three of them discussed "endlessly . . . the situation in the Gold Coast and what their man Kwame Nkrumah was up against."[36] Just a couple years earlier in January 1950, the British colonial government had arrested Nkrumah for participating in a protest seeking universal suffrage, that is, the vote without property qualifications. In February 1951, Nkrumah—while still incarcerated—and other CPP members ran for legislative offices and won in a British-sanctioned election. A month later, British authorities released Nkrumah from prison. Securing political representation, black residents of the Gold Coast colony traveled the road to self-governance and power. By 1952, the protest campaigns and electoral victory began to gain attention in the U.S. black community.[37] After Wright finished *The Outsider* and Dorothy Padmore convinced him to visit the Gold Coast colony, George Padmore helped arrange Wright's trip there. Anxious to go, Wright wanted to witness firsthand, as well as try to understand, what he had never seen—"a mass movement with a black leader" on the path to national liberation.[38] In emotive prose, Wright recounted driving with Nkrumah in a motorcade through the James Town "slum": "The passionate loyalty of this shouting crowd had put this man in power, had given him the right to speak for them, to execute the mandate of national liberation that they had placed in his hands; and, because he'd said he'd try, they'd galvanized into a whole that was 4,000,000 strong, demanding an end to the centuries-old thralldom."[39]

In 1954 Wright published *Black Power*.[40] To be clear, *Black Power* was not a book that embraced Africa as a U.S. black homeland. In some cases, Wright critiqued indigenous culture and African leaders. Nevertheless, the book provides a discrete moment for grappling with the political conditions that inspired the search for state power, and its relationship to broader critiques of U.S. democracy and Western society. While many black activists, domestically and internationally, discussed black nationalism and struggled mightily against racism, Wright's book stands out as one of the earliest public deployments of "Black Power" as a political phrase. (Robeson later wrote about "Negro power" and discussed "Black Power" in a 1957 interview in *Ebony* magazine and in his 1958 memoir.)

A travelogue documenting Wright's journey to the Gold Coast colony in the summer of 1953, *Black Power* presciently captures black leaders' concrete demands for black political power and economic control of the country's natural resources and wealth as remedies for challenging indigenous people's oppressive social conditions. Wright concluded *Black Power* this way: "Have no illusions," he warned Nkrumah, "regarding Western attitudes [. . .] Westerners, high and low, feel that their codes, ideals, and conceptions of humanity do not apply to black men."[41] He further advised Nkrumah to beware of foreign money, advice, and ideologies: "You have escaped one form of slavery; be chary of other slaveries no matter in what guise they present themselves, whether as glittering ideas, promises of security, or rich mortgages upon your future." Wright continued: "There will be no way to avoid a degree of suffering, of trial, of tribulation; suffering comes to all people, but you have within your power the means to make the suffering of your people meaningful, to redeem whatever stresses and strains may come. None but the Africans can perform this for Africa."[42]

Echoes of Garvey's "Africa for the Africans" slogan resound here. Wright, however, did not include transplanted black people in the diaspora as the appropriate wielders of power in Africa; he meant indigenous (even if Western educated) black African leaders. In fact, except for in the occasional reflection or commentary, American "Negroes" and U.S. racial politics remained peripheral in Wright's intellectual framing and analysis of Black Power. And, yet, clearly a U.S. social and political context (which he literally distanced himself from) shaped his racial subjectivity and analysis, as well as his journalistic description of "power" in black hands (even if in a specific African country). By the mid-1950s and into the 1960s, Nkrumah and an independent Ghana became an inspiration to those fighting racial oppression and white subjugation. Ghana also emerged as a symbol, a place worthy of visiting, and a literal home for numerous black militant progenitors and advocates of "Black Power" in the United States. This included the Du Boises, Garvin, Julian Mayfield, and Malcolm X.

Wright's *Black Power* did receive media attention. The *Washington Post* and *New York Times* published announcements or reviews of the book. Michael Clark writing for the *New York Times* dismissed Wright's book "more as a tract than as a considered study." He argued that Wright went to the Gold Coast with preconceived notions, particularly because Wright seemed "convinced that colonialism was wholly evil, convinced that the redemption of the African could be achieved only through the development of the black state and of black nationalism as a 'secular religion.'" Indeed, Clark seemed dumbfounded by the fact that Wright seemed "able to find some virtue in everything black but none in anything white," and accused him of caricaturing British colonialism.[43] A reader, Henry F. Wilson from Brooklyn, New York, wrote a letter to the editor taking Clark to task. Wilson called the book "a brilliantly absorbing if bitterly frank book" and stated: "It certainly was not Mr. Wright who drove the wedge between Africans and Europeans, and I for one find the 'mighty dose' of his 'emotional processes' more palatable than I find Mr. Clark's typically Western arrogance."[44]

In the mid-1950s, anti-colonial struggles struck out at Western hegemony not only in Africa but throughout Asia as well, and this equally fascinated the author of *Black Power*. Hearing of the conference of 29 African and mostly Asian nations to be held in Indonesia in April 1955, Richard Wright decided to attend and report on this world event. The attendees included representatives from the Communist People's Republic of China and the Democratic Republic of Vietnam (North Vietnam). The Bandung Conference brought together former colonies in a non-aligned movement that linked self-determination politics to culture and social transformation. In *The Color Curtain*, Wright discussed how "the burden of race consciousness" and oppression written in "blood and bones" led to "people yelling for freedom."[45] Robeson did not attend the Bandung Conference because his passport had been revoked. He, however, did send a message endorsing its calls for national self-determination as well as peace.

On June 12, 1956, the notorious Robeson appeared before the HUAC. By the time of the HUAC hearing, Claudia Jones, who had served nine months in the Federal Prison for Women in Alderson, had been released early for health reasons and deported. She set sail for London on the *Queen Elizabeth* on December 9, 1955. This was eight days after the arrest of Rosa Parks, which sparked the Montgomery Bus Boycott in Alabama. Testifying at the hearings to get his passport back, Robeson held his political ground. He told the HUAC that in 1949 in Paris—for these remarks stood at the center of the controversy: "I did say in passing, that it was unthinkable to me that any people would take up arms in the name of Eastland to go against anybody." James Eastland, a Democratic senator from Mississippi, opposed civil rights and believed wholeheartedly in racial segregation. In fact, shortly after the May 17, 1954 *Brown vs. Board of Education* Supreme Court decision outlawing "separate but equal" in public schools, Eastland argued that the Supreme Court had "destroyed" the U.S. Constitution, and he described segregation as "the law of nature" and "the law of God." Continuing his HUAC testimony, Robeson told McCarthy and others present: "What should happen, would be that this U.S. Government should go down to Mississippi and protect my people. This is what should happen."[46] What *should* happen and what *did* happen did not easily mesh—and in some ways the future witnessing and reckoning with what *did* happen by a younger, more willful generation would fertilize the nationalist as well as radical tendencies then under assault in the 1950s.

The same year the Gold Coast colony became the sovereign state of Ghana, Robeson did an interview with black journalist Carl T. Rowan for *Ebony* magazine.

Robeson remained internationally attuned. He also remained hopeful and inspired by Ghanaian, as well as the "prospects of Jamaican," independence. In the interview, Robeson shared his desire "just to sit for a few days and observe this black power."[47] Robeson's admiration of Black Power received attention in the press. *Ebony* publicized it by running a subscription ad announcing the publication of Rowan's article, "Has Paul Robeson Betrayed the Negro?" The *New York Age, Washington Post,* and the *Baltimore Afro-American* were among the newspapers that ran *Ebony's* notice. The September 1957 ad queried: "What happened to Paul Robeson, the 'Emperor Jones' with the big, bass-baritone voice that boomed out from the concert halls of the world? How did he become the isolated figure that he is today? Why is he shunned by Negroes and whites alike? What is his doctrine of 'Black Power' that he thinks holds the key to the freedom of America's Negroes?" Then the ad encourages newspaper readers to take a look at the "sensational, first person story" in the October 1957 issue of *Ebony.*[48] That same month the *Honolulu Record* published a story, "Paul Robeson Making Comeback; Gives Views for 'Ebony' Magazine."[49]

Robeson did give his views. He confirmed his admiration for the Soviet Union, whose very existence, he emphatically believed, placed undesired political pressure on U.S. and European colonial governments. He denied membership in the Communist Party and shared that when he visited Russia he, indeed, felt free of the racial animus pervasive in the United States. Robeson stumbled his way through questions about Josef Stalin, who, as the Soviet Union's supreme ruler, launched the Great Terror of the 1930s. (Robeson had received the Stalin Peace Prize and was denigrated by a black former Communist Party member as someone who had grand ideas of becoming a "Black Stalin" in 1949.)[50] Robeson challenged the claims that he was a stooge or part of a Communist conspiracy to take over the United States. He credited the British labor movement, alongside obviously U.S. racism, for making him a self-described "left-winger" and believer in socialism.

Positioning himself on the side of the black workers, not the black bourgeoisie, Robeson proclaimed the potential of the "power of Bandung" and "black power." He argued that black people's "unified voice" could counter southern racists and white supremacy. Black people "don't have to go begging to these people," Robeson asserted. For him, the "Negro masses" held the key; organized they represented "black power." The article ended with an arguably prescient vision of racial political upheaval. Wrote Rowan: "Robeson is convinced he will have the last laugh—even on those Negroes who 'betrayed' him—for he is sure that the day will come when American Negroes will find that 'black power' holds the key to their freedom."[51]

In his memoir *Here I Stand* published in February 1958, Robeson expounded upon the ideas of "black power" or "Negro power" further.[52] The FBI took notice of the book's release on February 3, its price in paperback and cloth, its dedication to Robeson's wife Eslanda, its printing by a union shop, and its availability—"to date only in Jefferson Book Shop, New York City, which deals in communist and front group literature." A February 11 intelligence memo described *Here I Stand* as a book that "purports to explain his dedication to winning freedom for the Negro." While the book held "no new information of intelligence value," the memo remarked that Robeson "apparently" sought "to incite the Negro into a form of concerted action for the purpose of fighting for Negro equality." In a March memo to the FBI director, the New York office noted "that county and regional committees want CP clubs to campaign for sale of 'Here I Stand.'"[53]

While seemingly more concerned about Robeson's Communist sympathies and affiliations—those moments when "red" ideology spread through "black" actors—the FBI memos of May 1958 provide a record of the reach and potential impact of Robeson's book. They take note of its dissemination at concerts, bookstores, college and church meetings, and lectures from Baltimore and New York City, to Portland, Oregon, to Los Angeles and San Francisco, California. The memos also expressed a measure of interest about the perceived influence of the book on rights activists such as A. Philip Randolph and Adam Clayton Powell—at least according to Robeson's fellow travelers Benjamin Davis Jr. and Lloyd Brown.[54] Brown believed that Robeson's view on black leaders' responsibility to the "Negro masses" and black people's fate being "in our hands" directly influenced Randolph. Similarly, Davis believed that Robeson's book "is going to be like Tom Paine's 'Common Sense' as far as Negroes are concerned."[55]

In *Here I Stand,* Robeson took his black liberation stand on the "Ten Principles of Bandung."[56] The principles included respect for "fundamental human rights"; "the sovereignty and territorial integrity of all nations"; national self-defense; "justice and international obligations"; "recognition of the equality of all races and of the equality of all nations large and small"; abstention from intervention and aggression; and the peaceful settlement of international disputes.[57] In fact, Robeson believed that such revolutionary independence struggles and the rise of African nationalism forced the U.S. government to confront, even if not address, its treatment of black people in the United States. Robeson wrote: "Here, then, in the changing bases of power abroad, is the main source of that pressure for changes at home."[58]

In the chapter titled "The Power of Negro Action," Robeson claimed that black people had "great moral power"; "the power of numbers, the power of organization, and the power of spirit"; and the legitimate right to evince power and to make demands without feeling that they had to pussyfoot or beg for "'favors' of the Big White Folks."[59] This is what Robeson laid out. He argued that gaining civil rights was only the first step, a necessity for bringing about racial equity and economic parity. Black leaders must have a "single-minded dedication to their people's welfare" that goes beyond a representational politics of individual advancement. The struggle must be built on independence steeped in responsiveness and accountability. While having white allies might be useful, what is critical is coordinated action among black organizations and the forging of a "Negro people's movement" that does not simply depend on favors from white powerbrokers and is "led by *Negroes,* not only in terms of title and position, but in reality." More women and "people from down below" must be in leadership for they would bring sources of "new strength and militancy," and organized labor must be challenged for its discriminatory treatment of black workers. He denounced a politics of gradualism and argued that "mass action—in political life and elsewhere—is Negro power in motion; and it is the way to win."[60]

Black people's search for power and the ingredients of Black Power politics germinated in U.S. black, African, and Third World radical writings, agendas, and activism in the 1950s. At times direct connections existed between political generations, other times not. Even so, the ideas and lessons of multi-faceted, anti-racist struggles circulated. While the oppressive power of the U.S. state did lead to the public diminution of radicalism in the country, such sensibilities were not fully extinguished. Black radicalism and nationalism remained strains of black politics. As such, they served as reminders, even if attenuated, that other routes to black liberation had existed and existed still. Through it all, the Janus face of U.S. democracy would be exposed.

Increasingly black domestic liberation politics in the 1950s publicly privileged battles—and a freedom rhetoric—that sought integration and legal reform of U.S. political institutions. This represented a more palatable anti-racist politics in that it adhered to U.S. geopolitics, at times adapted to "red" hysteria, and sought to navigate, even as it called to account, Robeson's "Big White Folks." In short order, direct mass action as a way to secure black people's civil rights followed. Whether true believers in the possibilities of U.S. democracy or strategists trying to figure out the best way forward, black people still challenged accepted racial boundaries. Brokering some success, such direct action desegregation efforts also fueled white intransigence, calls for patience and moderation, as well as outright white violence. These realities, contradictions, and continued black sufferance fed a lingering, as well as a newly seeded, spirit of black militancy in the mid-to-late 1950s and early 1960s. During these decades, new generations were raised up in revolt.

Raising a Generation in Revolt

During the 1950s, even as black radicals linked the national to the global, for a great number of black people in the United States, neighborhood politics and the daily travails of living commandeered their attention. The Cold War had something to do with that. Black racial liberals did not escape its clutches. They, too, accommodated and leveraged U.S. Cold War language of democracy, citizenship, and even at times anti-Communism to advance their agendas. In doing so, they helped intentionally and involuntarily to delegitimize black radical and internationalist activism. It was in this era that future civil rights militants and Black Power advocates came of literal and political age. One such advocate was Julius W. Hobson Sr.

For Hobson, the search for rights, and ultimately power, emerged in the capital of the free world—Washington, D.C. Originally from Birmingham, Alabama, Hobson had been christened at the 16th Street Baptist Church. There, in the near future, four black girls would lose their lives in an explosive hate crime that ignited the emotions of black people across the political spectrum. Hobson, as had these girls and millions of others, grew up in the midst of legal segregation. As a young boy, he worked at a library where he could not check out books because of his race. He attended the only black high school in town and could not drink from public water fountains or go to the public parks. His Pullman porter father died when he was young. His stepfather ran a dry-cleaning plant and drugstore; his mother was a teacher. Hobson enrolled in Tuskegee Institute where he earned his engineering degree after the Second World War.[61] He served during World War II, a time when black people braved fascism abroad and racism at home, flying 35 missions as an artillery spotter pilot in Europe and earning three bronze stars. Hobson earned a master's degree in economics at Howard University.

In 1950—while U.S. government officials revoked passports and issued deportation orders, and British officials in the Gold Coast arrested Nkrumah for organizing a massive strike that shut down the colony for 21 days—Hobson began working to desegregate public schools in D.C., the same year he began walking his son and namesake, Julius Jr., to school. Each morning, on the way, they passed by the white school. This concrete manifestation of inequality angered Hobson, as it would other parents in similar situations, as well as NAACP lawyers Charles Hamilton Houston and Thurgood Marshall, who fought to desegregate schools. Gardner L. Bishop was one of those other parents who as early as 1947 rallied black parents to boycott the overcrowded conditions of his daughter's D.C. school.[62] He helped form the Consolidated Parents Group to challenge "the whites, the highfalutin' blacks, the Board of Education—everyone." The parents' group led a school boycott in which 1,800 students participated.[63] The efforts in D.C., Delaware, Virginia, South Carolina, and Kansas were consolidated in 1952 into the legal campaign guided by Marshall that became the *Brown* desegregation case.[64]

A year after *Brown,* Hobson suffered a heart attack. In a letter to his mother that he penned from his hospital bed, Hobson shared a measure of what drove him to contest black oppression more vigorously:

> I feel as though the world will have been no better off by my having been here. I feel ashamed when other men have sacrificed, gone to jail, or even been executed for mankind . . . it's just that the injustice, suffering and cheating and all of man's inhumanity to man seems to be my personal problem. I cannot divorce myself from it. I will be ever unhappy if I cannot do something about it. I just hope this heart will last long enough for me to strike one blow at all the things around me which I detest.[65]

His heart would last him. He joined the Congress of Racial Equality (CORE), originally the Committee of Racial Equality. James Farmer and other University of Chicago students who joined the Fellowship of Reconciliation (FOR) co-founded CORE in 1942. As Hobson grew increasingly militant, the pacifist organization expelled him from its D.C. chapter. By the mid-1960s, Hobson had formed D.C. ACT (Associated Community Teams) and become a vociferous Black Power advocate, even helping to found the short-lived Organization for Black Power in 1965. As such—and to the chagrin of many—he would strike numerous blows at racially discriminatory institutions and push for an independent third party as well as reignite the call for D.C. statehood in an effort to open up and transform the local power structure.

The country's wrangling and foot-dragging over the implementation of the *Brown* decision would eventually spur black people to think more deeply about "what it meant to be black in white America," in the words of future Black Panther Party member Eldridge Cleaver. In 1954, however, Cleaver did not have "the vaguest idea of [*Brown v. Board*'s] importance." For in the immediate wake of the landmark case, the 18-year-old was otherwise preoccupied. Caught with a shopping bag of marijuana (he had been "smoking reefer four or five years"), Cleaver landed in the state prison in Soledad. Then not a year later, "an event took place in Mississippi which turned" the young Cleaver and many others "inside out."[66]

In 1955, Chicago-born 14-year-old Emmett Till was murdered in Money, Mississippi, for supposedly saying "Bye, Baby" to a white female storeowner on a dare by friends. On vacation visiting family, Till lost his life for naively breaching racial and gender social mores. His life taken, his body dismembered and sunk to the bottom of the Tallahatchie River, Till became a visual national and international symbol of U.S. southern racial terror and inhumanity after his mother Mamie Till held an open casket funeral and allowed photographers to take pictures and disseminate them around the world in *Jet* magazine and in newspapers. His white assailants, Roy Bryant and half-brother J. W. Milam, whose admission of guilt after the trial was published in a *LOOK* magazine article, had been acquitted after only one hour of deliberation by an all-white jury. When Paul Robeson told the HUAC a year later that the "U.S. Government should go down to Mississippi and protect [his] people," one can imagine that he surely must have been thinking of Emmett Till.

Till's murder deeply horrified Frances Beal, too: "I remember I was on the lawn, in the front yard, and thinking about this young boy. I can see it. My mother had this car—I can see the whole picture: me in the front yard, leaning on the car, thinking about Emmett Till. Because he was exactly the same age as I was. And it was a, I don't know, some sort of awakening of some—that I was so impacted, like, that could happen to me. . . . It created in you a feeling that something needed to be done about this."[67] Beal started her activist journey three years hence, beginning as a student at the University of Wisconsin–Madison. At that time, however, she was just becoming more familiar with the all-too-probable deadly ramifications of accidently flouting racial mores, let alone forthrightly contesting U.S. racism.

Indeed, the events of 1955 gave further credence to Malcolm X's assertion that "second-class citizenship" was an oxymoron that defaced the reality of black people's subjugation. It was also a year of responses. Audley Moore established the Reparations Committee of Descendants of U.S. Slaves in 1955 in New Orleans. The committee emerged out of an earlier movement to expose and eliminate state violence against black people, specifically black men facing the electric chair. The question arose: Who would pay for the costs, that is, the repercussions for all this black death? "Then we began to examine all the things they owed us for," recalled Audley Moore. The committee provided a model for 1960s reparations efforts. This included her own renewed call for reparations in the year marking the one hundredth anniversary of the Emancipation Proclamation, as well as campaigns launched by Black Power leftists, some of whom she would critique for "prostituting" the cause.[68]

This black militancy and nationalism operated alongside the struggle for integration and civil rights. In 1955, too, Rosa Parks, a political organizer and NAACP activist who in later years developed relationships with both Audley Moore and Mamie Till, refused to move further to the back of a Montgomery bus. Having witnessed decades of white violence against black people, including rape, beatings, and economic exploitation, Parks had "tired of giving in" to white hostility and brutality. Her decision—alongside the support of fellow NAACP stalwart E. D. Nixon and the pre-organizing efforts of black women professionals such as Jo Ann Gibson Robinson, a professor of English at Alabama State University and member of the Women's Political Caucus—helped launch the year-long Montgomery Bus Boycott and elevate the young Dr. King to prominence.[69]

The 12-year-old Angela Davis had heard of this Montgomery upsurge 100 miles away in Birmingham. There in Eugene "Bull" Connor's city, she lived—a preteen girl unknowingly on her way to becoming a black radical cause celebre who thousands of activists across the world would organize to free after a courtroom shootout and an FBI woman-hunt landed her in prison. But in 1955, the young Angela was simply another black youth experiencing one of the most familiar and concrete manifestations of racism—unequal education. She attended school in "beaten up wooden huts" or what the black students themselves called "shacks." She learned from textbooks that enshrined stories of how "black people much preferred to be slaves than free." This, however, did not register with Angela. The people she listened to and respected challenged exclusion with consistent vigor. She knew that the Birmingham NAACP had been declared illegal, and yet her parents as members kept paying their dues, even in the face of threats of imprisonment. They only stopped when the chapter dissolved. She knew that Rev. Fred Shuttlesworth's house had been blown up because he started the Alabama Christian Movement for Human Rights in 1956 and that he mounted a similar bus boycott. These daily assaults on black people made the young

Angela restless, and she wanted out of Birmingham. At age 14, she applied for two scholarships—one at Fisk University and the other sponsored by the American Friends Service Committee to bring black southern youth to an experimental Quaker high school in the Bronx. She occasionally visited New York in the summer with her mom, who had been working toward an advanced degree. After some consideration, Davis headed for the Bronx, and this decision—this migration, the first of many—quickened her politicization just as Robeson's trip to London had his and Beal's to Paris would hers.[70]

Military service, like migration and foreign travel, also had political impact. Returning to the United States as a war veteran, Robert F. Williams took over leadership of the fledgling Monroe NAACP in the mid-1950s; he built his membership base among black veterans and laborers by organizing, for instance, in beauty shops and pool halls. A too frequent fare of white violence and discrimination had motivated Williams—from the wrath of white mobs during the Detroit race riot of 1943, to his military experiences, and returning home to Monroe only to be faced with having to protect a friend's corpse from desecration by the KKK. His friend was executed for cutting the throat of his employer who had thrashed him for requesting his wages earlier in the day than usual. Successfully seeking to subvert his postmortem lynching, Williams and a group of black men armed themselves. Williams explains, "[This was] one of the first incidents that really started us to understand that we had to resist, and that resistance could be effective if we resisted in a group, and if we resisted with guns."[71] Soon enough, Williams became a public symbol of black self-defense, an advocate of militant civil rights struggle, a black internationalist, and an enemy of the U.S state.

In waging campaigns in the "uncivilized South" against Jim Crow, including black exclusion from the local swimming pool built with federal funds, Williams found it necessary to form armed defense units to protect black civil rights activists against not only KKK violence but also the police.[72] As has been charted, the history of armed defense and the belief in it to ward off white supremacist terror ran deep. Many black activists and organizations in the South had viewed armed self-defense as protection or literally picked up the gun after bearing witness to the cheapness of black life. Northern black activists supported Williams's rifle clubs and the Monroe NAACP, which the national office had expelled for its stance on armed self-defense. Supporters sent money and caches of weapons, and some even went to Monroe to join in the battle against Jim Crow. Willie Mae Mallory, herself originally a southern girl, was among them.

Mallory's militancy, including a desire for rights, economic and educational justice, and political power, is rooted in multiple regions, issues, relationships, and strategies. An only child, born Willie Mae Range in Macon, Georgia, in 1927, she was taught to defend herself against white bullying as a young child. In 1936 her mother brought her as a nine-year-old to the North to live with her grandmother in Brooklyn. At 17 years of age, Mae wed Keefer Mallory—whom she met through family members—apparently as the story goes not for love, but to escape an abusive stepfather.[73] The marriage did not last long. Within two years, Mae Mallory had two children and then filed for divorce. As a single mom, she moved into public housing and at times relied on welfare. In the 1950s Mae Mallory, who as a teenager had expressed concern about the unenviable social positions that black people found themselves in, joined and then left the Communist Party. She also visited meetings held by black nationalist organizations only to witness their "militant talk" alongside little action and a "contempt for the women."[74]

By 1956, against the backdrop of stateside and international black militancy, Mallory proudly referred to herself as a "maladjusted Negro" who refused to kowtow to racial inequality and discriminatory conditions.[75] This was particularly so within the Harlem schools where her children received a subpar education and had to stomach unsanitary conditions. There were only two bathrooms, both of them malfunctioning, for 1,600 students. She believed that teachers underestimated the intellectual abilities of her children, as well as other black and Puerto Rican children, and did not provide age-appropriate learning assignments. Counting pipes under the sink in fifth grade surely was not her idea of useful, engaging, or challenging work.

Disgusted by it all, Mallory joined with others to challenge school officials. She went to the headquarters of the New York School Board in Albany to complain. She also filed a lawsuit to challenge segregation and substandard education for black children. In the North, segregation might have been illegal, but it nevertheless existed. Attitudes and choices shaped where people lived. These residential patterns and school zoning policies influenced black children's access to quality education. Labeled "difficult," black schools had a higher percentage of emergency and substitute teachers. It was not unusual for teachers to resist being assigned to black schools, arguing they were not "psychologically prepared to teach children in such schools."[76] Other mothers, as members of the Parents Committee for Better Education in Harlem for which Mallory served as secretary, joined in the legal suit.

Black and Puerto Rican mothers also demanded the integration of neighborhood schools and orchestrated student boycotts of black schools to bring attention to unequal education and resources. Also known as the "Little Rock Nine of Harlem," evoking the courage of the nine children who sought to integrate a public school in Little Rock, Arkansas, in September 1957, the Harlem mothers kept their children out of the neighborhood schools. They boycotted junior highs 102, 136, and 139. A decade later, P.S. 139 remained a focus of parents, as well as drew the attention of members of the newly formed Black Panther Party of New York in 1966. To make sure their children still received instruction, the Harlem mothers established independent tutorial sessions at a local church. When the tutoring sessions were canceled, black lawyer Paul Zuber, as part of an already devised strategy, filed a lawsuit on behalf of Mae Mallory, Viola Waddy, Bertha Ware, and Dorothy Braun. Eventually, the school board was found to have perpetuated inferior education for black children.[77]

Such rights battles around schools pervaded the country. Sometimes they benefited black and brown students, other times not—given the complicated relationship of school access and quality education to residential and mobility patterns, school board and tax policies, parents' racial attitudes and choices, and other political decisions. For instance, white southern officials engaged in massive resistance by closing schools and establishing "choice" policies. On occasion, state and municipal officials attempted to equalize funding rather than desegregate schools. Even so, black parents continued to battle for quality education both through integration, and increasingly under the mantle of community control and self-determination in the era of Black Power politics.

Mae Mallory's concern for her daughter and other black children revealed an early militancy—one that, at times, bridged rights insurgencies with black self-determination and unveiled growing disgust with gradualism and accommodation. Driven by multiple philosophies and the concrete issues at hand, Mallory would become a cause celebre among some black radicals and internationalists by the early 1960s. Engaging in such battles had repercussions. Interestingly, in the late 1950s, soon after the New York court's landmark decision, the outspoken Mallory became the target of a welfare fraud case. Apparently, during a brief stint of work (six months), she had continued to receive Aid to Dependent Children checks. She was convicted of grand larceny, sentenced to 30 days in jail, and from then on also would have to contend with being labeled an "ex-convict."[78]

By this time, Malcolm Little had been released from prison and was on his way to becoming the charismatic minister of the NOI. Quite familiar with the world of work before prison (as a shoeshine boy, busboy, Pullman porter, and petty hustler) and in prison (making license plates and laboring in the coal warehouse and woodshop), Malcolm moved to Detroit and picked up different jobs. He worked in a furniture store and in different automobile assembly plant factories. He studied NOI doctrines; he also lived and moved among working-class and poor people, and became adept at conveying their pains. For this reason, the sandy red-haired Malcolm X quickly earned the respect of the masses, especially following the police beating of Johnson X Hinton. Now an iconic story, at that time, it was an unexpected incident that broadcast Malcolm X as a man with dangerously mesmerizing power.

On that April day in 1957, the 32-year-old Johnson X, a member of Temple No. 7, was watching a fight between two black men on 125th Street and 7th Avenue when he saw the police pummeling one of the black men whom they sought to arrest. Johnson X and two other NOI members intervened. Police turned their wrath on Johnson X, and then hauled all four men off to jail. In short order, 500 people crowded outside of the 28th Precinct, including cadres of black Muslims led by Minister Malcolm X. After seeing that Johnson X had sustained a head injury, Malcolm X demanded that police have him taken to the hospital. By the time the crowd marched to the hospital, it had swelled to 2,000. Doctors treated Johnson X for his injury, and then the police quickly returned him to jail.[79] Back outside the precinct, the crowd had swelled to 4,000. This flustered and unsettled the police. Only after Malcolm X gave a signal did the crowd disperse for the evening. That was too much power to behold.[80]

Under Malcolm X's leadership, the NOI became the fastest growing membership organization in urban areas. He provided visibility for low-income black people; he had genuine connections to both, having suffered poverty and prison and the neglect and stigma they produced. Malcolm X's story is not his alone, but a reflection and complex exposition of oft-forgot people, including black women and their impact on Black Power politics. While influenced by Garveyism, Malcolm X learned about Africa from Audley and Eloise Moore and Vickie Garvin. The NOI, although impacted by the UNIA and Marcus Garvey, had focused on the Asiatic black man. After Malcolm X and Audley Moore had a conversation, according to Audley Moore, he told her that he could not say the word Africa without clearance from Elijah Muhammad. So Audley Moore went to Muhammad's house in Chicago, sat at his breakfast table, and argued with him about the importance and centrality of Africa. Muhammad "didn't want to hear nothing about Africa," recalled Audley Moore. "We had to teach Malcolm, you hear, and that's how he was able to get a new insight, you see, put that to work."[81] Black activists even younger than Malcolm X came of age amidst these complicated politics. Some of them also drew inspiration from Garveyite, black nationalist, pan-Africanist, Third Worldist, and anti-colonialist revolutionaries and ideologies.

In May 1957, about a month after the famed Muslim minister–police standoff, the Rev. Martin Luther King Jr., who had risen to national stature because of the Montgomery Bus Boycott, headlined a prayer pilgrimage at the Lincoln Memorial. Paul Robeson attended to the chagrin of some civil rights leaders, who feared his attendance might cast a pall over the march. There, King and others demanded the ballot as part of black people's citizenship rights. After nearly nine decades since the passage of the Fifteenth Amendment, only one-fifth of the black population could vote.

Four months later, Republican President Dwight D. Eisenhower signed the Civil Rights Act of 1957 into law. The first legislation passed since Reconstruction to protect black civil rights, the 1957 act, however, was dramatically scaled back and placed the mechanisms of enforcement in the hands of local authorities. This helped to appease southern congressmen. The 1957 act, while limited, also had strategic importance for Vice President Richard M. Nixon. It served his Cold War concerns, by combating foreign critiques of U.S. race relations.[82] As head of the administration's Committee on Government Contracts, Nixon had argued that racial discrimination, including "in employment provides fuel for Communist propaganda." Black radicals' exposure of the U.S. Achilles' heel, in fact, did impact U.S. racial policy. Indeed, this would not be the last time that Nixon advocated limited racial reforms to preserve "internal tranquility," suppress black radicalism, and attract the support of black constituents even as he upheld segregation and notions of black inferiority.[83]

While some black leaders felt that no civil rights act would have been better than the 1957 act, Rev. King believed otherwise. King wrote to Nixon that he believed the limited bill "is far better than no bill at all," continuing, "Inadequate legislation supported by mass action can accomplish more than adequate legislation which remains unenforced for the lack of a determined mass movement."[84] A mass movement for civil and voting rights lay ahead.

Throughout the 1950s black struggles for equality unfolded. In 1958, Nkrumah visited the United States at President Eisenhower's invitation and to black fanfare; the Harlem mothers fought against school inequality in New York; and black activists launched a bus desegregation campaign in Memphis.[85] The Nashville sit-in at the five-and-dime store, in which John Lewis, Diane Nash, and Marion Barry participated, was just around the corner, as was intensified white congressional and citizenry resistance to desegregation. Even with the 1957 act, however, Eisenhower hesitated to protect black people's civil rights domestically. He had reluctantly sent federal troops to protect the Little Rock Nine. Such government reluctance and gradualism, alongside white massive resistance, only fueled civil rights and black militancy that watered the seeds of Black Power.

Increased Black Militancy: 1960–1962

In the early 1960s black civil rights militancy, nationalism, and anti-colonialism overlapped and informed visions of U.S. black liberation. On January 17, 1961, the assassination of Patrice Lumumba, the Belgian Congo's first African prime minister, sparked a protest of thousands at the United Nations. Mae Mallory and Lorraine Hansberry joined the protest organized by the Cultural Association for Women of African Heritage (CAWAH), an organization formed by black jazz vocalist Abbey Lincoln, Trinidadian-American trade union activist Rosa Guy, and writer-activist Maya Angelou among others.

Lumumba's assassination also inspired the launch of *Liberation* in March 1961, a six-page billet edited by Lowell P. Beveridge as the voice of the Liberation Committee for Africa, and founded by Daniel Watts and Richard Gibson. Two months later, it became *Liberator,* and in addition to discussing the Lumumba case, it advertised events such as a "Nationalism, Colonialism, and the United States" conference at the Martinique Hotel in New York City. That conference featured author-activist James Baldwin, progressive journalist William Worthy, Harlem Writers Guild and future Black Arts Movement writer John O. Killens, James Higgins, and a representative from the South African United Front—Vusumsi Make. The *Liberator* also shared that "[t]he United States was placed at the top of the list of 'perpetrators of Neo-Colonialism' in a resolution of the third annual All-African Peoples Conference meeting in Cairo last March."[86]

In just a year, the New York–based *Liberator* had grown to 16 pages and its advisory board featured the names of veteran proponents of cultural and economic black nationalism. For instance, Lewis Michaux, of the Harlem-based black bookstore; Captain Hugh Mulzac, the first captain of Garvey's Black Star Line; and Richard B. Moore of the race-first socialist ABB served on the advisory board. By then Daniel Watts had taken over as editor. Its May 1962 anniversary issue featured articles on the killing of NOI member Ronald Stokes in Los Angeles. While supporting black nationalism, the article critiqued Muslim inaction, clearly revealing the editor's differing stance on political strategy from that of the NOI. In the anniversary issue, a *Liberator* editorial also pointed out that despite a recent "sickening display of club swinging by New York City police against peace demonstrators, peace is now a 'respectable' issue in the U.S." The article continued, revealing a hint of sarcasm, "At least we have come a long way since Dr. W.E.B. Du Bois was handcuffed and led off to jail for advocating an end to the nuclear arms race." By the August 1962 issue of *Liberator*, editors had added a book service section, which provided a list of selected readings by, for instance, former Sojourners' member Alice Childress, Du Bois, Richard B. Moore, Langston Hughes, Alphaeus Hunton, Jomo Kenyatta, Kwame Nkrumah, and Haywood Patterson. The book service also featured albums by Abbey Lincoln and her husband, jazz musician Max Roach.

In the early 1960s, the *Liberator* had become yet another voice and intellectual venue for black militants and nationalists who theorized and participated in the freedom struggle. In years to come a burgeoning generation of activists—for instance, Donald Freeman, Max Stanford, Rolland Snellings, and Donald Warden—would publish in its pages, as well as engage in activism in their own cities and elsewhere. In doing so, they played a role in helping to foment burgeoning radical sensibilities and the rise of the Black Power era.

In the midst of this black militant ferment, SNCC formed, just a couple months after the widely publicized sit-in by four North Carolina A&T students at a Woolworth's lunch counter in Greensboro in February 1960. While the Greensboro sit-in initiated a new mass direct action struggle led by students, it was not the first sit-in to take place. CORE had held sit-ins at restaurants as early as its founding year in 1942 in Chicago, Illinois. CORE also had organized freedom rides and jail-ins to protest racial exclusion and discrimination. Just over a decade later in 1959, James Lawson, who was at the time a divinity student at Vanderbilt University serving as CORE's southern director, trained college students in Nashville, Tennessee, in nonviolent resistance and sit-in strategies.

Moving from the forefront of civil rights to the forefront of Black Power by 1966, SNCC did not emerge as an organization with inclinations toward achieving independent black political power, supporting anti-colonialism, or expressing a black consciousness sensibility. The latter, when conveyed, by SNCC members emerged through the harnessing of a sense of race pride that meant they, too, as black people deserved the spoils of U.S. citizenship. The early SNCC focused on access to the American Dream by pointing out the gap between rhetoric and reality and demanding integration, voting rights, and the dismantling of Jim Crow. In just six short years, however, this organization, which continuously confronted white power, even with citizenship rights in hand, grew into a bullhorn for Black Power. So would CORE.

The Greensboro sit-in took place in an era that heralded the establishment of 17 new African nations, and at a time when black people unapologetically struggled against white supremacist ideology and colonial oppression globally. Just a month after the Greensboro sit-in, a major slaughter was in the making. Across the Atlantic Ocean, the Pan-African Congress, harboring a belief in South Africa for black South Africans, had split from the African National Congress (ANC) over the ANC's multiracial vision. Soon thereafter, the Pan-African Congress organized a march in Sharpeville to protest laws requiring black South Africans to carry passbooks to gain entry to white cities. White South African police unreservedly fired into the crowd of 20,000 protestors, wounding 250 people and killing 67. The Sharpeville massacre, as well as the burgeoning U.S. sit-in movement, would inspire anti-apartheid and anti-racist activism in places as far away as Australia.[87]

A month after the Sharpeville massacre, SNCC was founded. In April Ella Baker organized the Southwide Student Leadership Conference in Nonviolent Resistance to Segregation with financial support from the Southern Christian Leadership Conference (SCLC) at her alma mater Shaw University in Raleigh, North Carolina.[88] This conference marked the founding of SNCC, which launched a new phase of civil rights activism. A veteran activist and theoretician, Baker had worked as the NAACP's director of branches and the SCLC's executive director. The SCLC had wanted the students to form a youth branch of its organization, but Baker, who believed in building cadres of grassroots leaders, told the students that they needed to determine their own platform and pathway. And so they did. They formed "a continuation committee to explore what kind of structure they might have," and that committee eventually became a permanent organization.[89]

A manifestation of the liberal civil rights ethos that gained new life in the Cold War era, SNCC followed a pathway of direct action and tactical nonviolence. Within two months of the initial protest, solidarity sit-ins occurred in 60 cities and by year's end had spread to 200 cities.[90] In Cleveland, Ohio, Donald Freeman, as a budding black radical, participated in one of those solidarity sit-ins. Freeman grew up in Outhwaite Estates, a public housing complex, with his parents and three brothers during the first 14 years of his life. His mother worked a short stint at an electrical company in the 1940s. His dad worked for a machine manufacturer, Freeman says, benefiting from Randolph's threatened March on Washington and the subsequent opening up of jobs to black people during the war. In 1953 the Freemans, Don and his "soul mate" Norma Jean, moved to their first house on Phillips Avenue in Glenville. Three years later, they moved to the house where they still live, having raised three sons there. At the time of the solidarity sit-in and mass demonstration at the Woolworth in downtown Cleveland, Don Freeman attended Western Reserve University. A member of the leftist National Student Association, he had already read Wright's *The Color Curtain* and would find his way to Robeson's *Here I Stand,* and the University of Wisconsin–Madison where he met Max Stanford. Together they would establish the Revolutionary Action Movement (RAM).

Other future Black Power era activists and theoreticians also participated in sympathy sit-in protests. These included Stokely Carmichael and Frances Beal. At the time, Carmichael was a senior in high school in the Bronx. Within the year, Carmichael, as a Howard University student, became a Freedom Rider and had become a leader of the campus's SNCC affiliate, the Nonviolent Action Group (NAG). In later years, he went South to mobilize in the Black Belt states of Mississippi and Alabama. There, he helped to organize the Lowndes County Freedom Organization, which established an independent black electoral party with the black panther as its symbol. It would be his bellowing of "Black Power" that garnered national media attention and helped to usher in the publicly acknowledged era of expansive Black Power politics.

A future fellow SNCCer during its nonviolent civil disobedience and Black Power phases, the teenaged Frances Beal was a student at the University of Wisconsin–Madison when she joined a sympathy sit-in protest at the local Woolworth's that, in fact, had already been hiring black workers. Born in 1940 in Binghamton, New York, Beal grew up around political radicals. Her father, Ernest Yates, of black and Native American ancestry, died of cancer when she was still young and her mother, Charlotte Berman Yates, the child of Russian Jewish immigrants, was involved in leftist politics. After her father died, Beal and her mother moved to the racially transitioning neighborhood of St. Albans in New York. Coming of age, Beal was deeply moved by her uncle fighting "fascism and evil things and deeds" such as Nazism during World War II.[91] She enrolled at the University of Wisconsin in 1958 and became involved in civil rights as a leader of the campus NAACP chapter and in socialist politics. Beal, like Hobson, Robert Williams, and others whose political expressions veered outside the acceptable moderate stances of the dominant integrationist organizations, found herself facing censure. After Beal's participation in the Woolworth's protest earned her a television appearance, the NAACP told her that direct action protest was "not the thing that we should be doing." Between her exposure to leftist politics at home and in college, the Till atrocity, and the burgeoning black student movement, however, her commitment to black liberation and radical politics only grew.

International travel radicalized her, as it did others, even further. Beal went to Paris in August 1960 with her husband James Beal, and during trips home she volunteered with SNCC. In Paris, where she spent six years, she further developed her feminist and anti-colonial, internationalist consciousness. There she met African students, learned about empire and the Algerian Revolution, and became familiar with Martinique-born psychiatrist Frantz Fanon's anti-colonial and revolutionary writings through people who introduced her to *Presence Africaine*.[92] She sponsored Malcolm X as a speaker to "an overflowing crowd," and she discovered "a better social security system" of medical care and vacation time in France versus the United States.[93]

On the ground, people's politics and networks, at times, were porous, even as real ideological differences shaped organizational strategies and goals. After returning stateside from Paris, Beal joined SNCC's New York chapter. By that time, SNCC had not only proclaimed Black Power, ushering in the Black Power era, but had started an international affairs committee. For a decade, Beal worked for the National Council of Negro Women (NCNW), in particular its organizing effort called Project Women Power and their newsletter *The Black Woman*. She went on to establish SNCC's Black Women's Committee and later the Third World Women's Alliance (TWWA) through which she met Louise Thompson Patterson and which she organized with Linda Burnham, the sister of black Communist and feminist Margaret Burnham. The Burnham sisters were childhood friends of Angela Davis.[94]

While the civil rights sit-ins politicized and mobilized many young people, others were not enthralled by or even aware of them. Numerous youth focused on school, friends, and striving to get ahead. In fact the majority of young people were likely just trying to figure out how to navigate their youth, home lives, communities, and, of course, have fun. The 13-year-old Joanne Deborah Byron (the future black revolutionary Assata Shakur) focused on running away from home, yet again. She rented a cheap room at a motel where she met Sister Shirley, a transvestite, who talked to her about the life-threatening dangers of hustling men on the street and got her a job as a barmaid. While sipping on a (nonalcoholic) cocktail and chatting with men, Joanne kept them drinking in order to generate profit. It was a safer hustle, if not "legal" since she was underage. She only returned home after a friend of her aunt Evelyn Williams, who Joanne had been staying with when she ran away, recognized her and told Evelyn, a lawyer, where to find her. It would be at least four more years before Joanne joined the Black Power struggle.

The sit-ins, which passed Joanne by, also generated debate about tactics and goals in black movement circles. For instance, while Malcolm X criticized the sit-in movement as passive, James Baldwin argued that maintaining calm in the face of vitriol "demands a tremendous amount of power."[95] On April 25, 1961, Malcolm X, LaVerne McCummings, and Baldwin discussed the sit-ins. Baldwin argued that far from simply seeking integration—or what Ella Baker described as struggling for more than a hamburger—black people were on a quest for power. "When the sit-in movement started or when a great many things started in the western world," began James Baldwin, "I think it had a great deal less to do with equality, than it had to do with power." Taking over the black literary mantle from the late Richard Wright, who died of a heart attack as an expatriate in Paris in November 1960, Baldwin argued that white people had not "suddenly changed or become more conscious of the black man's humanity." Instead, he said, "white power has been broken." This, for him, raised critical questions regarding the "distinction between power and equality" and "power and freedom." "And I know," Baldwin continued, "that in terms of Africa, that an African nation cannot expect to be respected unless it is free . . . unless it has its political destiny in its own hands which is what we mean by power."[96]

This question of power, particularly gaining political control shaped early considerations about whether SNCC should focus its energy on direct action campaigns like the sit-ins or organize for political rights. SNCC decided to do both. Robert Moses was one of many SNCC activists who believed in the power of the franchise and the importance of political voice for everyday people. He headed to Mississippi where he met local NAACP leader Amzie Moore, who envisioned electoral power as a critical pathway for achieving black equality. By 1961 SNCC had launched its statewide voter registration campaign in Mississippi. With the guidance, aid, leadership, and protection of local people, SNCC started in McComb and shifted to Greenwood, the seat of Leflore County. This set the stage for events—such as Freedom Summer, the formation of the Mississippi Freedom Democratic Party, and the tragic slew of activists' deaths at that hands of whites—that contributed to philosophical shifts and political splintering within the black liberation struggle.[97]

In another southern city further east, Monroe, North Carolina, social and economic agendas accompanied increased attention on voting. In August 1961, Robert Williams presented to the Monroe Board of Alderman a "Ten-Point Program" or "Monroe Program." According to Williams, "[T]he basic ill is an economic ill, our being denied the right to have a decent standard of living."[98] Mallory soon arrived in town to help the Williamses with the 20 Freedom Riders who would participate in local NAACP voter registration efforts at the Union County Courthouse. She would not go to the protests, however, because, as she indicated, "I couldn't follow any discipline of a non-violent demonstration."[99] She was an adamant believer in resisting violent attackers. The Freedom Riders' nonviolent civil disobedience had gained national publicity and sympathy, and their presence in Monroe had the potential to draw similar attention. Launched by CORE in May 1961, from Washington, D.C., the interracial cohort of Freedom Riders had sought to test a desegregation law in interstate transportation. Hostility and mob violence temporarily halted the effort in Alabama, until Nashville students led by Diane Nash, a founding member of SNCC and a direct action coordinator, and hundreds of other students rallied to continue the effort. They met intense brutality from white citizens and police, but they were intent upon breaking down the barriers that impeded their ability to achieve quality lives, questioned their humanity, and perpetrated racial oppression.

The arrival of the nonviolent Freedom Riders and an interracial cohort at that, according to Williams, instigated "a week of terror."[100] On Sunday, August 27, racial tensions exacerbated as white crowds expanded exponentially to a mob of thousands (the numbers range from 3,000 to 5,000) and attacked some 30 civil rights protestors outside the closed courthouse. With the willful neglect and active participation of some police officers, the demonstrations devolved into a racial melee—with black people scrambling to escape the white throng. James Forman was among them on that August day, experiencing the howls of "Kill the

Nigger!" and suffering a wound when a white protestor held Forman at gunpoint. Recounted Forman: "I can see down the barrel of the shotgun but I must be cool. I must not panic. Look the mother fucker straight in the eye and let him know he has lynched a strong black man." Forman argued that defying death—which many black men and black women would be called upon to do—was the "greatest act," one "necessary to make a revolutionary."[101] While Black Power activists would be criticized for their "gun barrel" politics, white elected officials did little when white vigilantes and police used violence against black people to undercut their liberation struggles.

As circumstances on the ground shifted—bodies inching, tempers flaring—armed black reinforcements arrived in a car. (This included Julian Mayfield, a journalist who worked for Robeson's *Freedom* magazine.) That's when Forman made his move. First he pushed a fellow white female Freedom Rider, Constance Lever, into the car. Then he felt the cold barrel of a shotgun crashing into his head, splitting open his skull and setting blood "gushing like a volcano in eruption."[102] Almost a decade later in his 1972 memoir *The Making of Black Revolutionaries,* Forman shared how being in the crucible of white anger and suffering the wounds of white brutality led him to embrace the need for self-defense: "Run red blood so that the world may see racism. Run red blood down my black, gritty, sweaty face. Run to the words of the poet McKay, if we must die let us die as men fighting with our backs to the wall."[103] The gun and white power were staring him right in the face and crashing down on him, and that's when he began to believe that force, violence, and power must be met with force, self-defense, and power.

The drama, however, did not end there. After a day of racial conflagration, Williams and other black activists found themselves trying to protect an elderly white couple driving through their neighborhood of Newtown. Their efforts turned fateful. The white couple Bruce and Mabel Stegall claimed that their would-be protectors were trying to kidnap them and ultimately filed charges. This set in motion more conflict, an indictment, and the physical flight of the Williamses and Mallory. The Stegalls would charge that a rifle-bearing Mallory ordered them to go to the Williamses' yard; Mallory alternately claimed that she was in the kitchen when the Stegalls appeared on the Williamses' porch. After two hours—the only point of agreement—the Stegalls left the house unharmed.[104] The next day, on August 28, 1961, the FBI office in Charlotte, North Carolina, issued a warrant charging Williams "with Unlawful Flight to Avoid Prosecution for the Crime of Kidnapping."[105] But, according to Robert Williams, fear of an indictment was not the primary reason that he and his wife Mabel, or even Mae Mallory, departed Monroe in a hurry. Instead, they were motivated by the anti-black tenor of white law enforcement, alongside death threats by North Carolina officials. By way of New York City and Canada, the Williamses fled to Cuba, and Mallory fled to Cleveland, Ohio, where she had family. Police arrested white Freedom Rider John Lowery, alongside 19-year-old Richard Crowder and 18-year-old Harold Reape—two black members of the Monroe Youth Action Committee.

The FBI issued "Wanted" posters for the fleeing black activists. Mallory's gave the following information: 180–200 pounds, black hair, brown eyes, dark brown complexion, scar on right knee, scar on left thigh, "reportedly speaks in loud manner, may wear glasses," and has a record of "grand larceny." The 30-day jail sentence she received came back to haunt her. The FBI also warned that Mallory "should be considered very dangerous," and "described [her] as having a violent nature, [. . .] she reportedly carries a .22 caliber pistol."[106] The FBI would trace Mallory to Cleveland through a postal letter sent by her lawyer, Conrad Lynn. They then set a trap to capture her, receiving help from her cousin's husband.

Mallory sometimes babysat for her cousins. On an evening in October 1961— the same month that Du Bois became an expatriate in Nkrumah's Ghana—her cousin's husband asked if she was available. According to the FBI field report, the arrest proceeded this way: About 9:35 p.m., Mallory sat on a couch in her cousin's living room with four black men, two on the couch and two in chairs. The FBI, seeing her through the screen, entered the house and asked her if she was Willie Mae Mallory. "Yes," she said. Lifting her up off the couch by her left arm, the FBI advised her that she was under arrest and walked her out to the front porch. About 15 minutes later, they arrived at the Cleveland FBI office, where she informed them of her attorney's name, Conrad Lynn. At 10:09 p.m., they asked her if she wanted water. "No, thank you," she replied. A minute later, they asked her if she wanted a Coca-Cola. "No, thank you," she said. At 10:11 p.m., they inquired whether she knew where Robert F. Williams was. "I don't know what you are talking about," she said. At 10:35 p.m., they photographed her, and there the report ends.[107] North Carolina wanted her extradited, and for three years she and members of the Monroe Defense Committee would fight.

Mallory wrote numerous letters from Cuyahoga County Jail. She clearly feared that some black radical activists and the public would forget her, particularly because the Williamses had escaped to Cuba. In August 1962 the *Liberator* published a letter that she wrote to editor Daniel Watts. Under the headline, "A Freedom Fighter Speaks from a Northern Jail," Mallory reminded Watts that she and others still remained imprisoned, and she urged the *Liberator* to publicize her case to African groups as well as ask them to write U.S. Attorney General Robert F. Kennedy to order North Carolina to drop the charges against her. She would write many letters of this kind to friends and colleagues domestically and abroad.[108] Ultimately in 1964 over the protests of activists in Harlem, Cleveland, Philadelphia, and even internationally, she would be extradited to North Carolina.

Her comrades, indeed, were safely in exile in Cuba. While on the island, Robert Williams wrote *Negroes with Guns* in 1962, published *The Crusader* (a title echoing that of Cyril Briggs's radical magazine in the early 1900s), and aired commentary on his "Radio Free Dixie" program. In *Negroes with Guns,* Williams called for the creation of "a black militancy of our own" and a self-directed struggle to "achieve our own destiny," and reaffirmed the necessity to counter white citizenry and state terror.[109] In this book, Williams detailed his struggles with white supremacist citizens and the state. He described black nationalism as "another label" just "as meaningless as the Communist label." Instead, he identified himself as an "Inter-Nationalist"—one concerned about the problems of humankind, including of Africa, Asia, and Latin America.[110] Williams also prepared a "Ten-Point Program" in the same expository style of the UNIA's "Declaration of Rights," the NOI's "Wants and Beliefs," and the Bandung Conference's "Ten Principles." His "Ten-Point Program" addressed socioeconomic marginalization, and called for the right to armed self-defense and black-led organizations. Each of these treatises preceded the Black Panther Party for Self-Defense's "Ten Point Program" in the mid-to-late 1960s.[111] His explicit denial of black nationalism, however, would earn him the criticism of black leftist and nationalist Harold Cruse. The future author of *The Crisis of the Negro Intellectual,* Cruse fashioned Williams as little more than an integrationist who willingly adopted self-defense as a tactic.

Williams's political exile and writings nevertheless captured the attention of young black militants, including Donald Freeman and another Ohio student, Max Stanford. Stanford grew up in Philadelphia. His family members were political—his paternal grandmother a Garveyite, his father an NAACP member, a maternal uncle a democratic socialist. He had a cousin in the NOI in the early 1950s. His young consciousness was shaped by political kin; the conflict he experienced with Italian youth and adults who called him a nigger growing up; the murder of Emmett Till; reading *Ebony, Jet,* and Richard Wright's novels; and hanging out with brothers in "street clubs" on different corners where they drank, boxed, sang, and discussed "how African Americans were going to get freedom."[112] Not only did Stanford become known as "Black Max" because he began to study black politics and history, including reading the *Communist Manifesto* and learning from former members of the Communist Party's Abraham Lincoln Brigade who fought in the Spanish Civil War, but also because he dubbed himself a "modern radical."

Freeman, a member of Students for a Democratic Society (SDS), who had now graduated from Western Reserve University, and Stanford, a student at Central State College in Wilberforce, Ohio, had met during the summer of 1961 at a National Student Association meeting at the University of Wisconsin–Madison.[113] That fall at Central State, Stanford helped to establish Challenge, which primarily focused on promoting political awareness among black students. The organization's mentor from 1961 to 1962, Freeman suggested that Challenge members read Harold Cruse's "Revolutionary Nationalism and the Afro-American," which discussed black people as comprising an "oppressed nation within a nation." The students then formed a broad coalition—the Reform Action Movement—to take over the student government. They won. Max Stanford and Wanda Marshall left Central State College and relocated to Philadelphia. There, Stanford would meet with Freeman, who took trips to the city, about organizing a black working-class nationalist movement. Recalled Freeman: "They had those snack places where you could get refreshments out of the vending machines. H & H's they called it."

Every afternoon for about a week Don and Max met and "over that time [. . .] formulated the foundation for RAM"—the Revolutionary Action Movement.[114] RAM formed in 1962. This was the same year that South African police arrested Nelson Mandela, the ANC leader and chair of its guerrilla arm *Umkhonto we Sizwe,* who went to prison for his part in a sabotage campaign targeting public buildings, utilities, and transportation networks. RAM linked the struggle of black Americans to the Third World liberation struggles. An organization more political and radical than the NOI, RAM deployed direct action without unquestionably adhering to nonviolence. Seen as "a revolutionary black nationalist direct action organization" that pointed to capitalism as an oppressive economic system, RAM sought to "change the civil rights movement into a black revolution."[115] Along with others such as Donald Warden and his Afro-American Association in San Francisco and UHURU in Detroit, the two RAM founders would engage in explicit discussions of Black Power as a concept and political praxis.[116] Wayne State University students Luke Tripp and General Gordon Baker, who "entered Detroit's black left through participation in the Detroit Robert Williams Defense Committee," founded UHURU (Swahili for "freedom").[117] As with Stanford and Freeman (whom the FBI would denigrate as "Black Stalin," echoing a similar characterization of Paul Robeson), the worldviews of Robert F. Williams and Malcolm X had influenced Tripp and Baker. So had Fidel Castro and U.S.–Cuba politics.[118] Stanford also studied with black women nationalists and militants Audley "Queen Mother" Moore and Ethel Johnson, the latter of whom initiated the grassroots newsletter *Did You Know?,* which Johnson published initially from Monroe, North Carolina, and then Philadelphia.

Johnson and Moore's tutelage was critical to Stanford's political development and RAM's organizational maturity. They helped him hone his revolutionary perspective, mentored him in the craft of organizing, and provided a safe space to escape the police and the volatility of street protests in which he participated.[119] In particular, Stanford recalled meeting Ethel Johnson. It was in 1962. A native of Monroe, Johnson had lived next door to Robert and Mabel Williams. When they fled Monroe, Johnson's son "drowned mysteriously." The community and family feared for her safety, feeling that "she would be targeted next."[120] So, she moved to North Philadelphia to live with her sister. Stanford secured Johnson's contact information through someone at the Philadelphia branch office of the National Student Association. Stanford knew she had organized with Robert Williams. He called her, and they met. Shortly thereafter, Stanford shared one of RAM's position papers that he drafted regarding building a black revolutionary internationalist movement. Ethel Johnson told him to leave it with her and then contact her after Thanksgiving. That is what he did, and then planned a Thanksgiving trip with his then-girlfriend and fellow activist Wanda Marshall to her parents' house in White Plains, New York.

Since they were going to New York, Stanford thought they should try to meet with Malcolm X. Marshall thought the idea "ludicrous," but called Temple No. 7 anyway. To her surprise, they were able to gain an audience with Malcolm X and

Benjamin 2X at Temple #7's restaurant. "[Malcolm] talked for about 45 minutes to me, and now I had been taught by black doctors degreed," Stanford reminisced. He continued with respect in his voice: "Malcolm put together black history from like before Ancient Egypt." Stanford had even seen Malcolm X on television, had a cousin in the NOI, and had read *Muhammad Speaks,* but listening to Malcolm X in person, he recalled, "Oh man! He just blew me away." After the lesson, Stanford asked Malcolm X whether he should join the NOI. Malcolm X told him no, saying he could "do more for the Honorable Elijah Muhammad outside of the Nation, and then he left."[121]

Upon Marshall and Stanford's return to Philadelphia, Stanford called Ethel Johnson to see what she thought about his position paper. Stanford recalled, "She said, did you write this? She said, are you serious? I said, yes. She said, come over." He went to her sister's house. That's when she told him, "If you're serious, I'll show you how Robert did it. . . . I'll show you how he organized."[122] One of the first things she told Stanford was this: "Every organizer has [a communications] organ," and she told him about Garvey, who he had begun reading having already visited with Thomas Harvey, president-general of the UNIA, as well as president of the Philadelphia division. Then she had Stanford read "What Is to Be Done?" by Vladimir Lenin. And he did, as did Don Freeman. "So I studied that," remarked Muhammad Ahmad (Max Stanford), continuing, "and came back . . . and she said, 'you pull together a study work group.' This is how we evolved between December of 1962 to January of '63." He and Marshall expanded their Philadelphia network, beginning with Stan Daniels, a local organizer who had dropped out of the University of Pennsylvania and led the Philadelphia Action Committee. Daniels already had a network, though he had purged members of the white Left because he felt they "were trying to manipulate and control." The two men "formed an all-African study group," and Johnson mentored them. Eventually, alongside the students, they brought in community people, including Mabel Holloway, who was in the Harriet Tubman Association with Audley Moore. Shortly thereafter, the Philadelphia-based RAM started on its path from studying theory toward action.[123]

Following Johnson's advice, they began identifying and working with sympathetic established black leadership. "You got to find who can you work with, the most progressive," Johnson told them. She was RAM's Ella Baker. Recalled Stanford:

> It was the same philosophy that Ella Baker was teaching. It's that you don't go in a community focusing around yourself. You go in a community and you start working with folks. . . . There's always indigenous leadership. Every community has leaders. But you have to go and create a process . . . to bring that indigenous leadership out, help them develop, and work yourself out of a job, where the community is no longer dependent on you. So that was our policy.[124]

Eventually they worked with Rev. Leon Sullivan, participating in the boycott against Tasty-Kake, which hired few and promoted even fewer black workers. Daniels and Stanford leafleted neighborhoods in West Philadelphia where they lived, and again they applied Ethel Johnson's advice. "Don't put a leaflet in every door," Stanford said she told them. "You put it in every other door, or every two doors. She said what happens is that a neighbor will say, 'Did you get this leaflet?' to the other neighbor and that will get the word out." Later, after getting approval from Johnson, the young RAM cadre began working with Cecil B. Moore, the president of the Philadelphia NAACP in 1963. The local chapter—as had others across the nation—was shifting from legal battles to direct action. As RAM built relationships with black leaders, RAM also worked to develop a program based on community needs. They went door-to-door in teams—a woman and a man—interviewing residents, many single mothers, to see what they thought the key issues were. But it was still difficult to gain the community's trust. A medical emergency helped them on this score, according to Stanford. "What happened right near our office was Ruth [Overton] who was [Johnson's] niece, she was a registered nurse. She goes in to knock on the door and the daughter, I guess, said, 'Is anybody, can [anybody] deliver a baby?' . . . . Her mother's water had [broken]." Stanford continued: "Ruth delivered the baby on the porch. (Laughs) And so, hey, we had the community from that point on. . . . We were invited to the neighborhood block committees and stuff" and began developing the "beginnings of a base."[125]

Ethel Johnson also introduced Stanford, Marshall, and other RAM members to Queen Mother Moore. At first Stanford and Marshall were a little nervous about associating with her. The Cold War was still hot, and black freedom struggles were still redbaited. However, once they grew to know her, she became an intellectual- and activist-bridge to a past and contemporary black nationalist history and community. In fact, in his memoir Ahmad (Stanford) dubbed her "RAM's second mother." He discussed spending many days reading her clipping files that documented social struggles from the 1930s to the 1960s. He, Marshall, Daniels, and others also would join Moore's African American Party of National Liberation (Robert Williams was its chair-in-exile) and participate in study collectives.[126]

The complex roots and routes of Black Power manifested in the alliances, as well as mentoring relationships, between veteran and neophyte women and men activists. Veteran black radical activists and organizations continued to labor for black freedom, and a cadre of black youth—who experienced the World War II years and the 1950s—was politicized, embarking upon grassroots and intellectual journeys among civil rights activists, black leftists, black nationalist formations, and sometimes all. While some black radical organizations were short-lived, individual members, their ideas, activism, or the context they helped to create inspired future generations of activists. As younger generations of activists came of age during the Cold War era and established their own organizations, they tapped into the wisdom of elders, gaining activist educations both in theory and praxis. They responded to the political landscapes that had their own roots in prior political developments, and recognized the United States' contradictory role as a supporter of domestic apartheid *and* self-described world leader of democracy.

Some 1950s black intellectuals, artists, and grassroots political activists knew, or grew to understand, the indubitable links between the two. Others only experienced its most quotidian expressions—that is, the social, political, economic, and physical insensitivities, insecurities, and inequalities that structured the daily lives of black people. These concerns provided the stuff of activism. They not only continued to feed demands for self-determination, but also produced increasing contempt for government recalcitrance, white citizenry resistance, and violence. In the early to mid-1960s, black revolts increased exponentially across the country, and as they amped up, participants—whether in planned campaigns or urban uprisings—grew increasingly impatient and less forgiving of circumstances that seemed to only bolster the racism that undergirded U.S. democracy.

Notes

1   Robeson, 89.
2   Donald Freeman, interview by author, October 24, 2013, Cleveland, Ohio.
3   Ibid.
4   Harold Cruse, "The Roots of Black Nationalism," *Liberator,* March 1964. Also see, Plummer, *In Search of Power.* She, too, argues that "black nationalist activity did not disappear but survived and gained ground during the era," p. 33.
5   Cedric Robinson, *Black Movements in America,* 134.
6   Evanzz, 15, 282–283. According to Evanzz, Malcolm X followed Robeson through radio broadcasts and newspaper articles, and wrote to Truman about his support of Robeson. The U.S. government voided Patterson's passport when he delivered the United Nations petition on behalf of the Civil Rights Congress. As a result, Patterson was forced to live for a time as an expatriate in Paris.
7   Some of the writers of the letters sent to the FBI identify themselves as "American Negroes" and articulate a fear of racial disunity and the volatile themes in his fiction. "Dear Sir" Letters sent to FBI, June–July 1945, Los Angeles, California, Part 1, Richard Wright, FBI File Number 100-157464, FBI Files.
8   In 1945, St. Clair Drake and Horace Cayton published *Black Metropolis* on Chicago.
9   Du Bois resigned from the NAACP in 1934, but returned for a short stint in the mid-to-late 1940s as the director of special research.
10 Plummer, *Rising Wind,* 153–156; Taylor, *The Veiled Garvey,* 151–154, 165–174; Von Eschen, 46.
11 Munro, 45.
12 Yohuru Williams, "They've Lynched Our Savior, Lumumba in the Old Fashion Southern Style," in *Black Power Beyond Borders,* ed. Slate, 147–168.
13 Birmingham, 4. Between 1935 and 1945 while in the United States, Nkrumah peddled fish for two weeks in New York while on vacation, then joined Father Divine's religious mission so he could eat more cheaply. "For entertainment, he listened to soap-box orators" in Harlem. Peter Kihss, "Harlem Hails Ghanaian Leader as Returning Hero," *New York Times,* July 28, 1958.
14 Lewis, 513.
15 Amy Jacques Garvey, *Black Power in America,* 33.
16 Ula Taylor, "Intellectual Pan-African Feminists," in *Time Longer than Rope,* eds. Payne and Green, 186, 190–191. Also see, Lewis, 513.

17 Meriwether, 75–76; Taylor, *The Veiled Garvey,* 166.
18 Wright, *White Man Listen!,* in *Black Power: Three Books from Exile.* The quotes appear on p. 780, the statistics on p. 797.
19 Robeson, 41.
20 Gilbert King, "What Paul Robeson Said," September 13, 2011, Smithsonian.com, www.smithsonianmag.com/history/what-paul-robeson-said-77742433/.
21 Davies; Weigand.
22 Claudia Jones, "On the Right to Self-Determination for the Negro People in the Black Belt," *Political Affairs* 25 (January 1946), 74.
23 Claudia Jones, "An End to the Neglect of the Problems of Negro Women," in *Words of Fire,* ed. Guy-Sheftall, 109.
24 Ibid., 110.
25 Ibid., 119.
26 McDuffie, "A 'New Freedom Movement of Negro Women'"; Charles H. Martin, 251–268.
27 Claudia Jones, "An End to the Neglect of the Problems of Negro Women," 119.
28 Davies; McDuffie, *Sojourning for Freedom.*
29 Editors of Freedomways, *Paul Robeson: The Great Forerunner* (New York: International Publishers Co., Inc., 1965), 147.
30 Plummer, *Rising Wind,* 16–17.
31 Baldwin, *No Name in the Street,* 29.
32 Carter, 41–47.
33 McDuffie, *Sojourning for Freedom.*
34 See film *Beah.* Other founders included Charlotta Bass, Alice Childress, Josephine Grayson, Sonora B. Lawson, Amy Mallard, Rosalie McGee, Bessie Mitchell, and Pauline Taylor. See also Davies, 82–83; and McDuffie, *Sojourning for Freedom.*
35 Gore, *Radicalism at the Crossroads,* 79. Also Strain, 29–30.
36 Rowley, 404.
37 Meriwether, 152. On Nkrumah, see Birmingham, 6.
38 Rowley, 423.
39 Wright, *Black Power,* 76.
40 Webb, 417. Webb noted in her 1968 biography of Richard Wright that his book title "anticipated the slogan of Stokely Carmichael by thirteen or fourteen years," chapter 25, endnote 10.
41 Wright, *Black Power,* 411.
42 Ibid., 419.
43 Michael Clark, "A Struggle for the Black Man Alone?" *New York Times,* September 26, 1954.
44 Letters to "Black Power," *New York Times,* October 31, 1954.
45 Wright, *The Color Curtain,* in *Black Power: Three Books from Exile,* 440.
46 Robeson, 42.
47 Edmondson, 711.
48 "Has Paul Robeson Betrayed the Negro?" advertisement, *Baltimore Afro-American,* September 21, 1957. The same ad also appears in the *Washington Post,* September 17, 1957 and *The New York Age,* September 21, 1957.
49 "Paul Robeson Making Comeback; Gives Views for 'Ebony' Magazine," *Honolulu Record,* October 17, 1957, Center for Labor Education & Research, University of Hawaii–West Oahu: Honolulu Record Digitization Project, www.hawaii.edu/uhwo/clear/HonoluluRecord/articles/v10n12/Paul%20Robeson%20Making%20Comeback%20Gives%20Views%20for%20Ebony%20Magazine.html.
50 "'Black Stalin' Aim Is Laid to Robeson," *New York Times,* July 15, 1949; "Testifies Robeson Wants to Be 'Stalin,'" *Washington Post,* July 15, 1949.
51 Carl Rowan, "Has Paul Robeson Betrayed the Negro?" *Ebony,* October 1957.

52 Amy Jacques Garvey made this statement in 1958 in the manuscript of *Garvey and Garveyism,* which was not published until 1963 because of limited financial resources. Quote appears in Amy Jacques Garvey, *Garvey and Garveyism,* 1.
53 Memo to Director of FBI from Special Agent in Charge (SAC), New York, Re: Paul Leroy Robeson, February 6, 1958; U.S. Government Office Memo to L. V. Boardman from A. H. Belmont, Re: Paul Leroy Robeson, February 11, 1958; Case Report to FBI Director from SAC, New York, Re: Paul Robeson, March 20, 1958, Section 15, Paul Robeson Sr., Part 20 of 31, Paul Robeson (FBI-HQ File 100-12304), FBI Files.
54 Audley Moore served as Ben Davis's campaign manager when he ran for the New York City Council in the 1940s. Raymond R. Sommerville, "Queen Mother Audley Moore," in *Notable Black American Women,* ed. Jean Carney Smith, 765.
55 Airtel to FBI Director from SAC, New York, Re: CPUSA—Political Activities and Paul Robeson, May 19, 1958, Section 16, Paul Robeson Sr., Part 21 of 31, FBI-HQ File 100-12304. Also see, U.S. Government Office Memo, New York Office, September 15, 1958, Section 17, Paul Robeson Sr., Part 22 of 31, Paul Robeson (FBI-HQ File 100-12304).
56 Robeson, 46–47.
57 Ibid.
58 Ibid., 84.
59 Ibid. The quotes appear respectively on pages 91, 92, 95.
60 Ibid., 102–107.
61 "Black Biography: Julius W. Hobson," www.answers.com/topic/julius-hobson.
62 Kluger, 511.
63 Ibid., 514.
64 Ibid., 508–523.
65 Cynthia Gorney, "Julius Hobson Sr., Activist, Dies at Age 54," *Washington Post,* March 24, 1977.
66 Eldridge Cleaver, *Soul on Ice,* 3–4.
67 Frances Beal, interview by Loretta Ross, March 18, 2005, Oakland, California, *Voices of Feminism Oral History Project.*
68 Audley (Queen Mother) Moore, interview by Cheryl Gilkes Townsend, 1978, in *The Black Women Oral History Project,* ed. Hill.
69 Theoharis, *The Rebellious Life of Mrs. Rosa Parks,* 71.
70 Davis, 101–103.
71 Timothy B. Tyson, "Robert F. Williams, 'Black Power,' and the Roots of the African American Freedom Struggle," *Journal of American History* 85 (September 1998), 548–549.
72 Robin D. G. Kelley, "Stormy Weather: Reconstructing Black (Inter)Nationalism in the Cold War Era," in *Is It Nation Time?,* ed. Glaude, 71.
73 Foong, 4.
74 Tyson, *Radio Free Dixie,* 189–190.
75 Foong, 14–15.
76 Benjamin Fine, "Northern Cities Confront the Problem of De Facto Segregation in the Schools," *New York Times,* February 10, 1957. Also see Fine, "Negro Sues City on School Zoning," *New York Times,* July 18, 1957; and Fine, "Zoning That Results in Segregated Schools Is Under Attack in the Courts," *New York Times,* July 21, 1957.
77 Leonard Buder, "Negro Pupils Stay Home for 3d Day," *New York Times,* September 11, 1958; Leonard Buder, "Harlem Parents Plea to State," *New York Times,* September 17, 1958; "Harlem Parents File for Million," *New York Times,* October 29, 1958. Also see Adina Back, "Exposing the 'Whole Segregation Myth,'" *Freedom North,* ed. Theoharis and Woodard, 64–91; and Foong.
78 Foong, 15–17, 25.
79 Eventually, Hinton who was fitted with a silver plate in his head won a $75,000 judgment from an all-white jury against the New York Police Department. Sales, 31–33.

80 Joseph, *Waiting 'Til the Midnight Hour,* 9–11; Marable, *Malcolm X,* 127–129.
81 Audley (Queen Mother) Moore, interview by Cheryl Gilkes Townsend, 1978. See McDuffie and Woodard, 11. On Vicki Garvin, also see Gore, *Radicalism at the Crossroads.*
82 Plummer, *In Search of Power,* 53; Weems and Randolph, "The Ideological Origins of Richard M. Nixon's 'Black Capitalism' Initiative," 51.
83 Weems and Randolph, "The Ideological Origins of Richard M. Nixon's 'Black Capitalism' Initiative," 51–52.
84 Rev. Martin Luther King Jr. to Richard M. Nixon, August 30, 1957, The Martin Luther King, Jr. Papers Project, http://mlk-kpp01.stanford.edu/primarydocuments/ Vol4/30-Aug-1957_ToNixon.pdf.
85 "Ghana Seeks Investors," *New York Times,* July 26, 1958; "Nkrumah in City for a 3-Day Visit," *New York Times,* July 27, 1958.
86 "The United States and Neo-Colonialism," *Liberator,* May 1961.
87 Clark, "The Wind of Change," 91–94.
88 Forman, *The Making of Black Revolutionaries,* 216.
89 Ibid., 217.
90 Lawson, 78.
91 Frances Beal, interview by Loretta Ross, March 18, 2005, Oakland, California.
92 Richard Wright was among the initial sponsors and supporters of the magazine.
93 Frances Beal, interview by Loretta Ross, March 18, 2005, Oakland, California.
94 Stephen Ward, "The Third World Women's Alliance," in *The Black Power Movement,* ed. Joseph, 122–123.
95 James Baldwin and Malcolm X Discussion, April 25, 1961, www.youtube.com/ watch?v=aNzMn2uhgFc.
96 Ibid.
97 Dittmer; Payne, *I've Got the Light of Freedom*; Umoja.
98 Robert F. Williams, *Negroes with Guns,* 40.
99 Foong, 35.
100 Robert F. Williams, *Negroes with Guns,* 38. Julian Mayfield, "The News That Wasn't Fit to Print about Monroe," *Liberator,* October 1961.
101 Forman, *The Making of Black Revolutionaries,* 200.
102 Ibid., 198.
103 Ibid.
104 Foong, 37.
105 Gallen, *Malcolm X: The FBI File,* 500.
106 A copy of the FBI "Wanted" poster appears in Foong, 69.
107 A copy of the FBI field report, October 16, 1961, appears in Foong, 70. In October 1961, two FBI agents also made a visit to James Boggs in Detroit, looking for Robert F. Williams. According to Boggs, he told them: "I am proud of Williams and I don't care who knows it." He, then, asked the FBI agents: "How is it that the FBI is so interested in Williams and yet in all the other cases . . ." His line trails off, and the young agent replies, "You mean Till?" Boggs replies, "Till, Charles Parker, and all the other lynch cases." See, James Boggs, "FBI Asks Me About Rob Williams," in *Pages from a Black Radical's Notebook,* ed. Ward, 70.
108 Willie Mae Mallory, "A Freedom Fighter Speaks from a Northern Jail," letter dated July 29, 1962, printed in *Liberator,* August 1962.
109 Robert F. Williams, *Negroes with Guns,* 78.
110 Ibid., 81–82.
111 Ula Taylor charts the "ironic" influence of the NOI's "Wants and Beliefs" platform on black student unions in California, as well as Huey Newton, co-founder of the Black Panther Party for Self-Defense. Taylor writes: "[i]t is somewhat ironic that the Nation of Islam's platform was interpreted as a 'Black Power' blueprint and that the waves of new members were former student activists, considering the fact that Elijah Muhammad never wavered from his conservative position that his followers eschew mainstream

politics." Taylor, "Elijah Muhammad's Nation of Islam," in *Freedom North*, eds. Theoharis and Woodard, 186.

112 Ahmad, xi–xiii.
113 Donald Freeman, interview by author, May 4, 2011, Cleveland, Ohio. Ahmad, 96.
114 Ahmad; Kelley, *Freedom Dreams,* 72–109.
115 Ahmad, 101. Also see, Kelley, *Freedom Dreams,* 62.
116 Just a year later, Freeman maintained that RAM would decide that Warden believed in bourgeois economic nationalism and "didn't have RAM's revolutionary political orientation" after a discussion at the March on Washington in 1963. Up until that dialogue, RAM and Warden were compatriots, but after that, they parted ways. Donald Freeman, interview by author, 24 October 2013, Cleveland, Ohio.
117 Mullen, "Transnational Correspondence," 195.
118 Gallen, *Malcolm X: The FBI File,* 500–501.
119 Muhammad Ahmad, telephone interview by author, November 18, 2013.
120 Ibid.
121 Ibid.
122 Ibid; Ahmad, 100–101.
123 Muhammad Ahmad, telephone interview by author, November 18, 2013.
124 Ibid.
125 Ibid; Ahmad, 101–103.
126 She had them read, for instance, James Allen's *The Negro Question in the United States and Reconstruction* (1936) and Harry Haywood's *Negro Liberation* (1948) on Marxism-Leninism and black self-determination. See Ahmad, 11, 113–114.

3

THE TIME IS ARRIVING NOW

Now is the moment. Come on, we put it off long enough. Now, no more waiting.
No hesitating. . . . The message of this song is not subtle. No discussion, no rebuttal.
We want more than just a promise. Say goodbye to Uncle Thomas. Call me naïve.
Still I believe. We're created free and equal. Now, now, now, now, now, now . . .

—*Lena Horne (1963)*[1]

In anticipation of the centennial of the Emancipation Proclamation, Audley
Moore, who co-founded the Reparations Committee Inc. (based in Los Angeles),
had filed a claim with the U.S. government for reparations on December 20,
1962. She and fellow activists had gathered one million signatures on a petition.
"I begged gas from station to station," Moore recalled. "I begged from farm to
farm. Once I was shot at by the Klan—three shots. They went on thinking they
had killed me, after my car went into the ditch. . . . You need assistance to do the
work. Work for black people."[2] Moore presented the petition to President John F.
Kennedy. He did not respond. In 1963 she published the pamphlet "Why Reparations?: Money for Negroes."[3] The opening paragraph read as follows: "After
244 years of free slave labor and the most inhumane, sinister and barbaric atroci-
ties which pass in magnitude any savagery perpetuated against human beings in
the history of the planet earth, and an additional one hundred years of so-called
freedom accompanied by terror, the Committee seeking Reparations for the
descendants of America's slaves, concludes that the payment of Reparations is an
absolute necessity if the Government of the United States is ever to wipe the slate
clean, redeem herself and pay for the damages she has inflicted upon more than 25
million American citizens."[4]

James Baldwin held a similarly critical view in the centennial year. In his article
"Not 100 Years of Freedom," published in the *Liberator* in January 1963, Baldwin

blatantly asserted that the nation, in commemorating the Emancipation Proclamation, really had little to be celebrating. Instead, he wrote, the centennial "harshly illuminates our failure to either end the Civil War or to recognize the Negro as a human being." Calling attention to Cold War rhetoric that stealthily undermined black liberation struggles by labeling activists Communist, Baldwin, however, boldly contended: "Our dangers do not exist mainly in the area of the Cold War. It is the irresolution with which we confront the political, social, and moral chaos of this country which is dangerous."[5] The slow implementation of the *Brown v. Board of Education* verdict, "disappointment with both political parties," continuation of housing discrimination despite President Kennedy's promise to end it "with the stroke of a pen," unfair lending practices by banks, and anti-black union and employer policies helped to explain why—even according to Dr. King—1963 became the year of the "Negro Revolt."[6] Ongoing gradualism and recalcitrance increasingly provoked criticism of equality and justice denied, and contributed to the milieu that would hasten the Black Power era.

As the centennial year unfolded, more vigorous calls for the establishment of black conduits of political power shared the public stage with interracial rights campaigns. These newly strident voices questioned a freedom orthodoxy that put faith in moral suasion and a federal government that moved slowly to dismantle racial and economic inequalities when it even did so at all. In the same issue of the *Liberator* in which Baldwin's article appeared, an editorial spotlighted "General Harriet Tubman"—described as "the real emancipator," the "fearless and persistent" conductor of the Underground Railroad. An escaped slave armed with a rifle and an anathema for slavery, Tubman sacrificed her own life many times over in order to liberate black people. "Harriet Tubman believed in a very personal God who served as kind of combination intelligence system and tactical advisor," the editorial stated and continued matter-of-factly that Tubman's God "did not insist that she love her enemy and offered no objection to her carrying a long rifle or side arm when the situation required it."[7] Imbued with the spirit of militancy, the *Liberator* clearly offered an alternative vision of what it might take to secure black liberation in a society striated by gradualism, racist defiance, and white power.

Black activists, intellectuals, and artists ramped up the black freedom rhetoric in a manner that also conveyed the urgency of their concrete demands: In addition to civil and voting rights, they desired rat-free neighborhoods, affordable rents, better schools, an end to police brutality, access to well-paid jobs, and socially just treatment by white landlords, banks, bosses and workers, teachers, and government officials. They wanted the ability to control black life and institutions. Black nationalism, independent power, and unified political and economic action became elevated catchphrases. In many ways, then, the centennial year of notorious civil rights protests, featuring the March on Washington for Jobs and Freedom, was also a remarkable year of ripening for Black Power.

This growing desire for black empowerment sprouted in communities across the country. In February 1963 in Rochester, New York, Malcolm X led a demonstration of 500 people to protest police treatment of NOI members. Then in May in Cambridge, Maryland, Gloria Richardson helped organize campaigns to expose the economic severity that made black living in the Upper South city (as it did elsewhere) a precarious proposition. In June, following the brutality in Birmingham, Alabama—where between April and May demonstrators protesting segregation were beaten, arrested, and jailed by police, including Dr. King and many children—over 100,000 people participated in the "March for Freedom" in Detroit.[8] Organized in order to not forget the racial violence that resulted in 34 deaths in the city in 1943, the Detroit march arguably served as a rehearsal for the March on Washington in D.C.[9]

All of these events not only exposed the existence of black radical and nationalist struggles in an era more identified and remembered for civil rights heroism, but also provide an inkling of the ideological and tactical tensions emergent within the black liberation movement. In the case of the Detroit march, advocates of integration and black political autonomy shared the same urban stage. For instance, the Rev. C. L. Franklin, who chaired the Detroit Council of Human Rights, stood on the dais with black Christian nationalist Rev. Albert B. Cleage Jr., who fused black theology and secular politics. Rev. Cleage also bridged race pride and concern for the poor to spiritual and institutional self-determination.[10] Indeed, black radicals' increased demands for black political and economic power would test the limits of this particular coalition.

By August 1963, an untold number of people had suffered tremendously in the struggle for freedom. This included paying the ultimate sacrifice. Such news traveled the world. Before the March on Washington, for instance, Chairman Mao, who had participated in the Afro-Asian Conference in Bandung and inspired black leftists in exile and in the United States, issued a statement criticizing U.S. racism and supporting black liberation struggles. He apparently did so at the insistence of Robert Williams.[11] The death of black freedom fighters—the human casualties of concrete demands for rights and economic justice—also troubled the March on Washington planning committee, which was comprised of representatives of the Big Five civil rights organizations—the NAACP, SCLC, National Urban League, CORE, and SNCC.

In the planning committee's second and last organizing manual, the following statement appeared: "The March will be a solemn and dignified tribute to Medgar Evers of the NAACP, William Moore of CORE, Herbert Lee of SNCC and the thousands of nameless heroes who have given their lives in the struggle for full equality."[12] After eight years of receiving death threats, Evers was murdered—shot in the back in the driveway of his Mississippi home.[13] Herbert Lee was a black farmer and founding member of the NAACP in Amite County, Mississippi. He worked with SNCC on the McComb County voter registration campaigns, and was shot dead in 1961. William Moore, a white postal worker turned civil rights activist, was killed in April 1963 in Alabama while on a solo march to protest racial segregation. Coincidentally enough, just a few years later, another solo march, James Meredith's "March Against Fear," would not only end violently, but also ignite a collective response that set the immediate stage for publicly changing the hue and cry of the black freedom struggle. That was still years away. The march that many people focused on at this time was the Bayard Rustin-organized mass march for jobs and freedom to be held in the nation's capital in order to seek government action "to help resolve an American crisis"—one "born of the twin evils of racism and economic deprivation."[14]

The March on Washington featured well-known black activists and labor leaders, artists, and intellectuals who lifted up the plight of the unemployed, as well as lambasted "reactionary Republicans and Southern Democrats" who held up racial progress and "came to power by disfranchising the Negro."[15] The stage was filled with the likes of A. Philip Randolph and James Farmer, Harry Belafonte and Sidney Poitier, Daisy Bates and Josephine Baker, among others. Gospel singer Mahalia Jackson bellowed a goose-bump rendition of "I've Been 'Buked, and I've Been Scorned." Over 250,000 marchers—about 75 percent people of color—participated, alongside 5,000 police officers.[16]

The public remembrances of that now historic day rarely focus on the content of the messages beyond Dr. King's hopeful and daring speech. Indeed, the 10 demands that Rustin highlighted at the Lincoln Memorial have tended to disappear into the shadows. These included creating "comprehensive and effective civil rights legislation"; "withholding" federal funds from programs that engaged in discriminatory practices; desegregating schools in 1963; enforcing the Fourteenth Amendment and reducing congressional representation for states where black people could not vote; establishing standards, federal action, and executive orders to ban discrimination in housing and employment; creating training and placement programs for all unemployed people; and establishing a minimum wage that promoted a decent standard of living.[17] The demands at the march and King's "I Have a Dream" speech—prominently recollected not simply because of his oratorical deftness, but because of the power of the media—did convey black people's hope in the promise of the United States. They thought it possible, and some deeply desired, to secure equal citizenship.

Upon closer inspection, the complex landscape that shaped the dynamics and context of the march exposed a sobering reality and provided glimpses of a growing black militant zeitgeist. The nightmares surrounding civil and voting rights campaigns represented a cocktail of oppression that some black radical activists increasingly refused to imbibe. This included, for instance, lawyer Conrad Lynn, who had served as a lawyer for Robert Williams and Mae Mallory. He attended the march and passed out leaflets publicizing the nascent all-black Freedom Now Party. Donald Freeman, too, made it a priority to attend the march, although he left the event before King even spoke, recalling: "I didn't see no militant struggle that day."[18] The teenaged Ericka Jenkins (Huggins), the daughter of working-class parents and resident of Southeast D.C., also attended the March on Washington. The march moved her, for it was after this experience that she "committed [herself] to moving from the sidelines to the frontlines in the global human rights movement."[19] In the next six years, as the fight for black liberation continued to rage, she would travel west, marry, and become a member of the Black Panther Party for Self-Defense.

Coincidentally, maybe prophetically, on the same day as the March on Washington, W.E.B. Du Bois died in Ghana as an expatriate. "The father of pan-Africanism" took his last breaths as a resident in the nation of the "father of African nationalism." "Buried on the grounds of Nkrumah's castle-home at Christiansborg," Du Bois decided to forever leave his birthplace (as had Richard Wright who died in exile in Paris) and claim a new homeland—the very act of which served as a penetrating critique of U.S. democracy and racial politics.[20]

That more signs of black radicalism did not emerge at the March on Washington might have had as much to do with who was allowed to speak and what they were allowed to say, as much as tempered hope. The March on Washington planning committee vetted the speakers—and by extension the message. As the story goes Baldwin, who authored *The Fire Next Time* (1963), was excluded as a possible speaker because he was "liable to say anything."[21] His penchant for fiery, unscripted critiques of racism and the U.S. government alongside his "unconcealed homosexuality" did not garner Baldwin favor. As it was, Rustin consciously sublimated his homosexual identity to stave off attacks on the movement. Like patriarchy, homophobia shaped black liberation struggles; and like sexism, heterosexism would not go uncontested, particularly by the late 1960s and early 1970s with women's and gay liberation movements. According to Baldwin's biographer James Campbell, King "did not want" Baldwin to speak at the march, believing that he "could not risk him."[22] As the planning committee reviewed their speakers' list, which included no women, a proposal to exclude John Lewis, SNCC's youthful chair, also emerged.

The planning committee threatened to exclude John Lewis because, while he advocated nonviolence and black people's citizenship rights, he also had a strident critique of the federal government's broken promises. He was preparing to publicly question whether the civil rights bill proposed by the Kennedy administration could effectively deal with the extensive economic deprivation and violence—state sanctioned and state ignored—experienced by so many black people. Ultimately, when the appointed hour arrived on that warm August day, however, Lewis had his time at the podium, but not before adjusting the bite in his remarks.

Still, the growing general sentiment of fed-up-ness seeped through. So, too, did a growing belief in self-determination even if it was not as far left ideologically as RAM's revolutionary nationalism or politically as the all-black Freedom Now Party. Lewis deleted from his remarks: "In good conscience, we cannot support wholeheartedly the administration's civil-rights bill," for it conflicted with the stance of the civil rights establishment. He also deleted the following: "We will not wait for the President, the Justice Department, nor Congress, but we will take matters into our own hands and create a source of power, outside of any national structure, that could and would assure us victory."[23] He, however, still questioned the bill's capacity to protect the lives of black people. Stated Lewis, raising the specter of Birmingham: "It is true that we support the administration's Civil Rights Bill. We support it with great reservation, however." As is, it would not "protect the young children and old women who must face police dogs and fire hoses." Then, before he left the microphone, Lewis exclaimed, "America, wake up! For we cannot stop, and we will not and cannot be patient."[24]

In 1963, dubbed the year of the "Negro Revolt," strides toward Black Power had indeed begun, and in the next year, Freeman, Stanford, and others would make their way south to Lewis and SNCC with the goal of building wider appeal for their ideas. Simultaneously, SNCC activists would begin to have their own internal debates regarding black consciousness, white involvement, and racial separatism. These augured ideological and tactical shifts to come.

While Lewis actually had an opportunity to speak at the March on Washington, Gloria Richardson, the more openly militant "Lady General," did not—not really anyway. The planning committee had invited her and other black activist women such as Daisy Bates and Rosa Parks to be publicly recognized but not to participate as main speakers—despite Anna Arnold Hedgeman's petitioning for just this.[25] Being present on the stage, then, did not mean one could command the microphone. The only word that the chair of the Cambridge Nonviolent Action Committee (CNAC) had an opportunity to utter before the microphone was summarily taken away was "hello." As if that were not enough, according to Richardson, organizers of the march then promptly escorted her and the black actress-activist Lena Horne off the platform before King spoke. Lena Horne, Richardson recalled, had been telling people that Rosa Parks, not King, really started the civil rights movement.[26] This was not necessarily a false statement or even an unviable analysis for those who witnessed Rosa Park's willful act—one that drew attention, engendered respect, and inspired hundreds of black people to protest. Still, Horne's purported narrative that featured prominently a black woman quite possibly pinched (borrowing activist Ella Baker's words) a few preacher egos.

As for Richardson, by the time of the March on Washington, her track record as an SNCC radical and grassroots activist had been well established. A woman disparately described by scholars as a civil rights militant and a harbinger of Black Power politics, Richardson took direct action, quests for political and social equality, and demands for economic justice to another level.[27] Independent minded, she did not unquestioningly take the counsel or follow the strategies of the civil rights establishment, especially if she did not think it would benefit local people. Indeed, a brief recounting of the shifting ideological and activist terrains that Gloria Richardson (among others) navigated exposes the concrete concerns, as well as the fluid and complicated relationships between civil rights advocates and black militants, as they waged the "Negro" (or "Black") Revolt in 1963 and marched toward the era of expansive Black Power politics beginning in 1966.

1963: The Year of Revolt

Cambridge is in Dorchester County on the eastern shore of Maryland. Not far from the seat of the nation's capital, the Upper South city arguably was as racist as cities in the Deep South. In the antebellum era, the tobacco town, which depended on slaves, was just down the road from Brick Town, where Harriet Tubman escaped from slavery. Gloria Richardson moved to Cambridge with her family during the Great Depression to live with her maternal grandparents. Racial segregation still thrived there (the city charter protected residential Jim Crow) and shaped the political, economic, and social relationships of its black and white residents. Richardson's great-grandfather and grandfather were "race men" and political powerbrokers who served on the Cambridge City Council from the all-black Second Ward. They also had a measure of economic independence as owners of local grocery stores. Despite their black middle-class status, race nevertheless structured their lives, as it did the city's other black residents. It circumscribed where they could live, how white society treated them, and even ultimately their physical well-being. These personal and community realities, alongside a growing awareness of "the evils of racism," would become ever more clear and disconcerting to Richardson. As a student at Howard University between 1938 and 1942, Richardson studied under Rayford Logan, E. Franklin Frazier, and Mordecai Johnson. There, she began to appreciate "black culture and achievements" and engaged in her first picketing campaign at a Woolworth's store.[28]

After SNCC came to Cambridge in 1961 (in the midst of the sit-ins on Route 40 that Stokely Carmichael also participated in), and her teenaged daughter Donna became involved in local campaigns, Gloria Richardson, too, took greater interest. CNAC formed in January 1962 at a community meeting at St. Luke's African Methodist Episcopal (AME) Church. Richardson's cousin Frederick St. Clair served as co-chair of CNAC with Inez Grubb. A divorced mother of two, Richardson and her cousin Yolanda St. Clair (Frederick's wife) went to Atlanta where they received training at an SNCC conference, and Richardson came back ready to organize. She became CNAC's co-chair with Grubb and garnered respect in the community for her tenacity.[29] Richardson wanted power for the black residents of Cambridge—a city like Birmingham where the White Citizens Council and police abetted inequality and racial terror; a city where both her father and uncle died because they could not access the specialized medical care in the whites-only hospital.

Several months before the March on Washington, Richardson and other CNAC activists in Maryland (similar to black radicals in Detroit and elsewhere) had been calling attention to the severity of black life including inequitable education, poor city services, deteriorating neighborhoods, police brutality, inadequate healthcare, and unresponsive elected officials. In Cambridge, the black unemployment rate was 50 percent, and in the Second Ward it was thrice that of the local white community's and six times higher than the national rate.[30] In Cambridge, local black activists organized protests to open up jobs in "factories, banks, and businesses with federal subsidies, since none of these places hired black people."[31] They also demanded low-income public housing.

Demonstrations in Cambridge in May 1963—the same month as the demonstrations in Birmingham—amplified the tensions in a city that drew student activists from Baltimore, Washington, D.C., and elsewhere. Between May and July, a season of protest had begun. Police arrested Gloria Richardson, among others, for sitting-in at local establishments such as the Dizzyland Restaurant. In June after a protest, tempers flared, fighting ensued, a Molotov cocktail was thrown, and Cambridge police arrested 20 people. The National Guard enforced a 10 p.m. curfew. In July, two carloads of white men (later identified as Maryland national guardsmen) drove through the black community, shooting willy-nilly out of their car windows. The first time, the black community, which was armed, did not respond. When the cars returned, "black people shot the cars out from under them."[32] These confrontations (eerily reminiscent in style if not cause with the East St. Louis riot in 1917) forced the Department of Justice to negotiate the "Treaty of Cambridge" to address de facto segregation and the black community's educational, housing, and economic concerns. Comprised of five points, the treaty was signed in Attorney General Robert Kennedy's office with Richardson and Mayor Calvin Mowbray of Cambridge.[33] The black community celebrated its victory at an evening rally at Bethel AME Church in Cambridge. This treaty, however, did not end local battles.

On the heels of Maryland's passage of a public accommodations bill, which also afforded Eastern Shore counties an opt-out provision through senatorial courtesy, CNAC demanded a comparable ordinance be included in the Cambridge city charter. White city officials, on the other hand, supported putting the issue up to a popular vote through a referendum. Richardson called for a boycott of the electoral process, arguing black residents would become party to a political farce in which indubitably white residents, who comprised two-thirds of the city's voting population, would quash the referendum and win the day: "Our position was that we were not going to put our rights up to a vote. Our rights were not based on the whim of the white majority."[34] Her call exposed the limits of the vote, as well as the potential to shield injustice behind the democratic process. The local decision drew fury from some national civil rights leaders who asked her to turn out the black vote. Her refusal to do so drew criticism. However, just as Richardson predicted, white residents easily defeated the public accommodations referendum.

Many months later the *Liberator* featured "Mrs. Richardson's Revolt." The editorial read: "The torrent of abusive attacks on Mrs. Richardson's character and motives during her boycott campaign would leave one to believe she was a combination of Robert Williams, Elijah Muhammad, and Dr. Du Bois. Why?"

The editorial answered its own question—because Gloria Richardson did not play by the rules, not even by those of the civil rights establishment that, black left-ists argued, sometimes prioritized peace over freedom. It was for this reason, the *Liberator* editorial continued, that black Americans must "develop a unified inde-pendent structure to fight and defend their own interests."[35] The "Lady General's" notable militancy, along with her willingness to challenge established black leaders, earned her new recognition in the *Liberator*. She now had a place at the table with the popular black male militants long recognized as forging the multiple streams of Black Power politics.

Further north in urban and industrial centers, black people protested the twin evils of racism and economic deprivation that pervaded the nation. Wherever black people lived, whether in Cambridge, Detroit, Birmingham, or elsewhere, black people needed work. The bosses of industrial, factory, or otherwise relatively well-paid and skilled employees, however, did not readily look to black or brown people. White private employers discriminated against people of color, even when they had government contracts. Some unions also excluded black workers and, in fact, labored hard to maintain white privileges in employment. This was nowhere more prevalent than in the construction and building trades.

In Philadelphia, RAM members joined the NAACP's fight to secure greater access to the construction trades. Max Stanford and Stan Daniels, who joined a picket line blocking white workers from entering, ended up in a violent melee. According to Stanford, when Daniels jumped "out of line to take a picture of [Stanford and Daniels] fighting these white construction workers," blackjack-wielding police "came down on both of [them]." As blood streamed from Daniels and Stanford's head wounds, they began "screaming, 'Let Africa see!'" Philadelphia police summarily arrested them. When Stanford received his one call, he phoned Malcolm X: "You [could] hear a rat piss on cotton (laughs)." He told Malcolm X: "Minister they beating us down here. . . . He said, 'Brother I'll see what I can do, but my hands are tied.'" Muhammad Ahmad (Max Stanford) continued: "What happened was he got on the radio in New York, and said, 'There is a mass dem-onstration in Philadelphia. They are beating our young brothers down there,' and called for support."[36] The Philadelphia campaign to protest exclusion of black workers from construction jobs would be one of the first and, according to histo-rians David Goldberg and Trevor Griffey, "helped launch a six-year, nationwide movement for 'affirmative action from below' that became rooted in Black Power and community control politics."[37]

Over the next couple months, RAM members traveled to different cities, meet-ing other activists and attending conferences. Daniels and Stanford went to the NAACP convention in Chicago where they talked about Robert Williams and Cuba and traveled to Detroit where they met Milton and Richard Henry, who were mobilizing protests to publicize police abuses and building the Freedom Now Party. They also participated in an "all-male" black vanguard meeting about a month before the March on Washington in D.C. Stanford recalled that "Wanda

[Marshall] hit the ceiling" when she heard only men could attend the meeting. In Ohio and Pennsylvania, Marshall supported RAM and yet her gender, in that moment, relegated her to the sidelines. According to Stanford, Freeman had made that decision, arguing that the presence of women would only "distract" them. There seemed to be no vigorous protest otherwise. Stanford, Freeman, John Bracey, and Rolland Snellings attended the meeting. There they discussed a strategy to "escalate the civil rights movement."[38] Within the next year, Stanford and Snellings traveled to Tennessee and then Mississippi where they would talk with John Lewis about testing their revolutionary nationalist ideas among student activists and SNCC members.[39]

In 1963 in New York, members of Brooklyn CORE also organized demonstrations protesting racial discrimination in the construction trades. For instance, between July 10 and August 8, Brooklyn CORE spearheaded a campaign to shut down the Downstate Medical Center project, which focused on expanding the State University of New York medical school campus. Black Christian ministers joined (and tried to usurp) the campaign. Ministerial participation brought a congregational following, but that had its price. When the ministers decided to disengage, their congregations followed suit. Losing numbers, Brooklyn CORE and their allies had to take radically creative actions.[40] People of different races, genders, and ages—black, white, Puerto Rican, Asian, men and women, adults and children—chained themselves together, blocked construction trucks by sitting in front of them with their arms and legs locked, and sent in children as protestors.[41] This was where the anti-racist activist Yuri Kochiyama, a Japanese-American woman formerly interned in U.S. prison camps during World War II, met the Muslim minister Malcolm X, who thought it foolhardy to put one's body in front of racist whites driving construction vehicles. A devotee of nonviolence who refused to consider self-defense as an option, Kochiyama began to reconsider her belief after meeting Malcolm X and later supported the Black Liberation Army. Her apartment became a gathering space for political salons that increasingly drew black militants such as Malcolm X and Max Stanford.[42] Ultimately, the Downstate Medical Center protest ended with black ministers brokering a compromise with municipal officials and employers. Unfortunately, it had little concrete impact on black employment.

So, the 1963 March on Washington remains a significant mass protest, one that signaled the hope of a new racial order. But, it actually represented a moment of discontinuity amidst a slew of confrontational protests challenging racial inequality, economic exclusion, and anti-black violence. Tragically, less than a month after Lewis asserted that Kennedy's proposed civil rights bill would not protect young children, the death bell rang, yet again—rendering his statement presciently accurate. On September 15, Cynthia Wesley, Denise McNair, Carole Rosamond Robertson, and Addie Mae Collins went to church dressed in their spiffy Sunday clothes. They "were preparing to speak about civil rights at the church's annual Youth Day program" as part of the Friendship and Action Meeting, a new interracial organization founded to promote "grassroots activism around school desegregation."[43] Instead on that Sunday, they met their tragic deaths when 22 sticks of dynamite planted by United Klans of America members exploded outside the basement of the 16th Street Baptist Church.

This horrific news traveled across the country and around the world. Donald "D. C." Cox, who became a Black Panther Party field marshal in San Francisco in 1967, remembered the explosion; it helped seed his growing anger. Instead of saving for and celebrating Christmas, Kochiyama donated money to southern movements and later took her children to visit the 16th Street Baptist Church.[44] Angela Davis, an exchange student from Brandeis spending her junior year abroad in Biarritz, France, picked up a newspaper on September 16. The headline announcing the slaying of the young girls caught her eye as she walked and listened to fellow exchange students. She knew the victims from her neighborhood. Then, in all its sickening awe, it struck her—the "objective significance of the murders." Davis wrote in her autobiography: "This act was not an aberration. It was not something sparked by a few extremists gone mad. . . . The people who planted the bomb . . . were not pathological, but rather the normal products of their surroundings." They reflected the "daily, sometimes even dull routine of racist oppression."[45]

The historic and contemporary experiences of black people across the country served as testimony to this—whether the 19-teens' East St. Louis, 1950s' Money, Mississippi, or 1963s' Cambridge or Birmingham. This reality not only provoked indignation and nourished diverse philosophical discussions, political strategies, and activist directions in black communities, but also rendered questionable the desirability of integrating into the U.S. political and economic system as-is. Under the persistent weight of inequality, hopeful yearnings and unflappable critiques grew into demands to expeditiously dismantle unfair systems and erase asymmetries of power.

Growing black militancy also revealed, and reflected publicly, the belief that social struggles required flexible strategies beyond nonviolence. Local power relations made a difference in how one responded. The first five decades of the century affirmed this reality. Gloria Richardson might have "believed in the need to hold nonviolent demonstrations," but she did not support allowing "people [to] come in and shoot up or firebomb our houses or shoot us and [we] not defend ourselves, because then the white attacks would just keep on."[46] While many black leaders and grassroots activists held firm to nonviolent civil disobedience, others such as Richardson, Robert F. Williams, Mae Mallory, Malcolm X, and so many unnamed and unknown ordinary people thought that nonviolence should not be protected as a tactical sacred cow. They deemed self-defense in the face of police and state repression as a quite reasonable, if not appropriate and necessary, tactic for black people engaged in struggles for both their lives and social transformation. Members of the future Black Panther Party for Self-Defense would agree.

In the November 1963 issue of the *Liberator* that featured Richardson on its front cover, an advertisement appeared for the Northern Negro Leadership Conference in Detroit. So, too, did an installment of Harold Cruse's "Rebellion or Revolution," and a "special department devoted to the new Third Party movement." In the inaugural essay, "Third Party: Facts and Forecasts," also by Cruse, he wrote: "It is evident the glorious March on the capital marked the end of an era. But with its passing have gone illusions which it is a pity we have taken so long to shed." He called attention to the circulation of Freedom Now Party fliers at the March on Washington, and then he issued a warning of the challenges ahead. For an all-black third party to have success, its "program must be a radical departure from the moderate stand of the old era," and its proponents must recognize that models of moderation, moral suasion, legalism, and dependency on white "good will" are inefficient. Echoes of Robeson's critiques, particularly of "Big White Folks" and all that meant, resound. Debate began immediately about what an all-black party really meant, in terms of membership, platform, issues, and impact in a predominantly white society. But there the concept was, publicly circulating more than a year before the formation of the Lowndes County Freedom Organization's all-black Black Panther Party that provided the name for the soon-to-be iconic grassroots Black Power–era organization.[47]

In November, Gloria Richardson made her way to Detroit for the Northern Negro Leadership Conference. While Richardson, like many others, was initially headed to the conference at Rev. C. L. Franklin's church, she actually ended up at the competing conference featuring Malcolm X, the contemporary apostle of black pride, power, and "by any means necessary." Richardson and Malcolm X's friendship began there in Detroit. This was the birthplace of the Nation of Islam and where Malcolm X's brother Wilfred headed the local NOI temple. Detroit, which experienced the most deadly race riot of the 1940s, also served as the hub of the automotive industry. In less than a decade black auto factory laborers would launch the revolutionary union movement (RUM) and the Marxist-Leninist League of Revolutionary Black Workers (LRBW). As Black Power-era formations, the RUMs and LRBW envisioned black industrial workers as the vanguard of the liberation struggle.

When Richardson arrived in Detroit for the leadership conference, someone told her that she needed to be at King Solomon Baptist Church. There, the Northern Negro Grassroots Leadership Conference intentionally competed with the event hosted by Franklin. Initially, only one conference had been planned. The existence of two conferences reflected the splintering among black activists who had just five months prior joined together in the March for Freedom. Ideologies, participants, and agendas divided them. Franklin and the municipal human rights council did not welcome as participants black nationalist and radical activists whose stances they viewed as working against liberal civil rights organizations in the city. Two weeks before the conference, then, the black radical cadre of the planning team broke with Franklin and his supporters, especially after they refused to endorse a black agenda that centered on "independent political action and regional and national economic action by united Negro communities." Franklin wanted to avoid such actions and all-black formations in order to prevent "at all costs" being "labeled a black nationalist like Marcus Garvey."[48]

Who were these radicals?—James and Grace Lee Boggs, Rev. Cleage, and Richard and Milton Henry. They also were members of the Group on Advanced Leadership (GOAL), an organization they founded in the early 1960s to protest the death of two black Detroiters—one at the hands of a police officer, the other killed by a white youth.[49] GOAL organized the grassroots leadership conference, relished the participation of black nationalists, and unabashedly forwarded an agenda that supported the Freedom Now Party, race pride (not sublimated to interracialism), black self-defense, asylum for exile Robert F. Williams and political prisoner Mae Mallory (described as a "militant Black grassroots freedom fighter"), and a discussion of alternative economic arrangements that elevated the labor question and critiqued capitalism.

How were these differences reflected at each conference? No political slouch (in fact, in just a few years, he would proclaim the need for "audacious power"), Rev. Adam Clayton Powell Jr., pastor of New York's Abyssinian Baptist Church, had already agreed to speak at the Northern Negro Leadership Conference. At the grassroots conference, Malcolm X spoke, as did others heralded for their piercing critiques of white power and attention to the travails of everyday black women and men. Freeman spoke before Malcolm X on RAM's worldview, "and when I sat down," Freeman recalled, "Malcolm went up to the podium and the rest is history."[50] Indeed, it was in the Motor City and the home of Motown that Malcolm X gave the famed "Message to the Grassroots" to a robust crowd, estimates of which range from 700 to 2,000 people.[51] In his speech he characterized the 1963 March on Washington as a "performance of the year," controlled "tight" to minimize its uncompromising liberation message. Malcolm echoed his earlier calls for a black united front built along the lines of Bandung, and called for a black revolution versus a "Negro" revolution. A black revolution would focus on solidarity, land, nation, and self-defense, and move beyond the framework of integration. These were some of the very ideas that undergirded anti-colonial struggles in Africa and Asia and excited Black Power advocates.

Activists converged on Detroit from several cities. The Cleveland-based Freedom Fighters attended the grassroots leadership conference. The Freedom Fighters challenged school segregation, picketed segregated public accommodations, and protested job discrimination. Korean War veteran Lewis G. Robinson described the Freedom Fighters, which he founded in 1960, as "Cleveland's most militant civil rights group." In his memoir he described the Freedom Fighters' decision to allow only black men to serve as officers (though white men could head committees) as their "black power of 1961, not 1966!"[52]

At the Detroit grassroots leadership conference, the Freedom Fighters and Cleveland CORE activists called on conference organizers and attendees "to consider a nationwide boycott and selective buying campaign against GM, Cadillac Division." For five months, the Freedom Fighters had been engaged in a picketing campaign against the dealership. In a resolution, the conference organizers avowed their support.[53] In this same resolution, they also upheld the principle of self-defense and made common cause with "colored oppressed people of the world," as well as instructed activists to prepare for a boycott of schools if necessary in order to protest "unequal inferior education."[54]

By the end of the centennial year, many of the general concepts, strategies, and political streams of Black Power existed and increasingly gained public footing, often in alternative leftist publications. In November–December 1963, RAM published *Black America*. The organization, which now had a communication organ as Ethel Johnson had advised, featured articles on internationalism, revolutionary nationalism, and the economics of oppression. Stanford pinpointed the nexus of power as the "Wall Street-military-industrial complex that chokes [the] American economy and forces thousands of babies to die in poverty while a few reap the benefits of its cold war products."[55] Rolland Snellings argued that the "Negro Revolution" was in its "second stage"—one that featured a call to "unite with self and kind NOW!" and required "cutting the West aloose."[56]

In "Integration, Separation, or What?" Wanda Marshall declared, "The real issues have seemingly been avoided by both movements." By this, she meant traditional civil rights and black nationalist organizations. Marshall continued: "Our struggle is not one of Separation or Integration, but rather a struggle to assure the survival of the black race in an automated economy."[57] Technological changes would increasingly lessen the need for industrial workers in increasingly black cities where numerous factories shut down or relocated to white towns and suburbs, taking jobs, tax bases, white people, and capital with them. This process of employment retrenchment, deindustrialization, and disinvestment in rustbelt and port cities had a tremendous impact on their economic stability and vibrancy.[58]

Marshall's emphasis on mechanization echoed the analysis of James Boggs, one of RAM's mentors, as well as conveyed the shifting structure of labor. Just months before, Boggs had published *The American Revolution,* which would subsequently be translated into six languages and garner him speaking engagements throughout the country. While the book critiqued the labor movement, his discussion of automation drew the most attention. Boggs argued that automation exposed the contradictions of capitalism by making work less necessary and the working class expendable.[59]

In the same issue of *Black America,* Freeman discussed the establishment of an independent black political party. It was a concept that Harold Cruse wrote about that same month in *Liberator,* and Detroit and New York black radicals had attempted to develop, in actuality, in the Freedom Now Party. Freeman wrote: "Neither the 'donkey' or the 'elephant,'" because neither intended "to emancipate us; to vote either Democrat or Republican is merely to 'champion Lucifer or the Devil.'" Instead, he believed only an independent party would give black people a reason to vote and pay attention to politics, as well as provide them "with a potent weapon to eliminate 'economic rape' (fantastic rents, retail prices and slave wages in the Black Ghetto), police brutality, "rat-infested' housing, and . . . deplorable school systems."[60] Those same months, in *The Illustrated News*, a grassroots Detroit newspaper run by Cleage, the reverend penned a three-part series about the "Black Revolt of 1963" and called for "undertaking a comprehensive program of independent black political action and independent black cooperative economic action." For him, this revolt served as a prelude to an expected "revolution."[61]

1964: Quit Saying We're Free

As the centennial year gave way to 1964, black militants, particularly radicals and nationalists, stood as the harbingers of that revolution. Local black activists helped to generate such concern. In Cleveland, the Freedom Fighters had seriously begun considering forming a rifle club. Their decision was spurred by white retaliation, or what they described as "hoodlumism," against black parents and an interracial, group of activists who challenged the segregation of black students in the previously all-white Murray Hill School.[62]

The idea of a rifle club was not new, nor did it register as outlandish to Robinson. He was 14 when he joined his first rifle club in his hometown of Decatur, Alabama, as a proactive measure: "We planned what we would do in case of a race riot," he said, because only 80 to 90 black families lived on their side of town.[63] For similar reasons some 20 years later in 1964, rifle clubs represented proactive protection in the face of white resentment. After about a month of consideration filled with discussions in basements and barbershops, and with colleagues in Detroit and Chicago, the Freedom Fighters had made their decision. They sent a press release announcing their new rifle club to the news media on April 3, 1964—the same day Malcolm X was to deliver a version of one of his most stirring and definitive speeches in Cleveland, "The Ballot or the Bullet."[64]

Word of his appearance attracted between 2,000 and 3,000 people to Cory United Methodist Church on 105th Street, one of the oldest African American churches in the city. His lecture was part of a symposium sponsored by Cleveland CORE titled "The Negro Revolt—What Comes Next?" In part, Cleveland CORE had invited Malcolm X to draw more attention to the ongoing school protests. Malcolm publicly supported local activists' desegregation efforts, not because he bore a newfound belief in integration or the miraculous healing capacity of black and white together, but because he felt such a move would remove from power school officials disinterested in black children's education.[65]

That April day in Cleveland, journalist and author Louis E. Lomax spoke first. Not quite a year before, Lomax had predicted in the introduction to *When the Word Is Given: A Report on Elijah Muhammad, Malcolm X, and the Black Muslim World:* "[O]n the whole the Black Muslims will have a healthy influence on our own social structure."[66] In fact while Lomax disagreed with the Nation of Islam on many points, he nevertheless sympathized with the NOI in its quest to protect black communities, and viewed his book as putting the white "Western man . . . on trial." Indeed, "the failings of Western society" gave birth and cause to groups like the Nation of Islam. Lomax wrote: "I know white people are frightened by Malcolm X and Elijah Muhammad; maybe now they will understand how I have felt all my life, for there has never been a day when I was unafraid; we Negroes live our lives on the edge of fear." Lomax continued in the book's introduction that he was optimistic about change because "Negroes are now determined to better their lot" and "white people are beginning to yield some of their power, and that—power—is what the argument is really about."[67]

At Cory United Methodist Church, the audience waited in anticipation for Malcolm X to speak. After thanking Lomax and "brothers and sisters, friends and enemies," Malcolm X addressed the symposium theme. Having just established Muslim Mosque, Inc., Malcolm X argued for political, economic, and social self-determination; control of community resources; black electoral power; and reeducation.[68] Malcolm said, "In my little humble way of understanding it, it points toward either the ballot or the bullet." Then he said, "I'm not here to argue or discuss anything that we differ about, because it's time for us to submerge our differences and realize that it is best for us to first see that we have the same problem, a common problem—a problem that will make you catch hell whether you're a Baptist, or a Methodist, or a Muslim, or a nationalist. Whether you're educated or illiterate, whether you live on the boulevard or in the alley, you're going to catch hell just like I am."[69] At the end of his "Ballot or Bullet" speech, Malcolm X addressed gun and rifle clubs. He did not suggest forming "battalions" and going on the offense. But he was clear, as was Ida B. Wells-Barnett, Nannie Louise Hansberry, Gloria Richardson, Robert F. Williams, and others: "[When] the government has proven itself either unwilling or unable to defend the lives and the property of Negroes, it's time for Negroes to defend themselves."[70] Within a number of days, Malcolm X gave another version of the same speech at King Solomon Baptist Church in Detroit. He was making his grassroots, urban rounds.

Malcolm X's sponsored appearance in Cleveland by CORE—one of the well-known civil rights organizations that promoted integration—signaled one among many steps on the path to the embracing of Black Power. Within the next couple of years, but particularly after SNCC's 1966 Greenwood moment, the national office of CORE formally adopted Black Power as its clarion call.[71] And Malcolm X—as well as his intellectual mentors Marcus Garvey and Audley Moore, alongside black people's quotidian experiences—would continue to have a profound impact on a generation of youth across the country.

Shortly after Mallory's extradition from Cleveland in 1964, Stanford returned to the city. He did not stay long. Freeman sent Stanford south to help organize an Afro-American Student Conference on Black Nationalism at Fisk University in May 1964. RAM knew people in Fisk's Afro-American Student Movement (ASM), including leaders Michele Paul and Betty Rush, who had agreed to host the conference.[72] Paul was their primary contact. It was she who secured "administrative permission to have the conference on Fisk University's campus," Freeman recalled.[73] The goal was to unite students in liberation organizations worldwide who supported a global black revolution. As Stanford traveled to raise money for and publicize the May conference, he met SNCC's Mississippi field staff and invited them to attend the black nationalism conference.[74]

The conference, echoing RAM's stances, positioned itself as part of a global, people of color, socialist struggle. In particular, the Bandung Conference, Mao's China, and Castro's Cuba had inspired RAM. Such stances drew the attention of the FBI, which put the group under surveillance. In an intelligence memo that appeared in Malcolm X's surveillance file, an FBI operative captured the truth of RAM's political position: "RAM is entirely non-white in membership, clandestine in nature, and owes its primary allegiance to the 'Bandung World,' that is, the non-white races of the world, rather than any national entity, as such."[75]

During the 1964 ASM conference, revolutionary black nationalist activists critiqued capitalism; questioned what they deemed at the time as the bourgeois reformism of SNCC, CORE, and the NAACP; and challenged orthodox black nationalist approaches that they deemed more rhetoric than action. These critiques echoed ideas in Marshall's 1963 essay on "Integration, Separation, or What?" in *Black America,* as well as Stanford's 1964 essay titled "Towards Revolutionary Action Movement Manifesto" in *Correspondence,* a magazine edited by Detroit radicals James and Grace Lee Boggs. The manifesto read in part: "As revolutionary black nationalists, we do not believe that standing on street corners alone will liberate our people. Revolutionary black nationalists must act as a vanguard to show our people how to seize power so that they may gain some control over their lives."[76] According to Ahmad (Stanford) in his memoir: "The consensus of the conferees was that African-Americans needed to control their own neighborhoods, similar to what Malcolm X was teaching at the time, but they also stated they realized that contemporary reality necessitated the use of a strategy of chaos that was advocated by Rev. Cleage."[77] In other words, mass disruption, or a more aggressive or "devastating civil disobedience," needed to take precedence over courteous civil disobedience.[78]

The summer was just heating up. After the ASM conference, SNCC launched Freedom Summer in Mississippi. Robert Moses helped develop the project, and James Forman served as its executive director. Sponsored by the Council of Federated Organizations (COFO), the voter registration project strategically focused on attracting white northern students to Mississippi. Established in 1961, COFO served as an umbrella organization for the NAACP, the National Urban League, CORE, SCLC, and SNCC. The project entailed setting up freedom schools, registering black residents to vote, and drawing media attention to these efforts. Recruiting white college and university students, who put themselves in harm's way, would do just that. Early on, Moses and others expressed concern about the focus on white students, both in terms of safety and the potentially disruptive impact on black leadership, but the project proceeded. That summer, some 1,000 mostly white students converged on Mississippi, and under the stewardship of black SNCC field secretary Charles Cobb Jr., 300 freedom schools opened, and some 3,500 students attended.[79] Even so, at SNCC organizing meetings, conversations about white students' participation in mobilization efforts continued to bubble up, presaging debates linked to black consciousness and racial separatism in the era of expansive Black Power.

Serving as a black revolutionary voice, RAM members Stanford and Snellings also went south to Mississippi with the goal of building a following for their precepts highlighted at the Fisk conference. Stanford recalled that SNCC chair John Lewis allowed him and Snellings "to test [their] ideas of building an all African-American black nationalist self-defense project"—even though Lewis did not agree with their approach. Lewis still believed in nonviolent direct action and integration as the primary strategy and goal of the black freedom movement. As part of Snellings's organizing and political education work in Greenwood, Mississippi, he opened a freedom school where he taught African and black history.

Snellings's activist credentials began as early as high school. Born in Raleigh, North Carolina in 1938, Snellings moved to Dayton, Ohio in 1944. Coming of age there, as a student at Roosevelt High School from 1952 to 1956, Snellings sang doo-wop songs as well as participated in a sit-in at his school. After a three-year stint in the air force, he moved to New York where he visited Lewis Micheaux's black bookstore, also known as the "House of Common Sense and the Home of Proper Propaganda," founded in 1932 on 7th Avenue in Harlem, and listened to the street sermons of Malcolm X.[80] A short year later, Snellings participated in the 1961 United Nations protest alongside the likes of Maya Angelou and Mae Mallory, and then in 1962 joined a collective of black artists and intellectuals. Using his creative talents in the movement, Snellings alongside others such as LeRoi Jones (Amiri Baraka) and Sonia Sanchez, a member of Brooklyn CORE and admirer of Malcolm X, helped to fuel the Black Arts Movement—dubbed the cultural arm of Black Power.

In Greenwood, Snellings witnessed the devaluation and cheapness of black life. Ever since SNCC arrived there, its members had experienced violence. After an attempt in 1964 to firebomb the home of Mrs. Laura McGhee, who believed in armed self-defense and was known to "take no shit," according to historian Akinyele Umoja, Snellings and other SNCC members in Mississippi responded.[81] They decided to patrol black neighborhoods in carloads and arm the freedom houses. According to Snellings, while Carmichael became the outraged face and blistering voice of Black Power years later, in 1964 he had not yet become that public revolutionary. When Carmichael arrived in Greenwood from Atlanta, he questioned local SNCC members about the patrols, and then told them in no uncertain terms, "Roland is not your leader. He's with RAM. SNCC believes in nonviolence."[82] In 1964 in this southern city of Greenwood, then, where extensive civil rights organizing was occurring, so was "revolutionary nationalist activity."[83]

Students who streamed to Mississippi for Freedom Summer worked toward voter education and securing political power within the established two-party system. For instance, COFO sought to organize state conventions to choose alternate delegates for the all-white Mississippi delegation at the Democratic Convention in Atlantic City in 1964. This helped spur the formation of the statewide grassroots political party, the Mississippi Freedom Democratic Party (MFDP), in April 1964. Shortly thereafter, MFDP opened an office in Washington and its co-founder and grassroots activist Fannie Lou Hamer, who also served as an SNCC field secretary, took the national stage. Just two years earlier, Hamer had been a sharecropper and timekeeper; she had worked for 18 years in Ruleville, Mississippi, but her employer fired her for trying to register to vote.[84]

The MFDP delegates arrived in Atlantic City for the Democratic Convention on Friday, August 21, 1964, and held a rally. The next day they held a breakfast and then presented their case to the Credentials Committee. Hamer testified, unveiling the racial subjugation, economic marginalization, political exclusion, and wholesale violence experienced by black Mississippians generally. She also gave an "emotional recounting" of the jail beating that she received after she returned from a voter education workshop in 1963. It was yet another example of state and gendered violence against black women. That particular day white law enforcement officials in Winona arrested her and five others and beat them. They cursed her, took her into "the bullpen," and ordered a young black male prisoner to beat her with a blackjack. As she lay on her stomach screaming, other white law enforcement officers joined in, pummeling the back of her head and ordering the black prisoner to hold her feet down. Yet another officer pulled her dress over her head. The experience was a horrifying expression of racialized sexual terror, and white power—unchecked, legal, and accepted.[85]

Hamer ended her Credentials Committee testimony by declaring: "If the Freedom Democratic Party is not seated now I question America. Is this America, the land of the free and the home of the brave, where we have to sleep with our telephones off the hook because our lives be threatened daily, because we want to live as decent human beings in America?"[86] The MFDP was not seated. Instead it was given two nonvoting seats—an offer which Hamer and her compatriots unblinkingly turned down. The Black Revolt and a sense of being betrayed by the government were fueled even further.

The summer of 1964 represented a critical turning point. It was a summer of urban uprisings (in August Harlem exploded), protest, dashed hopes, and new realizations. While Hamer was testifying, news confirming the deaths of three (two white and one black) Freedom Summer workers—Michael "Mickey" Schwerner, Andrew Goodman, and James Chaney—arrived. That same summer another four volunteers were wounded, 80 beaten, and more than 1,000 arrested. Thirty-seven churches and 30 homes were bombed, and MFDP had come home empty handed.[87] At that moment, what some had realized earlier had been newly confirmed: black activists could not depend upon U.S. government officials or civil rights and labor leaders. Nor was moral suasion necessarily sturdy enough to serve as the primary pathway to progressive social change.

Old questions emerged anew, and sentiments and efforts on the ground continued to shift. SNCC activists, MFDP participants, and Fannie Lou Hamer did not lay down their freedom plows. They challenged the white power structure in the South and North. Those two places were not all that different, according to Hamer, particularly when it came to black people living free and with dignity. On December 20, 1964, Hamer shared the stage with Malcolm X at Williams Institutional Christian Methodist Episcopal (CME) Church. Malcolm talked about needing a Mau Mau in Harlem, Alabama, Georgia, and Mississippi (something Medgar Evers, an admirer of Jomo Kenyatta and the Kenyan freedom struggle, had believed in). Warned Malcolm X: "If they don't want to deal with the Mississippi Freedom Democratic Party, then we'll give them something else to deal with." Hamer, too, criticized the federal government, saying while U.S. officials cannot seem to protect black people in Mississippi, "when a white man is killed in the Congo, they send people there." And lest black Harlemites think themselves better positioned than black Mississippians, Hamer proclaimed: "You're not free here in Harlem. I've gone to a lot of big cities and I've got my first city to go where this man wasn't standing with his feet on this black man's neck." She continued: "This is something we going to have to learn to do and quit saying that we are free in America when I know we are not free. . . . The people are not free in Chicago. . . . They are not free in Philadelphia. . . . And when you get it over with all the way around, some of the places is a Mississippi in disguise."[88] Hamer solicited Harlemites and northerners' support for black Mississippians' fight for electoral power. But even legally securing the vote would not automatically translate into the protection of black people—their rights or lives—or improvement of their material conditions whether in the South or North.

Around this same time, in the mid-1960s, New York teenager Joanne Byron (the future Assata Shakur) struggled, as did many other youth, with exactly how to live free and with dignity in a society that did not provide ample opportunities or even fully value her humanity. Byron returned to school after her brief stint working as a barmaid. She recalls her music teacher talking down to her and other black and Puerto Rican classmates. The teacher called them "names like hooligans and ignoramuses" because they were not as enthralled with symphonies and sonatas, and treated their music—Latin music, jazz, and R&B—as "trashy." For Byron, the teacher and her "so-called education in amerika" were racist and Eurocentric. She experienced this as she learned, through friends and independent reading, about the sit-ins, freedom rides, Medgar Evers, Jim Crow, the KKK, and the "trigger-happy nightstick-wielding police."[89]

Ultimately after completing several years of high school, Byron decided to quit before graduating, live on her own, and take a job in a secretarial pool. The low-paying job did not provide medical benefits, had "indecent" working conditions, and only paid her enough to buy "air sandwiches" after paying her rent. Byron described, in the words of Helen Howard, the "nitty-gritty" of poverty. Howard was a black resident and activist in Vine City, a poor segregated black community in Atlanta, where the SNCC cadre that most stridently espoused black consciousness would be based. "We (the poor) know what the 'nitty-gritty' poor is like," explained Howard in the *Southern Regional Council Magazine* in 1965, continuing, "The 'nitty-gritty' poor is the hopeless and bleakness we have to face night and day." Other black women and men also found themselves in dire straits trying to make ends meet by "hook or crook."[90] The majority of black women (and men) still worked in service, agricultural, and low-wage factory jobs.

While gaining access to white-collar work once off-limits to black women, Byron still faced discrimination as a black person, as a "low-level" secretary, and likely as an uppity young black female worker. "In the office there was a group of secretaries who worked for the company's president or vice-presidents," recalled Byron. "They looked down on those of us who worked in the general office and treated us like we were nothing."[91] Neither did her gender serve as a source of worker bonding. The rebellions, which captured the attention of her white female co-workers, amplified her outsider racial status. These women, who hardly ever paid her any attention, all of a sudden wanted to talk about the Harlem uprising. One white woman called "those people" who were rioting "stupid and dumb" for "tearing up their own neighborhoods and burning down their own houses," and then asked Byron: "Isn't it a shame?" Taken off-guard, Joanne reluctantly responded "yes" and then left. "Disgusted with myself," Byron said, she prepared a better answer just in case the issue came up again. It did a few days later, and this time, Byron shot back: "What do you mean, they're burning down their houses? They don't own those houses. They don't own those stores. I'm glad they burned down those stores because those stores were robbing them in the first place!" Eventually, she was fired, she said, to her own relief.[92]

Alongside the rebellions, conversations with African students who attended Columbia University (emblematic of historic and ongoing black diasporic intellectual exchanges as well as student activism on campuses), and seeing her friends "dying from OD and going into the army" further politicized Byron. Local conditions guided her grassroots actions and concrete demands. She, as had many others, began to question the ability of rights and integration to liberate black people. With the African students, she discussed their culture, traditions, the Vietnam War, democracy, and U.S. geopolitics. Over time she grew to understand how much she did not know, or how much of what she knew was either wrong or slanted. She learned that U.S. democracy was fallible, blood-tainted, and limited. As early as the mid-1960s, the belief "that integration was really the solution to our problems" disintegrated for Byron, and a new caveat guided her politics: "Never let your enemies choose your enemies for you."[93]

These critical years of political awakening, and state response to black people's rights struggles, as well as her political alliances, dramatically influenced her activist path. The 17-year-old Joanne Byron, soon to become Joanne Chesimard, would travel west to California in search of Black Panthers; meet American Indian and Asian-American radicals; return to Harlem; join the Black Panther Party; work in survival programs, schools, and health clinics; and later enlist in the radical Black Liberation Army. Still many years away, but soon enough, Joanne Chesimard would become famous—or infamous in the eyes of the state—as the radical black freedom fighter Assata Shakur.

Clearly, black people and burgeoning, and even veteran, activists began to grapple with what freedom looked like before and after the Civil Rights Act of 1964, the Voting Rights Act of 1965, "Bloody Sunday" in Selma, Alabama, and other mounting reality checks soon to follow. They were already pondering whether securing rights could protect black life, provide an antidote to the matrimony between racism and capital, change the daily concrete living conditions of black working-class and poor people, or transform power relations.

The same summer that MFDP fought for political representation in Atlantic City, RAM sought to extend its national reach. In fact, during that summer, Stanford went to Cuba where Robert F. Williams remained in exile. While there, Stanford met Ernest Allen, a Merritt College student and member of the Afro-American Association, who organized with other West Coast students. Freeman met their plane at John F. Kennedy airport. That's when Freeman first met Ernie Allen, who helped spread knowledge of RAM to California and establish the Soul Students Advisory Council (SSAC) with his brother Doug.[94] Initially, it was through the Afro-American Association that Bobby Seale and Huey P. Newton, two southern transplants, met at Merritt College in 1962. They joined the association and participated in efforts to establish courses on black history and culture, as well as began thinking about how to inform and get students involved in community issues. They also joined SSAC. In a matter of a few years, Newton and Seale would leave SSAC, work more directly in community, and later found the Oakland-based Black Panther Party.[95] RAM, however, would remain a relatively small cadre of primarily male activists.

Between 1964 and 1965, RAM members, including Stanford, Snellings, Freeman, and Charles "Chuck" Johnson (a member of UHURU), gathered in Detroit and engaged in revolutionary theorizing about black political independence and power. There, the literal home of the Boggses became a haven, as well as a creative site for the production of *Black America*. Freeman often stayed with the Boggses when he traveled to Detroit and brought copies back to Cleveland to distribute.[96] The fall 1964 issue cost 25 cents for 24 pages of political essays, quotes, and drawings celebrating black men as models of militancy. The issue's cover featured a watercolor of Marcus Garvey's ghost painted by Stanford. Excerpts from Du Bois, Garvey, Malcolm X, Elijah Muhammad, Cleage, and Robert F. Williams filled the journal's pages. No women made it to the front—no General Tubman or Lady General Richardson, no Audley "Queen Mother" Moore or Ethel Johnson, this despite the fact that Moore and Johnson were RAM's mentors and provided critical nuts-and-bolts knowledge regarding community organizing.

Shortly after the publication of the fall issue of *Black America,* Stanford, who was often in New York, arranged a meeting with Malcolm X to ask if he would help start the Organization for Black Power.[97] Malcolm X met in a coffee shop with Stanford, the Boggses, William Worthy, an *Afro-American* newspaper reporter who covered the revolutions in Cuba and China, and fellow *Afro-American* newspaper correspondent and Mount Vernon black feminist and socialist activist Patricia Murphy Robinson. Malcolm X, however, declined their offer.[98] Thus, even before its formal media coming out, Black Power, using those words, yet again, was being discussed as a strategy for securing black political self-determination, economic independence, and community control.

In the North, South, Midwest, and West of the United States, the currents feeding Black Power grew. This occurred against the backdrop of economic restructuring and hardship, amplified civil rights protests, and shifting national politics tempered by the assassination of President Kennedy in November 1963. The next year, Lyndon B. Johnson, who took over the Oval Office, signed the Civil Rights Act. Even so, the daily exigencies of black living still exposed harrowing circumstances influenced by local and national racial and class power structures. This ongoing reality continued to inflame people's passions and struggles. In 1964 racial uprisings occurred in eight cities. Harlem and Rochester, New York, were the first to start what would become four years of long hot summers. In the wake of these uprisings, the federal government and philanthropic foundations initiated programs to respond to and calm discontent. President Johnson, who had declared a War on Poverty in January 1964, established eight months later the Office of Economic Opportunity and its centerpiece, the community action program. Community action programs across the country helped to further ignite activism and politicize neighborhood residents despite the minimal budgets, political backlash, and ultimately the siphoning of funding to the Vietnam War. Indeed, such grassroots activism, predicated on the community action program's philosophy of "maximum feasible participation," would clash with municipal leaders' designs to maintain control of cities and programs, at all costs.

1965 Onwards: Get Power for Black People

At the beginning of 1965, Black Power stood on the horizon of the black liberation struggle. Its varied ideological and tactical seeds—civil rights militancy, black nationalism, and economic and international radicalism—had sprouted in the North, South, Midwest, and West. For the last few years, black nationalism and growing civil rights militancy had intermingled and operated alongside each other. In 1965, the willingness of the most widely recognized apostle of black nationalism to create a united front with rights activists, coupled with his tragic fate, further fertilized expressions of race pride, black consciousness, and critiques of white power.

In February Malcolm X appeared before 300 people at Brown's Chapel AME Church in Selma, Alabama. By this time, he had formed the Muslim Mosque, Inc. and the Organization of Afro-American Unity. At Brown's Chapel, he met Coretta Scott King and "praised [Martin Luther] King's dedication to nonviolence." He also, however, "advised that should white America refuse to accept the nonviolent model of social change, his own example of armed 'self-defense' was an alternative."[99]

Just two weeks later, on February 21, Malcolm X (El Hajj Malik El-Shabazz) readied himself for his early afternoon presentation in New York City's Audubon Ballroom. This time he stood before a crowd of over 200 people. Recently freed after a long court battle in the Monroe case that sent Robert and Mabel Williams into exile, Mae Mallory sat in the front row of the ballroom on that day. Mallory had been sentenced to 16 to 20 years, but on January 29, 1965, the North Carolina Supreme Court ordered her release and that of the other defendants on a technicality that broadcast civil rights violations and exposed racial inequality in the judicial system. The grand jury was segregated—that is, all white. Less than a month after gaining her freedom, Mallory—along with other civil rights, black nationalist, and grassroots militants, some of whom would lead the liberation charge in the Black Power era—waited eagerly to hear Malcolm X.

That's when the fatal and now familiar disturbance ensued. It was punctuated by the exhortation, "Get your hand out of my pocket," the pointing of a gun, and then the ringing shots. Malcolm X, the target, lay bulleted and bloody and dead—his head cradled by Kochiyama. Shaken by it all, Mallory remembered: a black hand pulled the trigger. Also in the audience that fateful day was Larry Neal, a soon-to-be voice of the Black Arts Movement. He was selling copies of RAM's *Black America*. Malcolm's comrade and activist Patricia Murphy Robinson was there too. An advocate for welfare and tenant rights activism in the 1960s and early 1970s, Robinson would help organize the New York–based group Black Women Enraged "to help the family of [the] assassinated leader."[100]

Eldridge Cleaver sat in a prison mess hall (which doubled as a theater) on that Sunday. He was watching *The Strangler* when a fellow inmate Silly Willie told him Malcolm X had been shot. Cleaver recounted: "For a moment the earth seemed to reel in orbit." He continued to look at the movie, thinking to himself that such a tragedy might just bring heightened attention to Malcolm's message, that is, until he found out Malcolm had died. It hit him hard, for Malcolm X symbolized hope for thousands who found themselves trapped in the vicious "PPP" cycle: prison-parole-prison. He gave "voice to the mute ambitions in the black man's soul." For Cleaver, Malcolm was like Patrice Lumumba of the Congo; he was to be gotten rid of; his assassination akin to "mad-dog butchery."[101]

In the days and months after Malcolm X's assassination, black militancy expanded in cities and hamlets across the country. Just one day later, LeRoi Jones (who changed his name to Amiri Baraka in 1967) founded with Larry Neal the Black Arts Repertory Theatre/School (BARTS). BARTS represented both a salvo to the slain leader's significance and a resolute desire to reach black youth, rally for black self-determination, and enact unity through the political weapon of the arts. BARTS followed in the rich legacy of groups such as Umbra, a collective of black writers established in 1962.[102] The theater/school opened in a brownstone in Harlem with black intellectuals, cultural workers, and activists as teachers and advisors, such as Cruse, Sanchez, Stanford, and Snellings, who also belonged to Umbra.[103] That same year, Jones penned a pivotal poem "Black Art," in which he wrote: "We want 'poems that kill.' *Assassin* poems, Poems that shoot guns." Neal's essay titled "The Black Arts Movement" echoed this sentiment: "Poetry is a concrete freedom, an action. No more abstractions. Poems are physical entities: fists, daggers, airplane poems, and poems that shoot guns."[104] BARTS closed six months after opening because of "ideological, aesthetic, and monetary crises," but it would later be acknowledged as an origination moment that launched the artistic arm of the Black Power movement.[105]

On February 27, just two days after Malcolm's assassination, Rep. Powell, the chairman of the House Education and Labor Committee, gave a speech at a fundraiser for the black Fourth District Democratic Organization in Baltimore. He argued black people needed to pursue "audacious power" in order to "control the affairs of [their] city and [their] state." His view was akin to seeing the city as the black man's land. Months later and for the first time Powell delivered his "Black Position Paper" at another banquet, this one in Chicago for Ebenezer Missionary Baptist Church. There, Powell discussed how "the Negro revolt must change into a Black Revolution."[106]

The heightened public attention and growing fear of black militancy exposed the fashioning of black self-determination and power agendas. For instance, militant activists proposed a unity conference in May 1965 in Washington, D.C. The FBI knew this and wrote memos warning of efforts to form a coalition of "militant Negro radicals." The FBI, not surprisingly, also linked such organizing efforts to "possible racial violence," paying little attention to the argument of proponents such as Julius Hobson and Harlem tenant rights activist Jesse Gray, who discussed assuaging black penury and powerlessness. "We have to address ourselves as the black power in the ghetto, black political power," stated Gray at a Detroit organizing meeting, which the FBI had infiltrated: "We're looking forward to the day when we're able to consolidate this black power . . . if we're united, 20 million of anything is a powerful attraction."[107] In May 1965, these black militants formed the short-lived Organization for Black Power, the group that they initially had asked Malcolm X to help build.[108]

In Los Angeles, California, Ron Karenga founded the cultural nationalist US (versus them) Organization. Born Ronald Everett in 1941, he grew up near Salisbury, Maryland, the youngest of 14 children, the seventh son of farmers. He moved to Los Angeles in 1958 and eventually enrolled at the University of California Los Angeles where he became interested in African and Caribbean culture, anticolonialism, and activism. A year after founding US, he created the black holiday

Kwanzaa to emphasize, teach, and celebrate black cultural renewal and revolution through seven principles or the *Nguzo Saba:* unity, self-determination, collective work and responsibility, cooperative economics, purposeful community building, creativity, and faith. US also would attempt to enact all of these principles through united front politics that over the years would hit bumps, some of them fatal in the Black Power era.[109]

In 1965, the year of the Voting Rights Act, SNCC turned toward organizing a locally based "all African-American political party in 1965."[110] Having experienced the supremacy of white political power at the Atlantic City convention and afterward, SNCC staffers devised plans to expand efforts to secure black political power for poor people throughout the Deep South. James Forman had suggested expanding the Mississippi Summer Project to the entire Black Belt at SNCC's October 1964 meeting in Atlanta. This occurred just three months after the formation of the Deacons for Defense. While it started in Louisiana, the Deacons for Defense eventually formed 21 chapters throughout Louisiana, Mississippi, and Alabama.[111] Disagreement in SNCC, however, spelled defeat for the Black Belt Summer Project; it never launched.[112]

Nevertheless, SNCC would help initiate an all-black campaign to develop an all-black political party to contend with white officials. Their efforts in Lowndes County began not even one month after Malcolm's death, two weeks after Bloody Sunday in Selma, and a matter of a day or two after the murder of 39-year-old white Detroit homemaker and mother turned activist Viola Liuzzo. Liuzzo had been shuttling marchers to Selma and was on her way back to Montgomery on March 25, 1965 when the Klan shot her to death as she drove through Lowndes County along U.S. Route 80. In that particular Alabama county, black people comprised more than 80 percent of the population. However, while there were 5,122 African Americans of voting age, not one was registered. Responding to Liuzzo's murder and the inhumane, anti-democratic, and marginalized conditions of black people, SNCC staff decided to work with black people there to organize the Lowndes County Freedom Organization (LCFO) with its visual symbol, the black panther.[113] Stokely Carmichael became the senior field secretary who went to Lowndes County the last week of March 1965.

There existed real hope that organizing a black political party and mobilizing the community to vote would secure the necessary power for black residents to influence policy and the decisions in their communities. Historian Hasan Jeffries identifies the LCFO as "the first major test of SNCC's most significant Black Power project," one which emerged out of lived experience and grassroots praxis.[114] At SNCC's November 1965 staff meeting, Courtland Cox, who worked with Carmichael and other SNCC staffers, gave a report on the mobilizing work in Lowndes County. He wrote something like "get power for black people" on the blackboard. Engaging the ideas that Cox reported, Forman then wrote on the blackboard, "Power. Education. Organization."[115]

In his memoir, Forman recalled: "From that time on, SNCC began to talk more and more about power for black people, organization, and political education. We had attained a whole new level of objectives, we were once again moving in harmony with the needs of the masses of black people."[116] In December 1965, Lowndes County activists with SNCC, established the all-black political party to contest the all-white Alabama Democratic Party that had a white cock as its mascot and a slogan that avowed "white supremacy for the right." The LCFO put forth a people's agenda, including the push for redistribution of wealth through tax reform. In fact, according to Jeffries, "the Lowndes County political program defined Black Power, which SNCC organizers understood to mean developing grassroots, independent political parties through which African Americans could win local office and secure a definitive say in the decisions that affected their lives."[117]

The growing desire to control political agendas, black communities, and ultimately decision-making authority also resulted in struggles over rural and urban community action programs and federal dollars. Within the next couple years, from Mississippi to D.C. and elsewhere, black grassroots activists raised questions about greater representation and employment of the poor in community action agencies. The self-described organization of militants, Associated Community Teams (ACT), a "living union . . . of people fighting together for their freedom (from fear, ignorance and want), their comfort and their human dignity," broached this issue in D.C. Led by Julius Hobson, ACT members asked why the District's anti-poverty agency had no poor people on its board of directors. The group would broach the following question in its first newsletter *The Activist,* which was "dedicated to the memory of Malcolm X."[118] The Organization for Black Power, which Hobson also helped initiate, adopted a resolution on July 4, 1965. It had harsh words for the anti-poverty program, describing it as incapable of dealing with "the immediate needs of the poor of this nation" and as "a bonanza of job exchange for the nation's middle-class social workers."[119] Jean Smith, a black Howard University student who joined SNCC and became an organizer in Mississippi, too, expressed concern, in her case about white Mississippians asserting control over the Child Development Group of Mississippi (CDGM), a Head Start program funded by the Office of Economic Opportunity (OEO), which black and poor people initially ran in 1965.[120]

The anti-poverty program, and the battles over it, politicized and galvanized local residents to demand changes in their neighborhoods and representation, even as it raised concerns about the ability of government to address black people's needs and protect their rights. For instance in Baltimore, public housing tenants and grassroots activists fought for representation on community action boards and to access financial resources to initiate programs with some (but too often limited) success. They struggled against veteran white and some black political officials and professionals—to be called the black bourgeoisie by economic radicals—who unabashedly angled to maintain control over the anti-poverty bureaucracy.[121]

For SNCC activist Jean Smith, the struggle over CDGM exposed this "paradox" that pitched grassroots activists and poor people against public officials: "The poverty program says it wants 'maximum feasible participation of the poor' but it *doesn't* want the poor to participate. For me it was a devastating paradox. It required me to abandon my last hope that American society would willingly make room for us." While she did not feel black people should simply relinquish the fight for integration, as the years passed she increasingly believed the following: "We [black people] have before us the objective of building strong black communities on which we and our children can depend and in which we can lead full, rich lives." When a conscious black community gains strength and power, then "the rules of the game may change."[122] Cadres of black people really began to question under what circumstances, if at all, inclusion could substantively alter their daily lives and power relations without their first garnering greater political and economic power for black communities.

The growing number of urban uprisings, which had increased five-fold, reflected the poverty and intensity of urban living. For the Boggses, the Watts rebellion in August 1965 signaled what they viewed as an emergent racial civil war. In the predominantly black Watts neighborhood in South Central Los Angeles, the arrest of a black male driver by a white police officer, alongside the commotion caused by the intervention and arrest of the driver's brother and mother, sparked unrest that lasted five days. The Watts rebellion ended in the death of 34 people, 25 of whom were black, more than 1,000 injuries, and millions of dollars in damage. Echoes of the racial violence and black deaths in Detroit in 1943 were profound and eerie. The McCone Commission, appointed by California's governor Edmund G. Brown to investigate the unrest, maintained that at the core of the urban explosion lay the deeply embedded issues of poverty, joblessness, racial inequality, and the circumventing of black people's rights at the state level. Black people's ongoing economic insecurity and lack of political voice and impact in rural and urban spaces became fuses for the amplification of Black Power philosophies and politics.

In 1965 the Boggses penned what became known as the "City as a Black Man's Land" thesis. By now an increasingly familiar refrain, their essay called for the development of independent black political power in majority black cities as a conduit for reorganizing the economy and transforming the faltering institutions of society. According to the Boggses, the "toughest battle" for black liberation was in and for cities, and would result in a "civil war between black power and white power."[123] Their essay by the same name published a year later in the April 1966 issue of the socialist magazine *Monthly Review* would spark a reply from fellow black radicals.

"The World is the Black Man's Land!" appeared in *Soulbook,* "the quarterly journal of revolutionary afroamerica." Responding directly to the Boggses, Willie Green made an even more strident political claim—one that ultimately challenged the Boggses' view of urban politics and the battle for power. Green argued that black people's position in cities mirrored their "colonized" status in the United States. In doing so, he linked black liberation to anti-colonial Third World struggles undergirded by a strident revolutionary ethos—as had others before him. Green also argued that in order for Black Power to be successful, and black governments to triumph in cities, "a black revolutionary government" had to be established "on a national level." All-black political leadership of cities was only a step in the process, but could not be the end goal of revolution.[124]

Black self-determination debates grew even more vigorous by early 1966, including in the nation's capital. During the 1960s Washington, D.C. had become one of the first cities in the nation to gain a black majority, with 54 percent in 1960 and 66 percent by 1965, but D.C. remained a federally controlled residential district. In the capitol of American governance, the District's residents, the majority of whom were African American, lacked political home rule. A predominantly white police force patrolled the District. D.C. residents could not even vote in the presidential election until the enactment of the Twenty-third Amendment in 1960, and even then they still could not elect a mayor or city council members. The president and Congress controlled the budget, municipal services, and the courts. Black residents in D.C. not only suffered racism and economic inequity, but they did so as wards of the federal government. This irony was not lost on black freedom movement activists who organized with CORE, initiated D.C. ACT, and would form the Free D.C. Movement.

While the Free D.C. Movement officially launched on February 21, 1966—on the one-year anniversary of Malcolm X's assassination—the path toward it had begun about three months before. In December 1965, the D.C. Coalition of Conscience responded to a letter that the Metropolitan Washington Board of Trades wrote and then sent to newspapers across the country as part of their anti-home rule campaign. The board's letter maintained that most Washington leaders disagreed with home rule in the District. The anti-home rule letter generated publicity, and subsequent letters supporting the Board of Trades' position flooded Congress. The D.C. Coalition of Conscience, an interracial alliance of churches and civil rights organizations including Washington chapters of the Urban League, NAACP, and SNCC, argued that the Board of Trades, which represented white male commerce and industry leaders, was out of step with the sentiment of D.C. residents.

Just a year prior in 1964, residents had voted nine to one for home rule in a local ballot initiative.[125] But home rule required a two-thirds vote of Congress, ratification by three-quarters of the nation's state legislatures, and even then home rule could be rescinded. In the wake of the Board of Trades' letter, the D.C. Coalition of Conscience, co-chaired by the black Rev. Walter E. Fauntroy and white Bishop Paul Moore Jr. of the Episcopal Diocese, requested a meeting with the Board of Trades. On January 11, 1966, coalition and Board of Trades members talked for about an hour in a closed meeting that only amplified the distance between their respective stances. Something had to be done. The coalition strategized. About six weeks later on February 21, the coalition held a press conference to announce the Free D.C. Movement campaign. Its leader and spokesperson was 29-year-old Marion S. Barry Jr., who had just moved to D.C. six months prior to head Washington SNCC.

The new director of Washington SNCC was born in 1936 in Leflore County, Mississippi. Barry moved to Memphis, Tennessee, with his mother and nine siblings after his father died. As a child, Barry worked numerous jobs, including picking cotton. In the late 1950s during the era of mounting civil disobedience, Barry attended the weekly workshops of James Lawson alongside the likes of Diane Nash and John Lewis.[126] With the formation of SNCC in 1960, Barry became its first chair. He also earned a master's degree in organic chemistry from Fisk University in 1960. In August 1961 during the voter registration campaigns in McComb, Mississippi, Barry, alongside Charles Sherrod and Dion Diamond, conducted workshops on nonviolence and direct action for community youth. In 1964 he spent time working at the SNCC office in New York. In 1965, Barry arrived in D.C. to head the local SNCC office, held a successful one-day boycott campaign in January 1966 to protest a D.C. transit bus fare hike, and within one month emerged as "the leader of the Free D.C. Movement," headquartered out of the SNCC office in a rowhouse on Rhode Island Avenue in Northwest D.C.[127]

His remarks at the February 1966 press conference castigated those who opposed home rule. He positioned the capital of the free world as a plantation and a place where white political and economic lords subjugated residents and kept black people, in particular, in socially dire straits. Charging the opposition with "keeping the City in 'political slavery,'" Barry continued: "We want to free D.C. from our enemies—the people who make it impossible for us to do anything about lousy schools, brutal cops, slumlords, welfare investigators who go on midnight raids, employers who discriminate in hiring and a host of other ills that run rampant throughout our city."[128] The Free D.C. Movement called for consumer boycotts of businesses that did not support home rule, labeling them "moneylord merchants" who allied with segregationists in Congress.

The Free D.C. Movement particularly criticized the Board of Trades, which in addition to launching the anti–home rule letter campaign, also had voted against a minimum wage, fair employment guidelines, "and everything else that would benefit poor people, white or black."[129] The Free D.C. Movement initially focused on a 13-block area of H. Street in the ninth district where primarily white small businesses operated in the predominantly black precinct. As Barry argued, in a city where black people did not have political power to impact the decisions shaping their lives, they had to use their economic power to make change.[130] Activists went from business storefront to business storefront delivering their message. They passed out leaflets that read, "In chains 400 years—and still in chains in D.C.," and had a drawing of a black person held in chains by two figures: the House District Committee chair John McMillan (D-S.C.) and Senate District Appropriations Committee chair (and former KKK organizer) Robert Byrd (D-W.Va.). A third figure represented the "D.C. Power Structure."[131] For organizers, the seat of U.S. freedom represented the nation's last official mainland "colony."

On March 12, 1966, after much controversy, the Free D.C. Movement held a victory rally. In less than three weeks, 11 members of the Board of Trades rejected the board's official position and articulated their personal support for home rule. Ninety percent of the businesses in the H. Street area put the orange and black "Free D.C." sticker in their windows for various reasons ranging from support of home rule to fear of reprisal. The campaign continued, extending to the predominantly black residential U. Street area, as well as the downtown Kann's department store.

The vitriol and dissension ratcheted up. The Board of Trades' president and lawyer F. Elwood Davis called the Free D.C. supporters "immoral, un-American, and unjust," and charged the interracial and integrationist D.C. Coalition of Conscience with "emasculat[ing] the English language by using the word 'conscience' in its name."[132] John R. Immer, of the Federation Citizens Association, echoed Davis's criticisms, but went one absurd step further, saying the efforts of the Free D.C. Movement "[are] exactly the way that Nazism got started in the days before World War II."[133] The Free D.C. Movement had garnered so much attention that the *Washington Post* did an expose on the two-month-old campaign in April 1966. The headline used memorable language: "The Genesis and the Exoduses of Free D.C. Movement: Already Left Mark. . . ."[134]

By the end of May 1966—still weeks away from the Meredith March—"new developments" would hurry the public rise and expansion of Black Power. A key epicenter was Atlanta, Georgia, one of the few places where SNCC had organized around urban-based issues. Based in Vine City, the Atlanta Project focused on low-income people's living conditions and mounted "a program of political organization and education" in an attempt to convince local people of the potential of political power to transform economic conditions and foster "human dignity."[135] They organized against slumlords and demanded quality affordable public and private housing. In fact, that's why Barry had been excited to go to D.C.: "During our early days in the South, we had very little experience in major urban centers, with the exception of Atlanta. We knew the day is coming when the vast majority of the Nation's population will live in urban areas, so we knew we had to get this experience. Washington, because it is the Nation's Capital and because it has some of the same problems and attitudes of the South, was chosen as a logical place to start."[136]

Indeed the issues at the grassroots in Atlanta were not unlike those in D.C., or for that matter, Cleveland, Detroit, Harlem, Baltimore, Oakland, and a long list of other cities. Black urbanites, while confronting their specific municipal leaders and local histories and politics, confronted generally similar social, economic, and political challenges. This included inadequate housing, unemployment, rat infestations, poor schools, and physical displacement through proposed and actual freeway and highway construction. The treatment of black working-class and poor people was shameful in the richest nation in the world.

Black self-determination and consciousness efforts emerged out of encounters with such concrete conditions—that is, people's travails, organizing efforts on the ground, and the political and economic decisions that disadvantaged poor people. In this way, black people's daily lives and politics were intricately connected to debates over white capital, privilege, supremacy, and power. SNCC members with the Atlanta Project prepared three position papers that invigorated a national black consciousness debate. Donald Stone, Bill Ware, and Snellings called for an all-black organization and asked SNCC's central committee to think about black nationalism versus integration as its guiding philosophical position. Spelman College student and Atlanta Project member Gwen Robinson (Zoharah Simmons) believed black people should lead and control their own organizations, campaigns, and communities—for she witnessed how the presence of even committed white activists could hamper the growth of indigenous black leadership.[137] The position papers also asked dedicated white activists to move the needle on race in white communities by providing educational experiences that challenged white supremacy. Finally, these theoreticians linked black liberation in the United States to anti-colonial movements for self-determination abroad.[138]

In May 1966, one week after LCFO's party convention to select its slate of candidates, the national SNCC office held its staff retreat in Kingston Springs, Tennessee. Over 100 members attended. Vigorous debates arose over the position of black self-determination, the role of white staffers in the organization, and the development of independent all-black political parties as the core of SNCC's ongoing fieldwork. These concerns had been percolating since 1964. Into this mix, Forman also introduced an internationalist perspective, arguing that SNCCers needed to have "an understanding of capitalism, imperialism, the class struggle, colonialism, and revolutionary nationalism." This met some intense opposition, particularly among those who felt because Marx was white, he "had nothing to tell [black people]." While Forman wholeheartedly believed racism still remained a primary foe of black liberation, he argued that black people, like other colonized peoples, also could face oppressors of the same color. Without understanding the relationship between race, class, empire, and power, poor black people and their allies would be unprepared to challenge the status quo.[139]

By the end of the Kingston Springs retreat, a more strident black consciousness stance emerged and an election ushered in new leadership to match. John Lewis, whose voice had represented a "militant" edge of civil rights at the 1963 March on Washington, now stood at the "conservative" edge of the black liberation struggle. More black nationalist-inspired SNCC members had moved the needle in a different direction. For instance, Lewis found himself in disagreement with the LCFO's political approach in Lowndes County; he did not support a third-party electoral strategy. Instead Lewis felt that black people needed to fight for representation within the established Democratic Party. Carmichael, who had initially contested the expulsion of white SNCC activists and even tamped down on the idea of self-defense (at least as conveyed in Snelling's remembrance of the 1964

Greenwood moment), now militantly advanced all-black leadership and control as a framework for organizing black people and communities.

The Kingston meeting and SNCC's strident black consciousness stance had reverberations. While the national SNCC's stance resonated with its strategy in Lowndes County, Alabama, it ran counter to the interracial D.C. Coalition of Conscience's campaign strategy for home rule. Given this, the coalition's acting chairman Rev. Channing E. Phillips wanted to know the relationship between the Free D.C. Movement and SNCC. Did the national SNCC control the local chapter, and if so, would its black consciousness leaning shape the tenor of the Free D.C. Movement? Barry responded that the local chapter had to establish its own way. "SNCC's newly avowed course of aggressive, all-Negro activity outside the white power structure" did not tie his hands. Barry, however, did agree ultimately that the black liberation movement should be black-led. Ultimately, the D.C. Coalition of Conscience deemed SNCC's increasingly "black nationalist stand" as "inconsistent with the Coalition's philosophy." While still supporting home rule, the coalition distanced itself from Barry and the Free D.C. Movement.[140]

The local battles for self-government and power exposed the fault lines of ideology and goals, as well as diverging approaches and agendas that governed struggles for black liberation. The split, for instance, in D.C.'s home rule campaign occurred just weeks before SNCC activists found themselves at a June rally and in the midst of a media frenzy that introduced Black Power to the mainstream and catapulted those grassroots activists aligned with it—or even operating within its rhetorical midst—to new tumultuous heights.

Notes

1 Months after the March on Washington, Lena Horne first performed at a civil rights benefit what would become her hit song "Now," which demanded equality without further ado. The record would sell 185,000 copies within a few weeks of its release, but radio stations nationwide refused to play it because they deemed it "controversial." "Lena Horne's Hit Disc," *The Illustrated News*, December 9, 1963. Listen to Lena Horne, "Now," *Here's Lena* album (1963).

2 "The Black Scholar Interviews: Queen Mother Moore," *Black Scholar* 4 (March–April 1973), 51.

3 On Nation of Islam, Taylor, *The Veiled Garvey*, 188. On Moore, McDuffie, "'I Wanted a Communist Philosophy, but I Wanted Us to Have a Chance to Organize Our People'," 187; Audley M. Moore, "Why Reparations? Reparations is the battle cry of for the economic and social freedom of more than 25 million descendants of American slaves," Los Angeles: Reparations Committee Inc., c. 1963.

4 Audley M. Moore, "Why Reparations?"

5 King, *Why We Can't Wait*, in a *Testament of Hope*, ed. Washington, 521; James Baldwin, "Not 100 Years of Freedom," *Liberator*, January 1963. James Baldwin served on the advisory board of *Liberator*.

6 King, *Why We Can't Wait*, 521–525.

7 "General Harriet Tubman: The Real Emancipator," *Liberator*, January 1963.

8 Joseph, *Dark Days, Bright Nights*, 64–65.

9 Thompson, *Whose Detroit?*, 8, 57.

10 Dillard.

11 Robert and Mabel Williams were in exile in Cuba, but would make their way to China after the Williamses lost faith in the revolutionary potential of Castro's Cuba. (See *Concrete Demands,* Chapter 6). Also, Kelley and Esch, 6–41; Robeson Taj Frazier, "Black Crusaders: The Transnational Circuit of Robert and Mabel Williams," in *The New Black History,* ed. Marable and Hinton, 91–98.

12 "Final Plans for the March on Washington for Jobs and Freedom," Organizing Manual No. 2, Civil Rights Movement Veterans, Tougaloo College, Tougaloo, Mississippi, www.crmvet.org/docs/moworg2.pdf.

13 The culprit Byron de le Beckwith would be arrested three times (1964, 1965, and 1991). He was finally convicted in 1994–31 years after the murder occurred.

14 "Final Plans for the March on Washington for Jobs and Freedom," Organizing Manual No. 2, 3.

15 Ibid., 3–4.

16 "March on Washington," Universal International Newsreel, PublicDomainFootage. com, www.youtube.com/watch?v=yWQ6EuKBxHw.

17 "Final Plans for the March on Washington for Jobs and Freedom," Organizing Manual No. 2, 4. Also, *Brother Outsider.*

18 Donald Freeman, interview by author, May 1, 2013, Cleveland, Ohio.

19 "Ericka Huggins: Biography," www.erickahuggins.com/Biography.html.

20 Birmingham, 124.

21 Joseph, *Dark Days, Bright Nights,* 24.

22 Campbell, 175, 176.

23 "Original Draft of SNCC Chairman John Lewis' Speech to the March," Civil Rights Movement Veterans website, Tougaloo College, Tougaloo, Mississippi, www.crmvet. org/info/mowjl.htm.

24 "Actual SNCC Chairman John Lewis' Speech to the March," Civil Rights Movement Veterans website, Tougaloo College, Tougaloo, Mississippi, www.crmvet.org/info/ mowjl2.htm.

25 No black women made speeches, and Hedgeman was the only female on the planning committee. While she petitioned for a woman speaker, she was denied. This she described as "bitterly humiliating" for black women. See Collier-Thomas, 458.

26 Gloria Richardson Dandridge, "The Energy of the People Passing Through Me," in *Hands on the Freedom Plow,* ed. Holsaert et al., 289.

27 Historian Sharon Harley, for instance, has argued that Richardson's activism and political stance marked the shift from "a nonviolent civil rights movement seeking integration and legal equality to a militant Black Power activism that supported self-defense and formidably challenged poverty and economic injustice." Sundiata Cha-Jua and Clarence Lang, however, argue that Richardson represented the militancy of civil rights, not Black Power.

28 Gloria Richardson Dandridge, "The Energy of the People Passing Through Me," 275–277; Annette K. Brock, "Gloria Richardson and the Cambridge Movement," in *Women in the Civil Rights Movement,* ed. Crawford et al., 121–144. Also, Hogan, 120–128; Levy, 15–16.

29 Gloria Richardson Dandridge, "The Energy of the People Passing Through Me," 278–279; Levy, 42–51.

30 Annette K. Brock, "Gloria Richardson and the Cambridge Movement," 123.

31 Gloria Richardson Dandridge, "The Energy of the People Passing Through Me," 279.

32 Ibid., 291.

33 The treaty's five points were "complete and immediate desegregation of the public schools . . . and hospitals"; construction of a low-rent black public housing complex; black employment in the post office and state Department of Employment Security; appointment of a Human Relations Commission; adoption of a charter amendment to

desegregate public accommodations. See Annette K. Brock, "Gloria Richardson and the Cambridge Movement," 136.

34 Gloria Richardson Dandridge, "The Energy of the People Passing Through Me," 282.
35 "Mrs. Richardson's Revolt," *Liberator,* November 1963.
36 Muhammad Ahmad, telephone interview by author, November 18, 2013.
37 Goldberg and Griffey, 2.
38 Muhammad Ahmad, telephone interview by author, November 18, 2013. I asked Don Freeman whether this was in fact the case. Since he could not remember having said this and Ahmad recalled that he did say it, Freeman stated he would not refute its accuracy.
39 Ahmad, 104.
40 Brian Purnell, "'Revolution Has Come to Brooklyn': Construction Trades Protests and the Negro Revolt of 1963," in *Black Power at Work,* ed. Goldberg and Griffey, 23–47. Also, Fujino, 119; Kochiyama.
41 Brian Purnell, "Revolution Has Come to Brooklyn," 24–41.
42 Diane Fujino, "Grassroots Leadership and Afro-Asian Solidarities," in *Want to Start a Revolution?,* ed. Gore, Theoharis, and Woodard, 294–316; Fujino; Maeda.
43 Joy James, "Introduction," in *The Angela Y. Davis Reader,* ed. Joy James.
44 Kochiyama, 48–49. A Japanese Nisei who, with her husband, raised six children in public housing in New York City, Kochiyama was also involved in the fight for Asian-American equality, Puerto Rican independence, school and housing equality, and political prisoners' rights. Fujino.
45 Davis, 130–131.
46 Gloria Richardson Dandridge, "The Energy of the People Passing Through Me," 291. For examinations of black self-defense and concepts of armed revolution across decades, see Strain and Umoja.
47 Harold Cruse, "Third Party: Facts and Forecasts," *Liberator,* November 1963.
48 "Differs with C. L. Franklin on Policy," *Illustrated News,* October 28, 1963.
49 "'GOAL': Takes New Tack," *Illustrated News,* November 13, 1961.
50 Donald Freeman, interview by author, May 1, 2013, Cleveland, Ohio.
51 William P. Jones, 215; Thompson, *Whose Detroit?,* 45.
52 Lewis G. Robinson, 58, 68. Also, Ryan Nissim-Sabat, "Panthers Set up Shop in Cleveland," in *Comrades,* ed. Judson L. Jeffries, 98.
53 "Resolution Passed at the Northern Negro Grassroots Leadership Conference," Detroit, Michigan, November 9–10, 1963, Folder: Northern Negro Grassroots Leadership Conference, Box 2, Mae Mallory Papers, Walter P. Reuther Library, Wayne State University, Detroit, Michigan.
54 Ibid.
55 Max Stanford Jr., "Revolutionary Nationalism and Afro-American Liberation Movement," *Black America* 1 (November–December 1963): 7–8.
56 Rolland Snellings, "Re-Africanization, Prelude to Freedom," *Black America* 1 (November–December 1963): 7–8.
57 Wanda Marshall, "Integration, Separation, or What?" *Black America* 1 (November–December 1963): 7–8.
58 Sugrue, *Sweet Land of Liberty,* 256–262. Also, Sugrue, *Origins of the Urban Crisis.*
59 It appeared first in essay form in the leftist journal *Monthly Review* during the summer, and later in book form by the Monthly Review Press in October 1963. James Boggs, *The American Revolution,* in *Pages from a Black Radical's Notebook,* ed. Ward.
60 Donald Freeman, "The Politics of Black Liberation," *Black America* 1 (November–December 1963): 7–8.
61 Albert B. Cleage Jr., "Unite or Perish: Part 3," *The Illustrated News,* December 23, 1963.
62 Lewis G. Robinson, 76.

63 Lewis G. Robinson, 15.

64 Ibid., 78.

65 Moore, 35–36.

66 Lomax, 11.

67 Ibid., 12.

68 Malcolm X, "The Ballot or the Bullet," in *Malcolm X Speaks,* ed. Breitman, 39.

69 Ibid., 24.

70 Ibid., 43.

71 On Brooklyn CORE and Malcolm X, see Brian Purnell, "Revolution Has Come to Brooklyn," 23–47.

72 Ahmad, 115. Also, Grady-Willis, 64; Sales.

73 Donald Freeman, interview by author, October 24, 2013, Cleveland, Ohio.

74 Mullen, *Afro-Orientalism,* 86.

75 Gallen, *Malcolm X: The FBI File,* 501.

76 Cited in "The Colonial War at Home," *Monthly Review* (May 1964): 6.

77 Ahmad, 117.

78 Ahmad, 117. Also, Sugrue, *Sweet Land of Liberty,* 301.

79 Ahmad, 57.

80 James W. Richardson, "Askia M. Touré," in *Oxford Companion to African American Literature,* www.answers.com/topic/askia-m-tour.

81 Umoja, 92.

82 Rhonda Y. Williams, Notes from the Black Power Conference, Smithsonian Institution, Washington, D.C., March 30, 2009. Also, Umoja, 94.

83 Ahmad, 54. Also, Grady-Willis, 65.

84 Lee, 85–102.

85 Ibid., 49–51.

86 Ibid., 89.

87 Ahmad, 59.

88 Fannie Lou Hamer, "I'm Sick and Tired of Being Sick and Tired," in *Speeches of Fannie Lou Hamer,* ed. Brooks and Houck, 64.

89 Shakur, 136–138. Quote, p. 138.

90 Helen Howard, "Am I My Brother's Keeper," in *Black Women in White America,* ed. Lerner, 311–312.

91 Shakur, 149.

92 Ibid.

93 Ibid., 139–152. Quote, p. 152.

94 Donald Freeman, interview by author, May 4, 2011, Cleveland, Ohio.

95 Yohuru Williams, *Black Politics/White Power,* 107–108. Also, Murch.

96 Donald Freeman, interview by author, May 4, 2011, Cleveland, Ohio.

97 Ibid.

98 Grace Lee Boggs, 134. Also, Roth, 87; Grace Lee Boggs, "The Malcolm I Remember," *The Michigan Citizen,* May 20, 2012.

99 Marable, *Malcolm X,* 411–412.

100 Roth, 87; Ongiri, 108.

101 Quotes in Cleaver, *Soul on Ice,* 50–51 and 58–60, respectively.

102 Kaluma ya Salaam, "Historical Overviews of the Black Arts Movement," Modern American Poetry Website, www.english.illinois.edu/maps/blackarts/historical.htm. Also, see, Smethurst.

103 Woodard, 63–68.

104 Ongiri, 101.

105 Ibid., 89.

106 Rhonda Y. Williams, "The Pursuit of Audacious Power: Rebel Reformers and Neighborhood Politics in Baltimore, 1966–1968," in *Neighborhood Rebels,* ed. Joseph,

215–241. Also, Art Pollock, "'My Life's Philosophy': Adam Clayton Powell's 'Black Position Paper,'" *Journal of Black Studies* 4:4 (June 1974): 457–462.

107 Airtel to Director FBI from Special Agent in Charge (SAC) Detroit, "Proposed Conference to Form Coalition of Militant Negro Radicals Washington, D.C. 5/30–31/65," May 4, 1965, Organization for Black Power (FBI-HQ 157–3022), FBI Files.

108 Grace Lee Boggs, 136; Ahmad.

109 Scot Brown.

110 Ahmad, 59.

111 Lance Hill.

112 Forman, *The Making of Black Revolutionaries*, 418.

113 Forman, *The Making of Black Revolutionaries*, 443; Hasan Kwame Jeffries, *Bloody Lowndes*, 51–54.

114 Hasan Kwame Jeffries, *Bloody Lowndes*, 180–181. Also, Ahmad, 63.

115 Forman, *The Making of Black Revolutionaries*, 444.

116 Ibid.

117 Hasan Kwame Jeffries, "Organizing for More than the Vote: The Political Radicalization of Local People in Lowndes County, Alabama, 1965–1966," in *Groundwork*, ed. Theoharis and Woodard, 155.

118 "War on Whose Poverty?" *The Activist* 1:1 (n.d., circa February/March 1965), Folder: ACT—Activist Newsletters, Box 4, Collection 1, Julius W. Hobson Papers, The Washingtoniana Collection, D.C. Public Library, Washington, D.C.

119 "Resolution Adopted by the Organization for Black Power," July 4, 1965, Folder: ACT—Black Power, 1965–1966, Box 1, Collection 1, Julius W. Hobson Papers.

120 Jean Smith, "I Learned to Feel Black," in *The Black Power Revolt*, ed. Barbour, 207–218.

121 Rhonda Y. Williams, *The Politics of Public Housing*.

122 Jean Smith, "I Learned to Feel Black," quotes on p. 215–216 and p. 218, respectively. Also, *The War on Poverty*, ed. Orleck and Hazirjian; on CDGM, see Amy Jordan's chapter, "Fighting for the Child Development Group of Mississippi," 280–307.

123 The speech was later published in April 1966 in the *Monthly Review*, a socialist magazine. Boggs, *Racism and the Class Struggle*, 41.

124 Willie Green, "The World Is the Black Man's Land," *Soulbook* 2:1 (Summer 1966). Donald Freeman, Isaac Moore, Ernie Allen, Leo R. Huey, Alvin Morrell, Kenn M. Freeman, Carroll Holmes, and Bobb Hamilton were on the editorial board.

125 Willard Clopton, "The Genesis and the Exoduses of the Free D.C. Movement: Already Left Mark . . . ," *Washington Post*, April 24, 1966.

126 Jaffe and Sherwood, 36.

127 Dan Morgan, "Barry Finds Home Rule a Frustrating Battle," *Washington Post*, July 25, 1966.

128 "Store Boycott Planned by New Rights Group Supporting Home Rule," *Washington Post*, February 22, 1966.

129 William Raspberry, "Barry Is New Catalyst for Change Here," *Washington Post*, March 9, 1966.

130 Ibid.

131 Willard Clopton, "2 Boycott Leaders Meet to Refine Plans," *Washington Post*, February 28, 1966.

132 Sue Cronk, "Free D.C. Movement Termed Immoral, Un-American by Trade Board Head," *Washington Post*, April 5, 1966.

133 Richard Corrigan, "Home Rule Debated by Immer and Barry," *Washington Post*, April 7, 1966.

134 Willard Clopton, "The Genesis and the Exoduses of the Free D.C. Movement," *Washington Post*, April 24, 1966.

135 Grady-Willis, 84.

136 William Raspberry, "Barry Is New Catalyst for Change Here," *Washington Post,* March 9, 1966.
137 Zoharah Simmons, interview by author, May 30, 2014, Chicago, Illinois. See Grady-Willis.
138 Grady-Willis, 88–90.
139 Forman, *The Making of Black Revolutionaries,* 450.
140 Dan Morgan, "Barry, Rights Units Rift Seen Developing Here," *Washington Post,* May 25, 1966.

PART II
The Expansive Era

4

INTO THE PUBLIC'S EYE

The call for black power touched the depths of my soul.

—*Gwen Patton (1966)*[1]

"Hey Jim, I got an idea. I want to know what you think of it." It was Willie Ricks, the young SNCC field secretary who had acquired a reputation as a brilliant organizer of young people in Birmingham, Americus, and other hot spots in the South. He had stopped in the Atlanta office on his way to Mississippi, and he had a question for James Forman. The renewed Meredith March in June 1966 was underway and Stokely Carmichael had asked Ricks to join him in Greenwood, Mississippi.

"Suppose when I get over there to Mississippi and I'm speaking, I start hollering for 'Black Power'? What do you think of that?" Ricks asked. "Would you back me up? You think it would scare people in SNCC?"

"'Black Power'—sure, try it," I told him. "Why not? After all, you'd only be shortening the phrase we are always using—power for poor black people. 'Black power' is shorter and means the same thing. Go on, try it."[2]

SNCC's executive secretary Ruby Doris Smith Robinson stood in the crowd on the evening of June 16 in Broad Street Park where the marchers had received "grudging permission from the city" to gather. John Lewis, James Forman, and Willie Ricks were there too. It had been a long day of walking and organizing to carry on the solo March Against Fear started by James Meredith—now hospitalized after being ambushed and shot by a would-be assassin.[3] The violent assault on Meredith led SNCC members to re-evaluate his campaign, which they had initially agreed to not participate in. They thought the idea of a March Against Fear was "madness" and politically vague. But SNCCers eventually decided that their absence from a march that would pass through parts of Mississippi where they had spent years organizing might be hard to explain to local people.[4] Moreover, the march could provide an opportunity to register more voters and thereby demonstrate their will to control their destinies. So, they entered the fray. Indeed, their presence would have dramatic impact.

June 16, like other days, would be long. Once night began to fall and organizers and marchers started arriving in Greenwood, they would need food and rest. Part of the advance team, Carmichael and others started preparations at the Stone Street Negro Elementary School. Although the school was in the black community, white school board officials refused to allow marchers to use the black school as a campground. Here—starkly and concretely—emerged the issue of black community control, or the lack thereof. Not only had white officials prevented black school officials and residents from using the public facilities in their community as they wished, but white police showed up to uphold that decision. Even in the face of white authority, Carmichael began preparing the campground. That's when the police commissioner arrested him and two others.[5] Ricks, who had begun testing out the phrase "Black Power" in the community, had supposedly advised Carmichael to let the police arrest him. He then told Carmichael: "We'll get you out of jail, and you come and make the speech tonight."[6]

Tonight arrived at Broad Street Park where marchers, this time, successfully erected tents. Impatience and excitement pervaded. Upon release from jail, Carmichael made his way to the rally and to the podium. Ricks followed closely behind: "Drop it now," he advised SNCC's sinewy chairman. "The people are ready. Drop it now."[7] The crowd roared. Carmichael avowed rapturously that he would be arrested no more. He told black people to stop taking what white police meted out and insisted that black police should be in charge. Then, he shouted, "What we gonna start sayin' now is 'black power!'"

Ruby Doris Smith Robinson stood there and soaked it all in—the exasperation with the racial status quo and the pregnant desire for something better. Now, for sure, was not the time to retreat. It was the time to renew one's commitment. Known for her seriousness, Ruby Doris Smith Robinson was already a six-year movement veteran by her early twenties. As a teenager, Spelman College student, and member of the Committee on Appeal for Human Rights, she attended SNCC's founding conference at Shaw University in 1960. She went to Rock Hill, South Carolina, where she, at age 18, served 30 days in jail alongside fellow SNCC activists Diane Nash, Charles Sherrod, and Charles Jones. Soon thereafter, she joined the Freedom Rides, spending 45 days in the infamous Parchman Prison in 1961. Back in Atlanta, her birthplace, Ruby Doris Smith joined protesters at Grady Memorial Hospital to challenge its segregation policies in 1962. She helped to build SNCC chapters in McComb, Mississippi; Charleston, South Carolina; and Nashville, Tennessee. In 1964 she went door to door organizing and took charge of the Sojourner Truth motor fleet for SNCC's summer voter registration campaign in McComb. That's where she met her husband, Clifford Robinson, who worked as a mechanic for the fleet. They married that year, and in 1965, their son Kenneth Toure was born.

On that day in Greenwood in 1966, Ruby Doris Smith Robinson's commitment to SNCC and against racial oppression radiated when she, alongside Forman, Ricks, and hundreds of others in the crowd, followed Carmichael's public lead and chanted "Black Power." In fact, the three SNCCers strategically positioned themselves "directly behind a mass of people who were in front of news cameras and joined in raising the cry of Black Power."[8] She would remain opposed to racial separatism, but she unapologetically believed in black consciousness and racial solidarity. While Carmichael became Black Power's publicly recognized champion, the "hardworking, clear, and decisive" executive secretary continued to dedicate herself to SNCC and a black-led liberation struggle by firmly managing the day-to-day organizational work—at least until her sickness and premature death from cancer at age 25.[9]

Black Power both scared and moved grassroots people and activists—veterans and neophytes, known, not so known, and unknown. The cry resonated in a society where white men such as Aubrey James Norvell felt empowered to load, aim, and fire a 16-gauge shotgun in order to kill a black man who walked across Mississippi for the right for black people to exercise the vote without fear. The cry resonated in a nation where the absence of power resulted in policies, practices, and institutions that maintained, perpetuated, and expanded inequality. In Greenwood, for instance, widespread hunger and poverty were endemic for African Americans.[10]

Gwen Patton remembers when the call came for Black Power. It was in the midst of the escalation of the student movement at Tuskegee Institute in 1966. At Tuskegee, where Patton had become the first woman student body president, she met Carmichael and Ricks, read Frantz Fanon's *Wretched of the Earth* and Jomo Kenyatta's *Facing Mount Kenya,* and learned about South Africa's anti-apartheid struggle.[11] In 1965, she and other students had formed the Tuskegee Institute Advancement League (TIAL), which supported desegregation and voter registration campaigns. Sammy Younge Jr., a 20-year-old Tuskegee Institute student and U.S. Navy veteran, served as TIAL's liaison to SNCC. Younge organized both on campus and in the community. He pushed for Macon County officials to accept a much needed surplus food program, struggled to secure expanded access to low-rent housing for black residents, and spearheaded picketing campaigns at the local A&P store to protest employment discrimination. The first effort succeeded; the latter two failed. Recalled Patton, Younge raised "some very basic questions that upset a lot of people in the community." This included not just white people, but also black middle-class people, whether business persons or college officials.[12]

Younge and the more militant members of TIAL also had supported SNCC's effort to help launch an independent black political party in Lowndes County and later Macon County in Alabama. According to Patton, however, the majority of TIAL members did not think starting such a political party was plausible "because of the structure of the community. The bourgeois people and the poor people didn't have any unity."[13] This tension existed in Younge. He struggled over whether to pursue status and forgo the movement or stay engaged. In December 1965, he recommitted himself to his dungarees and the battle for grassroots power. Shortly thereafter, in January 1966, a travesty occurred. One late evening, a white Standard Oil gas station attendant shot the 21-year-old Younge in the back of the head for trying to use the white restroom.[14]

His murder distressed SNCC members, "precipitated" the issuance of their first official anti-war statement, and gave rise to their now familiar chant, "Hell No, We Won't Go."[15] Gloria House of SNCC drafted the statement, which began: "The murder of Samuel Younge in Tuskegee, Alabama, is no different than the murder of peasants in Vietnam, for both Younge and the Vietnamese sought—and are seeking—to secure the rights guaranteed to them by law."[16] The link made between the Vietnam War and racism, as well as stateside and foreign aggression, was a divisive issue among black Tuskegee students, but it made sense to many. Patton, in fact, would help found SNCC's National Black Anti-War and Anti-Draft Union (NBAWADU). After all, what was the point of putting one's life on the line for a country that did not respect, or protect, that life on its own soil?

Patton believed that black people should no longer have to beg for access, prove their humanity, or wait on the slow pace of change. Black people needed to demand and gain power. Recalled Patton: "If we had had Black Power, my uncle would be alive; my grandfather, an unbent businessman; my father, a prosperous businessman and a city father in a predominantly black city; my mother, alive in cancer remission with the best of rehabilitation treatment; and me, never to have suffered the mental and emotional humiliation of being captive in a sanitarium. *Yes,* Black Power was the answer." While focusing on very "personal experiences," Patton indubitably raised the specter of systemic exclusions. In fact, her experiences as a student as well as her family's experiences exposed the limits of racial liberalism premised on assimilation. Black Power called into question this American creed by pointing out the gap between the promise of individual opportunity and the trenchant reality of structural inequality that still impacted the majority of black people's lives. These concrete reasons expressed why for many women and men "the call for black power," as Gwen Patton put it, "touched the depths of [their] soul."[17]

What the quest for Black Power actually looked like in terms of strategy and impact would proliferate in the days, months, and years ahead. Acolytes operated along a continuum of self-determination that privileged race-based politics, pride, autonomy, control, and even sovereignty. They took advantage of their newfound access to the media to make visible and legible the tragic conditions of black people living in a wealthy nation. In this intensified phase of the black freedom movement, some old organizations shifted their rhetoric and agendas and new organizations formed; at the same time activists held all-black conventions and rallies, authored histories of black struggles, and developed black position papers and manifestos. All unapologetically questioned the foundations of U.S. democracy as they raised the battle cry of black people as oppressed, colonized, and poor in an era rife with social movements and domestic and global wars. Indeed, between 1966 and 1968, the first two years of the era of expansive Black Power politics, the longings expressed over multiple generations, the nationalist and leftist visions of post-World War II black liberation, and the acceleration of discontent opened up pathways onto the public scene.

Black + Power = What?

Black Power gained public cache and celebrity quickly. That evening at the Greenwood rally, black people had responded enthusiastically. This was likely not only because SNCC field organizer Willie Ricks (now Mukasa Dada) primed people beforehand, but also because battles for equity and human dignity remained ever pressing. Patton and many Black Power advocates and sympathizers really felt "the revolution was just around the corner."[18]

While Black Power as a race-first slogan resonated, it also evoked immediate concern. Shortly after the Greenwood rally, King met with Carmichael, Floyd McKissick (who took over CORE's reins from James Farmer), and members of their staffs in Yazoo City. Only men attended the meeting, at least from the information at hand. Not even Ruby Doris Smith Robinson, who as SNCC's executive secretary handled "the real heavy lifting, day to day," was present.[19] Like at the March on Washington, primarily black men still manned the national gates of the most recognized black freedom organizations. During the gathering at the Catholic parish house, King expressed his concern: "For five long hours, I pleaded with the group to abandon the Black Power slogan."[20] For, as he argued, "The words 'black' and 'power' together give the impression that we are talking about black domination rather than black equality."[21]

For Black Power activists, however, achieving self-determination and control of political, social, and economic institutions required securing power. If white people could not distinguish between the desires of black people to make decisions controlling their institutions, communities, and lives versus the oppressive exercise of white power that produced inequalities and undermined black self-determination, this was not their problem. On June 19, just days after the Greenwood rally, Carmichael appeared on CBS's *Face the Nation* and explained Black Power: "Where black people were the majority, as in Lowndes County, Alabama, and other southern localities, they should be in political control. They should organize, register to vote, and vote. If this did not work, then other tactics, including violence, may be required."[22] Black Power was not up for negotiation.

Nor was it a wholly new idea, even if it signaled a new phase of the freedom struggle that emerged out of specific political circumstances. Even King acknowledged that the concept and phrase, Black Power, "had been used long before by Richard Wright and others." But in Greenwood, King noted what he deemed a signal difference: "Greenwood turned out to be the arena for the birth of the Black Power slogan in the civil rights movement," as well as for its expansion locally, nationally, and internationally.[23] The media coverage helped.

Almost overnight journalistic and popular discussions of Black Power proliferated. The media seemed simultaneously mesmerized and troubled by the phrase. White and black detractors waxed critical, presenting the call as bombast, as a black predilection to violence, and demagoguery, or at minimum undefined and elusive. The black sociologist Nathan Hare would write in "How White Power Whitewashes Black Power": "The lexicographic confusion over the term 'black power' is, then, but a whey-eyed conspiracy to defame it and its philosophy."[24] In some ways, these public debates echoed centuries-old efforts to de-legitimize black militancy and radical thought. This included post-World War II black radicalism which, in bridging "Negro power," anti-colonialism, and anti-capitalist quests, challenged the ideological underpinnings of U.S. national and global supremacy and threatened consensus in the Cold War era. Indeed, by the mid-1960s, the ethos that privileged individualism, democracy, markets, and paternalism was so entrenched that some white liberals not only expressed surprise about black people's public cry for power, according to William Sales, but also felt "that there was something basically unfair, unwarranted and un-American about Black Power demands."[25] Despite this critique of Black Power, the age-old search for racial and ethnic power was unquestionably very American, and for black people generations in the offing.

For several years, SNCC members, in particular, had been organizing around self-determination, motivated by racial pride, and seeking political power. CORE, too, already had a focus on building black community power. In 1965 at its annual convention, CORE argued that it could not depend on "cajoling political units toward desired actions." CORE's members continued, "We must be in a position of power, a position to change those political units."[26] Less than a month after Greenwood, on Independence Day in 1966, CORE officially adopted its Black Power resolution.[27]

While Black Power unsettled the white liberal establishment and white civil rights activists, some of whom had committed years of their lives to the civil rights struggle, not all white allies took offense. In Chicago, for instance, some white radicals actually supported the mandate that white activists concentrate on building an anti-racist agenda among poor and working-class white people. Peggy Terry was a white Chicago resident and activist with JOIN (Jobs or Income Now), an organization founded in Chicago by the Students for a Democratic Society (SDS) as part of its interracial Economic Research and Action Project (ERAP) in 1963. She participated in Meredith's renewed March Against Fear and personally witnessed Carmichael exhort Black Power. Acknowledging that "she had been witness to an incredible moment," Terry, who migrated to Chicago from

Appalachia and had organized with poor white and black activists in the Windy City, remembered: "We reached a period in the civil rights movement when Black people felt they weren't being given the respect they should have and I agreed." Despite the vigorous debates circulating in the March Against Fear camps, Terry stated: "There was never any rift in my mind or my heart. I just felt Black people were doing what they should be doing."[28]

JOIN activist Mike James similarly responded without anathema or seeming affront. James was a student who had spent a year organizing poor whites in Chicago's Uptown. He acknowledged the efforts of white radicals to do what Black Power activists advised. "Given Black Power's challenge to white activists to go organize their own communities," James maintained, "JOIN provides an example to be emulated, for it is unfortunately one of the few attempts being made to organize permanent bases of radical opposition among whites in general, and poor whites in particular."[29]

Even when criticism saturated the airwaves and newsprint, white people did not hold the monopoly. As suggested by Dr. King's early response, black leaders also expressed concerns. Bayard Rustin not only argued that "great passions are involved in the debate over the idea of black power," but also saw "its propagation" as "positively harmful."[30] He and others worried that a turn to Black Power jeopardized their efforts to garner white support for the black freedom struggle. This pragmatic concern was not totally unwarranted. In fact, as SNCC and CORE officially adopted Black Power as their organizational philosophy, financial resources dwindled. This decrease in black freedom organizations' coffers unarguably and ironically provided yet more evidence of the reach of white economic power to impact black political organizing efforts. Others worried that forming all-black groups, even if focused on elevating race pride and cohesion, might reify white conservative agendas and undermine the struggle to achieve a more racially just society. Black Power, these critics feared, could spur resentment, hatred, and violence.

Such concerns regarding Black Power surfaced at the NAACP's annual convention in Los Angeles in July 1966—not even a month after Greenwood and the same month as CORE's convention in Baltimore. In no uncertain terms, Roy Wilkins lambasted Black Power. After calling attention to the non-strategic and counterintuitive "published posture" of self-defense, he identified "the more serious division" as a divergence in goals signaled by the call for Black Power. He described it as "anti-white power," which some Black Power advocates no doubt would have agreed with on some level, depending on whether "anti" modified white or white power. "It has to mean 'going it alone,'" stated Wilkins, continuing, "It has to mean separatism." What does it offer? he pondered out loud, answering: "Little except to shrivel and die." The "only possible dividend" was "a tremendous psychological lift."[31]

At the NAACP convention, Ohio's black state legislator Carl Stokes also expressed "great concern" at the "new concept receiving wide press."[32] Soon to emerge as the first elected black mayor of a major city in the country, Stokes recognized that power and politics are intertwined. Indeed, Stokes and other aspiring black politicians, who were attempting to break the color bar in municipal offices, paid acute attention to the racial temperature of their potential white constituents and opponents. In Cleveland, Stokes had just lost his initial bid for mayor by one percent of the total vote. He did not want to alienate white support. At the convention, Stokes argued for "the attainment of absolute equality of citizenship rights for all our people, Negro and white, neither to the exclusion or advantage of the other." He continued: "Black power as a rallying cry, symbol or label of civil rights activities is to introduce an additional self-imposed burden which only hurts and does not help," because it might stymie "a real partnership with like-minded whites" and threaten the coalescing of "progressive forces" into an "EFFECTIVE political majority in the United States."[33] In his estimation, "the vast and overwhelming majority of Negroes have no desire to create a 'black power structure' in America."[34]

Positions counter to Stokes and Wilkins, however, did emerge at the convention. A *Washington Post* reporter wrote, in fact, that Black Power "generated considerable support among [NAACP] members."[35] Rev. James Jones, a Los Angeles school board member, believed the NAACP should support the concept of Black Power: "An organization such as the NAACP should not be scared into a position of defense by the power structure with regard to the question of black power." Jones articulated a mantra similar to that of Joanne Chesimard (aka Assata Shakur): never let your enemies choose your enemies. Jones continued: "The NAACP must accept the challenge of defining black power and making it honorable and a factual part of the total power spectrum in America."[36] Rev. Jones's statement drew cheers at the NAACP convention.

It was complicated, this move to garner power for black people. Even in Stokes's case, the public denouncement of Black Power as a slogan did not temper his belief in all-black political clubs. In fact, after his initial campaign loss, Carl Stokes provided advice to other electoral campaigns seeking to explicitly elect black mayors. He went to Newark in 1966 with comedian and rights activist Dick Gregory to help Kenneth Gibson, a black engineer, with his ultimately unsuccessful first mayoral bid.[37] A similar move was afoot as early as 1965 in Gary, Indiana—a steel mill city on the south shore of Lake Michigan and the second major industrial city to elect a black mayor. In this case, black businessmen from Gary, who desired to help Richard G. Hatcher run, gathered signatures in barber and beauty shops. They also traveled to Cleveland to seek counsel from Carl Stokes.[38]

There were differences, however, among these varied political strategies to gain Black Power. All-black political clubs, for instance, did not necessarily call into question the soundness of the two-party system, at least not in the same ways as had Black Power advocates' efforts to establish an independent third party in Detroit in 1963 or Lowndes County in 1965. In fact, all-black political clubs could be more easily stomached as an acceptable strategy for black middle-class leaders to secure access to the political process while also assimilating into the U.S. political system. While black electoral politics also provoked racial hostility and fear, in contrast, it offered a more palatable anecdote for mediating ongoing black outrage.

In Cleveland, just two weeks after the NAACP convention, the city exploded in racial turmoil. This, in fact, elevated Stokes's value as a potential racial mediator. It was dusk on Monday July 18 outside a bar at 79th and Hough in Cleveland. A predominantly black working-class neighborhood, Hough suffered from industrial and economic flight. Even so, white people still owned many of the businesses in the community. A crowd began to gather after the owners refused to serve water to a black man who had just purchased a bottle of wine; an argument ensued with a black woman, and a sign appeared in the window that read: "No Water for Niggers." The owners called police, armed themselves with shotguns, and patrolled their front entrance. When the police arrived, their presence further ramped up tensions. As in other urban and rural black communities, police–community relations were quite contentious. In Hough, the situation elevated into rock throwing and supposedly chants of Black Power, and, then, the emotional dam broke. The uprising raged for six days, ending with four deaths, 30 critical injuries, 275 arrests, and at least $1 million in property damage.[39] This uttering of Black Power during an urban uprising further nourished negative depictions of unstable inner cities occupied by pathological black residents who turned to a violent political philosophy.

Even if the rebellions registered general dismay, they, however, did not simply elicit the same reproach from neighborhood people. At the time, 7-year-old Charlise Lyles lived on 123rd Street with her mother. She remembered her "Momma," freshly home from work as an elevator operator at a downtown Cleveland department store, talking "about the politics of the riot." She sat in front of the television; "her voice was dry with disgust."[40] She emphatically stated: "None of this would have happened if they had gotten rid of that damn Mayor Ralph Locher and let Carl B. Stokes be the mayor." Her mother continued: "Negroes are mad enough to fight and burn down their own neighborhoods and that Mayor Locher is trying to pretend not a thing is wrong."[41] By the third day of the uprising and her mother's unfailing commentary, the curious Charlise asked her mother why "Negroes want to fight." Her mother responded: "The white man don't want to treat Negroes right no matter what we do."[42] For many black residents, then, Locher, his municipal policies, and the response of the police were at the root of the black community's problems.

Retired black steelworkers who gathered outside the neighborhood corner store where Charlise bought candy also conversed about the uprising and what it meant. She overheard Mr. Willie Joe explaining the cause of the Hough rebellion this way: The "police didn't want them colored children over at the John F. Kennedy House [the JFK House actually stood for the Kenyan anti-colonial freedom fighter Jomo "Freedom" Kenyatta], learnin' *a lot* abut Negro history,

Africa, and what's his name? Jomo Kenyatta."[43] Freedom Fighters' founder Lewis Robinson established the JFK House, a black nationalist center at 8801 Superior Avenue. He opened it in September 1964 to fulfill a two-fold purpose: "to support the parents and businessmen in the Wade Park-Superior neighborhood in curbing juvenile delinquency by providing a neighborhood recreation and cultural center" and "to promote civic, political, and economic responsibility and cooperation between the varied economic and cultural groups of the immediate vicinity."[44]

Black nationalists operating in cities across the country in the Black Power era, however, were not widely beloved by white authorities. They were often blamed for fueling and orchestrating undesirable urban unrest, whether they did so or not. A white-led county grand jury in Cleveland blamed Robinson and Harllel Jones for agitating and organizing the uprisings against "the uneasy backdrop" of "poverty and frustration." The grand jury report, in linking the men to RAM, the Deacons for Defense, and Communists, disparaged and sounded the alarm about black radical organizations. Even in its recognition of appalling social and economic conditions, the grand jury rooted blame in "black power apostle[s]."[45]

The business elite's desire for a "safeguard against black unrest" and their feeling that Carl Stokes, as a black politician, might be able to deliver the promise of calm created a fortuitous electoral opportunity.[46] The next time Stokes ran for mayor in 1967, he emerged victorious over Locher in the Democratic primary and over white Republican contender Seth Taft in the general election. Carl Stokes made history. His brother Louis Stokes, too, would make history when he became Cleveland's first black congressional representative from the twenty-first district—the same year his brother won office.

The passage of the Voting Rights Act of 1965 and electoral expressions of Black Power had impacted the hue of political representation. Black representation increased and this provided an opening for black politicians to steward relationships with white powerbrokers. Black communities often pinned their hopes for change on black politicians, but racial representation did not automatically translate into power to transform everyday people's conditions. In other words, black inclusion in the political arena neither decentered nor operated independently of white party politics or economic power. Moreover, black politicians, just like their white counterparts, could very easily privilege individualistic efforts for advancement or further entrench patronage politics. In fact, this was one reason why Rustin, a critic of Black Power refused to champion all-black independent parties. For him, "the relevant question [was] not whether a politician is black or white, but what forces he represents." Rustin continued: "What I am saying is that if a politician is elected because he is black and is deemed to be entitled to a 'slice of the pie,' he will behave in one way; if he is elected by a constituency pressing for social reform, he will, whether he is white or black, behave in another way."[47] In either case, representation was only a first step. Ideology, agendas, goals, strategies, and accountability mattered as well. So would access to economic resources.

"Let Us Take Our Destiny"

The first two years witnessed not only a shift in goals of familiar organizations, but also the growth of new groups and platforms. In the same month that Black Power emerged as a media sensation, Max Stanford called Stokely Carmichael to see if they could "use the name Black Panther in forming another support branch of the Black Panther Party" and potentially a national organization.[48] So it was that the New York Black Panther Party formed many months before the Oakland-based party of the same name. The latter party, which experienced intense and deadly government repression as it labored to advance a community-based agenda and revolutionary nationalist stance, became the iconic Black Panther Party. Both urban-based Panther parties, however, uplifted the political party symbol of the southern and rural Lowndes County Freedom Organization. The cadre of black radicals who formed the New York Black Panther Party envisioned it as a coalition of those who held Marxist-Leninist stances as well as supported black political empowerment, Third World solidarity, and armed self-defense.[49]

The New York Black Panthers garnered support from veteran black radical and nationalist activists. In Harlem, Audley Moore held weekly recruitment meetings, or Black Nationalist Action Forums, for the new organization.[50] Yuri Kochiyama, who had met Stanford in 1964, offered her public housing apartment to the cadre to hold political education sessions and draft their organizational platform.[51] Operating out of a basement office at 2409 7th Avenue near 140th Street, the party supposedly had 30 "hardcore enthusiasts" and up to 100 overall members by August.[52]

In the midst of the media blitz about Black Power, these new northern Panthers received their share of attention. The *New York Times* not only described them as "articulate young militants who reject integration," but also unsurprisingly begged the question whether they sought to exclude white people.[53] The liberation slogan conjured such concerns in a way that drew attention away from black people's affirmative associations, or their defiance of white supremacy. Even when Black Power activists focused on black unity and voice, they often ended up having to refute depictions of "Klanism in reverse" and "black supremacy." After being asked the question about excluding white people, a New York Black Panther responded to the *New York Times* reporter by steering his response toward black consciousness thusly: "Our party will be by black people, of black people and for black people."[54]

Truth be told, many advocates of Black Power had little faith in white people or more importantly the white power structure to bring justice to black people. That was one of the reasons why they wanted to build Black Power. This meant acknowledging the ways in which integration did not transform black people's conditions. For others it also meant retreating to the safety of black communities in a society where, despite battles for desegregation, race continued to structure geographical space and people's place. Given this, it made sense to accentuate the need to improve black people's quality of life and economic conditions in black-controlled spaces. This reality, while not necessarily comforting or palatable to white society, represented a legible response to ongoing resistance to black equality, the racial politics of the day, and the concrete conditions impacting black people's daily lives.

"Black Power is a working philosophy for a new breed of cats—tough, proud young Negroes who categorically refuse to compromise or negotiate any longer for their rights," argued Adam Clayton Powell Jr. He continued, "[They] reject old-line established white-financed, white-controlled, whitewashed Negro leadership."[55] Nor did they desire to counsel to white people's feelings. Even Rosa Parks spoke to this reality. After moving to Detroit in 1957, Rosa Parks remained active. An admirer of Ella Baker, Malcolm X, and Robert F. Williams—someone who trained with Septima Clark, and organized with King and the Henry brothers—Parks "observed that the increase in black militancy derived from white obstructionism."[56] Black Power rebuked white paternalism, white conservatism and violence, and new sleight-of-hand political arguments that claimed black unity, anti-racist struggles, and race-conscious strategies to advance black people were somehow racism in reverse. On the day Malcolm X's house was bombed and seven days before his assassination, he gave his last public message. In it, he called such arguments "tricky logic" and "skillful manipulating" that makes "the victim look like the criminal and the criminal look like the victim."[57]

In this context, comparing Black Power advocates to white supremacist organizations or describing Black Power demands as *a priori* reverse racism was spurious at best and illegitimate at worst, particularly in the absence of historically nuanced understandings of how power operated. Black Power acolytes did not have a history of hanging, maiming, beating, raping, drowning, firing, indebting, or otherwise intimidating communities of white people, not like Citizens Councils, Klan members, or other hostile whites knowingly did to black people for centuries, often unimpeded and supported by police and government officials. They did not have the weapons of power, such as deportation, revocation of passports, redlining, urban renewal, counterintelligence, contracts, or other government policies in their reach or toolkits. Nor did the majority of Black Power advocates who critiqued structures of domination characterize white people as biologically or inherently culturally inferior, even if they lambasted white cultural practices and assumptions they deemed deleterious to the black community and found it increasingly difficult to imagine a racially harmonious future.

As the weeks and months passed, Black Power increasingly began to take on more organized forms in communities across the country. On July 26, 1966, Rep. Powell and Carmichael held a press conference in congressional offices to announce a plan to hold a Black Power conference. This occurred about 10 days after Powell had his 17-point "Black Position Paper" entered into the *Congressional Record*. Carmichael sat to the immediate left of Powell. Powell, who held to his beliefs in nonviolence and integration, explained that the proposed Black Power conference will "let the black masses themselves define black power. . . . In other words, this is a people's movement." Powell continued, "And we've just got to come face to face with the fact that the white power structure, as I said before, is no longer acceptable to 12% of the American citizens." Carmichael then took the chairman's seat and Powell stood behind him. Carmichael explained that in talking with McKissick before he left for Cambodia, they together decided that they "needed to have a conference of black people across the country, all black who have some semblance of leadership in this country to come together to discuss what black power means." Carmichael continued, "We're just a little bit disturbed about the way white people in this country are projecting it." They decided Powell would be "best to convene" the conference because he has "national visibility," he speaks up for black people, and "is not afraid at anytime to call any white man down."[58]

In Washington, D.C., on Labor Day, September 3, 1966, 169 delegates representing 37 cities, 18 states, and 64 organizations attended the closed-door event. An eclectic group of people gathered, including grassroots activists, reverends, dentists, lawyers, leaders of local civic clubs and national liberation organizations, students, teachers, professors, and politicians. They came from primarily the Northeast, East Coast, and Midwest as delegates and observers and represented organizations such as CORE, the Negro American Labor Council, Harlem Lawyers Association, the Harlem Parents Council, the United African Movement, the Baltimore chapter of the National Council of Negro Women, local NAACP chapters, and economic neighborhood development and community action groups. Ron Karenga, of the cultural nationalist US organization, attended. So did Milton Henry, of Detroit's GOAL, and Julius Hobson, of D.C.'s ACT. James Meredith, Jesse Gray, Nathan Wright, Cecil Moore, and black feminist and radical lawyer Flo Kennedy were all in attendance to begin considering the "definitions," "guidelines," and "goals" for a national Black Power conference.[59] A continuations committee carried out the planning for what resulted in the Newark-based Black Power Conference almost a year later in July 1967.

Soon after the September 1966 planning meeting, Powell, who had been on the radar of the FBI since 1942, allegedly for having Communist affiliations, gained a new kind of public notoriety as the target of a congressional investigation. Flo Kennedy, who would provide counsel to Black Power activists such as H. Rap Brown and Assata Shakur, believed that because Black Power was so scary to white politicians and their constituents, it represented "the beginning of [his] downfall."[60] Proving that Powell's avowal of Black Power per se led to his being investigated may be hard to confirm. Powell had been involved in political graft (as had many white elected officials), but of course timing is everything. His support of Carmichael, as well as his hosting a gathering in his Washington office to plan a

Black Power conference, could not have won him many supporters among white politicians, whether racial liberals or conservatives. Investigators accused Powell of unnecessarily delaying an anti-poverty bill, which had to pass through his House Education and Labor Committee, as well as making unwarranted demands on Sargent Shriver, the anti-poverty program director. Powell also faced charges of embezzlement and other ethical violations. Protesting the investigative proceedings, some 150 people showed up wearing Black Panther insignia and Black Power buttons. The protest was one of many that appeared in the media.

Around the same time as the Black Power planning meeting in Washington, D.C., the Black Panther Party in New York participated in a drive led by black parents and other New York activists to boycott the Harlem schools.[61] Black parents had threatened the boycott to highlight poor school conditions and limited resources, argue for neighborhood control of schools, and to protest the lack of black history and teachers in the classroom. The boycott stood as one among many in a decades-long struggle to improve school conditions for black and brown students. It echoed the struggles waged by Mae Mallory and the Harlem mothers in 1956, as well as the experiences of the young Assata Shakur. These struggles elevated the framework of community control and racial pride—two hallmark expressions of Black Power politics. One Harlem-based Panther Party member said: "Neighborhood schools gave Harlem James Baldwin and Claude Brown," the black author of *Manchild in the Promised Land*. This fact, he continued, "proves that you don't have to integrate to make it."[62]

Black Power politics also prioritized the desire for quality education in schools where primarily black and brown children attended. Activists and parents wanted teachers and a culturally relevant curriculum, and they wanted resources whether or not black and brown children went to school with white students. On Monday, September 12, New York Black Panther Party members gathered at P.S. 139, a five-story, red brick junior high school on W. 140th Street near 7th Avenue where, according to a party member, many of them had actually gone to school themselves. It was also one of the schools that the Harlem Nine mothers, including Mallory, had boycotted in the late 1950s.

Not far from the headquarters, Black Panthers arrived at 7:30 a.m.[63] Just 45 minutes after the protest began, and party members had tried to prevent students from entering the building, police arrested and charged them with disorderly conduct. These members included Eddie Ellis, 25, and Walter Richie, 27, organizers for Harlem Youth Opportunities Unlimited (better known as HARYOU); Ted Wilson, 24; Larry Neal, 27, an architect of the Black Arts Movement; and Donald Washington, a 30-year-old former aide to Malcolm X who had participated in the Downstate Medical Center protests.[64] Within a matter of months, the New York Black Panther Party disintegrated into factionalism.[65] Parents nevertheless continued their battle for community control of local schools, and a second New York-based Black Panther Party would emerge in a couple of years and produce the New York Panther 21.

On September 22, 1966, not quite two weeks after the school campaign, an article by Carmichael titled "What We Want" appeared in the *New York Review of Books*.[66] The charismatic SNCC leader made his case for Black Power, saying it conveyed the "tone" of the black community using "the words they want to use," despite the press's attempt "to stop the use of the slogan by equating it with racism or separatism." Exposing some of its historical roots and early forerunners, Carmichael argued that Black Power emerged out of a "nationalist tradition that extended from Martin R. Delaney through Malcolm X." Moreover, Black Power signified an attempt to address two major problems—being black and poor in a racist, capitalist society.[67] Carmichael, then, described SNCC's path toward Black Power by delineating its efforts to win "political power for impoverished Southern blacks." Despite all the criticism from white and black people who disagreed with the pronouncement of Black Power, according to Carmichael, SNCC remained on message, if no longer in step with the precepts of U.S. liberalism or privileging integration as the panacea for black oppression.

Defiance, a new assertiveness, and a desire for black people to control their destinies, agendas, and decision-making comprised the core of politics in the Black Power era. This dovetailed with efforts to radicalize liberation struggles nationwide. Just as RAM had taken deliberate steps to convey its black revolutionary nationalist stance to SNCC cadres in 1964 and then, in 1966, harnessed SNCC's Panther Party political activism, SNCC sought to extend its new rallying cry and organizational reach from the South nationwide. SNCC members continued to run voter registration campaigns and support independent political parties in the South and North in order "to elect representatives and *to force those representatives to speak to their needs*."[68] Of course, Black Power "will take time to build, and it is much too early to predict its success," Carmichael wrote, continuing: "We have no infallible master plan and we make no claim to exclusive knowledge of how to end racism; different groups will work in their own different ways."[69]

On the question of poverty, Black Power advocates held a range of ideas. They argued that black people had to demand the reallocation of land. Here, echoes of Garvey, the "Black Belt" thesis, the Nation of Islam, and Malcolm X abounded and inspired Black Power formations yet to emerge such as the Republic of New Afrika. Revolutionary nationalists such as RAM and the Black Panther Party were anti-capitalists and anti-colonialists. For them, neither the liberal agenda of access nor integration would necessarily cure poverty, dismantle economic inequality, or liberate "the colonies of the United States." The description of black communities or "ghettos" as colonies became a hallmark critique of revolutionary nationalists and pan-Africanists. Wrote Carmichael: "For a century, this nation has been like an octopus of exploitation, its tentacles stretching from Mississippi and Harlem to South America, the Middle East, southern Africa, and Vietnam. . . . This pattern must be broken."[70] Black Power adherents, as well as people who did not identify as Black Power activists but mobilized during the Black Power era, set out to break such patterns in their own myriad and often times conflicting ways.

During the same summer months of 1966, Black Panther parties (BPPs) formed on the West Coast as well. In August 1966, for instance, a RAM-affiliated BPP chapter emerged in San Francisco, and in October a group of radical students sponsored a Black Power conference in Berkeley.[71] Sometime shortly after that, Huey P. Newton and Bobby Seale founded the Black Panther Party for Self-Defense (BPP-SD) in Oakland—a city that Reginald Major later dubbed "a cracker town" and "a 44 percent black urban plantation" in his book *A Panther is a Black Cat*.[72] Working at the Bay Area Community Action Program in the North Oakland Anti-Poverty Center, Newton and Seale pooled their wages to open their first BPP-SD headquarters.[73] The story goes that Newton saw a flier, which had been most likely handed out as students prepared for the October Black Power conference. The flier featured the Lowndes County Freedom Organization and its electoral logo, a black panther. Having left SSAC to work more closely with the community, Seale and Newton decided that they, too, would use the logo.[74]

The Oakland-based Black Panther Party waged a multi-pronged fight against poverty, poor education, inadequate healthcare, and police brutality. Their Ten Point Program demanded full employment or a guaranteed income, exemption from military service, freedom for incarcerated men, trial by peers, and "land, bread, housing, education, clothing, justice and peace."[75] Moreover, this Black Panther Party, which proclaimed, All Power to the People, believed in the political potential of the lumpen proletariat and did not forgo the possibility of multiracial coalitions, as had some cultural nationalist or pan-Africanist Black Power organizations. In fact, the Panthers built (sometimes strained) alliances with white left, Puerto Rican, Chicana/o, Asian-American, and Native American activists. This Black Panther Party, which took the nation and world by storm, became the national base and inspiration for the disparate, indigenous chapters proliferating across the country, and became a model for young revolutionary activists inside and outside the United States.

The proliferation of organizations that identified with Black Power over the next couple years exposed some activists' efforts to operationalize the rallying cry on the ground. It would not be an easy road, or even one road, to travel. Different strategies and internal conflicts, from both pre- and post-Greenwood, punctuated these efforts. Within SNCC, for instance, activists continued to grapple with the ideological and tactical path forward that began as early as 1964 and came into relief in the black consciousness debates and elections of early 1966. But new concerns emerged as well, particularly given the media's attention to Black Power and its proponents. Ruby Doris Smith Robinson expressed concern about "Carmichael's instant media access" and his espousal of views that did not fully represent what other SNCC members believed, even with the organization's official turn to Black Power. SNCC activist Fay Bellamy, too, questioned the effectiveness and potential impact of Carmichael's frequent appearances.[76]

Bellamy believed that SNCC staffers and field organizers needed to talk directly to the people. Experience had shown, she argued, that the press was not above misrepresenting their positions. "It makes me wonder if we are addicted to the press," she queried in her "A Little Old Report," continuing, "The press doesn't ask about the Free D.C. Movement, or what we plan to do in Chicago or anywhere else that we may be working. They don't ask what it is we plan to do in Vine City or Philadelphia. They don't ask what our future plans are as far as our projects are concerned. What are the questions they do ask? 'Are you nonviolent?'"[77] Furthermore, she said, "[T]he people who work these projects and the dangers that still exist for them have been ignored by many of us." She called for discretion on organizational stances, and refocused attention on local people's concrete demands: "It is my hope that we will refrain from letting the press or anyone else bind us into thinking or feeling what they want us to. I would argue for a little more talking to black people and less talking to the press."[78]

A subset of Black Power activists also believed it equally important to understand local people's struggles within the broader framework of the United States' reach globally. This meant exposing the connections between the operation of racial subjugation, empire, violence, and power. Black revolutionary nationalists, in particular, had been describing black people as "subjects" of the United States and black communities. D.C. gained special attention as the nation's "last colony" in newspaper exposés. At least, or so the argument went, U.S. territories such as the Virgin Islands, American Samoa, and Puerto Rico were gaining "some voice in their own government."[79] As it stood in the majority black D.C., white elected officials from the South controlled the municipality through the House District Committee. Home rule advocates viewed such congressional representatives as part-year settlers ruling over indigenous residents, and even more starkly as white politicians willfully excluding a majority black city from self-governance while upholding racially discriminatory practices and policies.

In the midst of Washington's ongoing struggle for home rule and the expanded United States' presence in Vietnam, Stokely Carmichael addressed about 150 people at a Sunday gathering in late August 1966 in Anacostia Park in D.C. In what became his increasingly familiar and explosive discourse, Carmichael conjured armed struggle as a method to fight against imperial forces whether at home or abroad: "We're going to organize and fight for our free elections in the District the way the boys in Vietnam are fighting for elections over there."[80] In the first years of the era of expansive Black Power, such discourse became all too familiar.

So, too, did the interconnections between the war and black poverty. In 1965 the "Moynihan Report" had blamed, to great black public furor, black poverty on so-called black matriarchs and emasculated men. Named after its author, the assistant secretary of labor, Daniel Patrick Moynihan, "The Negro Family: The Case for National Action" argued that one way to right the situation was through the military. There, black men were "as equals" and occupied an "utterly masculine world." Continued Moynihan: "Given the strains of the disorganized and matrifocal family life in which so many Negro youth come of age, the Armed Forces are a dramatic and desperately needed change: a world away from women, a world run by strong men of unquestioned authority."[81] Not a year later in October 1966, under President Johnson's administration, Department of Defense Secretary Robert McNamara initiated Project 100,000, which targeted poor unemployed urban youth for recruitment into the military. It was billed as a Great Society and anti-poverty program. About 41 percent of those recruited through the program were black.[82] As the critiques of racism and poverty ratcheted up and the Vietnam War escalated, with a disproportionate number of poor black people serving in combat platoons, so too did vociferous debates, national mobilizations, and the formation of separate, all-black, anti-war groups.

A little over a year after its founding in response to Malcolm X's assassination and less than six months after the exclamation of Black Power, Black Women Enraged had turned its attention to the Vietnam War. At the time, Patricia Murphy Robinson, who had been interviewed about Malcolm X for an Italian book on Black Power, worked at Planned Parenthood in upstate New York. That is how she met the low-income mothers (who became known as part of "Pat Robinson and Group"). They had expressed growing interest in social and political issues, including the war because "some of [their] young men began to come home in boxes."[83] Shortly thereafter, this group of black women raised their voices, particularly as they learned more about the Vietnam War. They read "material from the Vietnamese fighters" and "compare[d] it to what [they] were being told by the Man"—that is, white male powerbrokers and the U.S. government. In the process, they grew increasingly disturbed that black mothers allowed their sons to fight and that black men enlisted in the military to earn "bread," "to get away from home," or just "to be big and bad like John Wayne" (modeling the representation of a white cowboy in the exertion of their manhood) without even knowing "the Vietnamese peoples' [sic] side."[84] Robeson's 1949 statement at the world peace conference and SNCC's lament after Younge's murder echoed here: Why take up arms for a government that oppresses you?

With children in tow, black middle-class women and poor mothers picketed at an army-air force recruiting center in Harlem.[85] Black Women Enraged prepared and distributed fliers printed with help from SNCC, CORE, and the black radical lawyer Conrad Lynn. One leaflet addressed "Black Women!!" and another "Black Men!!" The leaflet targeting black women queried, "WHAT THE HELL ARE BLACK MEN DOING IN VIETNAM . . . !!" In a prescient summation, the flier anticipated some of the issues wrapped up in late 20th- and 21st-century cradle-to-prison pipeline campaigns. Black people suffered from police brutality as well as poor schools that failed to teach black children, who were then labeled as "DROP-OUTS," "HOODLUMS," and "CRIMINALS." Dope saturated black communities and worked *"TO LULL US TO SLEEP!"* and *"KEEP US CRIPPLED FROM THE CRADLE TO THE GRAVE!"* The flier declared, *"LET US TAKE OUR DESTINY IN OUR OWN HANDS!!!"* Then, echoing McKay's poem "If We Must Die," the flier argued that if black men *"MUST FIGHT, LET IT BE FOR THEIR DIGNITY AS BLACK MEN,"* who *"PROTECT US, THEIR*

WOMEN AND CHILDREN FROM THE MURDER AND RAPE OF THE WHITE RACIST."[86]

The flier addressed to "Black Men!!" was much shorter. In part, it declared: "Choose jail. Stay here and fight for your manhood," and then promised black women's support.[87] Over the decades numerous black men, both unknown and well known, had chosen jail, including Elijah Muhammad, Malcolm X, and Bayard Rustin during World War II and, more recently, heavyweight boxing champ Muhammad Ali.[88] According to the flier: being conscientious objectors took great courage because it meant not only taking a stand against the U.S. state, but also, at times, aligning rhetorically with the struggles of Third World revolutionaries.

The era of Black Power clearly overlapped with, what historian Paula Giddings has labeled, the "masculine decade"—a time of increased attention to countering public attacks on black masculinity, particularly exacerbated by the Moynihan Report.[89] Both leaflets provided a prevailing and familiar view of what black manhood meant in the era of militarism, geopolitical battles, and racial wars over power and sovereignty at home and abroad. If black men were going to fight, then they should protect their own families and communities, as well as stand up against a racially oppressive and imperial state. Such calls for black men to contest white authority on behalf of kith and kin need not be fatally sexist. However, when such calls fomented posturing premised upon controlling, minimizing, or relegating black women to specific roles as women, then it easily could and often did slip into male chauvinism that upheld patriarchal authority.

On January 21, 1967, representatives of black anti-draft groups gathered at the Harlem Unemployment Center for the Eastern Black Anti-Draft Conference. The conference aimed to promote national cooperation among black anti-draft activists and establish mechanisms to respond to campaigns of suppression, the likes of which had just occurred in Atlanta. The protests there had begun the year before when white Georgia legislators had refused to seat Julian Bond, who as SNCC's information director and a newly elected state representative, spoke out against the Vietnam War. SNCC's Atlanta Project led these anti-war protests. After a week of such protests outside an Atlanta induction center in August 1966, being called "nigger" by white counter demonstrators, and clashes with military personnel and police, 12 Atlanta Project members—10 men and two women—were arrested, jailed, convicted, and sentenced.[90] Bond would finally be sworn in as a Georgia legislator in January 1967—on the same day that Powell lost his congressional seat (not to be regained for two years) as a result of the investigation.

Conference attendees proposed numerous actions in order to build a strong, autonomous black resistance movement that forthrightly critiqued the "racist aspects of the war." They suggested expanding the reach of Black Women Enraged, given that "the experience of Black Women picketing in New York and Atlanta has shown us that women are a powerful force."[91] In Atlanta, black girls had taken to the streets to raise money for the Atlanta 12's legal defense, and a small group of black women staged a protest. Like in 1917 when black people demonstrated to bring attention to the racial travesty in East St. Louis, these Atlanta women marched in silence. They wore black veils and carried signs that broadcast the racially gendered violence against black men, such as "We Mourn the 400 Years of Lynching and Castration of the Black Men in this Country" and "We Mourn the Drafting of Black Men."[92]

The anti-draft conferees in Harlem proposed opening regional and local offices geared toward dissuading black youth from joining the military for "economic advantage." They also suggested forming community alert patrols (possibly modeled after the Community Alert Patrol established in 1965 in Watts that also influenced the Black Panther Party for Self-Defense). They wanted to start physical fitness classes, establish "liberation schools," work on solutions for community problems such as housing, jobs, and education, and establish their own information networks. Robert Allen, Conrad Lynn, and Michael Simmons (one of SNCC's Atlanta Project workers and one of the 12 arrested in Atlanta) spoke.[93] Volunteers from New York, Philadelphia, and Cleveland formed a national coordinating committee to move the work forward.

In February 1967 SNCC activist Gwen Patton published an article in *Liberator* on "Black People and Wars" and wrote two position papers "laying out the rationale to establish a black anti-war movement."[94] About a year later, she served on the SNCC central committee when SNCC voted to establish NBAWADU. Much of this black anti-war ferment, relatively invisible in the historical narrative, took place prior to Dr. King's famed anti-Vietnam War speech. Months later, at the Riverside Church in New York City on April 4, 1967, King made the "connection between the war in Vietnam and the struggle [he], and others, have been waging in America," and further argued there comes a time "when silence is betrayal." He delivered this speech exactly one year before his assassination.[95]

The loud roars of Black Power in the first two years of its expansion not only critiqued U.S. foreign policy, but also traveled globally. It lured Angela Davis back stateside from France in 1967. Davis wrote in her autobiography, "The struggle was the life-nerve; our only hope for survival. I made up my mind. The journey was on."[96] Once back in the United States, Davis joined radical student and anti-war groups at the University of California San Diego, where she continued her studies under philosopher Herbert Marcuse. Then she joined the Black Panther Political Party—distinct from the BPP for Self-Defense. She had first heard of the latter Black Panther Party, led by Newton and Seale, when she lived in Frankfurt, Germany. Davis remembered that while she lived "hidden away in West Germany the Black Liberation Movement was undergoing decisive metamorphoses," beginning with the Black Power slogan springing forth in Greenwood and the transformation of SNCC and CORE. "Everywhere there were upheavals," she wrote. Davis read about how the Black Panther Party entered "the California Legislature in Sacramento with their weapons in order to safeguard their right (a right given to all whites) to carry them as instruments of self-defense."[97] When legislators passed the Mulford Act, also known as the Panther Bill, they ended the right to carry loaded weapons in public. This undercut the Panthers' primary activist strategy.[98] The man who signed the bill into law, California governor and anti-communist Ronald Reagan would soon become Davis's nemesis and a late 20th-century Republican Party darling and U.S. president.

The Black Panther Political Party—the BPPP—was "a small cadre group which felt its role was to develop theoretical analyses of the Black movement, as well as to build structures within the existing movement."[99] Both Davis and Elaine Brown met its leader John Floyd in 1967. Brown, the Black Panther Party's future chair, worked with Floyd through the Black Congress, a "united front" organization in the Los Angeles area. The congress included the US organization, the Afro-American Association, black anti-war and anti-draft groups, black student groups, and welfare rights activists. Brown credited Floyd with teaching her "the language and the ideas of . . . the left or militant wing of the Black struggle for civil and human rights."[100] Davis met Floyd at a house meeting in Los Angeles. There she heard James Forman and field secretary Ralph Featherstone report on their trip to Tanzania. Davis also would have future conversations with Forman and her childhood friend Charlene Mitchell about the revolutionary theorist and activist Amilcar Cabral and his liberation struggles in Guinea-Bissau and the Cape Verde Islands. Cabral talked more about transforming popular consciousness, warned of romanticizing the gun and armed revolution, and became known for his 1969 mantra: "Tell no lies. Claim no easy victories."[101]

By 1968 a Los Angeles chapter of the Black Panther Party had formed. The former Slauson gang leader Alprentice "Bunchy" Carter led the affiliate "military wing." He had served four years at Soledad State Prison for an armed robbery and became a follower of Malcolm X in prison. It is unclear when Bunchy Carter met Newton, but whenever he did, Bunchy "pledged devotion."[102] In the wee hours of October 28, 1967, police had arrested Newton for allegedly killing police officer John Frey in an early morning confrontation that also left Newton wounded. His arrest spurred the "Free Huey" campaign. The party formed a defense committee on the advice of William Patterson, and the newly arrived Kathleen Cleaver, with help from artist Emory Douglas, launched a campaign through the *Black Panther* newspaper.[103] The publicity campaign brought immeasurable attention to the Black Panther Party and helped build a following nationwide.

With the proliferation of chapters, conflict over who rightfully had "black panther" naming rights in California quickly emerged. Supposedly at the end of 1967 at a Black Student Association poetry reading, Bunchy Carter walked into the auditorium with his officers duded up in leather jackets and armed with weapons. Then, he told Floyd that he could not use the name "Black Panther" unless he had permission from the BPP-SD's central committee. With militaristic bravado, Carter continued: "Nobody will speak about Black Power or revolution unless he's willing to follow the example of the vanguard, willing to pick up the gun, ready to die for the people."[104]

For about two months, SNCC facilitated a measure of unity between the two California Panther parties. SNCC leaders took on roles in the BPP–SD. Carmichael became prime minister, H. Rap Brown became minister of justice, and Forman became minister of international affairs. By 1966 SNCC had already formed its New York–based International Affairs Committee, which Fran Beal, who had returned from Paris, helped to steward. SNCC also negotiated an affiliation agreement with the BPPP under the name Los Angeles SNCC. By mid-1968, however, SNCC's "merger with the Panthers had all but dissolved."[105]

In 1969, Carmichael resigned from SNCC (now the Student National Coordinating Committee). Within the next couple years SNCC waned as a Black Power organization, but in 1967 that had not yet happened. Black Power was ramping up, with SNCC still in the mix, and fervent debates arose among a host of academics, activists, and organic intellectuals who backed Black Power and grappled with the concept.

Writing Black Power

As supporters authored Black Power on campgrounds, in black neighborhoods, and at rallies and conventions, they also created and memorialized its ideas and practices through the written word. The number of books, articles, treatises, manifestos, and literature proliferated. In Detroit James Boggs published "Black Power: A Scientific Concept Whose Time Has Come" in the April–May 1967 edition of the *Monthly Review*: "Black Power. Black Power. This is what is being written about and talked about in all strata of the population of the United States of America. Not since the spector [sic] of Communism first began to haunt Europe of one hundred years ago has an idea put forward by so few people frightened so many in so short a time." Boggs continued, "Liberals and radicals, Negro civil rights leaders and politicians, reporters and editorial writers—it is amazing to what degree all of them are fascinated and appalled by Black Power."[106]

Stokely Carmichael and Charles Hamilton's *Black Power: The Politics of Liberation* (1967) became the premier manifesto of the era, reaching from Howard University as far away as Sweden where Carmichael spoke and signed books. Carmichael decided to write *Black Power* after an invited public debate with Bayard Rustin. In the audience was Toni Morrison, who had taught at Howard University and then worked as an editor at Random House. As Carmichael recalled, Morrison approached him about producing a book-length "discussion of the concept, free from media distortion."[107] Given Carmichael's schedule, he approached Hamilton, a political scientist at Lincoln University, as well as sought help from others. The book, according to Carmichael, "was in many ways a collective SNCC project. A lot of folk—Elizabeth Sutherland Martinez, Ivanhoe Donaldson, Courtland Cox, Jim Forman—all contributed to different sections."[108]

Echoing the title of Richard Wright's 1954 book on Ghana, Carmichael and Hamilton's *Black Power* appraised what happens when black people operate from a base of powerlessness—electoral, economic, and social. Their message reflected the present-day situation of U.S. black people, and asserted that they needed to create new political structures. The authors believed, however, that alongside white institutional power, black people's "politics of deference" would make establishing such structures difficult. They argued that "white society devised the language, adopted the rules and had the black community narcotized into believing that the language and those rules were, in fact, relevant."[109] This meant the black community had to be de-narcotized. According to *Black Power:* "The point is obvious: black people must lead and run their own organizations. . . . They must achieve self-identity and self-determination in order to have their daily needs met."[110] This meant that political agendas must emanate from the community, not "'downtown' machines."[111]

In her memoir almost three decades later, Nina Simone recalled of *Black Power* and Carmichael: "Stokely . . . had been working out his answer to the 'where do we go from here' question; he and Huey Newton combined all sorts of related ideas about economic, social justice and political resistance under the general heading of 'Black Power.'" Known for her signature 1963 song "Mississippi Goddam," the "high priestess of soul" read and embraced *Black Power.* Simone continued: "I just wish some of the opponents of Black Power had bothered to read it too, because they would have understood that Black Power was a lot more than black men with guns—it was a way of returning the black man's pride."[112]

The link between black self-determination and restoring black men's pride pervaded *Black Power,* so much so that even when the authors mentioned women, they tended to do so in the context of explaining men's absence of power and their desire to regain it. Carmichael and Hamilton aptly critiqued the "paternalistic attitude" of public and private social welfare agencies" that "dehumanize[d] the individual and perpetuate[d] *his* dependency."[113] They also highlighted how merchants, who extended credit, victimized welfare recipients by "threaten[ing] to tell the caseworker if a recipient . . . [wasn't] meeting *his* payments."[114] Important critiques withstanding, in each instance black women vanished behind a discussion of what it meant for men to be heads of households and breadwinners. Indeed, *Black Power* did not offer a sustained discussion of black women's relationship to the "politics of liberation." It was a stark absence, given black women's critical roles in SNCC and in waging battles against social welfare, educational, and other public institutions.

The now famed *Where Do We Go From Here?* also appeared in 1967. In the book, King wrestled with Black Power as a movement slogan, while simultaneously critiquing the "simple explanation" that blamed the Watts rebellion, as "the voice of Black Power," for birthing the white backlash. Black Power would not become the patsy here. As King stated (and history reveals), "The change in mood had preceded Watts."[115] In fact, King continued, the "cries of Black Power and riots are not the causes of white resistance, they are consequences of it."[116]

The latter point undoubtedly resonated with others such as Nathan Wright. The reverend and former CORE field secretary took over leadership of the national

Black Power conference's planning team from Powell, who was fighting corruption charges. In addition to ongoing white resistance, Wright also pointed out how the changing job market such as the decrease in agricultural jobs, low-wage work in cities, and automation reinforced economic marginalization. Poverty was not disappearing, the racial income gap was broadening, and residential and school segregation still existed. All had not been, and still was not, right for many black Americans—not in the North, South, Midwest, or West, not in rural communities or cities.[117] By July 1967, however, the upsurge of urban uprisings and Black Power protests, alongside decades of jail going for breaking unfair laws, had contributed to the perception (even if specious) of black people as criminal and a threat to law and order.

Coincidentally, one day after the Black Power conference's planning team (which included Amiri Baraka and Flo Kennedy) had announced that the conference would be held in Newark, that city exploded in racial turmoil. Conference planners, nevertheless, refused to cancel or delay the event. They moved forward, and thousands arrived in the city between July 20 and 23. This included Queen Mother Moore, who bristled at the presence of some white women at Flo Kennedy's workshop. While Moore wanted them gone, Kennedy told them to keep their seats, and they did. Kennedy had invited the young feminists because she thought they could learn something from Black Power.[118] Clearly, multiple visions of what Black Power could achieve existed at the conference.

Around the same time as the Newark conference, Nathan Wright's *Black Power and Urban Unrest* hit bookstores. In his book, Wright asked the question: "To what strategic ends—aside from eventual growth and increased self-respect—can the movement toward Black Power lead?" He answered his own query in four ways: Black Power would result in changed status, help "America to save itself from the folly of a myopic vision of what America in human terms is destined and called to be," call "attention to the neglected dimensions of meaning of democracy," and require that "the life of our cities . . . be redeemed."[119] In particular, Wright advocated a moderate economic agenda for the black community. He argued that Black Power had a creative and sellable potential, which would be achieved when black people as individuals received their shares.

Black revolutionary nationalists such as Robert Allen, however, would critique the positions of Nathan Wright and others similarly minded. Allen argued that such a Black Power as "black capitalism" approach primarily benefited the black middle class and propped up an unjust economic system. A lawyer, ordained priest, and feminist who coined the term "Jane Crow," Pauli Murray also would critique Wright. However, she targeted his "myopia" with regard to women whom he barely mentioned. She argued that his "Black Power" presented the struggle "in terms of black males and black manhood."[120] These internal debates, which exposed competing beliefs and strategies, proliferated as Black Power did.

Months after the 1967 conference, the continuations committee released the "Black Power Manifesto and Resolutions," a 26-page report.[121] The manifesto reflected the eclectic gathering of people and ideas. Conferees passed resolutions on economic, political, and cultural development; black youth; artists, craftsmen, and communications; general welfare; as well as individual resolutions from the floor. Not surprisingly, black women were often cast in traditional gender specific roles in the black nation. The section "Black Women and the Home" largely reinforced, as did other Black Power writings and public statements, a conception of women tied to the home or broader community. It read: "As sisters, mothers, teachers and nation builders," black women should lead "intensified efforts and programs . . . to stabilize the Black family Unit by emphasizing security, protections, love and respect for each family member." Other resolutions included black women making "black homes . . . centers of learning and growth," exposing "genocidal practices by racist societies," and declaring war "against narcotics" by outing "pushers" and helping addicts to secure medical treatment.[122] Black women were tasked with getting their communities' houses in order.

The Black Power Manifesto also linked U.S. blacks to worldwide freedom struggles. It continued: "Black people who live under imperialist governments in America, Asia, Africa and Latin America stand at the crossroads of either an expanding revolution or ruthless extermination." They needed to wrest control of their communities from "white supremacist oppressors." The conferees expressed their broader concern for anti-imperial struggles in the section on international affairs. Directives included cementing ties and developing cooperation with the Organization of African Unity and establishing "an Institute of African Studies in each state, and every community, where possible." The manifesto endorsed "the revolutionary struggles against South Africa, Mozambique, Angola, Zimbabwe and all other colonized African territories."[123]

In the late 1960s numerous books on black resistance tapped into the desire to document the repression and continuum of black militancy over at least a century if not more. In doing so, these books identified and anthologized, in particular, the genealogy and nationalist roots of Black Power. Venerating mostly black men, these books included Floyd Barbour's *The Black Power Revolt* (1968), SNCC activist Joanne Grant's *Black Protest* (1968), and Harold Cruse's *Rebellion or Revolution* (1968). Historian Lerone Bennett Jr. wrote *Black Power U.S.A.* (1968) on the "human side of Reconstruction" from 1867 to 1877 when the first group of black men served in elected and appointed offices and the threat of their access to political power resulted in Redemption, as well as Jim Crow and economic marginalization.[124] Powell's former aide and black journalist Chuck Stone also narrated a story about black political struggle. A future supporter of the D.C. statehood movement initiated by Hobson and others as an expansive phase of the District's quest for self-determination, Stone wrote *Black Political Power in America* (1968). Stone's book not only examined black people's contemporary presence in government positions, but also explored how the ability to access and wield power influenced decision-making and patronage politics.[125]

Black indignation and assertiveness pervaded writings of the Black Power era. Julius Lester's book *Look Out Whitey! Black Power's Gon' Get Your Mama!* grew out of his 1966 article titled "The Angry Children of Malcolm X," which was published in *Sing Out* magazine. A folk singer and newly hired photographer for SNCC in 1966 working in the basement of the Atlanta office, Lester expanded his article into the book—the name of which snubbed and challenged white power by conspicuously positioning black men as subduing "Whitey's mama." Illustrative of the book's tone, Lester wrote in the culminating chapter that Black Power must confront white power and destroy America "as it now exists."[126] No topics were off limits. Referencing three astronauts who died in the Apollo 1 spacecraft during rehearsals at Cape Kennedy in January 1967, Lester argued of the program, they "were spending money that blacks needed. White folks trying to get to the moon, 'cause it's there. Poverty's here!" In July 1969 the United States did reach the moon. Federal dollars invested in the space program, and the Vietnam War, however, provided political grist for black activists. Space and guns vied against bread-and-butter issues.[127]

Black religious leaders and congregants authored Black Power as well. The National Committee of Negro Churchmen issued a "Black Power Statement" in 1966.[128] Forty-five men (Nathan Wright was among them) and one woman, Anna Arnold Hedgeman, who worked with the National Council of Churches, signed the statement. The Black Power Statement addressed the "Leaders of America" on "power and freedom," "White Churchmen" on "power and love," "Negro Citizens" on "power and justice," and the "Mass Media" on "power and truth." It was a frank calling out of hypocrisy, one that took issue with the "assumption that white people are justified in getting what they want through the use of power, but that Negro Americans must, either by nature or by circumstances, make their appeal only through conscience." According to the signatories, "powerlessness breeds a race of beggars."[129] As black nationalists and radicals had argued before, so too did they: black people needed power.

Rev. Albert Cleage, of Detroit's Shrine of the Black Madonna, who helped organize the Northern Negro Grassroots Leadership Conference, had much to say about black theology and race pride as well. By the end of 1968, Cleage had written and published *The Black Messiah*. In it, he portrayed Jesus as a black man—a belief that steeled the righteousness of black people's power demands, as well as helped to make the black church, as he wrote later in *Black Christian Nationalism,* "relevant to the Black Liberation Struggle."[130] In 1969 James Cone wrote *Black Theology & Black Power* for "the voiceless black masses."[131] Trying to reconcile a belief in King's nonviolence, Malcolm X's critique of Christianity, and emergent Black Power politics, Cone described the white church as an agent of repression, and maintained God and Jesus were on the side of black liberation.

While black men may have emerged more frequently as the politicians, religious leaders, and public chroniclers of Black Power politics in the masculine decade, black women, too, authored the movement and pushed at its edges. Black religious women such as black Catholic sisters wrote themselves into this Black Power dialogue through the formation of an all-black federation, their community-based activism, and public statements at conferences in the late 1960s. In 1968 Sister M. Martin de Porres (Patricia Muriel Grey) organized a conference for black nuns, also referred to as black women religious. Black priests already had met in Detroit in April to organize a Black Catholic Clergy Caucus. Some five months later, the National Black Sister's Conference (NBSC) met in Pittsburgh. They publicly and unapologetically avowed black pride and race consciousness and decried racial oppression in the church.[132]

A year later the NBSC issued a position paper, "Survival of Soul," at its second annual conference at the University of Dayton. In the position paper, they pledged themselves "to work unceasingly for the liberation of black people." They exalted "the gift of [their] womanhood, that channel through which the Son of God Himself chose to come into the human race." And they declared their blackness as a "gift" to deliver humanity, and black people, "from the intolerable burden . . . of white racism."[133] Exemplary of this "new breed of black nuns," Sister Sylvia Thibodeaux, who taught black children in Roxbury, Boston, even maintained, "Every kid coming out of a black school ought to know how to organize a rent strike by the eighth grade."[134] Years later, her cousin Sister Mary Roger Thibodeaux wrote *A Black Nun Looks at Black Power* (1972), in which she stated: "Black Power is not foreign to Yahweh and Yahweh is not foreign to Black Power. There is a covenant of friendship there. The cause of Justice is and always will be in strict accordance with the Will of God."[135]

🖋 An activist, architect, chronicler, and leader of black nationalist struggles since the early 1900s, Amy Jacques Garvey published *Black Power in America* from Kingston, Jamaica, in 1968. The pamphlet and title essay, in its very existence, exposed some of the linkages—the sources and courses—that fed the desire and protest traditions of Black Power. Always attuned to keeping the torch of Garveyism alit, Amy Jacques Garvey wrote that several leaders who committed themselves to black pride and unity in order to challenge white supremacy and defend black humanity were "understudies" of Garvey's teachings. She shared an excerpt from a 1964 letter written by Thomas Harvey, president-general of the UNIA. From Harvey's perspective, and seemingly from Amy Jacques Garvey's as well: Marcus Garvey "paved the way for all local leaders who have emerged since his death."[136] Her examples included Elijah Muhammad and Malcolm X.

Lest it be forgotten, Amy Jacques Garvey also chronicled "the awakening of the Negro in the deep South, and in the industrial North"—the "militant," "courageous," "New Negro" who was "suspicious of local leaders who are backed by white people" and brazenly contested white supremacy. She called attention to the impact of Garvey's philosophy on Malcolm X's mother and father, and shared that Dr. King recognized Garvey as "the first man of colour in the history of the United States to lead and develop a mass movement."[137] She reminded people that in the United States, "unequal integration" has "humiliate[d] Negroes." While acknowledging "sympathetic white people who hate the injustices meted out to Negroes," Amy Jacques Garvey reinforced the black nationalist foundation of Black Power: "The Negro must have an All-Negro organization, and evolve his own self-sacrificing leaders—who will refuse white hand-outs; preaching always self-denial, self-help and self-determination."[138]

Amy Jacques Garvey believed that the break from "conservative INTER-RACIAL GROUPS" such as the NAACP and Urban League by "Freedom Fighters" to "demand BLACK POWER" was a necessary "drive to mobilize the black communities." She begged the question: "What's wrong with that?" Even as she avowed "BLACK UNITY IS BLACK POWER," she did not wax on romantically about Black Power without calling to attention some of the likely pitfalls. One must not dismiss the potential of "abuse of this power by individuals—frustrated, despised and under financial pressure by the white majority." In fact, this was to be "expected," as was the possible "misuse of this power by splinter groups to wreak vengeance on others." She continued: "Human nature under pressure is unreasonable and unpredictable," and people will try to find the ways they can to "fight back." Sometimes that would be targeted externally, other times internally. The solution was to get rid of the causes and national and community violence that fed black men and women's suffering.[139]

Other black women activists also conjured the "sources and courses"—or roots and routes—that influenced the continuum of Black Power philosophies and politics. In particular, those in the black women's radical tradition wrote pioneering expositions elaborating on sexism and classism. The founder of the women's caucus in SNCC, which grew into the Black Women's Liberation Committee and provided the roots for the Third World Women's Alliance, Fran Beal penned the first draft of "Black Women's Manifesto: Double Jeopardy" in 1968. Becoming one of the most anthologized black feminist essays, "Double Jeopardy" directly addressed the analytical shortcomings of virile Black Power ideology, as well as its dissonance with black women's real life experiences. Patricia Murphy Robinson and Group wrote position papers on poor black women's struggles, and Toni Cade edited what would become a testimonial tome of black women's voices—*The Black Woman*—in 1970. The volume featured other black women in SNCC, the Black Arts Movement, and community organizing. Prioritizing black women's voices and concerns, they and other black women grassroots activists challenged black women's oppression, and some of them would emerge at the forefront of black feminist, Third World, and welfare rights struggles. In this way, they shaped the meaning, agendas, and struggles in the Black Power era.

The publication of newspaper and journal articles, books, and position papers on the new media darling and bogey—Black Power—proliferated. Its allure, and the conditions that gave it life, fostered a wellspring of theoretical and political conversations, ones that would continue at conferences, on campuses, and in communities. Similarly, black culture, art, and aesthetics reproduced Black Power. Cultural politics bore witness to black struggle, took up the psychological battle against perceived and believed black unworthiness, and dignified black life. While an unrepentant proclamation of black pride, black cultural politics, however, also revealed divergent ideologies and identities that complicated achieving black unity.

Black Aesthetics: From Homecoming Queen to Killer Poems

During the fall semester of 1966, for the first time, a contestant for homecoming queen wore an Afro in competition. Her name was Robin Gregory. Black law students asked Gregory, who they knew to be politically active, to run. They wanted her to challenge "old values" and "to make a statement about the black aesthetic."[140] In the midst of national and local debates galvanized by the recent call for Black Power, the Afro hairstyle brought newfangled, but not newfound attention to Howard University in Washington, D.C.—where black student activists had formed the Nonviolent Action Group (NAG), participated in rights campaigns in Baltimore and Cambridge, traveled to the South to join CORE's freedom rides, and organized with SNCC in Mississippi and Alabama between 1964 and 1966.

Robin Gregory had enrolled at Howard University in 1962, and in 1963 she served on the March on Washington committee to set up local logistics. As a work-study student in the Moorland Foundation library where many African students from other universities studied, Gregory met Carmichael. He would go there to work on his papers. A year later, Gregory joined SNCC, serving as the liaison between SNCC's D.C. office and the field staff in Mississippi. When Gregory attended the Democratic National Convention in Chicago in 1964, she met some Mississippi women who wore natural hairstyles.[141] When she returned to Howard University, she too began wearing a natural, joining only one other black woman (whom she could remember anyway)—Mary Felice Lovelace.

"At least two and a half years before the 'Afro style' would sweep the African community," Lovelace, a member of NAG, "had decided to wear her hair in public as the good Lord made it." At that time, Lovelace's decision sent dorm mothers reeling. They refused to let her leave the dorm, calling her hair a "wild African bush" and a "rat's nest." They also told her if she did not have enough money, they would give her some "to get it done." Said Carmichael, who was dating Lovelace at the time: "It was a sho-nuff crisis and a battle of wills." Fired up that "the first love of [his] young manhood" had been treated so disdainfully, Carmichael supported "throwing up a picket line around the woman's dorm." Dean Patricia Roberts, who in later years became the first black woman to occupy a presidential cabinet position as secretary of Housing and Urban Development in President Jimmy Carter's administration, intervened in order for Lovelace to gain permission to leave the dorm.[142] A personal decision that rose, intentionally and unintentionally, to the level of political statement, the Afro would resonate as the hairdo of female freedom fighters.[143]

Gregory, as had Lovelace, intentionally entered the fray of cultural politics when she decided to run for homecoming queen. After she won, people celebrated on and off campus with chants of "Umgawa, Black Power."[144] In recalling the moment, Gregory stated, while it may seem "superficial" to some, it was significant "for anybody who lived through . . . years of self denial and abnegation" because "of the way black people looked."[145] As bell hooks has argued about black beauty and Black Power, "[M]ilitant leaders of the black liberation struggle demanded that black folks see ourselves differently—see self-love as a radical political agenda."[146] Bolstering black pride and decolonizing the mind rested at the center of psychological freedom, or as Gwen Patton explained: Black Power included the struggle of "black people to rid themselves of internal oppression and hatred."[147]

Visual symbols of blackness, however, were not enough. One had to be careful, lest black people's complicated history devolve into romanticism and distortions or mask conservative gender and class politics. The first black woman to sit in the U.S. Congress had something to say about it all. "Black is Beautiful. You hear that phrase a great deal," maintained Shirley Chisholm. However, she cautioned against shallowly connecting to racial identity (which is what revolutionary nationalists often critiqued cultural nationalists for) by "adopting the outward manifestations of African dress and appearance." That was superficial. Exploring "African heritage" required learning "about contemporary Africa and its people." Moreover, Chisholm argued: "Black is beautiful in what you do to contribute to the building of a strong black community throughout this country."[148]

Gregory's activism did not end with winning homecoming queen. The two-year veteran of SNCC, as a student activist in the Black Power era, joined anti-war protests—as had Gwen Patton, Angela Davis, and numerous other leftist students mobilizing across the country. On Howard's campus, this resulted in a demonstration against General Lewis B. Hershey, head of the Selective Service. After the Atlanta protest and Harlem-based anti-draft conference, Hershey came to Howard—a campus that Gregory compared to a plantation on the bigger plantation of D.C. where black people still "could not vote." Like the city, Howard University, also, received allocations from the House District Committee. "And so, there were these white, southern senators who were essentially very racist, who were telling us what we could and could not do on campus," stated Gregory. Hershey, well, he was "part and parcel of that whole thing." It was around these issues that Gregory believed "sleeping middle class students at Howard University should wake up."[149]

This same semester, students formed a Black Power group. On the morning of March 22, 1967, representatives including Gregory stood in front of Crampton Auditorium with their advisor Nathan Hare, an assistant professor of sociology who had been on the faculty for six years. The students wanted to "overthrow the Negro College" and replace it with "a militant black university which [would] counteract the whitewashing black students receive[d]." They also supported abolishing ROTC and bridging the black community and campus.[150] Within six months, Hare was fired from Howard University and would resurface at San Francisco State College.

As at Howard University, black college students elsewhere increasingly became radicalized too. They confronted the politics of their university administrations, as well as made common cause with community residents. The Black Panther Party stands as a primary example, with Merritt College students Newton and Seale explicitly deciding to focus attention on black communities beyond the campus. At Columbia University, black students successfully protested the university's efforts to gain more land by expanding into the nearby lower income black neighborhoods of Morningside Heights and Harlem. At Princeton and elsewhere, hundreds of students challenged apartheid, and anti-war mobilizations captured the attention of black and white students from the East Coast to the West Coast.[151]

The Black Studies movement emerged in 1966 at the instigation of the SSAC also at Merritt College. Within two years, mobilizations for Black Studies programs proliferated in Oakland, San Francisco, Chicago, and New York. Black high school and college students insisted upon the creation of Black Studies curricula, and community-based Black Power organizations supported them. Not surprisingly, the Black Panther Party helped to mobilize students on college campuses, including San Francisco State College. There, a vigorous and fraught campaign known as the Third World Strike, which included Asian-American, Latina/o, and black students, went on for five months, ending with the creation of "a new academic discipline."[152] Hare served as the strikers' advisor, and helped to draft the proposal for what became the first Black Studies program in the country. He later founded *The Black Scholar* journal.

The new appreciation of blackness—as a hue with a history—challenged negative racial stereotypes. The legacy of race pride embedded in New Negro identity and the black arts and intellectual movement of the Harlem Renaissance endured into the era of expansive Black Power politics. Race pride and unapologetic critiques of black subjugation showed up in the arts, just as it had in churches, schools, neighborhoods, books, magazines, and grassroots organizations.

Community-based cultural centers, theaters, and literary presses proliferated from 1966 to 1968. While itself fleeting, BARTS helped spur this trend. A poet, foundry worker, postal clerk, and graduate of Wayne State University, Dudley Randall founded Broadside Press in Detroit. Poets Gwendolyn Brooks (who was in Richard Wright's South Side group in the 1930s) and Don L. Lee (Haki Madhubuti) established the Afro-Arts Theater and Organization of Black American Culture in Chicago. Lee also established Third World Press in 1967 with the help of Johari Amini (nee Jewel C. Latimore) and Carolyn M. Rodgers. A student of Gwendolyn Brooks, Rodgers's first volume of poetry, *Paper Soul,* was published by Third World Press in 1968. Sonia Sanchez published her first books of poetry with Broadside—*Homecoming* (1969) and *We Baddddd People* (1973)—and Third World Press—*Love Poems* (1973). Black Arts West emerged in San Francisco guided by Marvin X and Ed Bullins, and Kalaamu ya Salaam (né Val Ferdinand) established the BLKARTSOUTH community action and writers workshop at the Free Southern Theater in New Orleans.[153]

The public amplification of Black Power and the establishment of black arts institutions in 1967 set the stage for a generation of cultural workers. Nikki Giovanni, who had attended the Detroit arts conference where she met Black Power and radical activists, published her first volume of poetry, *Black Feeling, Black Talk* in 1968. While a student at Fisk, Giovanni (nee Yolande Cornelia Giovanni Jr. in 1943) deepened her connection to her black identity and the struggle. Giovanni had helped to reestablish the SNCC chapter on campus, enrolled in writing workshops with John O. Killens, and met black authors such as Amiri Baraka and novelist Margaret Walker, also a former member of Wright's South Side group. In 1967 Giovanni, who hailed from Lincoln Heights, Ohio, and attended Columbia University (for its MFA program), moved to Cincinnati where she initiated the Black Arts Festival and established the black indigenous New Theatre. In *Black Feeling, Black Talk,* she wrote poems dedicated to "HRB" or Hubert "Rap" Brown, Don L. Lee, Dudley Randall, as well as "For All the Beautiful Black Panthers East."[154] Giovanni, alongside black artists and intellectuals, also formed a group called Black People in Defense of Angela Davis in 1970.[155]

Baraka and Neal would team up to bring to the public *Black Fire!*—an anthology of black revolutionary writings in 1968.[156] The anthology included essays, poetry, fiction, and drama—mostly featuring men. Snellings and other artists penned writings that put them in the crosshairs of racism, imperialism, and colonialism and took up the question of black people's oppression across the world. A quartet of struggle, four of Snellings's poems appeared in *Black Fire!* They evoked the concrete—real people, places, situations, and confrontations—alongside cultural positions and political worldviews. *Sunrise!!, Mississippi Concerto, The Song of Fire,* and *Earth* were all poems that called to action constituencies in the anti-racist struggle. *Sunrise!!*—written for "Al Hadji Malik El Shabazz and the Afro-American Nation"—screamed the "Song of the Race" and urged, "Sing out our Destiny to your sons, to your warrior sons—in the ghettoes, on the tenant farms, in the swelling cities by the Western Sea."[157] *Mississippi Concerto,* written for Mary Lee Lane and the Southern Black People," called for "defy[ing] the Rope, the Gun, the Alabaster Plague" and a recommitment to "reclaim[ing] your Song."[158] *The Song of Fire* dedicated to "Africa, Asia, and Latin and Afro-America—the Wretched of the Earth" evoked Frantz Fanon's famous black revolutionary tome and rallied around the unity of people of color globally to respond to empire and colonial subjugation.[159] In his final poem, *Earth,* for "Mrs. Mary Bethune and the African and Afro-American Women," black women were undeniably valued as the "mothers of the world." While acknowledging the centrality of black women, particularly as the nation's "womb," Snellings called black men to task for being absent "warriors." Black men needed to step up and protect the black nation.[160] The consistently gendered discourse that shaped mindsets and behaviors—alongside black women's leadership, activism, and eventually critique—would help spark the creation of alternative, oppositional spaces for black women's radical voices related to every aspect of Black Power, including as artists and intellectuals.

The year 1968 brought even more fire: intellectual, political, and literal flames. Having traveled to Memphis, Tennessee, to support the sanitation workers' strike, King was killed on the balcony of the Lorraine Motel. His assassination on April 4, almost four years after Malcolm X's "The Ballot or the Bullet" speech and King's own anti-war speech, lit the fuse of long, hot summers in more than 100 cities. At the time of his death, Dr. King and SCLC had been planning the Poor People's Campaign in Washington, D.C., to demand economic justice and power for poor people. The campaign would have to—and did—proceed without its charismatic spokesman. And throughout the 1960s and into the 1970s, people girded up and became embroiled in grassroots power struggles in cities across the nation.

Notes

1 Gwen Patton, "Born Freedom Fighter," in *Hands on the Freedom Plow*, ed. Holsaert et al., 581.
2 Forman, *The Making of Black Revolutionaries*, 456.
3 In June 1966, James Meredith, who braved white mobs and broke the color bar at the University of Mississippi four years prior, decided to protest black people's fear to exercise their constitutional rights in Mississippi by engaging in a one-man March Against Fear from Memphis to Jackson along Highway 51. Fleming, 165; Garrow, 475–477.
4 Carmichael with Thelwell, 489.
5 Ibid., 506–507; Garrow, 481; Goudsouzian, 133–134, 140–141.
6 Ricks quoted in Joseph, *Waiting 'Til the Midnight Hour*, 141.
7 Carmichael with Thelwell, 507.
8 Forman, *The Making of Black* Revolutionaries, 457.
9 Carmichael with Thelwell, 486. According to Fleming, while Smith Robinson garnered respect, the responsibilities that came with being executive secretary, including exercising power over male colleagues and her no-nonsense administrative style (she tolerated no tomfoolery), gave her status as "one of the boys." This, alongside juggling family and activist work, made for challenging times. Cynthia Griggs Fleming, "'More than a Lady,'" in *Unequal Sisters*, ed. Ruiz with DuBois, 551–562. Also, Dorothy M. Zellner, "My Real Vocation"; Debbie Amis Bell, "A Young Communist Joins SNCC"; and Faye Bellamy, "Playtime Is Over," in *Hands on the Freedom Plow*, ed. Holsaert et al.
10 According to Plummer, 90 percent of 26,000 people receiving surplus food in Mississippi in 1962 were African American, and medical teams found many black children suffering near-starvation conditions. Plummer, *In Search of Power*, 245.
11 Gwen Patton, "Born Freedom Fighter," 580.
12 Forman, *Sammy Younge Jr.*, 125.
13 Jimmy Rogers of SNCC initiated the effort to start a Black Panther Party in Macon County and discussed it with Younge, who shared some ideas. Forman, *Sammy Younge Jr.*, 180.
14 Forman, *Sammy Younge Jr.*, 192.
15 On the precipitation of SNCC's anti-war statement, see Allen, 46; Sellers with Terrell, 149–150. On the rallying cry, see Hogan, 233–234.
16 Forman, *Sammy Younge Jr.*, 223; Gloria House, "We'll Never Turn Back," in *Hands on the Freedom Plow*, ed. Holsaert et al., 510–512.
17 Gwen Patton, "Born Freedom Fighter," 581.

18 Ibid.

19 Carmichael with Thelwell, 486.

20 King, *Where Do We Go From Here: Chaos or Community?* (1967), in *Testament of Hope,* ed. Washington, 573.

21 Ibid., 574.

22 Carmichael quoted in U.S. Government Memo to Mr. Wick from Mr. Jones, Re: Stokely Carmichael, June 20, 1966, Part I of 5, Stokely Carmichael (FBI File HQ 100–446080), FBI Files.

23 King, *Where Do We Go From Here,* 573.

24 Nathan Hare, "How White Power Whitewashes Black Power," in *The Black Power Revolt,* ed. Barbour, 183.

25 Sales, 45.

26 Allen, 69; Rhonda Y. Williams, *The Politics of Public Housing,* 157.

27 Allen, 65.

28 Sonnie and Tracy, 53.

29 Ibid.

30 Bayard Rustin, "'Black Power' and Coalition Politics," *Commentary* 42 (September 1966): 35–40.

31 Roy Wilkins, "Address to NAACP Convention, 1966," in *Black Protest Thought in the Twentieth Century,* ed. Meier, 597.

32 Carl Stokes, Speech at Annual Convention of NAACP, Los Angeles, California, July 7, 1966, Box 1, Carl B. Stokes Papers, Western Reserve Historical Society, Cleveland, Ohio.

33 Ibid.

34 Ibid.

35 Nicholas von Hoffman, "Black Power Called Racism by Humphrey," *Washington Post,* July 7, 1966.

36 Ibid.

37 Stokes, 270. While Gibson lost this round, he would win election in 1970 and serve for 16 years. In 1967, Gregory would himself run unsuccessfully for mayor of Chicago.

38 Paul Galloway, "Gary's Mayor Hatcher: He's Proud of His Grimy Steel City," *Cleveland Press,* January 16, 1979.

39 Michney, "Race, Violence, and Urban Territoriality," 415. Also, John Baden, "Residual Neighbors: Jewish-African American Interactions in Cleveland from 1900 to 1970," MA thesis, Case Western Reserve University, 2011, 66–68.

40 Lyles, 52.

41 Ibid., 52.

42 Ibid., 53–54.

43 Ibid., 55.

44 Lewis G. Robinson, 22–23, 113, 124.

45 Moore, 48.

46 Ibid., 6.

47 Bayard Rustin, "'Black Power' and Coalition Politics," *Commentary* 42 (September 1966).

48 Ahmad, 167.

49 Carmichael quoted in Ahmad, 167.

50 Ahmad, 167.

51 Fujino, 163.

52 Thomas A. Johnson, "3 Groups Claim Victory, Drop P.S. 175 Boycott," *New York Times,* September 3, 1966.

53 Thomas A. Johnson, "3 Harlem Schools Facing Boycotts," *New York Times,* August 26, 1966; Johnson, "3 Groups Claim Victory, Drop P.S. 175 Boycott," *New York Times,*

September 3, 1966. Also, "Black Panthers Picket a School," *New York Times,* September 13, 1966.

54 Thomas A. Johnson, "3 Harlem Schools Facing Boycotts," *New York Times,* August 26, 1966. Also, Yohuru Williams, "From Oakland to Omaha: Historicizing the Panthers," in *Liberated Territory,* eds. Williams and Lazerow, 1–2.

55 Richard L. Lyons, "Rep. Powell Defines Black Power: 'Equality,'" *Washington Post,* July 19, 1966.

56 Theoharis, *The Rebellious Life of Mrs. Rosa Parks,* 202.

57 Malcolm X, "After the Bombing," in *Malcolm X Speaks,* ed. Breitman, 165.

58 "Bridge to Black Power: Adam Clayton Powell, Jr. [W/Kwame Ture]," YouTube video, www.youtube.com/watch?v=bWTz5P-aIvg.

59 Chuck Stone, "The National Conference on Black Power," in *The Black Power Revolt,* ed. Barbour, 190; "Black Power Conference—Attendance List," September 4, 1966, Folder: ACT-Black Power, 1965–66, Box 1, Collection 1, Julius W. Hobson Papers, The Washingtoniana Collection, D.C. Public Library, Washington, D.C.

60 Kennedy; Sherie M. Randolph, "'Women's Liberation or . . . Black Liberation, You're Fighting the Same Enemies,'" in *Want to Start a Revolution?,* eds. Gore, Theoharis, and Woodard, 225–226.

61 Ahmad, 71.

62 Thomas A. Johnson, "3 Groups Claim Victory, Drop P.S. 175 Boycott," *New York Times,* September 3, 1966.

63 "Schools in City Open Smoothly Despite Protests," *New York Times,* September 13, 1966.

64 Thomas A. Johnson, "Black Panthers Picket a School," *New York Times,* September 13, 1966.

65 Ahmad, 170.

66 Joseph, *Waiting 'Til the Midnight Hour,* 163; Ahmad, 71.

67 Stokely Carmichael, "What We Want," *New York Review of Books,* September 22, 1966. Also, Allen, 47.

68 Stokely Carmichael, "What We Want," *New York Review of Books,* September 22, 1966.

69 Ibid.

70 Ibid.

71 Bloom and Martin, 43; Kelley, *Freedom Dreams.*

72 Major, 1.

73 Bloom and Martin, 48; Nelson, 55. Also, Murch; Donna Murch, "When the Panther Travels," in *Black Power Beyond Borders,* ed. Slate, 57–78.

74 Bloom and Martin, 43–44. Also, Ahmad, 72.

75 Bloom and Martin, 71.

76 Fay D. Bellamy, "A Little Old Report," circa 1966, Folder 1–15: News clippings and Miscellany, 1966, Student Nonviolent Coordinating Committee, Vine City Project (Atlanta, Georgia) Records, MSS 347, Wisconsin Historical Society, Madison, Wisconsin. On Smith Robinson, see Fleming, 179.

77 Bellamy, "A Little Old Report."

78 Ibid.

79 Raoul Kulberg, "The Last Colony—I," *Concern,* July 1–15, 1967, in Folder: Politics and Government: Home Rule, 1966–1967, Vertical Files, The Washingtoniana Collection, D.C. Public Library, Washington, D.C.

80 Raoul Kulberg, "The Last Colony—II," *Concern,* September 1, 1967; William Raspberry, "Civil Rights Not Won by City Flames," *Washington Post,* August 29, 1966, both in Folder: Politics and Government: Home Rule, 1966–1967, Vertical Files.

81 Daniel Patrick Moynihan, "The Negro Family: The Case For National Action," Office of Policy Planning and Research, United States Department of Labor, Washington, D.C., 1965.

82 Lang, 203; Pulido, 265n35. For statistic, Jonathan Sutherland, *African Americans at War: An Encyclopedia* (Santa Barbara, CA: ABC-CLIO, Inc., 2004), 502.

83 "The Revolt of Poor Black Women," in *Lessons from the Damned,* 93; Letter to Vilma Sanchez from Pat Robinson, December 17, 1966, Folder 1–2, Joan Jordan Papers 1966–1972, MSS 197, Wisconsin Historical Society, Madison, Wisconsin.

84 "The Revolt of Poor Black Women," in *Lessons from the Damned,* 93.

85 Ibid., 94.

86 "Black Women!!" and "Black Men!!" fliers attached to Letter to Vilma Sanchez from Pat Robinson, December 17, 1966, Folder 1–2, Joan Jordan Papers 1966–1972, MSS 197.

87 "Black Men!!" flier attached to Letter to Vilma Sanchez from Pat Robinson, December 17, 1966, Folder 1–2, Joan Jordan Papers 1966–1972, MSS 197.

88 On Ali, see Marqusee.

89 Giddings, *When and Where I Enter.*

90 Eventually, personal clashes and internal dissension over organizational strategy resulted in the expelling of Atlanta Project members from SNCC. See SNCC Atlanta Project Report & Affidavits, Folder 1–6: Project Position Papers, circa 1966 and "Atlanta's Black Paper," August 25, 1966, Student Nonviolent Coordinating Committee, Vine City Project (Atlanta, Georgia): Records, 1960–1967, MSS 347. Also, Grady-Willis, 101–113.

91 "Minutes of the Eastern Black Anti-Draft Conference—January 21, 1967." Recorder: Joanne Eubanks, Folder: National Coordinating Committee of Black Organizations against the Draft, Box 32, Social Action Vertical File c. 1960–1980, MSS 577, Wisconsin Historical Society, Madison, Wisconsin. Robert Allen would write *Black Awakening in Capitalist America.*

92 "Atlanta's Black Paper," August 25, 1966, Folder 1–7: Publications and Near-Print Materials 1966–1967, Student Nonviolent Coordinating Committee, Vine City Project (Atlanta, Georgia): Records, 1960–1967, MSS 347.

93 "Minutes of the Eastern Black Anti-Draft Conference—January 21, 1967." Robert Allen would write *Black Awakening in Capitalist America.*

94 Gwen Patton, "Born Freedom Fighter," 583.

95 Martin Luther King Jr., "Address to the Clergy and Laity Concerned, Riverside Church, New York City, April 4, 1967," in *Testament of Hope,* ed Washington, 231–232.

96 Davis, 145.

97 Ibid., 144.

98 Bloom and Martin, 69.

99 Davis, 145, 163.

100 Elaine Brown, 106–107. On US and other Black Congress affiliates, see Scot Brown, 83–84.

101 Angela Davis, "Memories of Black Liberation," in *Claim No Easy Victories: The Legacy of Amilcar Cabral,* ed. Firoze Manji and Bill Fletcher Jr. (CODESRIA & Daraja Press, 2013), 463.

102 Elaine Brown, 119–120.

103 Horne, *Black Revolutionary,* 196. On Newton's arrest and the "Free Huey" campaign, see Bloom and Martin, 100–101; Joseph, *Waiting 'Til the Midnight Hour,* 204–240; Murch, 151–168.

104 Elaine Brown, 124.

105 Davis, 170. Also, Yohuru Williams, "American Exported Black Nationalism," 13–14.

106 James Boggs, "Black Power: A Scientific Concept Whose Time Has Come," in *Racism and the Class Struggle.*

107 Carmichael with Thelwell, 548.

108 Ibid.

109 Carmichael and Hamilton, 51.

110 Ibid., 46.

111 Ibid., 47.

112 Simone, 109.

113 Carmichael and Hamilton, 18. Italics added.

114 Ibid., 21. Italics added.

115 King, *Where Do We Go From Here,* 556.

116 Ibid., 562.

117 Nathan Wright Jr., "The Crisis Which Bred Black Power," in *The Black Power Revolt,* ed. Barbour, 103–118.

118 Sherie M. Randolph, "Women's Liberation or . . . Black Liberation, You're Fighting the Same Enemies," 231–232.

119 Nathan Wright Jr., *Black Power and Urban Unrest,* 19–21.

120 Pauli Murray, "The Liberation of Black Women," in *Words of Fire,* ed. Guy-Sheftall, 189.

121 "National Conference on Black Power" Memo, October 30, 1967, Folder 1: ACT—Black Power, 1965–66, Box 1, Collection 1, Julius W. Hobson Papers. The memo was from Nathan Wright Jr. and other continuation committee members: Chuck Stone, Karenga, Omar Abu Ahmed (HARYOU-ACT in New York City), and Isaiah Robinson (Harlem Parents Council).

122 Ibid.

123 Ibid.

124 Bennett.

125 Chuck Stone, *Black Political Power in America.* Numerous other books followed after 1968. For instance, *Black Nationalism in America,* co-edited by John H. Bracey Jr. (himself a black nationalist activist who knew and organized with Stanford among others) and white professors Meier and Rudwick.

126 Lester, 137.

127 On race, the space program, and NASA, see Plummer, *In Search of Power,* 242–245.

128 National Committee of Negro Churchmen, "Black Power Statement," appendix in Nathan Wright, *Black Power and Urban Unrest.*

129 Ibid.

130 Cleage, xvi.

131 Cone. Black womanist theologians took to task male-centered black liberation theologians. Jacquelyn Grant, "Black Theology and the Black Woman," in *Words of Fire,* ed. Guy-Sheftall, 320–336.

132 "Negro Nuns to Form All-Black Federation," *Washington Post,* August 10, 1968. Also, Shannen Dee Williams; Collier-Thomas, *Jesus, Jobs, and Justice.*

133 National Black Sisters' Conference, 155.

134 Edward B. Fiske, "Finding Identity, Black Nuns Put Soul into Religious Life," *New York Times,* August 15, 1970.

135 Quoted in Rhonda Y. Williams, "Black Women, Urban Politics, and Engendering Black Power," in *The Black Power Movement,* ed. Joseph, 93.

136 Amy Jacques Garvey, *Black Power in America,* 5. Alongside Queen Mother Moore and Ethel Johnson, Stanford also met with Thomas Harvey during the course of his self-education.

137 Amy Jacques Garvey, *Black Power in America,* 7.

138 Ibid., 9.

139 Ibid., 11.

140 Robin Gregory, "Reflections on an Era: Black Consciousness," in *American Experience: Eyes on the Prize: America Civil Rights Movement 1954–1985,* American Experience/PBS; Transcript of Interview with Robin Gregory, *Eyes on Prize II* Interviews, October 12, 1988, Washington University Digital Gateway, http://digital.wustl.edu/e/eii/

eiiweb/gre5427.0883.061robingregory.html. Also, Craig, 73–74; Valk, *Radical Sisters,* 116–117.

141 Ford, 625–658; Laila Haidarali, "Polishing Brown Diamonds: African American Women, Popular Magazines, and the Advent of Modeling in Early Postwar America," in *Unequal Sisters,* ed. Ruiz with DuBois, 535–550.

142 Carmichael with Thelwell, 266.

143 On the personal choices and politics of the Afro, Fleming, 173–176; Ford, 625–658.

144 Valk, *Radical Sisters,* 116.

145 Robin Gregory, "Reflections on an Era: Black Consciousness," in *American Experience: Eyes on the Prize.*

146 bell hooks references Frantz Fanon and Albert Memmi as scholars and activists who informed Black Power–era critiques of internalized racism. hooks, 119.

147 Gwen Patton, "Born Freedom Fighter," 584.

148 Shirley Chisholm, "Speech at Howard University," in *Say It Loud!,* ed. Ellis and Smith, 108.

149 Transcript of Interview with Robin Gregory, *Eyes on Prize II* Interviews, October 12, 1988.

150 Don Robinson, "College 'Black Power' Group Formed," *Washington Post,* March 23, 1967.

151 On black student and campus movements, see Biondi; Bradley; Countryman; Rogers. Also, see Donna Murch, "A Campus Where Black Power Won," 91–105 and Jeanne Theoharis, "W-A-L-K-O-U-T!: High School Students and the Development of Black Power in L.A.," 107–130, both in *Neighborhood Rebels,* ed. Joseph.

152 Rojas, 45.

153 Woodard, 66–67. For more detail on the Black Arts Movement see Smethurst.

154 Giovanni, 37.

155 Aptheker, 28.

156 Kaluma ya Salaam, "Historical Overviews of the Black Arts Movement," *Modern American Poetry* Website, www.english.illinois.edu/maps/blackarts/historical.htm.

157 Rolland Snellings, "Sunrise!!," in *Black Fire,* ed. Baraka and Neal, 322.

158 Rolland Snellings, "Mississippi Concerto," in *Black Fire,* ed. Baraka and Neal, 324.

159 Rolland Snellings, "The Song of the Fire," in *Black Fire,* ed. Baraka and Neal, 325.

160 Rolland Snellings, "Earth," in *Black Fire,* ed. Baraka and Neal, 328.

5

GIRDING UP URBAN POWER STRUGGLES

Gird up your armor. Face up to reality. For whether we get beat up in the alley by a cop, whether our kids go without an education and end up in Vietnam, whether they work or eat, whether they sleep in a decent house or in a rat-infested shack, whether they are tossed into a river with irons around their necks or whether they sit in the halls of Congress or in the White House or in a general's seat at military headquarters is a question of power. And we shall have power, or we shall perish in the streets.

—James Boggs, "Power! Black Power!"[1]

Cities teemed with protests and people in the years following the Civil Rights and Voting Rights acts. Citizens organized to access places and opportunities beyond the confines of restaurants, theaters, and voting booths. Their struggles had roots in the successes and limits of rights campaigns to transform the hardships of everyday life. In increasingly disinvested black communities, residents confronted inadequate housing. Black youth, for the most part, continued to attend poorly resourced and racially segregated schools. Black men and women labored at low-wage jobs or lacked jobs in the face of automation and business relocation. Illegal drug economies began to grow, police brutality infiltrated everyday life, and urban discontent escalated. Indeed black people struggled to survive, find opportunities, and enjoy life in cities where integration faltered; and political, economic, and cultural changes of all sorts were afoot. In the midst of it all, some people girded up their armor and took to the streets—and parks, shop floors, welfare offices, churches, community centers, and legislative halls—to wage battles for self-determination. Urban power struggles went prime time, and this included in the nation's capital.

The Nation's Capital Colony

After 1965 in the seat of the "Free World," residents of D.C. could neither elect their local leaders nor have a say in directing the municipality's finances. The struggle for elected representation and by extension the chance to influence municipal decisions remained especially charged in the District. The federal government's denial of home rule in the chocolate city smacked of racial exclusion. For many black and white residents, U.S. democracy stood indicted, an example of what Julius Lester would call false-faced America.

Advocates of home rule in the District chafed at federal rule over municipal affairs, but entrenched congressmen and white business elites wielded significant power. And these white powerbrokers were not going to relinquish control easily. This made for quite a taxing battle. So much so that in July 1966, even SNCC veteran and Free D.C. Movement leader Marion Barry pined for the moment when Congress would break for the summer. This did not mean Barry forfeited his belief in D.C. residents' right to electoral self-determination. He, however, began to question where he should expend his energy.

Eventually the home rule controversy provoked a presidential response. In August 1966 President Johnson suggested a new governance plan for the District. He removed unilateral power from the House District Committee, and established a mayor-commissioner and nine-member city council. While the nation's chief executive had intervened, the solution was a far cry from democracy in action. Residents—black or white—still could not elect their own leaders. For under the president's plan, Johnson nominated officeholders and the Senate confirmed them. Furthermore the mayor-commissioner neither had budgetary authority or political respect. When the black politician Walter Washington became the first mayor-commissioner in 1967 and submitted his first budget, he was met with this response. The white southern House District Committee chair John McMillan, who had let bills proposing home rule die in his committee as early as 1950, sent Walter Washington a truckload of watermelons.[2]

Soon enough, in fact before President Johnson announced the District's new governance plan, Barry had decided to shift gears from trying to convince white politicians and corporate interests to support residents' political power to ostensibly seeking access to their economic purses. While the Free D.C. Movement had provided "an issue around which to build a local 'black power' force in the national SNCC image," according to the *Washington Post,* on another level the "self-government goal" registered "as a complex, remote problem in contrast with their more immediate needs of housing, welfare, and jobs."[3] Barry increasingly agreed. In early 1967 he resigned his position as Washington SNCC director and devoted himself "full time to solving the problem of the District's 'black people.'"[4] He hoped to do this through Pride Inc.

Pride Inc. focused on building race and community pride by providing unemployed black male youth (girls were not included) with jobs cleaning up their neighborhoods. The program was based on an idea developed by the District's black community renewal director and native resident Carroll Harvey. The Department of Labor under Secretary Willard Wirtz, who wanted to keep D.C. free of racial uprisings, provided an initial $300,000 for a five-week pilot program. Over the next five years, Pride Inc. received millions in federal funding and expanded its enterprise to include a landscaping business and gas stations. Barry and Mary Treadwell, who knew Barry from Fisk University and joined D.C. SNCC in 1966, served as co-directors.[5]

Pride Inc. launched on August 5, 1967, at Terrell Junior High School. Six hundred boys met there for orientation. After taking physical exams, they received uniforms. The 20-year-old Rufus "Catfish" Mayfield, a high school dropout and the son of a numbers runner, became Pride Inc.'s chairman. He had become active in the community after police killed his friend Clarence Brooker. As Pride Inc.'s chair, Mayfield counseled young men to keep their cool and work proudly as they helped to "clean up rat-infested areas and beautify littered spots" throughout the District. In this way, Mayfield stated: "We gonna prove something to the white power structure . . . that we, as black people, can stand up on our own."[6] But relying on federal funds to show the white power structure that black people could stand up on their own was complicated.

In the years when federal anti-poverty and community action programs met Black Power, black grassroots activists not only sought access, but also control over the government resources entering their neighborhoods. Securing federal funds afforded them this potential opportunity. The federal government's underwriting of community efforts, however, also brought with it risks. Challenging the racial or political status quo could (and did) result in the withdrawal of funding, as well as provide direct and indirect channels for municipal powerbrokers to control programs.

Funding black self-determination organizations and initiatives in the 1960s and 1970s (and even now) presented quandaries. How were activists in the Black Power era to financially sustain their struggles? The Black Power conferences in Newark and Philadelphia accepted corporate sponsors. Some local black nationalists and grassroots organizations received grant support from non-profit foundations such as the Ford Foundation, and black-led business ventures such as McKissick's "Soul City" in North Carolina depended on federal support.[7]

What did this all mean for Black Power? Some black activists believed that it was being co-opted, defused, or at worst anesthetized. For instance, Black Power leftists deemed McKissick a traitor, not simply for receiving funding, but also for switching his political allegiance to the Republican Party and buying into black capitalism as an end goal. Others, however, viewed corporate, non-profit, and government resources merely as a means to accomplish their agendas, and they used the money they received how they wanted. Still others believed that whatever money they received was simply their due—indeed long overdue. In other words, self-determination politics did not automatically have to mean releasing government from its responsibility to black people and communities. In fact, the question of who could access what kind of government resources spoke to the critical issues of fairness and power. White citizens benefited from government subsidies all the time, as did corporations. In both instances, they unapologetically partook in the often racially exclusive bounty of the state. Why should black people, as U.S. citizens and taxpayers, not receive government funding as well to address their needs and promote black advancement?

Barry, Treadwell, and Harvey viewed themselves as "militant pragmatists," garnering resources to advance community empowerment. And they believed that creating "viable" businesses could break down "social and class barriers" and produce "economic self-reliance among Washington's low-income Negroes." Pride Inc. touted employing 1,200 black youth, most of whom had dropped out of high school, 80 percent with police records, and 20 percent battling drugs. By June 1968, Rufus Mayfield had resigned from Pride Inc., feeling it had lost its grassroots focus, while the U.S. Conference of Mayors praised it. A year later, the ever politically attuned Barry continued his quest for government funds, in part by arguing that black neighborhoods resembled "economically underdeveloped island countr[ies]" and needed short-term aid if they were to develop businesses that ultimately did not have to rely on government support.[8]

While aware of Pride Inc.'s stated purpose, Hobson, D.C. ACT's chair, counseled caution regarding the program. He maintained that in the long run neither racial pride, nor a black-owned business that provided primarily low-wage summer or year-round jobs, could "clean up" black people's economic woes. "It should be put in perspective and not billed as a solution to what we know to be a grave and deep problem," argued Hobson. As far as he was concerned, the solution had to include opening up well-paid employment and vigorously enforcing anti-discrimination laws. Hobson also acknowledged, "We're going to have to hurt the rich to help the poor."[9] In other words, Hobson ultimately believed in the redistribution of resources and wealth. This also meant that black people had to devise solutions that did not simply focus on advancing liberal beliefs in changing individual behavior or creating black capitalists, even under the mantle of race pride. One had to attack structures of inequality, or poor people would remain poor in the nation's "last colony" and the country no matter who held power.

Attempts to achieve black political power in D.C. and elsewhere also took the form of building operational unity. In early 1968, fueled by his pan-Africanist sensibility, Carmichael stewarded such an effort in the District. On Tuesday, January 9, Carmichael hosted a closed meeting. One hundred people attended that "beautiful, very spirited" gathering of the country's first Black United Front (BUF) at the New School for African American Thought on 14th Street. The school sat directly across the street from SNCC headquarters. The BUF had precursors in the 1930s' National Negro Congress, Malcolm X's politics, the Los Angeles–based Black Congress (defunct by 1969), and the Black Power conferences. "We invited *evrahbody* [sic]," Carmichael recalled—the NAACP, Washington Urban League,

SCLC, CORE, NOI, youth, Masons, and the black Greek and community organizations. Among the attendees were Barry, Hobson, Hare, Rev. Phillips, Stone, and a black woman named Willie J. Hardy, whom Carmichael described as "a tough, respected community leader."[10]

Carmichael held the BUF's founding meeting in D.C. because he knew the place. As a college student, he had joined the Nonviolent Action Group at Howard University. He had built his activist toolkit with the help of Hobson, "who had schooled" him and other student activists "in direct action," and through subsequent campaigns, Carmichael had also met Rustin, Richardson, and Malcolm X.[11] Finally, Carmichael believed that "the Capital" presented "the clearest contradictions of black and white in America." Given this, he said, "Washington must begin to represent to people around the world what this country is all about."[12]

One month later, the Kerner Commission released its report on national civil disorders. Specifically spurred by the racial disturbances of 1967, the commission recognized the harrowing daily conditions propelling black people to rise up, and declared that the United States "is moving toward two societies, one black, one white—separate and unequal." Truth be told, race and white supremacy had produced social distance and oppression, if not always rigidly spatial segregation, since the country's founding. The report actually acknowledged this by noting that "racial violence was present almost from the beginning of the American experience."[13]

The Kerner Commission also acknowledged how the post–World War II "revolution of rising expectations" led to feelings of hope and ultimately betrayal.[14] In particular, the commission honed in on economic and social inequalities in cities. Yet, even in recognizing "the major unsolved questions," including the "failure of direct action" to transform schools, "slum housing," and "police brutality" among other issues, the report deftly shifted blame away from unfair systems to the community's "social disorganization." The report maintained: "The culture of poverty that results from unemployment and family breakup generates a system of ruthless, exploitative relationships within the ghetto." It continued: "Prostitution, dope addiction, and crime create an environmental 'jungle' characterized by personal insecurity and tension. Children growing up under such conditions are likely participants in civil disorder."[15] The reproof about ignoring structural inequality seemed quite appropriate here.

King and the SCLC focused on just that when organizing the multiracial Poor People's Campaign. They labored to bring to light economic inequality, as well as poor people's hardships and humanity. Initially proposed by Marian Wright Edelman, then director of the NAACP Legal Defense and Education Fund, the Poor People's Campaign ignited people's fervor. Willie J. Hardy, the feisty D.C. resident, mother, and grassroots activist, was one of them. Her activism bears witness to the ways in which urban, women's, anti-poverty, home rule, and local and national black liberation struggles overlapped during the Black Power era.

Hardy was one of 16 children. She was born in St. Louis in 1922. Her mother, Willie V. Dixon White, was born in Aberdeen, Mississippi, and she moved to D.C.

with her husband James in the year of the great stock market crash. James worked as a carpenter, and the elder Willie taught sewing and canning at the Nannie Helen Burroughs School in D.C. in the 1930s, and drove a truck to and from the school's farm in Maryland. The elder Willie also volunteered at the juvenile court, mended clothes for youth, served as PTA president, and formed the first Junior Civic Association in D.C. For Hardy, her mother's example and people's daily pains and needs inspired her activism. A mother of seven, Hardy founded the Metropolitan Community Aid Council in the early 1960s.[16] The council operated with a few dedicated staff and volunteers including her own children who helped out in the office after school. The organization provided emergency shelter, clothing, and services to those in need, including job placement.[17] By the mid-to-late 1960s Hardy had become a well-recognized advocate for welfare recipients and public housing tenants.

The only black woman on the BUF's steering committee in March 1968, Hardy readied herself for the poor people's "camp-in." Other Black Power apostles also supported the campaign—some with words, others through participation, still others by merely remaining neutral. Carmichael fell into the latter category.[18] In a *Washington Post* article, Hardy expressed her views on Black Power. "For hundreds of years you've taught me to be patient and wait," she explains of white society, "but as soon as I say I won't wait any longer, you tell me I'm violent." Hardy, as did many Black Power advocates, bristled at the hypocrisy of white critics who seemed to ignore white terror against black people while counseling black patience.[19]

For her, Black Power was not anti-white, nor did it equal violence. Black Power meant black people in leadership roles. It meant white people speaking "with [black people] and not for [black people]." It meant launching an assertive, frontal battle for power and equality—"the kind that goes deeper than laws and legislation." Hardy said, "We want power to participate, to make decisions." Hardy's protestations against the narrow and negative presumptions bound up in the words Black Power reflected debates prevalent at that time.[20] Before Hardy and others, however, could march with King in D.C., a white assassin's bullet felled him. Two days later, Hardy remarked: "When white America killed the father of non-violence," it amounted to "a declaration of war."[21]

Just six weeks after King's assassination, people from across the country converged in the District. It was a rainy Sunday, May 12, 1968, Mother's Day. Organized by the National Welfare Rights Organization (NWRO), the Mother's Day march served as a prelude to the Poor People's Campaign. There, in the stadium of the historic Cardozo High School, Coretta Scott King joined Ethel Kennedy, the wife of presidential candidate Robert F. Kennedy; Johnnie Tillmon, NWRO chair; Etta Horn, first vice chair of NWRO and chair of the D.C. affiliate; and many others.[22] Together, they rallied for women's power and the power of mothers, and laid bare the obscenity of physical and economic violence. Coretta Scott King described violence against poor and minority people as "routine" in the United States where children face starvation, cultures are suppressed, medical needs are ignored, and there is contempt for those impoverished. She rallied for jobs, a guaranteed income, and the repeal of President Nixon's freeze on the welfare budget. "In America, we say that every individual is entitled to life, liberty, and the pursuit of happiness," Coretta Scott King stated, continuing, "To translate this into simpler language, everybody has a right to live."[23]

A day after the Mother's Day March, campaigners erected plywood shanties on the Washington Mall, establishing Resurrection City. Suffering incessant rain downpours and the accompanying mess of mud, the "tent city" within the "colony" in the capital of the nation dramatized poverty. On May 25 at Terrell Junior High—the same school at which Pride Inc. had held its orientation almost seven months prior—24 black women campaigners from other cities met with about 50 poor and moderate-income black women residing in the District. They agreed on a range of problems: "welfare laws, poverty, lack of consumer protection, unemployment, daycare centers, discrimination."[24] Not surprisingly, however, they differed on the strategies for change. Their suggestions reflected the continuum of activists and thinking in the Black Power era.

Some argued that change would come from promoting black inclusion and garnering decision-making power. Others like Andrea Hill from the National Council of Negro Women (in seeming contrast to the early stance of NCNW's leader Dorothy Height) believed the "American dream [was] one great big nightmare." Echoing the critique of Malcolm X, Hill argued for building independent black economic and political power. Still others such as Miami activist Mae Rene Christian maintained the system was so "sick" it needed to be destroyed and remade. The Black Women of Washington, an informal group of black women made up of housewives as well as government, welfare, and poverty workers (including Hardy and Roena Rand, a former Freedom Rider and the D.C. CORE leader after Hobson), issued their critiques against black people who "made it" for "turning their backs on the poor." Another woman, leveling a critique of class and status politics within the black community, maintained: "Some of the Negro people here are in places where they can change things for the poor. They sit on the same boards as the white establishment. It's time they stopped sitting on their furs and realized we're all black sisters. We've got to find out what the poor want, and stop telling them what they ought to want."[25]

For the most part, the demands of marchers went unmet. For days on end, the conferees visited federal officials, as well as held issue-specific rallies. While some experienced measures of sympathy and limited successes, others encountered the literal force of the state—police and jail.[26] On June 19 or "Juneteenth," solidarity marchers rallied at the Lincoln Memorial. It was just one day after Coretta Scott King's fifteenth wedding anniversary. She delivered a strident message with her children aged 12, 10, 7, and 5 looking on. She told the government "to stop uttering 'pious platitudes and faulty promises' to the poor," called for a campaign of conscience, and told women to "unite to produce a solid block of womanpower" in order to save the nation's soul.[27]

Five days later, the federal government refused to extend the SCLC permit and ordered the park police to tear down Resurrection City. By 1969—after the Poor People's Campaign ended and "normalcy" returned to D.C.—home rule struggles entered a new phase. During a March news conference, Stone, Rev. Jesse Anderson, and Rev. Doug Moore read from a prepared statement: "Statehood for the District of Columbia is a natural right which can no longer be denied and must be achieved by whatever means necessary by the people."[28] Moore was also a BUF member with Stone and Hardy.

A vigorous movement for D.C. statehood, however, did not happen until some two years later, when black radicals Hobson and Josephine Butler shepherded the establishment of the Statehood Party. Butler moved to D.C. in the 1940s. A laundry worker and labor organizer, Butler was blacklisted from government employment opportunities in 1949 because of her leftist associations. She left the Democratic Party after the crackdowns on anti-war and civil rights protesters by police at the Democratic Convention in Chicago. As D.C. CORE chair, Hobson had led campaigns for open housing and fair rental housing and challenged police brutality. He opposed segregation in the Washington Hospital Center by "climbing into a hospital bed in a white ward and refusing to leave."[29] He spearheaded a rat campaign by threatening to release rats in white sections of D.C.[30] He also sued Carl F. Hansen, the superintendent of D.C. schools, to challenge the tracking system, or what Rimsky Atkinson, vice chair of D.C. ACT, called the "scarlet mockery of the 1954 Supreme Court decision."[31] The D.C. case raised the question of how to dismantle de facto segregation or, quite frankly, whether that should be the primary concern in increasingly black cities. Instead, Hobson focused on the type and quality of education black students received. In 1967 the court ordered under-enrolled white schools to open to students from over-crowded black schools, and abolished the tracking system.[32] In 1968, Hobson was elected to the D.C. school board.

Three years later, Butler and Hobson founded the D.C. Statehood Party and focused on running their candidates for elected offices in the District.[33] Similar attempts to establish such political third parties had been tried from Detroit to Lowndes County. D.C. Statehood advocates, too, desired more than municipal representation through existing parties, and they were keenly aware that D.C. still had no elected official in the Senate, or a vote in the House of Representatives even with a sitting delegate.[34] According to Sam Smith, a white journalist and former participant in the statehood movement, the demands for statehood exceeded those of the Free D.C. Movement: "Decentralist, environmentally committed, strong for human freedom and against the abuse of power, the early Statehooders, led by Julius Hobson—who would never rest his faith on the election of some benevolent ruler—perceived the need to define home rule as more than a mere transfer of power."[35] At one time an aggressive demand, home rule had become the moderate choice by the early 1970s.

After years of grassroots protest and political and economic jockeying, D.C.'s Home Rule Act passed in 1973 and was approved in a special referendum in 1974. That year, when Nixon resigned in disgrace over Watergate, black and white District residents elected their first mayor and city council. Walter Washington, the first mayor-commissioner, became D.C.'s first elected mayor. And at least three community activists on the continuum of Black Power became city council members: Barry, Hardy, and Hobson. The latter had run on the Statehood ticket.

Even with home rule now granted and a Statehood Party candidate in office, the battle for self-determination and statehood itself continued. For many, such as Hobson, home rule ultimately did not go far enough, for it still left many decisions in the hands of white congressmen unsympathetic to the interests of the District's year-round residents. In May 1974 at the National Black Political Assembly convention in Little Rock, Arkansas, one particular agenda item—alongside support for African revolutionary movements, black political prisoners, and still a black third party—revealed this. It was a call for "self-determination for the District of Columbia."[36] While D.C. residents could now elect a mayor and council members, the District's budget still required congressional approval. D.C. and its black (and white) residents had secured electoral power, but it still was a District. The campaign for statehood would remain an issue into the 21st century, as would economic justice for the masses of the District's black residents.[37]

Cleveland "Revolutions"

The growing number of black elected officials reflected a concrete measure of black political power. However, black electoral representation proved to be no panacea. The political realities were messier and more difficult than that. Swaying the balance of power in cities and towns across the country would take more than a sole or even a few black elected officials. For even when elected, those black mayors walked fine political lines in order to neutralize white anti-integrationists and enlist white liberal and financial support. Black politicians confronted the possibility of being crudely perceived as too racially militant by some whites, and too forgiving and cozy with white powerbrokers by black leftists. Black leftists, in fact, argued that white power elites more willingly accepted black people in municipal politics who could stymie black militancy and take the edge off of calls for black revolution. No doubt there was truth to this.

Black politicians also had to manage the divergent needs of their black constituents. Social class and ideology complicated political agendas and alliances. Being a black politician, then, brought opportunity as well as heightened scrutiny in the age of changing race relations and urban economies. In Cleveland, as in other cities, deindustrialization and disinvestment dovetailed with calls for black self-determination. The loss of white population, businesses, and tax bases dovetailed with demands for black community control and economic stability. Cleveland had a 15.5 percent unemployment rate, which was over six times that of the country. These urban realities, unsurprisingly, created in the words of Donny Hathaway "trying times."

Cleveland luckily escaped the uprisings immediately following King's assassination, and city officials wanted it to stay that way. Initiated in April 1968, Cleveland Now! seemingly offered the best strategy for redevelopment, community control, and "racial peace."[38] Stokes's "centerpiece" program aimed to improve housing, employment, youth services, and the health and welfare of residents in 10 years.[39] But the program still had to contend with tensions born of residential segregation, strained police–community relations, and employment discrimination including a lack of access to police and civil service jobs. In just three months, sparked by an armed confrontation between black militants and police, the Glenville section of Cleveland erupted and shattered the presumption of racial peace that accompanied Stokes's election. At the center of this turbulent Glenville affair was Fred "Ahmed" Evans and the Republic of New Libya.

Born in Greenville, South Carolina, in 1931, the young Fred Evans moved to the east side of Cleveland in the mid-1930s with his family. Like Carl Stokes, Evans dropped out of high school and made his way to the army in 1948. Evans had what some would consider a spotty military career, which included hard labor as punishment for striking his commanding officer. But other fed-up black men also struck out against fellow and commanding military officers, including Robert F. Williams and future Kansas Panther Felix "Pete" O'Neal Jr. In that sense, Evans's response was not all that remarkable. After the military, Evans worked for the Pennsylvania Railroad. The 1959 lynching of Mack Charles Parker moved Evans, who became intensely aware of racialized violence and, alongside his military experiences, the power of the state and its support of racist sensibilities. In 1962, after claiming to see a UFO at 79th and Kinsman, Evans began studying astrology. He was 33 years old.[40]

Two years later, Evans joined the Republic of New Libya and took the name "Ahmed." By 1966, he became its leader. Lecturing on history, culture, economics, and self-determination, Evans opened the African Cultural Shop in March 1967 in Glenville. Outside, he hung a red, green, and black liberation flag, a lasting symbol of Garveyism and the UNIA. Over the next year, a series of troubling incidents marked Evans's life: police harassment, loss of his cultural shop for nonpayment of rent, and eviction from his Glenville apartment. People thought him a tad off-kilter. His publicly expressed belief in armed revolution may not have helped matters, but he was not as out there as some may have thought—at least not on that question.

Revolution was in the air. Numerous white and black radical activists—men and women—believed that revolution just might require picking up the gun. Some black leftists felt such an approach sometimes failed to accurately assess the particular political conditions of the United States and romanticized gun barrel politics. Even so, groups like the Freedom Fighters had a self-defense rifle club. RAM had an underground arm, and so did the Black Panther Party. A radical offshoot of the white leftist Students for a Democratic Society (SDS), the Weath-ermen talked about forming "a white fighting force" and preparing for the armed struggle.[41] Anti-colonial struggles worldwide whether in Kenya, Algeria, Cuba, China, or Vietnam did not happen sans force or pressure. Whether similar revo-lutions were deemed realistic or not in the United States, the mere idea of black people with guns, exhortations of revolution, and threats of urban unrest were enough to compel government responses, including the crushing power of local police forces and J. Edgar Hoover's FBI.

As the story goes Evans supposedly traveled to Detroit and Pittsburgh around July 22, 1968, to purchase weapons that he stockpiled in his Glenville apart-ment on Lakeview and Auburndale. The police put the apartment under public police surveillance. Drawing on the account of Cleveland police sergeant Bosie Mack, Mayor Stokes recounted in his political autobiography *Promises of Power* the build-up to the Glenville uprising of 1968: Word on the street had it that Evans was planning a major assault on the police, who supposedly received the news two weeks prior to the scheduled event—July 23, 1968. Evans, too, suspected an assault, but from police. Sgt. Mack had asked the police department to provide a moving detail to watch Evans.[42] When Evans saw the stationary police cars, the situation escalated. Shortly thereafter gunfire erupted between those inside the house and police.

The "Glenville shootout" had begun. In the end, three police officers and three New Libya members lay dead and a community in turmoil. The 38-year-old Evans eventually surrendered and a jury convicted him of multiple counts of first-degree murder in May 1969. He received the death penalty and subsequently a stay of execution as his lawyers Stanley E. Tolliver and Charles W. Fleming fought for a new trial. Evans died in the Ohio State Penitentiary before he could either be executed or freed.[43] According to historian Yohuru Williams, the "violent con-frontation between black militants and police in the city of Cleveland . . . would serve as a catalyst for congressional investigations into the [Black Panther] party between 1969 and 1971." In Detroit, black radicals wrote about the Cleveland incident in the leftist *Inner City Voice*. The title of the article on Evans and the Glenville shootout was: "Was July 23 Part of the White Power Conspiracy?"[44]

In the aftermath of the shootout, Glenville exploded. In the midst of the melee, police–community relations further devolved. Reports included stories of police cornering and fondling black women in a local tavern, beating and shooting black men, and firing bullets in the black community that forced residents to stay home or duck for cover while on the streets.[45] As a child, East Cleveland resident Angela Benson remembers riding in the car with her family through the epicenter at 125th and Superior. "And I can remember the police on the loudspeakers saying, 'Don't get out of your cars. Stay this place, stay that place,'" recalled Benson, con-tinuing: "I can remember seeing cars overturned burning. . . . I saw people getting shot down in the middle of the street. My dad had to pull under a streetlight. He made us all lay down on the floor of the car." Finally a police officer driving by told them "to go." Benson said, "I can remember going home and we were just like, 'Oh my God, what did we just experience?'"[46]

In an effort to quell the disturbance, which resulted in 63 businesses destroyed and $2.6 million in damage, Mayor Stokes pulled white police officers out of the black neighborhood. He, then, turned to black police (who only were 165 out of a total force of 2,186), and black nationalist leaders—called the Mayor's Committee—to calm the area.[47] Baxter Hill (who ran Pride Inc. in Cleveland), DeForest Brown, and Harllel Jones led the patrols. They all had avowed in their own ways black pride and nationalism, economic self-determination, and armed self-defense.[48]

They, too, represented the new breed of leaders that Adam Clayton Powell had described in 1967. On October 9, 1968, the *Cleveland Press* newspaper echoed this language, saying the hallmark of "new breed ghetto leaders" was their search for black self-determination today, not tomorrow. The newspaper article continued: "They have tired of the long, slow road toward an integrated society of black and white together, which liberal whites and moderate Negroes have been trying to open. They feel they don't have time to sit by and wait for white persons to accept Negroes as equals while the masses of the black poor remain in the ghetto."[49]

The slogan, "Be black, think black, and act black" served as a mobilizing and unifying mantra. In Cleveland, grassroots committees such as those focused on hospital grievances, the Tenants Union, and the Welfare Rights Movement not only formed, but also united into a Poor People's Partnership. Jones was elected its leader. As described in a 1966 *Cleveland Press* newspaper article, these activists were less concerned about accessing economic or housing opportunities for a few middle-class black people. "The issue to them is . . . whether a mother and children on relief have to live with rats and whether the black youth who isn't educated in his ghetto school will have some place to go other than a street corner."[50]

DeForest Brown, who had dropped out of East Tech High School, was a community organizer. He grew up in Cleveland's central neighborhood and had held numerous low-wage jobs such as a hauler of ice and coal, a painter, and a hospital maintenance worker. Eventually he became an anti-poverty program employee working with unemployed high school dropouts and youth. Brown augured that "self-determination or nationalism is beginning to replace the civil rights stage in the black community. . . . This recognizes that the ghetto is where we live and where we should center our efforts." And yet he did not imagine black nationalism as being at odds with integration. Improvements of black people's everyday conditions laid the groundwork for power sharing, respect, and integration. He continued: "Integration will come only when my street is good enough so you'll want to live on it."[51]

DeForest Brown became executive director of the Hough Area Development Corporation (HADC), which formed in 1967 to keep tabs on how urban renewal and anti-poverty money was spent in black communities. The HADC graduated to piloting an economic development project with a Cleveland Now! grant, and eventually became the "most well-funded" community development corporation in the nation. It received a $1.5 million OEO grant in the same month as the Glenville uprising in July 1968. According to historian Nishani Frazier, HADC privileged collective wealth over purely free market principles and individual entrepreneurship.[52]

In its work as an all-black development corporation, HADC benefited from Operation Black Unity's (OBU) picketing campaigns at four McDonald's restaurants in Cleveland in July 1969. The Afro Set's Harllel Jones primarily led the protests. One of 11 children, Jones, later known as Harllel X, admired Malcolm X. As had HADC, Jones also secured a Cleveland Now! grant with which he founded the Project Afro University, or Afro Set, in 1968 at 81st and Superior.[53] Like Evans's African Cultural Shop, Afro Set hung outside its storefront building a red, green, and black flag, and painted the walls inside the same colors. The cultural nationalist center sold African art; it also employed youth and educated them about Garvey, Lumumba, Robert F. Williams, and Malcolm X. Jones himself taught a class entitled "The Search for Human Dignity."[54]

At the time of OBU's picketing campaigns, McDonald's corporation had a policy against establishing black-owned franchises. HADC and OBU wanted this changed. In this effort, Stokes collaborated with local black nationalists. He not only counseled OBU and HADC, but also intervened with corporate leaders on their behalf. Continuous grassroots pressure and these operational alliances ultimately resulted in HADC becoming the first all-black entity in the country to own a McDonald's franchise. HADC's success was short-lived, however. The alliances fractured over whether to advance individual black entrepreneurs or black communal ownership and wealth. The former group won out. The question remained, then, whether the current economic system really could work, and if it could, for whom.[55]

By the time of the 1968 Glenville uprising and the 1969 picketing campaigns at McDonald's, Jones was no newbie to local activism. He had already gained notoriety as a "tall, slim, goateed and belligerent" 20-something-old, alongside Robinson of the Freedom Fighters, during the Hough uprising in 1966.[56] Back then Jones lived at 97th and Hough, worked for Cleveland's division of water pollution, and served as a lieutenant in Robinson's JFK House, just seven blocks away from where the Afro Set would open.

The black grassroots patrols led by Hill, Jones, and Brown in the wake of the Glenville shootout brought relative, but not total, peace to the neighborhood. The melee continued. Under mounting pressure, Mayor Stokes dismissed the black nationalist patrols, deployed the National Guard, instituted a curfew, and sent in "integrated" police patrols comprised of one black and two white officers.[57]

While Stokes had attacked Evans as "a loud neurotic who enjoyed having followers," the mayor did not hold all black militants in the same negative esteem. His measure seemed to be whether he could work with them.[58] Stokes wrote in *Promises of Power* that Jones "was disciplined in the way that Bernadette Devlin and the Irish Republican Army are disciplined." He continued: "Men like Harllel are not to be understood in the simple-minded sensationalism of crime journalism, but in acknowledging the abiding and deeply personal willingness to die that is common to the real leaders of any oppressed people."[59] Stokes continued: "People who do not live under the oppressed conditions of the ghetto simply cannot comprehend the force such a man develops, nor can they understand that that man has to be understood as a member of a social force, not as a criminal."[60]

Within a matter of a couple years, Afro Set had established a fairly robust chapter in Columbus, Ohio, which the police department's intelligence unit or Red Squad kept under surveillance. Afro Set members openly carried guns and, particularly in Cleveland, "had a reputation" among law enforcement not as leaders of oppressed black people but "as the most vicious gang roaming the streets of the city's east side."[61] Allegedly as part of their neighborhood clean-up campaigns— or what the FBI called shakedowns—the Cleveland Afro Set targeted prostitutes and addicts and in Columbus they allegedly staged bank robberies. While Stokes described Jones—who he knew was dangerous— "as a valued ally," law enforcement viewed Jones simply as a criminal, a trainer of black urban guerrillas, and the Afro Set as "almost a black version of the Mafia."[62]

Jones expressed no love lost for police or white people generally. In March 1969, as a featured speaker at the esteemed City Club, he told the audience that white people had no basis for critiquing black nationalism: "Black Nationalism . . . is black people trying to do for themselves what white people have failed to do—get them out of poverty and misery."[63] He believed that "civil rights [was] a big hoax." Continued Jones: "We are trying to create black business, a black police force, a city within a city and a nation within a nation." Redeploying a commonly heard conservative response—"if you don't like it here go back to Africa"—to black people's critiques of U.S. racial politics and exclusion, Jones countered with "if you don't like what we are doing, go back to Europe."[64]

This similar attitude led Jones to critique the Black Panther Party for organizing with white people.[65] The Oakland-based Panthers, while primarily addressing the problems of poor black people in cities, upheld the tenet of "all power to the people." In 1968 entering the arena of electoral politics, Eldridge Cleaver ran for president of the United States on an interracial Peace and Freedom Party ticket with the white Chicago grassroots activist Peggy Terry. She left SDS's JOIN to run as his vice president, and across the country Black Panthers built coalitions with white radicals. In Chicago, 21-year-old Fred Hampton (who was murdered with Mark Clark in a joint Chicago police and FBI counterintelligence program operation) initiated the original Rainbow Coalition, bringing together the Illinois Black Panthers with the Puerto Rican Young Lords, white Appalachian-born Young Patriots, and Rising Up Angry, a cadre of middle-class white youth from Chicago's north side co-founded by Mike James (also formerly of SDS's JOIN).[66] While not to Jones's liking, the Oakland-based Black Panther Party would profoundly inspire cadres of young people in the United States and internationally.

These varied Cleveland revolutions profoundly bespoke the explosive potential of decades of black disappointment. During these times, Stokes's mayoral appeal and political cache waned. Moreover, the discovery that Evans too had received a $10,000 grant from Cleveland Now! and, as rumors had it, had purchased the weapons used in the shootout with those funds, resulted in attacks on the program. Efforts mounted to cut Stokes's budget, a campaign that Jones described as "a racist move directed against a black mayor." During his City Club presentation, Jones stated: "Look at the vote—it was almost all black councilmen for the funds and almost all white councilmen for cutting the budget while people are living in rat traps and the city has all kinds of problems."[67] A multi-million dollar budget, aimed at addressing the concrete demands of Cleveland's black citizens, was in jeopardy. Stokes might have been mayor, but the debate over municipal budgets (like in D.C.) raised questions about where real power resided, and what it meant to really shake up the political and economic status quo.

These questions of power raised not only the specter of racial politics, but also social class. Stokes's plans for income tax reform spurred concern among white businesses and white suburbanites who worked in Cleveland but lived elsewhere, and his hopes for scattered low-income housing provoked opposition from black middle-class residents.[68] They wondered how their neighborhood, which as they argued already struggled to provide adequate services, would be able to support low-income residents—residents whom some deemed unworthy because they received government subsidies. It revealed the existence of notions of cultural deficiency that shaped class politics within the black community, as well as the tenuous nature of black economic stability.[69]

Shrinking blue-collar job markets, and residential discrimination amplified the challenges of securing prosperity in black communities. Black politicians and residents had to navigate rigid status quo politics. Intransigent white employers, unresponsive unions, and negative assumptions about welfare policies also undermined black economic security. Given this, battles for economic repair and power took divergent forms including creating capitalist enterprises and business cooperatives, transforming labor and economic relations, and calling for the dismantling of capitalism and its oligarchy of corporate and political power. While these economic battles burgeoned in places across the country, they conspicuously escalated in the increasingly black industrial city of Detroit.

Battles for Economic Repair and Power

Detroit was a hotbed of Black Power era militancy. The city was home to a diverse group of black radicals and power activists including the Boggses, Richard and Milton Henry, and Rev. Cleage. It was there that events spawned during the year of the Black Revolt in 1963. And numerous harbingers of the Black Power era participated in political events held in Detroit, including Powell, Richardson, Malcolm X, Stanford, and Freeman. Black militants in Detroit also convened the short-lived Organization for Black Power.

In March 1968, as the Poor People's Campaign ramped up, the Henry brothers brought together hundreds of people to consider the creation of a sovereign black nation in the South's Black Belt. Echoes of the Communist Party's 1928 Black Belt thesis were stark. The Henry brothers' activism grew out of their black radical roots and relationships in Detroit. As members of GOAL, they helped organize the grassroots leadership conference featuring Malcolm X in 1963, as well as co-founded Detroit's short-lived, all-black Freedom Now Party. Five years later, the Henry brothers believed that justice could not be had under the U.S. government, not even through an all-black independent third party. Ultimately, black people needed to govern their own territory. This did not necessitate relocating to a homeland outside the United States as in Garvey's Back-to-Africa call or becoming an expatriate. Neither did it simply mean politically managing the "ghetto." Their call for a sovereign black nation even went beyond either establishing a black town (as the Kansas Exodusters attempted in the late 19th century and as McKissick would attempt in the 1970s with "Soul City"), or receiving recognition as a fifty-first state within the United States as with the D.C. statehood movement.

The Republic of New Afrika (RNA) sought self-determination as racial separatism achieved through spatial sovereignty. Influenced by a blend of cultural nationalism, resonant with the Nation of Islam's territorial stances, and Malcolm X's and Robert F. Williams's self-defense and internationalist philosophies, the RNA sought claims to U.S. land. This included the right to defend black people and establish a self-sufficient economy based on a Tanzanian socialist model of cooperation. After all, black people had built the wealth of the U.S. nation, and as far as RNA leaders were concerned, black people not only deserved freedom and political self-determination, but also were owed financial repair in the form of the wealth and the land that they helped to make profitable. The political handprints of Queen Mother Moore were present as well, including her knowledge of the Black Belt thesis and beliefs in black self-determination and reparations. In fact, she maintained that RNA was born out of an idea she had proposed but initiated much sooner than she would have suggested.[70]

Changing their names to Imari (Richard) and Gaidi (Milton) Obadele, the Henry brothers wrote a declaration of independence, became RNA's citizens, and requested recognition from the U.S. State Department. They then demanded $400 billion, partly in land in the Black Belt including Mississippi, Alabama, Louisiana, South Carolina, and Georgia. The State Department ignored them, but the RNA refused to give up. As a next step, they established a settlement in Jackson, Mississippi, and a provisional government that revealed their ideological influences and inspirations.[71] Queen Mother Moore was one of the first to sign the declaration of the provisional government. Still in exile, Robert F. Williams became honorary first president, Gaidi Obadale first vice president, and Betty Shabazz (Malcolm X's widow) second vice president.

In New York, RNA held gatherings at Mt. Addis Ababa on 254 acres of undeveloped land in the Catskills. Queen Mother Moore served as president of the Mt. Addis Ababa Corporation that owned the land, and her sister Loretta Langley served as secretary-treasurer. Concerned with the impact of automation on black people, Queen Mother Moore viewed land and the skills connected to land as sources of economic self-sufficiency and power. RNA's minister of health and welfare, Moore secured funding from the New York Board of Education to sponsor a youth camp there. A white journalist criticized the youth camps as indoctrination programs. Furthermore, he maintained, given RNA's revolutionary stance against the United States, accepting federal money to support its programs seemed quite contradictory. No doubt, Queen Mother Moore and RNA viewed such funding as legitimately owed to black people for generations of unpaid labor. While the under-resourced upstate New York development eventually faltered, Moore's vision had included building a school and giving "the children skills that automation could not erase—skills like soil conservation, skills like pruning trees, like landscaping, like poultry rearing, and so on," which would enable them to survive as well as share their skills with black people, including those in Africa. For the white reporter, however, such revolutionary "extremism" represented by Queen Mother Moore's Mt. Addis Ababa Corporation, RNA, Robert F. Williams, the Henry brothers, and other Black Power, "Castroite," and "Maoist" types only caught cities and working-class people in a "phantasmagorical maze."[72]

The RNA issued a call for black people to leave the false promises of the United States behind. Virginia Y. Collins (who changed her name to Dara Abu-bakari) was among those who answered. While in 1953 she thought there was hope "that maybe black and white people together could solve all the problems," by the late 1960s, she firmly declared: "I'm a separatist now." A nurse and mother of 10 children who attended segregated schools, Collins had struggled for quality education for more than 20 years. Also a member of the Women's International League for Peace and Freedom who became a vice president of the RNA, Collins argued: "The only thing you can aspire to is nationhood. We are a nation within a nation."[73] Still growing and as of yet without access to the land demanded in the early 1970s, RNA organizers, in the interim, resorted to a familiar strategy to build power. They wanted to control elected offices and the police. For them, it was part of a phased plan (not an endpoint) that they imagined would bring racial justice.

A hub of the "Big 3" auto industries, Detroit became a hot spot for black labor insurgency as well.[74] The auto plants hired black workers, but like in other industries, black laborers held the dirtiest, most dangerous, unskilled, and relatively lower wage jobs. By 1971 in the Chrysler Dodge main plant black workers represented 60 percent of the labor force, but they primarily labored on the assembly lines and in the foundries.[75] This state of affairs helped to set the stage for the emergence of the black revolutionary union movement (RUM).

The treatment of 24-year-old black worker General Gordon Baker Jr. provided the immediate spark. A Wayne State University student, Baker had co-founded with Luke Tripp UHURU on campus. Baker also knew black radicals from the *Inner City Voice* and traveled to Cuba as part of the Fair Play for Cuba Committee where they met Castro. In Detroit, Baker took a job at the Chrysler Dodge main plant, where he and four other black men walked out in sympathy with white women workers who initiated a wildcat strike in 1968. He was summarily fired—a less deadly yet financially devastating way to thwart interracial gender alliances and challenges to white corporate managers. His dismissal, however, did not end his protest. Baker joined forces with colleagues, including Chuck Wooten, grassroots organizer Marian Kramer, artist and laborer Glanton Dowdell, and Mike Hamlin of *Inner City Voice*. Together they initiated the Dodge Revolutionary Union Movement (DRUM) in May 1968. They called the plants "plantations" since whites occupied an overwhelming majority of positions of power in the United Auto Workers (UAW) union and skilled factory jobs: 99 percent of general foremen, 100 percent of superintendents, and 90 percent of skilled apprentices.[76]

In the following months, black workers at auto industry plants began forming their own RUMs. Eventually, the revolutionary union movement extended beyond the auto plants and the city of Detroit, spreading to the transit, railway, and steel industries.[77] By 1969 the RUMs cohered into the League of Revolutionary Black Workers (LRBW). They organized stoppages to fight for better jobs, pay, and safety in the plants, as well as staged protests against the UAW.

The LRBW also reached beyond shop-floor politics, primarily because of Kramer. She intentionally worked to build networks between industrial laborers and other laborers who did not work in the plants.[78] She was heavily influenced by her grassroots organizing experience in the Michigan Welfare Rights Organization, founded in 1966, and in the West Central Organization, a community-based organization that formed to fight urban renewal.[79] Often referred to as "Negro removal," urban renewal uprooted and displaced the majority of black people living in areas targeted for redevelopment. When Kramer met Baker (who became her husband) and the others, she persistently argued that mobilizing efforts should go beyond the point of production and extend into the communities where black laborers and their families lived and struggled to survive. Kramer recalled: "We were always in the streets, fighting urban renewal, organizing against slum landlords, forming tenants' unions, protecting people against police brutality, and so forth."[80]

Kramer helped tenants facing rent hikes in the Jeffries public housing complex organize against the housing authority. The Black Panthers helped as well. The strike started in early 1968 with Jeffries' residents joining those in Brewster-Douglas, Herman, and Parkside public housing complexes. Operating expenses were skyrocketing in part because of increasing managerial salaries and maintenance costs for old and poorly built public housing. To resolve this budgetary crisis, managers increased rents arbitrarily. This took place at a time when the value of real wages stagnated or decreased—a real concern if one had a job. Residents wanted less steep rent hikes, control over the majority of commissioner appointments, resident management opportunities, and jobs through the modernization program ("four and one half million dollars could lead to a lot of jobs for tenants").[81] Access to jobs was a serious issue whether in public housing or the auto industry, but it represented one strategy of economic repair and redress.

Soon after LRBW's formation, Forman made his way to Detroit. Hamlin, who had read Forman's writings, had invited him. Coincidentally, SNCC member Dorothy Dewberry also had invited Forman to speak at the National Black Economic Development Conference (NBEDC). The Interreligious Foundation for Community Organization (IFCO), a coalition of Protestant denominations that dispersed money to community organizing groups, sponsored the conference. Initially, Forman declined participation. He disagreed with IFCO's belief in capitalist solutions and had little love for religion. "Religion," he said, "fucked up my young life."[82] As a boy, white nuns told him at school "that heaven was like a city, with suburbs for the rich and slums for the poor, and you were rich or poor according to how much good you did on earth."[83] Such stories echoed the experiences of religious black women.[84] But Forman eventually decided to accept the NBEDC invitation so that he could finance his trip to Detroit. He met Hamlin and other league members, and together they drafted what became the Black Manifesto.

Before the manifesto was unveiled at the conference, however, Robert S. Browne took to the podium. He focused on increasing investment in local job creation and small business development, thereby giving voice to the hope of individual black entrepreneurship.[85] Since 1968 President Nixon had elevated the concept of black capitalism as a way to "quell and coopt 1960s black militancy," according to Robert Weems and Lewis Randolph. Black leaders' acceptance of black capitalism exposed the competing ideologies among black people seeking solutions to the pressing economic needs and inequalities shaping black life.[86]

Black capitalism proponents included McKissick and Roy Innis of CORE. McKissick formed McKissick Enterprises in 1968 and began laying the groundwork for the founding of "Soul City" in North Carolina. Innis supported "African American ownership of 'capitalist instruments'"—an idea that laid the cornerstone for the failed Senate bill on community self-determination, which called for "federally chartered community development corporations." Dunbar S. McLaurin, another black economist who owned the New York-based consulting firm Ghettonomics Inc., argued, as had revolutionary nationalists, that black communities were "underdeveloped nations." (Marion Barry argued similarly in making his case for Pride Inc.) Espousing the Ghetto Economic Development and Industrialized Plan (GHEDIPLAN), McLaurin believed that inner-city economies should be put under black control. In other words, capitalism did not need dismantling. It just needed to work for black people too.[87] All of these particular suggestions for economic reform emerged in 1969, the same year Nixon established the weak and minimally funded Office of Minority Business Enterprise. Ultimately, such black economic development strategies gained the upper hand, but Nixon's promise to deliver jobs and entrepreneurial opportunities, or black power through black capitalism, not surprisingly would go unmet.

Later that evening at the conference on April 26, Forman presented the Black Manifesto, which documented "the human misery of black people under capitalism and imperialism" and provided what it deemed a reasonable solution: "All control of church money should be placed in the hands of those opposed to capitalism and dedicated to building a socialist society, a cooperative society, a communal society."[88] He labeled black people who promoted "all types of schemes for black capitalism" as "black power pimps and fraudulent leaders."[89] He no doubt was referring to, at the very least, Innis, McKissick, and maybe Browne, who had just spoken earlier.

As Forman spoke, his intensity increased. He made common cause with Africa *and* criticized African leaders who were "duped into following the lines as laid out by western imperialist governments." He indicted the United States as "the most barbaric country in the world," and maintained "time is short." Continuing, he said: "Caution is fine, but no oppressed people ever gained their liberation until they were ready to fight, to use whatever means necessary, including the use of force and power of the gun to bring down the colonizer."[90] He linked corporate power to U.S. imperial ventures in Africa, Asia, and Latin America, particularly comparing General Motors's operation and labor practices in apartheid South Africa with white UAW leadership and its treatment of black workers in the United States. Forman argued that wealth must be taken out of the hands of "rich white exploiters and racists who run this world" such as the DuPonts, Rockefellers, Mellons, Chrysler, and Ford, redistributed, and controlled by the state for the benefit "of all people."[91]

Finally, came the piece de resistance, maybe for some the coup de grace—the Black Manifesto's concrete demands. The Black Manifesto, which demanded reparations for black exploitation, discussed the roots of U.S. wealth; the relationship between racism, class inequality, imperialism, and militarism; and the structural impediments to black economic success. Then Forman outlined the demands. They wanted money to implement a program to establish alternative, oppositional institutions controlled by and to benefit poor black people. This included a research center on the problems of black people; a training center for community organizing and communications; four television networks based in Detroit, Chicago, Cleveland, and Washington, D.C.; four publishing and printing businesses based in Detroit, Atlanta, New York, and Los Angeles; a southern land bank to seed cooperative farms; money to work with the National Welfare Rights Organization to mobilize welfare recipients; and a Black Labor Strike and Defense Fund.[92] To achieve this he asked for $500 million in reparations—a drop in the bucket compared to RNA's demand of $400 billion—but as Forman said provocatively, it was more than reasonable at "fifteen dollars a nigger."[93] The phrasing no doubt evoked the auction block.

Eight days later, the strategy—to begin interrupting church services to present the Black Manifesto—came to fruition. The first stop: May 4, 1969, at Riverside Church in New York, the same church at which Dr. King had delivered his anti-war address. Forman began thinking about Christians as architects of slavery and as rapists of black women. He viewed the founding fathers as people who dehumanized black people and enshrined inequality in the U.S. Constitution through the three-fifths clause. As he "mounted the steps of Riverside Church and walked into the monument to 'Christianity' that John D. Rockefeller had built with the millions he stole from poor people, the millions he made with oil stolen from the earth—the people's earth," he became even more emotional. He thought about "the temple of the liars" in which he included "quick-talking, double-dealing John F. Kennedy, Lyndon Bloodbath Johnson, Richard Tricky Dicky Milhous Nixon, and Funky Spiro Agnew—all these Americans who prayed to their white gods, their white popes, their white Billy Grahams, their white sweet lord Jesus, while they sent napalm to burn our sisters and brothers in Vietnam."[94] Then he delivered the Black Manifesto, stunning the clergy and congregants. Within a week Riverside Church leaders warned that anyone who "interfered with a worship service" would face a civilian restraining order. But they also acknowledged the need "for rapid improvement" of disadvantaged people's conditions. They, however, would offer the programs, not give millions of dollars to Black Manifesto leaders.[95]

The Black Manifesto was not the first, nor would it be the last, call for reparations. It joined a tradition of seeking economic repair for the unjust seizure of black labor and wealth in slavery and "freedom." Such realities had led individuals and organizations, across generations, such as Callie House and those in the ex-slave pension association, the Nation of Islam, and Queen Mother Moore, to ask for compensatory damages. Moreover, just as Moore had criticized RNA, she too expressed a measure of disapproval of the Black Manifesto. Moore argued that Forman neither consulted her as "the source" of the modern-day reparations struggle, nor did he take into account the needs of future generations when issuing his pecuniary demands.[96] Her rationale revealed the links and ruptures between activist generations, as well as the way in which black women nationalists as architects were also at times invisible in the struggle.

Reparations struggles also reflected black people's enduring quest for material resources, economic security, and land. Fannie Lou Hamer started her Freedom Farm on 40 acres near Ruleville, Mississippi, in 1969, primarily to produce vegetables to feed poor black families and cash crops such as cotton and soybeans to help subsidize the cost. The farm incorporated and added 640 more acres of property in Drew, Mississippi, but this black-controlled enterprise was a rough row to hoe. Incorporated as a non-profit a couple years later, Freedom Farm struggled to earn enough to underwrite its collective ownership, subsistence, and social service goals for Sunflower County's black poor.[97] Returning to the South and abandoning the cities such as Detroit, which Rosa Parks called "the northern promised land that wasn't," however, was not totally desirable or fully feasible, especially given the numbers of people, finances, and racial politics of place.[98] Black people's battle for land would remain as arduous inside the South as it would outside of it. Moreover, one just could not forget that the majority of black people now were city folks.

Survival and Fatigue Coast to Coast

Days before the rallying cry of Black Power, Baltimore's Mother Rescuers from Poverty formed in June 1966. Margaret "Peggy" McCarty, "a citizen who [had] a job to do," served as its first chair.[99] Not a Black Power organization but operating in the era of urban power struggles, Mother Rescuers was a part of a broader grassroots chorus demanding dignity, rights, and economic and political power for poor people in the city. As I have previously written, these struggles for survival expressed "a localized parlance of power politics."[100] Such agendas included the basics—affordable housing, employment, income or money to support families, health care, and good schools, as well as representation and voice—and drew on the support of different struggles including Black Power. Local campaigns also reaffirm the critical roles that women played in advancing survival coast to coast. McCarty's activist journey, among others, provides one rich example.

As a child, Peggy McCarty hailed from Virginia, where her family took in laundry. McCarty recalled, "We children would stomp the clothes" in tubs of water before the beating and scrubbing on a washboard. While the children had fun "playing" in the water, laundry work did not pay well. "My parents brought me to Baltimore," she said. "They felt like they needed a change because in Virginia there were no opportunities for black people to have a better life." In Baltimore they stayed in a small, dark, and dreary house on Low Street on the east side. But her father could not find work, so she and her brother went back to Virginia to stay with their grandparents until their parents came back for them. They were back and forth for a while until her dad secured a job at Bethlehem Steel and then did a stint in the military, where as she recalled: "[T]here was a lot of prejudice, a lot of hardship for them 'cause my father would talk to my mother about it. He wasn't happy." Home from the marines, her father went back to work for Bethlehem Steel only to lose his job again. That's when her mother went to work outside the home.[101]

Times grew hard. "We had to ask for charity from the grocery store so that we could eat," McCarty said. The family grew to five children. Her mother did day work to make ends meet. Her dad, unemployed, began "drinking heavy." Then her maternal grandparents moved in and, from her memory as a child, her grandmother lavished criticism on her father and a stern hand on her grandchildren. It was a very emotional time in McCarty's life and, as she recounted the story, she began to tear up: "It was hard. Our family began to fall apart."[102] Daily survival was a challenge. While she liked school, she dropped out at age 14. That's when she became pregnant. She took a job at Read's drug store. She had her second son at age 16 and she married the father. He was 19, still young, and prone to partying. When she was pregnant with her third child, she left her husband and in order to support herself and her three children, she "had to get on welfare."[103] Her husband moved in and out, drinking and working construction and odd jobs. After two more babies, she witnessed abusive behavior toward their children and she had her husband committed for alcoholism. She said, "It was very hard for me to do that, but I wasn't going to let him abuse those children."[104]

Circumstance and serendipity brought her to Union for Jobs or Income Now (U-JOIN) and welfare rights, just as they would to the Black Panthers. The house she lived in at the time had a coal stove. She had no coal and no money for coal, so she and her two oldest sons, with their red wagon, went scavenging for fuel sources. "And there was this big sign that said, it said U-JOIN, but it said free wood and coal. I said hold on," laughing gleefully as she remembered. "I said to my son, nobody gives you anything for free. I said but we going to go in here and we going to check it out."[105] That's when she met Walter Lively, a black organizer, and two white organizers, Joan Berezin and Rusty Gilbert. U-JOIN members not only delivered the wood and coal, but they lit her furnace for her. Thus began her relationship with U-JOIN, the local SDS-ERAP initiative.[106]

In the meantime McCarty began working, but then had another child, became ill, and sought additional help from the welfare office. They told her to go back to work. She told Joan, who then asked her what she wanted to do. She replied, "Something because I'm tired of being pushed around." McCarty continued: "I think it came out of a need, a need and just sick and tired of people putting you down. Let me see what word would I want to use for that? (Pause) . . . Fatigue. I was just tired, tired of not being able to get any justice." Her strength came from years of having to stand up for her brothers and sisters and take care of her son, and her sense of powerlessness and maltreatment drove her to action. Together McCarty and Berezin made some fliers and went down to the Department of Social Services and passed them out. McCarty recalled, "[T]here were a lot of women going through what I was going through. And we had our first meeting at the U-JOIN office." They named themselves Rescuers from Poverty, McCarty said, "because that's who we were, rescuing other women from poverty."[107]

As low-income black women, they consistently contested the ridicule and disrespect they received at the hands of others, including government officials. McCarty upbraided one Maryland legislator in the newspaper. Senator Robert P. Dean (D-Queen Anne), who chaired the Legislative Council's subcommittee on welfare costs, asserted during a subcommittee hearing, "Negroes . . . have the brains of rabbits. They're all Congolese to me. They're all from the jungle." This undoubtedly was a racist ascription of savagery, one that also failed to acknowledge white power and the recent assassination of the democratically elected Congo leader Patrice Lumumba in 1961. His murder had provoked black militants to protest at the United Nations in New York City. McCarty responded: "If this were slavery times, he just might make it. . . . This is the Twentieth Century and he had better wake up."[108]

Mother Rescuers "argued the evil of insultingly low welfare grants" and demanded that they be raised. They wanted to be able to choose between jobs that provided adequate wages and the ability to be stay-at-home mothers and raise their children.[109] In December 1966 just months after the formation of the Oakland-based Black Panther Party, which eventually advocated and worked with welfare rights activists across the country, McCarty joined other low-income women welfare recipients from 11 East Coast states in Pittsburgh to form a national organization. They discussed the need for more job opportunities and training. "If people on welfare are given a better chance to get decent jobs, then the welfare roles can be reduced a lot," McCarty said. The group decided to work out the specifics at a national convention in February 1967 in Washington, D.C.[110] These meetings and actions bespeak the roots of the NWRO, which sponsored the Mother's Day March in D.C. in 1968, established scores of affiliate organizations, and would push against Nixon's Family Assistance Plan (FAP) as they battled for a guaranteed annual income that could actually support families.

Nixon's attempt to establish FAP and the NWRO's battle against it might confuse some. After all, Nixon proposed a guaranteed annual income. His proposal of $1,600 for a family of four, however, did not confuse NWRO and their allies. In most cities, except the South, $1,600 represented a substantive reduction in benefits, as well as food stamps and food distribution programs, which were already insufficient to support recipient families and children. Nixon's plan also required recipients to enroll in job training and accept employment found by caseworkers. It did not matter whether recipients found the work fulfilling or desirable, or whether it paid a living wage. NWRO felt "the bare minimum" for a guaranteed income should be $5,500. Detroit WRO activists captured the sentiment: FAP would not provide an "adequate income," "create dignity," or for that matter "justice and democracy."[111] With "Zap FAP" campaigns attacking Nixon's plan on multiple fronts, FAP died.

In Baltimore, McCarty met Black Panthers while engaged in anti-poverty and welfare rights organizing. She became friends with Baltimore Panther Charles Wyche, who was arrested in a police roundup of Panthers for allegedly torturing and murdering the 20-year-old suspected police informant Eugene Leroy Anderson. This roundup included Donald "D. C." Cox, Panther field marshal and central committee member who believed in the redistribution of wealth "so the poor people [have] power" and "we might have peace."[112] McCarty testified on Wyche's behalf, saying that he along with many others had attended her birthday party. While McCarty never formally joined a Black Power organization, she liked what Black Power "stood for: black awareness." She continued: "And I felt like black people should have power. Power to decide their own destiny, power to be involved in politics, elections." The strident, "too militant" critiques, including of police officers, is what kept her at bay—particularly because some police were kind to her and she felt that some of them, too, "were caught up in the system."[113] The immediacy of violence, including at the hands of police, could not have been easy to navigate. Given McCarty's relationship with Wyche and the attacks waged on Black Panthers, reticence (or even dissemblance) was not an unfathomable response.

Indeed, violence resulted in the injury and death of black liberation activists whether through clashes with white resisters, assassination, police brutality, urban rebellions, and even internal fracturing and counterrevolutionary violence. Local police and FBI cooperated in secret counterintelligence program operations (COINTELPRO) to intentionally spur dissension and carry out assault campaigns that resulted in the death of Black Power radicals. The Black Panther Party especially experienced enormous repression and death. This included police killing the first youth member of the Black Panther Party, 17-year-old Bobby Hutton, as well as Black Panthers Fred Hampton and Mark Clark. Police violence would remain a serious concern as branches of the Black Panther Party turned their attention and energy from armed patrols of police in black neighborhoods to establishing survival programs to meet community needs.

Like the Atlanta Project in Vine City, D.C.'s Pride Inc., Mother Rescuers from Poverty, and public housing tenant activists, the Oakland-based Black Panther Party and its affiliates strove to address the material realities of black people. They did so by dreaming up solutions and enacting projects to speak to people's bread-and-butter needs. They also sought to expose the power relations that made their survival programs necessary. Black Panther Party leaders critiqued the U.S. state and, as McCarty and Coretta Scott King had, publicized the daily and systemic marginalization of black and poor people. According to the Black Panther Party: "The people must come to understand that when we talk about moving against those who oppress us daily this is not violent. It's violent when we go [to] these fools and ask them for food and clothing for our children and they refuse, it's violent when we beg for shelter and it is denied us. Because it is the right of every man, woman and child to have the best man and technology can give."[114]

While responding to the concrete conditions of the people, the Panther Party's community programs also reflected their political ideology. The programs, in serving the people, enacted self-determination and collectivism in the fight for human rights. The Black Panthers imagined their community efforts as part of a radicalizing and revolutionary journey. The ultimate goal: dismantling imperialism, capitalism, and racism and establishing a socialist government that universally benefited what Frantz Fanon characterized as the wretched of the earth. This meant establishing alternative, oppositional institutions and supporting national liberation of Third World "colonies" inside the U.S. and globally, as well as revolutionary struggle against white hegemony.

Their militancy influenced other U.S.-based activists of color engaged in their own primarily urban-based liberation movements. Chicana/o and Native American activists, for instance, took cues from Black Power activists, particularly the Black Panther Party. The honorifics emerged through naming and programs. For instance, the Brown Berets, young Mexican-American nationalists who organized in the barrios in California, worked with gangs, against police brutality, and for education. They dubbed their struggle the Chicano Power movement. Similarly, Native Americans christened their struggle the Red Power movement. The intersections extended beyond naming. There was ideological cross-pollination as well. In San Francisco the Black Panther Party also encouraged a young group of Chinese Americans to start a revolutionary party and suggested they read the works of Che, Mao, Fanon, and Castro. Similar to the Black Panthers and other Black Power formations, the Red Guard Party, which took its name from Mao's Red Guards, minimized requests for assimilation and sought to strengthen community and cultural institutions. This represented power.[115]

As much as the Black Panther Party inspired racial pride, self-determination, and grassroots activism, its vision of society provoked tremendous resistance from the government. It also fomented a mixture of acceptance, concern at the violent media image, and even dismissal in black communities where integration remained desirable, reform still seemed plausible, and explicit public analyses of systemic inequality were scarce or vilified as anti-American.

Even so, no matter where they operated, the Panthers confronted similar bread-and-butter issues and understood that "in order to fully develop the human capital of a community, the day-to-day needs of the people must be addressed."[116] In the richest nation in the world hundreds of thousands of black children could not even afford to eat breakfast, let alone access healthcare and good schools. Following the national organizational mandate, BPP chapters across the nation established free breakfast, clothing, pest control, and busing-to-prison programs. They not only had ministers of information, culture, and defense, but they had ministers of health. Within two years, the Oakland Black Panther Party required its chapters to establish People's Free Medical Clinics, and women were at the center as administrators and staff, running the day-to-day programs. By 1972, the Panthers added to their platform the demand for free medical care for all black and oppressed people. According to Alondra Nelson, the Panthers' desire to serve the people "body and soul"—to reach them with practical programs and political knowledge that could enable change—"exposed the limits of civil and social rights for the black poor in particular."[117]

Survival first, consciousness-raising next, then, maybe "the revolution to produce a new America" could be had—that's the formula Newton articulated.[118] Seale also made clear that it was critical to address the travesties and injustices of "millions of people . . . who are living below subsistence; welfare mothers, poor white people, Mexican-Americans . . . Latinos, and black people."[119] In West Oakland, St. Augustine's Episcopal Church housed the first Free Breakfast for Children Program and parishioner Ruth Beckford-Smith oversaw it.[120] From the program's inception in 1969, party members recruited mothers on welfare, grandmothers, and guardians in the black community to help both women and men Panthers serve neighborhood children.[121]

Breakfast programs proliferated; they sprang up in Chicago, Los Angeles, Kansas City, New York City, and Des Moines, Iowa. Between 1969 and 1971, more than 35 programs fed tens of thousands of children. Black girls and boys arrived at churches and centers before school started. They sat at tables, perched for hot breakfasts that many of them previously had to do without even with a War on Poverty being fought. Black Panther Party members and community volunteers served young people sausage, eggs, toast, orange juice, and even vitamin pills.

Health inequalities were prevalent in the black community. Poor nutrition and food choices were par for the course, and impacted physical wellness. The commodification of medicine amplified racial, social, and economic inequality. Many black people received inadequate, often deplorable, medical care, or had no access to medical treatment at all. They could not afford a doctor. Others did not trust the medical establishment. Neglect, abuse, and death—these were watchwords in the black community.[122] The critiques of Gloria Richardson, Ruby Doris Smith Robinson, Gwen Patton, Julius Hobson, and so many others echo here. Panthers opened healthcare clinics across the country, in Brooklyn, Boston, Cleveland, Philadelphia, Seattle, and Chicago among other cities.[123] One of the first people's clinics or "ghetto care centers," the Bobby Hutton Community Clinic, opened in Kansas City, Missouri, in 1969.

The Kansas City BPP chapter was started by the wiry, goatee-wearing, ex-convict, 28-year-old Pete O'Neal Jr., who credited the Black Panthers' revolutionary concept with not only saving others' lives, but his own. O'Neal grew up in segregated Kansas City, dropped out of high school, and decided to enlist in the U.S. Navy instead of go to reform school. He served from 1957 to 1960, and was thrown out "after he plunged a butcher knife into another sailor's chest over an insult."[124] Sentenced to five years, he went to prison from 1960 to 1962. Learning of the Black Panthers, as well as the example of Malcolm X, helped him walk away from pimping and hustling—a life that advanced him financially (he wore $300 Italian suits), but undermined the black community's health and safety. Many decades later from his place of exile in Dar-es-Salaam, Tanzania, O'Neal would tell a freelance journalist for *African Affairs:* "I was a useless piece of shit who thought I was smart. . . . I was on the edge of an abyss. If I had fallen in I would have never gotten out." The party "turned my life around."[125]

The Black Panthers' stated commitment to the people also impacted young D.C. native Ericka Jenkins. She learned of the party while studying at Lincoln University where she was among the first cohort of women students. After reading an article in *Ramparts* about Huey Newton being shot by Oakland police, the soon-to-be Ericka Huggins knew she would go west. She recalled, "I decided that day I was going to go to California and join the Black Panther Party. It was October."[126] The next month, to the disconcert of her mother, a secretary in the State Department "who was using her hard-earned money to send [her daughter] to school," Ericka Jenkins left school and traveled to Los Angeles with John Huggins, a fellow student and navy veteran. She went to help an organization that she felt put community first. She knew about other liberation organizations already—SNCC, CORE, the Deacons for Defense, and RAM, but none of these organizations had moved her enough to join.[127]

Arriving in California during Thanksgiving in 1967, John and Ericka stayed with his cousin in Venice Beach and worked in an auto parts factory. John worked in the main branch of Buy-Rite Auto Factory, and she worked in the women's branch where she did piece work. "I soldered pieces for car tachometers," recalled Ericka, continuing, "And any car, ANY car that has a tachometer I soldered, is in trouble." After pinching a nerve on the line, Ericka joined the union to try to organize around the "horrible" conditions, but did not have much success. She and John soon began volunteering with the Black Panther Party in Los Angeles. Within a couple months, they became full-time Panthers, laboring to bring "all power to the people."[128] At age 19, now married to John Huggins, Ericka Huggins had became one of the principal leaders in the Los Angeles chapter where youth education, but especially political education, would remain one of her passions.

Just over a year after arriving and within a month of giving birth to their daughter Mai, a deadly encounter altered Ericka and John Huggins's lives and activism. John Huggins and Bunchy Carter were killed in what would later be described as a FBI-orchestrated conflict that resulted in a shootout with US members on UCLA's campus on January 17, 1969. Widowed and with a newborn daughter, Ericka Huggins went to New Haven, Connecticut, to bury her husband. Asked by Yale University students and community members to start a Panther chapter there, she stayed in New Haven and did just that. Within a matter of months, police arrested Ericka Huggins, Bobby Seale, and a dozen others; they became known as the New Haven 14. Police charged them with the torturing and killing of Alex Rackley, a suspected police informant.[129] Ericka Huggins spent two years in jail—14 months in isolation and the last six months in the general population—before the charges were dropped. Finally free but living under the daily stress of wondering whether she would live "to see another day!" Ericka Huggins made her way back to California, started the Intercommunal Youth Institute in 1971, and became deputy minister of education. The institute expanded into the Oakland Community School and operated for more than a decade with Ericka Huggins as its director. It closed in 1982.[130]

In Los Angeles where, according to Ericka Huggins, "the police force was one of the most racist in the country," black people equally felt the weight of political inequality, especially in the realm of criminal justice. Street-level hustles, ideological profiling, and the consistently steroidal and disparate policing in black communities resulted in arrests. And, unfair indeterminate sentences expanded the black prison population. This was a preview for the law-and-order explosion of massively incarcerating black and brown people. While black freedom fighters crossed the threshold of jails and prisons more frequently, politically unengaged poor black and brown people also gained more intimate knowledge of the U.S. penal system. The criminalization of race by delegitimizing protest and urban rebellions was accompanied by, according to historian Heather A. Thompson, the "criminalization of urban space." In 1965, the same year the Voting Rights Act was passed, Congress also passed and President Johnson signed the Law Enforcement Assistance Act (LEAA). The Crime Control and Safe Streets Act followed three years later. These acts opened the door to greater federal intervention, more funding, new technologies, and increased arrests in black and brown communities.[131] Whatever their route to lockdown, families were fractured and separated over long distances and, in not so many decades, inner cities would begin to feel the devastating impact. During the Black Power era, as these political realities unfolded, the Black Panther Party established free busing-to-prison programs as a response.

The first busing-to-prison programs started, like the breakfast programs, on the West Coast. The Seattle branch of the Black Panther Party started its program in July 1970. Families and friends could not afford transportation to prisons many hours away.[132] On July 11, 1970, Black Panther and community members met at the Seattle Community Information Center, the name for local party offices, to go to Monroe Prison. On the drive up, party members discussed how prisoners fared on the inside, as well as the reasons they ended up in prison. Some did not have fair hearings, others were "railroaded," still others were "not judged by a jury of their peer group." Party members argued that not only were "the trials . . . brief and one sided"; they also usually took place "at the mercy of racists and bigots who have no understanding of the average Black man in the Black community."[133] The Panthers' southern California chapter also launched a busing program to Soledad State Prison where Black Panther George Jackson was serving his indeterminate sentence of one year for stealing $70.20. On a Sunday, August 9, 43 people took the first bus to Soledad.[134]

Two days after Christmas in 1970, Panthers in Cleveland initiated their bus-to-prison program. It made its first trip two days after Christmas to the Ohio Penitentiary. Cleveland Panther Jimmy Slater stated: "After so many comrades and Black Nationalists and people we knew were in prison . . . we knew we had to organize something to get families out, you know, to see their loved ones. And so the busing program sort of stemmed from so many of us going to jail, really."[135] Initially coordinated by Cecile McBride and Lewis McCoy, the job was passed on to a new Panther member in 1971, JoAnn Bray, who actually expanded and sustained the program for more than a decade. Bray joined the local Panther Party after the "tragic day" when guards killed George Jackson who had been advocating for prisoners' rights. Moved by this, Bray wrote a letter to the editor in the black newspaper the *Call & Post:* "White newspapers and the white power structure succeeded in executing George Jackson. Before I go on let me explain that I am not a militant revolutionist or a professional agitator. These are names given to those who speak out against injustices regardless of cost." Ashamed, Bray confessed that she did not "believe in anything or anybody enough to suffer physical or mental discomfort" and was simply "like millions of others . . . too busy with the everyday mechanics of life," that was "until Saturday."[136] After Saturday, this now "disgusted black woman" began to think about her legacy and decided to join the fray. In August 1971, she decided to become a Panther "and recruit in East Cleveland."[137]

JoAnn Bray lived in an apartment on Emily Street in a racially transitioning inner-ring suburb. East Cleveland bordered Glenville, where the uprising had exploded in 1968. Originally an all-white suburb that boasted the home of the nation's first billionaire, John D. Rockefeller Sr., the neighboring municipality underwent an extraordinarily quick racial (and later lengthier class) transformation. In a matter of a decade, the city shifted from two percent black in 1960 to 58 percent by 1970.[138]

Despite her initial aspirations to organize in East Cleveland, however, JoAnn Bray expended much of her energy working in the Panthers' headquarters on East 79th Street in the Cleveland neighborhood of Hough. She had been wheelchair bound since she was 13 years old. Motivated by the concept of keeping families together, Bray knew the pain of familial separation. An Alabama native, Bray was brought by her parents to Cleveland at the age of six for treatment for juvenile rheumatoid arthritis. She recalled, "I was running barefoot in the red clay (of Alabama) and tending farm animals. All of a sudden, I'm in hell."[139] She stayed in a suburban hospital until she was 16 years old, receiving weekly visits from her mother, who divorced, lived on welfare, raised eight children, and traveled in from the "bowels of society where [her] family lived."[140] Bray graduated Cleveland Heights High School at age 19, worked for what she described as an unfulfilling year at the Cleveland NAACP, and then, eventually, she said: "I went radical."[141] She became the coordinator for the free bus-to-prison program.

Grandmothers, mothers, children, and friends; physically and economically challenged—they were all passengers. The program served four men's prisons and the one women's reformatory. Chillicothe State Correctional Institution on the first Saturday. Mansfield State Reformatory on the second Saturday. Marion State Correctional Institution on the third Saturday. The Ohio State Penitentiary on the fourth Saturday. Marysville State Reformatory for Women on the first Sunday. Eventually the program would expand to the new penitentiary in Lucasville, as well as juvenile detention centers. In the wake of the Cleveland Black Panthers' demise in 1972, JoAnn Bray (25 years old at the time) took over the bus program herself, renaming it the People's Busing Program. She renamed herself too. In 1974, she became "Azadi"—Arabic for "freedom"—and legally changed her name one year later.[142] Azadi would work tirelessly, more than 10 to 12 hours a day. She used her own money for gas and applied for grants to keep the program afloat as long as she could. The loss of resources meant, however, that she had to begin charging for weekly visits. Eventually she cobbled together support from fares, donations and in-kind support, and grants.

Unbeknown to advocates like Bray—or even prisoner rights activists inside the cement, brick, and wire-fence walls—jails, prisons, and juvenile detention facilities in Ohio and across the nation would proliferate throughout the late 20th century,

becoming growth engines for local public and private coffers. Inner cities continued to be the targets of disparate policing, and that disparate policing accompanied
by arrests further fueled the growth of the prison-industrial complex. In fact, mass
incarceration would become a major grassroots issue of the 21st century, raise the
wizardly curtain on policing practices and drug policies, and expose the impact of
criminalizing black and brown people.[143]

Most advocates of community-control and survival programs—whether initiated by Black Power organizations or those seeking self-determination through
other grassroots routes—were unheralded and unknown. In fact, the majority of
men and women even in celebrated organizations such as the Black Panther Party
were not famous, nor were most grassroots activists necessarily affiliated with publicly noted groups. Yet, they too sought full participation and fair treatment as
citizens, claimed the right to be self-determined, and questioned the structure of
power that enforced systematic exclusion and marginalization in the United States,
and globally.

Notes

1 James Boggs, *Racism and the Class Struggle,* 69.
2 Jaffe and Sherwood, 62. On home rule bill, see p. 28.
3 Dan Morgan, "Barry Finds Home Rule a Frustrating Battle," *Washington Post,* July 25, 1966.
4 Jean R. Hailey, "Barry Quits SNCC Post to Aid Poor," *Washington Post,* January 19, 1967. Also, Jaffe and Sherwood, 55.
5 Jaffe and Sherwood, 58–59; Valk, *Radical Sisters,* 13–14. Treadwell and Barry married in 1973; they would divorce.
6 Hollie I. West, "600 Pride Inc., Volunteers Show Up to Work," *Washington Post,* August 6, 1967. Also, Jaffe and Sherwood, 53–54.
7 For recent scholarship on liberalism and Black Power, see Fergus; Ferguson; Self.
8 "Pride Inc. Gets Cleaning Job at Clifton Terrace," *Washington Post,* January 7, 1968; Willard Clopton Jr., "Pride Inc., Looks to a New Landscape," *Washington Post,* March 9, 1968; Peter Braestrup Washington, "Pride's Job Program Goal. 'Piece of the Action' for Ghetto," *Washington Post,* March 23, 1969.
9 Transcript, Theodore Granik's "Youth Wants to Know," October 22, 1967, Folder: ACT— Hobson Testimony and Interviews, Box 4, Collection 1, Julius W. Hobson Papers, The Washingtoniana Collection, D.C. Library, Washington, D.C.
10 Carmichael with Thelwell, 642–643.
11 Ibid.
12 Robert Maynard, "Urban League Wary of Black United Front," *Washington Post,* January 18, 1968; "The 'Black United Front,'" *The Washington Post,* January 12, 1968.
13 The official name of the Kerner Commission was the National Advisory Commission on Civil Disorders. See National Advisory Committee on Civil Disorders, *Report of the National Advisory Commission on Civil Disorders* (Washington, D.C.: Government Printing Office, 1968), 208.
14 Ibid., 226.
15 Ibid., 14.
16 Hardy was married twice. Her first husband and the father of three of her children, DeSales Carter Sr., died in the late 1940s or early 1950s. In 1954 she married Lloyd Hardy, a taxi driver, and they had four children together.

17 William Raspberry, "Samaritan Seizes Every Chance to Wage Own Poverty Program," *Washington Post,* October 17, 1965.

18 Carolyn Lewis, "Black Front 'Sweetheart' Looks for Unity," *Washington Post,* February 23, 1968; "Stokely, Rap Won't Take Part in March," *Washington Daily News,* March 5, 1968; Charles Conconi, "Militants Wait for King's Way to Fail," *Star,* March 10, 1968. Also, Carmichael with Thelwell, 646–648; Jackson, 349; Mantler, 125.

19 Carolyn Lewis, "Black Power Leader Endorses the 'Camp-In,'" *Washington Post,* March 10, 1968.

20 Ibid.

21 Carolyn Lewis, "Women Leaders Mourn Loss of Dr. King," *Washington Post,* April 6, 1968.

22 Elsie Carper, "Mother's Day Parade Opens Drive by Poor," *Washington Post,* May 13, 1968. Just a couple decades before, the school was the all-white Central High School. It became an all-black business high school in 1950 and was named after Francis Lewis Cardozo, a clergyman and educator who hailed from Reconstruction-era South Carolina. Cardoza became the first black person to hold a statewide office in the United States, and founded the black business school. His granddaughter, and an internationalist anti-racist activist in her own right, Eslanda Goode married Paul Robeson. Ransby, *Eslanda.*

23 Elsie Carper, "Mother's Day Parade Opens Drive by Poor," *Washington Post,* May 13, 1968. Also, Sobel, 28–29.

24 Carolyn Lewis, "Resurrection City Women Confront D.C. Counterparts," *Washington Post,* May 26, 1968.

25 Ibid.

26 Nadasen, 74–75.

27 William Steif, "Coretta Seeks Womanpower," *Washington Daily News,* June 20, 1968.

28 "D.C. Statehood Party Headquarters/ Julius Hobson/ Josephine Butler, African American Heritage Trail," Cultural Tourism D.C. Website, www.culturaltourismdc.org/portal/d.c.-statehood-party-headquarters/julius-hobson/josephine-butler-african-american-heritage-trail#.VB2kYucfshk.

29 Cynthia Gorney, "Julius Hobson Sr., Activist, Dies at Age 54," *Washington Post,* March 24, 1977.

30 Jaffe and Sherwood, 50.

31 "ACT Opposes Track System in D.C. Public Schools" *The Activist* 1:1 (n.d., circa February/March 1965), Folder: ACT—Activist Newsletters, Box 4, Collection 1, Julius W. Hobson Papers; Beatrice A. Moulton, "Hobson v. Hansen: The De Facto Limits on Judicial Power," *Stanford Law Review* 20 (1968): 1249–1268.

32 Cynthia Gorney, "Julius Hobson Sr., Activist, Dies at Age 54," *Washington Post,* March 24, 1977.

33 Hamil R. Harris, "City Loses A Force for Statehood," *Washington Post,* April 17, 1997. Not quite a decade later, Butler would found the Paul Robeson Friendship Society and serve as a member of the All People's Congress national advisory board. Cynthia Gorney, "Julius Hobson Sr., Activist, Dies at Age 54," *Washington Post,* March 24, 1977.

34 Given D.C. was not a state, it did not have an elected official in the Senate, or a vote in the House of Representatives even with a sitting delegate.

35 Sam Smith, "1985: Ten Years of Home Rule," http://prorev.com/dcstdhr10th.htm.

36 Johnson, 179. The Georgia resolution at the National Black Political Assembly was even more expansive. Its support of a third party raised the issues of community control of schools, advocacy for black workers, black women's struggles, and challenging police repression. Johnson, 180.

37 In 1976, Hobson died of cancer. Two years after that in 1978, Barry, at the time a District council member, succeeded Walter Washington as mayor, promising a "partnership with the people"; and in 1981 Hardy left the city council, started her own

consulting firm, and became a lecturer in University of District of Columbia's Urban Studies Program.

38 Moore, 73, 75.

39 Ibid., 72. Also, Leonard Moore, "Carl Stokes: Mayor of Cleveland," in *African-American Mayors,* ed. Colburn and Adler, 88.

40 Moore, 80.

41 Elbaum, 71. Yohuru Williams describes violent confrontation "as emblematic of the Panther story . . . in the Midwest generally." See Yohuru Williams, "Give Them a Cause to Die For," in *Liberated Territory,* ed. Williams and Lazerow, 246.

42 Stokes, 206–215.

43 Edward P. Whelan, "Hearing Set on Ahmed Trial," Cleveland *Plain Dealer,* October 18, 1969; "Ahmed Evans Wins Delay for Appeal," Cleveland *Plain Dealer,* December 9, 1969; Bob Modic, "Civil Liberties Charges: Police Violence in Glenville Incident Never Probed," *Cleveland Press,* March 19, 1970; Moore, 95.

44 Detroit workers and revolutionary union movement activists Mike Hamlin and John Watson, inspired by a Lenin pamphlet, started the *Inner City Voice* in 1967. Hamlin with Gibbs, 17. Yohuru Williams, "Give Them a Cause to Die For," 247. The July 23, 1968, Glenville shootout in Cleveland gained widespread attention among revolutionary nationalists. "Was July 23 Part of the White Power Conspiracy?" *Inner City Voice,* October 9, 1969.

45 Leonard Moore, "Carl Stokes: Mayor of Cleveland," 91.

46 Angela Benson, interview by Nancy Nolan-Jones, April 2, 2013, Voicing & Action Project.

47 Yohuru Williams, "Give Them a Cause to Die For," 247.

48 Moore, 88.

49 Bob Modic, "New Black Leaders Strive to Put Opportunity in Ghetto," *Cleveland Press,* October 1968; Bob Modic, "New Black Leaders: New Breed Ghetto Leaders Seek Today—Not Tomorrow," *Cleveland Press,* October 9, 1968, both in Folder 844, Container 45, Newspaper Clippings on Black Nationalism, Carl Stokes Papers, Western Reserve Historical Society, Cleveland, Ohio.

50 Bob Modic, "New Black Leaders: New Breed Ghetto Leaders Seek Today—Not Tomorrow," *Cleveland Press,* October 9, 1968.

51 Bob Modic, "New Black Leaders Strive to Put Opportunity in Ghetto," *Cleveland Press,* October 1968.

52 Nishani Frazier, "A McDonald's That Reflects the Soul of a People: Hough Area Development Corporation and Community Development in Cleveland," in *The Business of Black Power,* ed. Hill and Rabig, 68–75.

53 Moore, 48.

54 Bob Modic, "Black Nationalists Say They Favor Good Po . . . ," *Cleveland Press,* October 12, 1968.

55 Nishani Frazier, "A McDonald's That Reflects the Soul of a People."

56 Sam Giaimo, "Rifle Practice," *Cleveland Press,* July 28, 1966.

57 Moore, 89.

58 Stokes, 276.

59 Ibid.

60 Ibid., 277.

61 Kerby, 61.

62 Stokes, 277. Kerby, 68. While significant research needs to be done on the history of Afro Set, the description of the organization as a "gang" of people who at times hurt their own community also emerged in an oral interview with Christopher Williams. Christopher Williams, interview by Hank Smith, July 16, 2013, Voicing & Action Project. Also, Hank Smith, interview by Misty Luminais, July 2, 2013, Voicing & Action Project. The Afro Set's leader, Harllel Jones, did go to prison for murder, but

was released five years later when a judge decided Jones had not received a fair trial. Mary Taugher, "Harllel Jones is on the Offensive," *Cleveland Press*, February 14, 1982.

63 Bob Modic, "City Forum Hears Harllel Jones on Black Nationalism," *Cleveland Press*, March 14, 1969.

64 Robert G. McGruder, "Jones 'Nationalism' Charms City Club," *Cleveland Plain Dealer*, March 15, 1969.

65 Carl Kovac, "Jones Speaks at Municipal Program: Separation Urged for Blacks," *Cleveland Plain Dealer*, July 27, 1970.

66 News Release, National Organizing Committee, Peace and Freedom Party, October 1, 1968, Folder 2: Peace and Freedom Party Campaign, 1968, Box 2, Peggy Terry Papers, MSS 1055, Wisconsin Historical Society, Madison, Wisconsin. On Fred Hampton and Rainbow Coalition, see Jakobi Williams, 125–166.

67 Bob Modic, "City Forum Hears Harllel Jones on Black Nationalism," *Cleveland Press*, March 14, 1969.

68 Leonard Moore, "Carl Stokes: Mayor of Cleveland"; Michney, "Constrained Communities."

69 Leonard Moore, "Carl Stokes: Mayor of Cleveland," 93–101.

70 Audley (Queen Mother) Moore, interview by Cheryl Gilkes Townsend, 1978, in *The Black Women Oral History Project*, ed. Hill.

71 Berry and Blassingame, 418; Joseph, *Waiting 'Til the Midnight Hour*, 278.

72 Victor Riesel, "Extremists Taught Kids at Outings Paid for by US," *Milwaukee Sentinel*, October 15, 1968; "The Black Scholar Interviews: Queen Mother Moore," *Black Scholar*, 50.

73 Dara Abubakari, "The Only Thing You Can Aspire to Is Nationhood," in *Black Women in White America*, ed. Lerner, 555.

74 Thompson, *Whose Detroit?*; David Goldberg, "Community Control of Construction, Independent Unionism, and the 'Short Black Power Movement' in Detroit," in *Black Power at Work*, ed. Goldberg and Griffey, 91–92.

75 Thompson, *Whose Detroit?*, 105.

76 Elbaum, 81. Thompson, *Whose Detroit?*, 109–110. On the RUMs and the league, see Geschwender.

77 Thompson, *Whose Detroit?*, 110. Also, Elizabeth Kai Hinton, "The Black Bolsheviks," in *The New Black History*, ed. Marable and Kai Hinton, 211–228.

78 Elbaum, 82; Thompson, *Whose Detroit?*, 172.

79 Marian Kramer, *Detroit Lives*, ed. Mast, 103.

80 Ibid.

81 Robert Holland, "Public Housing Rent Strike Report: City of Detroit," 3–4, Commission on Community Relations, July 1969, Folder 15, Box 30, Detroit Commission on Community Relations (DCCR). Also, Shaw; Rhonda Y. Williams, *The Politics of Public Housing*; Rhonda Y. Williams, "'Something's Wrong Down Here,'" in *African American Urban History since World War II*, ed. Kusmer and Trotter.

82 Forman, *The Making of Black Revolutionaries*, 544. On IFCO and BEDC, Dillard; Michael O. West, "Whose Black Power?" in *The Business of Black Power*, ed. Goldberg and Griffey, 277–283.

83 Forman, *The Making of Black Revolutionaries*, 546.

84 Shannen Dee Williams.

85 Weems and Randolph, "The National Response to Richard M. Nixon's Black Capitalism Initiative," 69.

86 Weems and Randolph, "The Ideological Origins of Richard M. Nixon's 'Black Capitalism' Initiative," 57.

87 Weems and Randolph, "The National Response to Richard M. Nixon's Black Capitalism Initiative," 68–75.

88 "The Revolutionary Line for the National Black Economic Development Conference," courtesy of David Goldberg, actual flier, circa 1969, in author's possession; Forman, *The Making of Black Revolutionaries*, 545.

89 "The Black Manifesto," in *The Black Seventies,* ed. Barbour, 296.

90 Ibid., 297–298.

91 Ibid., 299.

92 Forman, *The Making of Black* Revolutionaries, 547.

93 Ibid., 301.

94 Ibid., 547.

95 "A Chronological Digest of the Response of the Churches to 'The Black Manifesto,'" New Jersey Council of Churches Council News, September 1969, Folder 10: Black Manifesto, Box 15, Interreligious Foundation for Community Organization Records (hereafter IFCO), Schomburg Center for Research in Black Culture, New York Public Library, New York.

96 Audley (Queen Mother) Moore, interview by Cheryl Gilkes Townsend, 1978.

97 Freedom Farm Corporation, Status Report and Request for Funds, Prepared March 1973, Folder 26: Freedom Farm Corp. (1973), Box 28, IFCO.

98 Theoharis, *The Rebellious Life of Mrs. Rosa Parks,* 166.

99 Rhonda Y. Williams, *The Politics of Public Housing,* 194.

100 Rhonda Y. Williams, "We're Tired of Being Treated Like Dogs," 31.

101 Margaret "Peggy" McCarty, interview by author, June 21, 2003, Baltimore, Maryland.

102 Ibid.

103 Ibid.

104 Ibid.

105 Ibid.

106 On Lively, see Rhonda Y. Williams, *The Politics of Public Housing.*

107 Margaret "Peggy" McCarty, interview by author, June 21, 2003, Baltimore, Maryland. On similar struggles in Las Vegas, see, Orleck.

108 "Welfare Leader Criticizes Dean," *Baltimore Morning Sun,* October 16, 1966.

109 Rhonda Y. Williams, *The Politics of Public Housing,* 205.

110 Christopher Gaul, "National Welfare Clients Union Planned," *Baltimore Evening Sun,* December 21, 1966. On the history of the NWRO, see Nadasen.

111 Detroit Welfare Rights Organization, "A New Beginning in the Struggle for Poor People's Survival in 1972," Folder: The Struggle for Poor People's Survival (1972), Box 144, New Detroit Inc.

112 Charlotte Curtis, "Black Panther Philosophy Is Debated at Bernsteins," *New York Times,* January 15, 1970; Rhonda Y. Williams, "Black Women, Urban Politics, and Engendering Black Power," in *The Black Power Movement,* ed. Joseph, 96.

113 Margaret "Peggy" McCarty, interview by author, June 21, 2003, Baltimore, Maryland.

114 Rivera, "Welfare Oppression in Mount Vernon, N.Y.," *The Black Panther,* August 21, 1970.

115 Maeda; Jeffrey Ogbar, "Rainbow Radicalism," in *The Black Power Movement,* ed. Joseph, 206. On the complicated politics regarding Mao, the Red Guards, U.S. Chinese radicals, and Black Power, see Robeson Taj Frazier, "Black Crusaders," in *The New Black History,* ed. Marable and Kai Hinton, 91–98; Robeson Taj Frazier, "Thunder in the East," 931.

116 JoNina Abron, " 'Serving the People': The Survival Programs of the Black Panther Party," in *The Black Panther Party [Reconsidered],* ed. Charles E. Jones, 174.

117 Nelson, 50.

118 JoNina Abron, " 'Serving the People': The Survival Programs of the Black Panther Party," 178.

119 Ibid., 183.

120 Bloom and Martin, 182.

121 United States House of Representatives, Committee on Internal Security, *Gun Barrel Politics,* 62. Also, Angela D. LeBlanc-Ernest, " 'The Most Qualified Person to Handle the Job': Black Panther Party Women, 1966–1982," in *The Black Panther Party [Reconsidered],* ed. Charles E. Jones, 304–334.

122 Nelson, 15.

123 Don Reeder, "Militants Give Pupils Breakfast," *Washington Post,* April 20, 1969; for quote on "fire-breathing Marxist revolutionary," see James C. McKinley Jr., "A Black Panther's Mellow Exile: Farming in Africa," *New York Times,* November 23, 1997. Also, Nelson, 75; JoNina Abron, " 'Serving the People': The Survival Programs of the Black Panther Party," 184.

124 Christopher Goffard, "Former Black Panther Patches Together Purpose in African Exile," *Los Angeles Times,* January 29, 2012.

125 Jeremy O'Kasick, "An Interview with Pete O'Neal," *African Affairs* 102 (October 2003): 632.

126 On being one of the first women, see Ericka Huggins, Interview by Michele Russell, April 20, 1977, Oakland, California, courtesy of Robyn Spencer. For quote, see "Ericka Huggins: From Black Panther to AIDS Activist," in *Sixties Radicals, Then and Now,* ed. Chepesiuk, 202.

127 Ericka Huggins, Interview by Michele Russell, April 20, 1977, Oakland, California.

128 "Ericka Huggins: From Black Panther to AIDS Activist," 202.

129 Yohuru Williams, *Black Politics, White Power.*

130 Ericka Huggins and Angela D. LeBlanc-Ernest, "Revolutionary Women, Revolutionary Education: The Black Panther Party's Oakland Community School," in *Want to Start a Revolution?,* ed. Gore, Theoharis, and Woodard, 161–184.

131 "Ericka Huggins: From Black Panther to AIDS Activist," 206; Thompson, "Why Mass Incarceration Matters," 703–734; Weaver, 244–247.

132 "Washington State Free Bussing Program," *Black Panther,* August 21, 1970.

133 Ibid.

134 "Bussing Program to Soledad Prison," *Black Panther,* August 21, 1970.

135 Ryan Nissim-Sabat, "Panthers Set Up Shop in Cleveland," in *Comrades,* ed. Judson L. Jeffries, 125.

136 JoAnn Bray, "A Tragic Day," *Call & Post,* September 4, 1971.

137 Ryan Nissim-Sabat, "Panthers Set Up Shop in Cleveland," 126.

138 Keating, chapter 5. On racial and neighborhood transformation linked to real estate practices in East Cleveland, see James Taylor, interview by Jeannie Joy (Lady Red) and Brandon King, 26 June 2012, Voicing & Action Project.

139 Tom Breckenridge, "Azadi Fills Bus with Love, Hope," *Cleveland Plain Dealer,* March 28, 1988.

140 Christopher Evans, "Women's Dream Is Road to Hope for Inmates," *Cleveland Plain Dealer,* March 17, 1985.

141 Tom Breckenridge, "Azadi Fills Bus with Love, Hope," *Cleveland Plain Dealer,* March 28, 1988.

142 "Invalid Runs Bus to Prisons that Black Panthers Ran Free," *Cleveland Plain Dealer,* March 31, 1972; Terry Pederson, "Plight of Prison Bus Eclipses Other Work," *Cleveland Plain Dealer,* January 20, 1974; Tom Breckenridge, "Azadi Fills Bus with Love, Hope," *Cleveland Plain Dealer,* March 28, 1988.

143 Thompson, "Why Mass Incarceration Matters." Also, see Alexander.

6

THE WORLD CRIES FREEDOM

We going to take this world through changes, not the other way around. . . .
It's the Third World Revolution, and we're standing at the gate.
You can add to the solution while the world is changing shape.
—*Gil Scott-Heron and Brian Jackson (1978)*[1]

When Charles Anderson wrote to Mae Mallory in March 1963, he was living in Anaheim, California. An artist, Anderson had worked in a Mexican Bracero camp on the Tijuana border until he no longer could bear the "low pay" and "slavery conditions." At the time, Mallory was still fighting extradition to Monroe, North Carolina. After apologizing to Mallory for not being in better touch, Anderson then told her (clearly in response to a query she made) that securing scholarships for her "two children in Mexico" was highly likely "because of political 'sympathy' or what ever word fits better, (admiration)."[2] Anderson also told Mallory about the articles he had written about her case for a few Spanish-language newspapers and magazines, and expressed his hope that they would be published. Then he turned to the poem that he included with his letter. Written several months before, a portion of "Forcast Storm" had already appeared in the Los Angeles *Herald-Dispatch*. Screaming global liberation, the poem critiqued white supremacy and imperialism and warned the "happy little white man" who was "out waterin' [his] lawn" (likely a response to white suburban bliss and leisure) to "look up":

You must open your eyes.
The world cries FREEDOM—
Uhuru,
And their pushin' at you!

He continued: Mae Mallory is "in prison—but not her cause." He counseled black women to shed "few tears." And he counseled the "little white man" to beware: "Sister Mae has caught the freedom song . . . your jail won't hold her long." Then, just a couple lines later, linking literal imprisonment and containment of ideas to social revolutions, Anderson penned: "Then there's Fidel Castro 90 miles from home./Does he threaten Florida Jim Crow?"[3]

For two more typewritten pages, Anderson celebrated anti-imperial struggles in the Third World: Mexico, Latin America (Brazil, Guatemala, Argentina, Bolivia, and Venezuela), Mao's China, and Africa (Nkrumah's Ghana, Kenya's Mau Mau, and South Africa's Johannesburg). The international and the national intermingled—and both turned around revolutionizing power relations. Anderson counseled: Don't blame Robert Williams for the goings-on in Mississippi and watch out for Audrey Proctor (of the Monroe Defense Committee) in Cleveland who "sets quite a pace" and "may turn out to be the leader of the race." At the end of it all, Anderson posits that the debts for the many crimes against people of color and the exploitation of their countries' resources would have to be paid:

> Don't you know your future is almost gone?
> And soon you'll have a cotton sack on your back
> paying your crimes
> to a government that'll be all black![4]

Mallory thanked Anderson for his comradeship. In other letters, she thanked Lorraine Hansberry for her $150 donation and England's Sir Bertrand Russell for writing to the Ohio governor on her behalf. She expressed appreciation for the "terrific" letter that Richard Gibson sent as well. A co-founder of the Fair Play for Cuba Committee, Gibson resided in Paris and served on the editorial board of *African Revolution*. Mallory asked Gibson whether he thought Algerian president Ahmed Ben Bella and "V.I.P.'s in Switzerland" might sign a petition against her extradition. She wrote to Robert and Mabel Williams, and queried Ethel Johnson about how Max Stanford and Stanley Daniels of RAM fared in the Philadelphia protests at construction sites to open up jobs for black people.[5] Mallory also exchanged letters with the U.S. journalist Julian Mayfield, who penned an "Open Letter to an American Governor" in the *Ghanaian Times*. Living in Ghana, Mayfield wrote: "Mrs. Mallory's case has been well-publicized here in West Africa where it is hoped that the proud state of Ohio will not sully her record by cooperating with the ugly Americans in North Carolina."[6] In this instance, none of these petitions and letters actually prevented Mallory's extradition, but they do reveal the international sympathies and reach of black liberation struggles.

In 1970, five years after Mallory's release—and amid the proliferation of electoral, labor, anti-poverty, welfare rights, black student, anti-war, and prisoners' rights campaigns—another militant black female activist was at the center of a quite stunning global campaign. Angela Davis, who had returned to the United

States from her studies overseas to participate in the Black Power struggle, joined the Che Lumumba Club of the Communist Party. By 1970, she sat in jail awaiting trial on murder conspiracy charges.

The necessity to "Free Angela Davis" was set in motion when 17-year-old Jonathan Jackson walked into courtroom No. 1 in the Marin County Courthouse on August 7, 1970. For 10 years, his brother George Jackson had been incarcerated in Soledad State Prison. As an inmate advocating for prisoners' rights and the founder of a prison-based Black Panther Party chapter, George Jackson stoked the ire of prison officials; they falsely charged him, Fleeta Drumgo, and John Clutchette with killing a prison guard. A defense committee formed for these three men who became known as the Soledad Brothers. Fed up and desiring to draw greater attention to his brother's case and prison abuse, Jonathan Jackson organized a dramatic event. He took over that Marin County courtroom, armed the three prisoners there, and took hostage the judge, the prosecutor, and three jurors. Things turned tragic quickly as the guards opened fire and killed Jonathan Jackson, the judge, and two of the three prisoners. The third prisoner, Ruchell Magee, survived.

Investigation into the deadly shooting shifted rapidly when authorities discovered that the weapons used by Jonathan Jackson had been registered to Angela Davis. At the time, the 26-year-old Davis was fighting to save her job in the Philosophy Department at UCLA. The anti-Communist governor of California, Ronald Reagan, sought her dismissal because of her Communist Party affiliation. She was also working on the Soledad Brothers' defense committee. Although Davis had not been present, authorities still indicted her for murder. She went underground and became the focus of an FBI woman-hunt. After nearly two months on the run, Davis was caught by the FBI on October 13, 1970. Davis later recalled, "There was a trip to a musty police precinct office, where I was officially booked as a prisoner of the State of New York. Forms, fingerprints, mug shots—the same routine."[7]

Very quickly, family, black radicals, and Communist Party comrades rallied. Childhood friends and activists Margaret Burnham and Charlene Mitchell worked to mount her defense. In Europe, James Baldwin published an "Open Letter to My Sister Angela Y. Davis" in the *New Statesman* in which he wrote: "I have been making as much noise as I can, here in Europe, on radio and television."[8] Louise Thompson Patterson also made noise in Britain, as did Ella Baker at the first stateside rally in January 1971. Both of these veteran activists knew Davis's mother from their early activist days. Harboring gratitude for everyone's support, Sallye Bell Davis thanked William Patterson at his birthday party in Chicago in 1971 for working "tenaciously" on her daughter's behalf. The man of "We Charge Genocide" fame and Thompson Patterson's husband helped to organize the defense campaign, and Thompson Patterson served as the executive secretary of the New York Committee to Free Angela Davis.[9]

"Free Angela" campaigns sprung up in Europe, Asia, Africa, and Latin America. Tens of thousands of people from the Federal Republic of Germany mailed letters to the Marin County Jail. Davis had studied at the socialist Institute for Social Research at the University of Frankfurt with Herbert Marcuse between 1965 and 1967. The same year that Black Power ferment lured Davis back to the United States, the Newark and Detroit uprisings spurred the Socialist German Student Union to "officially declare its solidarity with 'black power' at its twenty-second national convention."[10] Reminiscent of the Communist Party campaigns mounted to defend the Scottsboro Nine in the 1930s, the party this time formed the National Committee to Free Angela Davis and All Political Prisoners and provided additional legal counsel to rally mass support to win Davis's freedom. According to Bettina Aptheker, "By February 1971, five months after Angela's arrest—there were two hundred local committees in the United States and sixty-three in foreign countries."[11] Davis's trial began on February 23, 1972, and five months later on June 4, 1972, an all-white jury acquitted her. In a separate trial, however, a jury convicted Magee.

While numerous years apart, the cases of Mallory and Davis expose the astonishing breadth of networks across activist cadres, generations, and geographies, and thereby bring to life the soul-stirring evocation the "world cries freedom." Ideas and people traveled multiple, complex, and bumpy routes from the early 20th century, through the 1950s and early 1960s, into the Black Power era. This coursing of global revolution stirred and complicated black radical dreams of self-determination and social transformation. Mallory's and Davis's activist journeys and twining communication networks, then, are not theirs alone, but illustrative and revelatory. In confronting the U.S. state, as had black nationalists and radicals before them, Mallory's and Davis's stories represent two among many that broadcasted Third World sympathies, networks of exchange, and the raging political storms of their eras that took aim at white power.

Forecasting Third World Storms

Anderson's poem positioned Mallory's case within a constellation of Third World struggles. The Cuban Revolution was one of them. In 1959, after three years of war, Fidel Castro and his band of revolutionaries overthrew the dictator Fulgencio Batista, a U.S. ally. From that moment on, Cuba became a national concern, particularly given its geographical proximity, its nationalization of U.S. assets on the island (including the mafia's), and its turn to Communism and the Soviet Union. Within two years, President Kennedy authorized sending a force of CIA-trained Cuban exiles to Cuba in an attempt to overthrow Castro. That invasion known as the Bay of Pigs failed. Within a year came news of the installation of Soviet missiles in Cuba and yet an additional concern—the clash of world superpowers and the threat of nuclear war.

When news of the Cuban missile crisis reached a young Angela Davis, she was sitting in the front row of an auditorium at Brandeis University. She had arrived early to get a good seat to hear James Baldwin. "But he had hardly gotten into his lecturing when the news broke that the world was teetering on the edge of the abyss of World War III," she recalled. "Baldwin announced that he could not continue his lectures without contradicting his moral conscience and abdicating his personal responsibilities." Students disbanded in fear and anger. Others organized a rally, and that's when Baldwin once again took to the stage, along with Davis's professor and mentor Herbert Marcuse.[12]

While Davis sat in that university auditorium and Mallory sat in a jail cell, Mallory's compatriots Robert F. and Mabel Williams were actually in Cuba. They had made their way to Cuba with the help of Julian Mayfield, who in 1960 had accompanied Robert F. Williams and the Fair Play for Cuba Committee on a trip to Cuba. Now two years later, Robert Williams published *The Crusader*, as well as broadcasted Radio Free Dixie from there. Shortly after the Williamses left the United States, Mayfield, too, had left the country for Accra, Ghana. In Accra, Mayfield became President Nkrumah's advisor and speechwriter. He also lived next door to husband-wife W.E.B. Du Bois and Shirley Graham Du Bois, who lived there among other expatriates, including poet-activist Maya Angelou and radical trade unionist Vicki Garvin. After W.E.B. Du Bois's death and during the coup that overthrew Nkrumah, Graham Du Bois moved to Cairo, Egypt, and made numerous trips to China, where the Williamses moved in 1965. Such migrations built on already existing transnational political routes and further linked U.S. black struggles to Third World radicalism.

Just as in the 1950s, black activists served as liberationist ambassadors and publicists of black oppression. As they traveled, they shared information and found inspiration. Malcolm X journeyed outside of the United States for the first time in 1959 when he went to Cairo, Egypt, then Saudi Arabia, Ghana, and Algeria. Throughout his journeys, Malcolm X shared the story of black people's oppression in the United States. In April 1964, after delivering his "The Ballot or the Bullet" speech in Cleveland, Malcolm X traveled to Mecca, Jeddah, and Beirut, and throughout Africa. He stopped in Cairo, Alexandria, Lagos, and arrived in Ghana on May 10, where he met with Mayfield and other black expatriates. He stayed in Ghana, which by this time experienced internal political dissension marked by rising authoritarianism, corruption, and declining democratic processes. Then he headed to Casablanca and finally Algiers.[13] He returned to Africa in July 1964 and stayed for two months.

In September 1964 after the betrayal of the Mississippi Freedom Democratic Party's vision at the Democratic National Convention in Atlantic City, a cadre of SNCC activists traveled to Conakry, Guinea. Harry Belafonte had suggested the trip as a "recuperative getaway."[14] Fannie Lou Hamer, James Forman, John Lewis, Julian Bond, Ruby Doris Smith Robinson, Bob and Dona Moses, Donald Harris, Prathia Hall, Matthew Jones, and Bill Hansen traveled to the second independent nation in Africa. Forman described the trip as SNCC's "first major move in the international arena."[15]

The visit supplied psychological girding for some black activists in the United States. Guinea deeply moved Forman. Standing "alone on the verandah of the

Villa Silla, looking out into the dark night" of Guinea, Forman began thinking about the many forms of white rule and black protest. He began with slavery, the Middle Passage, the KKK, Jim Crow, massive resistance to *Brown vs. Board of Education,* the sit-ins and freedom rides, and McComb and Atlantic City in 1964. Similar sentiments spilled out years later when Forman delivered the Black Manifesto. Of Guinea, Forman wrote: "We had come from years of living as blacks in an enemy white world to this land of black people with black socialist rulers." Hamer, too, maintained there was power in just seeing all-black communities with black leaders heading "the government, industry, everything." Yet as much as they might have felt free or connected there, Forman maintained that: "We had to stay [in the United States] and struggle" against "the daily grind of racist poverty." Once back in the United States, Forman and Ruby Doris Smith Robinson fought "vigorously for an understanding of economic exploitation—not merely race—as part of the problems that black people faced."[16]

Three years later in May 1967 Forman visited Dar es Salaam, Tanzania (the country where Mallory and her daughter would live for some years). This visit moved him just as much as his trip to Guinea had. Forman traveled to Tanzania for a United Nations conference on apartheid, racism, and colonialism in southern Africa. SNCC's legal advisor Howard Moore Jr., who three years later became one of Angela Davis's lawyers, accompanied him. With "no illusions" of the United Nations' desire to advance black liberation, Forman nevertheless believed, as had many other black nationalists and leftists before him, "that pressure upon the United Nations could be useful . . . in shaping public opinion."[17] While there, Forman met President Julius Nyerere who believed that anti-colonial struggles arrested "the suffering of a whole chunk of human beings" and "challenged and discredited" white colonial rule and arrogance.[18] Nyerere also believed the "growing gap between the haves and have-nots" required establishing a polity that had as its primary goal advancing human equality.[19]

The Arusha Declaration of 1967, which Nyerere drafted and Forman found so profound, expressed this primary goal. The declaration avowed state socialism undergirded by the "twin principles of liberty and equality" alongside "individual rights and collective well-being."[20] Recalled Forman: "This declaration was under intense discussion in political circles. The freedom with which people talked of socialism, armed struggle, the liberation of Africa, was a liberation in itself for Howard and me, coming as we did from the repressive atmosphere of the United States."[21]

At this United Nations conference, SNCC presented a position paper, "The Indivisible Struggle against Racism, Colonialism, and Apartheid," and announced the Black Power movement "with SNCC in the lead." Forman argued that "a defeat for racism and colonialism in southern Africa would hasten the destruction of these institutions in the United States, and vice versa." He drew attention to U.S. corporate giants such as Chase Manhattan Bank that invested in apartheid South Africa.[22] SNCC's position paper preceded by a handful of years the solidarity struggles of the Black Workers Organizing Committee in the Bay Area and the Detroit-based Black Workers Congress (BWC). Stewarded by Hamlin, the BWC would form to extend the League of Revolutionary Black Workers' national reach in the early 1970s.

Just as Third World struggles stirred black leftists in the United States, U.S. Black Power and Third World struggles simultaneously influenced other U.S. racial and ethnic liberation movements. For instance, the Black Panthers impacted the Puerto Rican Young Lords. In 1968, the Young Lords, a Chicago gang, became a revolutionary nationalist organization under the leadership of Jose "Cha Cha" Jimenez, and joined the local Panther Party as Rainbow Coalition members. That same year, the Young Lords established a branch in New York, a city where one million Puerto Rican migrants had settled between 1930 and 1960.[23] In July 1969 the Young Lords in New York gained notoriety for their "Garbage Offensive" to protest poor sanitation in their neighborhoods. The moniker echoed the "TET Offensive" of the Vietnam War—an operation by North Vietnamese rebels and regular army forces to strike at strategic targets in order to spur popular uprisings in South Vietnam to overthrow Saigon authorities.[24] The Young Lords expanded to other cities such as Philadelphia, Milwaukee, and Los Angeles, and chapters also sprang up in prisons on the east and west coasts.

These mainland Puerto Rican power activists were also guided by Puerto Rico's specific colonial relationship with the United States. Not quite a decade earlier, the Marxist Movimiento Pro Independencia (MPI) formed and established a branch in 1959 in New York City where the first wave of Puerto Rican immigrants had arrived during the late 19th century. The Cuban Revolution also had aroused activist ferment in Puerto Rico. In the years preceding MPI's formation, the Puerto Rican Nationalist Party had already begun protesting U.S. control of Puerto Rico. The most incendiary campaigns included the failed assassination attempt of President Truman in 1950 and an armed takeover of the U.S. Congress by Lolita Lebron and others in 1954, the same year as the *Brown* decision.[25] In 1965, two months after Malcolm X's assassination, Puerto Rican Nationalist Party leader Pedro Albizu Campos died. In the wake of such losses, pro–independence activists continued to challenge U.S. political control and corporate exploitation on the island.

By the late 1960s, the conditions of Puerto Ricans in the U.S. barrios, alongside ongoing desires for homeland autonomy, led to campaigns championing their self-determination struggles on the mainland and in Puerto Rico. Puerto Rico was a U.S. Commonwealth, not a state. And like Washington, D.C., it had a representative in the U.S. Congress, but no vote. The New York–based Young Lords included in its 13-point program community control, armed self-defense, self-determination for Puerto Rico and all Latinos, liberation for Third World people, and a socialist society.[26]

Black radical articulations and global political sympathies, however, did not always translate into nuanced understandings, or widespread knowledge, of other nations' internal and external affairs. Nor did organizational associations automatically mean that activists fully comprehended or appreciated the intricacies of other U.S. racial and ethnic groups' culture, or social, political, and economic conditions. This, at times, could produce tensions and strain international and multi-racial alliances. Yet, Black Power internationalists cast their lot with the oppressed at home and abroad.

Huey Newton's proclamation on "intercommunalism" reaffirmed a general commitment to grappling with injustice globally. Newton "asserted that imperialism had reached such a degree that sovereign borders were no longer relevant and that oppressed nations no longer existed; only oppressed communities within and outside artificial political borders existed."[27] Not everyone agreed with Newton. Assata Shakur challenged this idea, saying: "Somebody had forgotten to tell these oppressed communities that they were no longer nations."[28] In his rhetorical erasure of borders, Newton had expressed an idea for uniting the massive numbers of oppressed people worldwide. However, while white supremacy and imperialism had little respect for borders, the nation-state still held governance power in the world. Even anti-colonial revolutions for sovereignty and self-determination did not challenge this presumption.

In this age of world revolution, Third World nations frequently held an allure for U.S. Black Power radicals.[29] This allure fueled revolutionary imaginations and expectations, sometimes untenable, and served as a geographical guide to presumed politically sympathetic landing sites for U.S. blacks who sought to flee abroad, build networks, organize, and initiate revolutions. Indeed, countries such as Cuba, Algeria, Ghana, and Scandinavia did welcome black radicals, but in some cases only for a time and under certain political conditions.

Casting Abroad

When Angela Davis took flight to escape arrest in connection with the Marin County courthouse shooting, the FBI must have worried that she might find safe haven outside the United States. She had traveled internationally, including to Cuba, in 1969. By 1970, black expatriates lived in France and Ghana as a result of voluntary and politically driven emigration. Richard Wright said goodbye to the United States and moved to Paris in the 1950s. Garvin, Angelou, the Du Boises, and Mayfield had moved to Ghana in the first decade of its independence. In the era of expansive Black Power politics, still others fled the United States. Theirs revealed a different kind of revolutionary exile—the desire to escape potential imprisonment. Like Robert and Mabel Williams, some sought asylum in Cuba, exalted as a beacon against racism, "capitalist exploitation, imperialist aggression and fascist suppression." The one-time tourist destination had now become a political destination for black radicals and exiles.[30] In 1968 Eldridge Cleaver became one of them.

That year the Black Panther Party minister of information had decided to run for U.S. president on the Peace and Freedom Party (PFP) ticket. The PFP was a left-wing coalition of black, Latino, white, feminist, and anti-war activists. Out on parole for his engagement in the shootout that resulted in Bobby Hutton's death, Cleaver jumped his $50,000 bail. He arrived in Cuba on Christmas morning full of grand plans to mount an armed struggle against U.S. imperialism from this new tropical base. Over the next decade, numerous black radicals made Cuba their primary home in exile. Newton became a fugitive and lived there from 1974 to 1977, and the most famous political exile—Assata Shakur—arrived there after her escape from Clinton Correctional Facility in 1979.[31]

Cuba did not heartily welcome all black exiles, however, particularly those arriving on the island through airline hijackings or stridently publicizing their desires to export revolution to the United States. Many of these arrivals, instead of finding freedom, became familiar with Cuba's criminal justice system. There were black hijackers who spent anywhere from two months to over 11 years in prison. Some, such as a 19-year-old former marine Richard Duwayne Witt, who had tired of U.S. racism, ended up in a halfway house for hijackers in a suburb of Havana. Others such as Vietnam veteran Everett White and Black Panther Party member Garland Grant, who feared Milwaukee's "'terrorist police' and felt hopeless about life for a black man in a white society," worked off their sentences (ranging from four to eight years) cutting sugarcane or digging ditches.[32] The reality was that hijackings produced weighty concerns for Cuban national security. Quiet arrivals could be handled differently than very public skyjackings that involved dozens, even hundreds, of unsuspecting passengers. A relatively new phenomenon, "air piracy" was happening too frequently and drawing quite a lot of attention. By January 1969, 10 planes had been hijacked and forced to land in Cuba.[33] In response, Cuban officials began arresting and jailing hijackers.

"Factional struggles" also existed "among Cuba's leadership."[34] Those like Che Guevara, who supported armed insurrection and believed in protecting revolutionaries from the long arms of capitalist empires, had to contend with Cuban Communist leaders who increasingly labored to avoid U.S. retribution and military might.[35] The more moderate Moscow-aligned faction included Fidel Castro's brother Raul Castro and the chief theoretician of the Popular Socialist Party, Carlos Rafael Rodriguez.[36] Che (the namesake of the Che Lumumba Club), who sought to make another Vietnam, was executed in Bolivia in 1967, and by the late 1960s the moderate faction in Cuba had gained greater control.

Eldridge Cleaver arrived in Cuba in the midst of these political goings-on harboring hopes of training U.S. black radicals for armed revolutionary struggle. While Cuba had not relinquished its revolutionary commitment, this did not occur. Cleaver became so disenchanted that he described Cuba as "a San Quentin with palm trees, an Alcatraz with sugar cane."[37] Finding himself in conflict with Cuban officials, he ultimately left the island for Algeria in 1969.

The allure of Algeria as a destination for Black Power–era radicals had its roots in Frantz Fanon's writing and that nation's armed struggle against French imperialism. More than 12 million Algerians, 4.5 million of whom lived in poverty and 2 million in concentration camps, lived under French autocratic rule.[38] The black radical theoretician from Martinique had fought in the Algerian Revolution and become an icon for black radicals. In 1961, the same year that the 36-year-old Fanon died while in the United States seeking treatment for leukemia, he published *Wretched of the Earth*. The book became an essential tome of revolutionary philosophy for Black Power militants.

Forman recounts that after a disappointing visit to an Organization of African Unity (OAU) meeting in Congo Kinshasa in 1967, he turned to Fanon's writings for insight. Forman had traveled to the OAU meeting to seek an audience for SNCC executive secretary H. Rap Brown with African heads of state. OAU officials declined the opportunity. Deemed "the sword and shield of the African masses in their struggle for genuine independence, real unity and for the total liberation of the continent," the OAU had disappointed Forman.[39] By this time, the OAU also had begun to temper its revolutionary stance. However, in the OAU's case, unlike with Cuba, it was not necessarily the threat of nearby military might that explained caution over controversial activism, but the receipt of U.S. aid and the leadership of increasingly conservative heads of state.[40] It was at this moment that Forman began reading and re-reading Fanon's essay "Concerning Violence," and grappling with the questions of colonizer over colonized, economics, and the military-industrial complex.[41] He credited Fanon with helping him to understand the dangers of "reactionary" or "bourgeois" nationalism that reconstituted power in the hands of middling classes and professionals who worked in league with former colonial authorities.

Just as in the 1950s, Asia and Africa—from Bandung to Algeria—continued to inspire ideas of global racial and anti-imperial solidarities. In Ethel Johnson's *Did You Know?* newsletter, a July 24, 1965 column read:

> From Bandung to Algiers. Separated by oceans and great spans of lands these two cities although so far apart have everything in common. Common in outlook and destiny these two cities represent the feelings and hopes of the whole Afro-Asian world.

The column maintained,

> Ten years ago it was the flower city of Bandung which was the centre of the world. It was here where the historic ten principles of Bandung were formulated. It was here where for the first time Afro-Asian heads of States [sic] came together and found common ground and common weapons to headlong meet the common enemy of mankind, especially of Afro-Asia.

Referencing the Afro-Asian non-alignment conference in Bandung, Indonesia, in 1955, the column continued: "The ten principles of Bandung have no doubt influenced all our thinking" and "acted as the rallying point for all our activity, for all our thoughts. Now we meet once more in Algiers a city which was once riddled with colonialists." The column also referenced the June 19, 1965, coup against President

Ahmed Ben Bella of Algeria, who led the war against the French.[42] The coup seemed to come just as Ben Bella—operating initially under a one-party state and alienating the Communist Left—was mending relations and, according to scholar Vijay Prashad, moving toward a more inclusive and progressive poor people's agenda.[43] Colonel Houari Boumedienne, who led the coup and later became OAU president, firmly controlled the state (with the military) "in the name of socialism."[44] By the late 1960s, the socialist state project had become "a state capitalist one" with the country entering into billion dollar deals with American corporations.[45]

This is the Algeria in which the Black Panthers, including Eldridge and Kathleen Cleaver and other Black Power advocates, arrived in 1969. Under Boumedienne, Algeria hosted the First Pan-African Cultural Festival. Black Power cultural workers such as singer Nina Simone, playwright Ed Bullins, and black studies scholar Nathan Hare attended. So, too, did Carmichael. The Black Panther Party had an office out of which it organized an official exhibit for the cultural festival.[46] With the Cleavers' arrival, Algeria became the base for the International Section of the Panther Party by 1970. The party, in fact, received "accredited movement status" on par with South Africa's African National Congress (ANC) and the Palestinian Liberation Organization (PLO). Such recognition brought with it a multi-level villa that had been "formerly occupied by the National Liberation Front of South Vietnam," as well as an operating budget.[47]

The Panthers' International Section became an activist beachhead and, for a few years, a safe haven for other Panthers as well. The "highly competent Panther organizer," Donald "D. C." Cox arrived in Algiers in 1970. He had gone underground to avoid arrest in the alleged torture and murder case of a Baltimore Panther member rumored to be an informant. Cox was a Black Panther field marshal based out of San Francisco and regularly penned a column in *The Black Panther* newspaper "on guerrilla strategies and tactics."[48] Fearing infiltration of government provocateurs, which bred dissension, Newton had sent Cox to Baltimore to clean up the local chapter. Cox did his job. He held hearings and expelled suspected renegade Panthers. While there, Cox had become implicated in the alleged torture and murder of the Baltimore Black Panther. The case subsequently blew wide open when investigators discovered that the human remains belonged to a white man. However, before the case even got that far, Cox had fled the United States and surfaced in Algiers where he helped build the International Section.

Black Panther Michael "Cetewayo" Tabor also surfaced in Algiers in 1971. Born in Harlem in 1946, the same year that Malcolm X went to prison, Tabor joined the Black Panthers in its early days. As a party member, he met Connie Matthews, who had served as Newton's personal secretary as well as the Panthers' international coordinator in 1969. She worked in Scandinavian countries where she mobilized, fundraised, and educated people "about poor black and oppressed people's revolutionary struggle from the Panthers' vanguard position."[49] In 1971 Tabor fled the United States, as did fellow defendant Richard Moore (Dhoruba Bin Wahad), after being charged for plotting to kill police and bomb public buildings.

Tabor and Moore were part of the New York Panther 21. The men became fugitives in the U.S. government's eyes, and enemies of the people in Newton's eyes. The dissension between the party's East and West Coast factions, and between Newton and Cleaver, accelerated and played out in the streets, courtroom, news media, as well as videos produced by the International Section. At the time Tabor left the country, the New York Panther 21 trial was four months old; it eventually ended in acquittal. Tabor, like Cox, however, left the United States forever. Within a year of his arrival in Algeria, Cox disassociated himself from the Panthers. By 1971, Newton had expelled the New York Panther 21, and the Black Panther Party had formally split into two factions. The split, Cox believed, only aided the FBI's counterintelligence operations and undermined the party's revolutionary potential.[50] Eventually Cox moved to Paris where he died.

Fellow Panther Pete O'Neal also found his way to the International Section. He was among a handful of Panther sympathizers who hijacked his way there. In 1970 just a year after founding the Kansas City chapter, O'Neal, who supposedly wore a .30 caliber bullet around his neck to symbolize "that political power comes from the barrel of a gun," had charged Kansas City police chief and later FBI head Clarence M. Kelley with funneling firearms to right-wing organizations at a Senate inquiry in October 1969. In a matter of two weeks, police had arrested O'Neal for transporting a shotgun across state lines as an ex-felon. He was sentenced to four years in prison. While out on appeal, O'Neal fled to Algiers (by way of Sweden) with his wife and fellow party member Charlotte Hill. According to a newspaper report recounting the couple's escape, they "crawled out the backdoor of their house at 3 A.M. and into the trunk of a colleague's car, which carried them to St. Louis where they caught a plane to New York, then on to Sweden, with the help of fake passports given to them by New York City Communists."[51] O'Neal had lived in Algiers for about two years when Eldridge Cleaver resigned as leader of the International Section in January 1972. O'Neal then became leader of the section, but only for nine months before moving to Tanzania where the Sixth Pan-African Congress would be held in 1974.

While for decades black male Panthers had been celebrated for their daring and even fugitive status, female Panthers proved quite crucial as well, not only to stateside, but also foreign, operations of the party. Kathleen Cleaver served as the communications secretary for the International Section. "Searching for someplace to take collective action against the repressive social conditions" and inspired by the assertiveness of black women activists, such as Gloria Richardson, Diane Nash, and Ruby Doris Smith Robinson, who stood their grounds literally in the face of white power, the young Kathleen Neal had joined SNCC on the cusp of its ideological transition to Black Power.[52] Within the next year, she had moved to California to participate in the "Free Huey" campaign. As the stateside communications secretary, she had become the first woman on the party's Central Committee. In Algeria, Kathleen Cleaver provided critical political and creative guidance for the party's communication network. She also emerged as a celebrated advocate for black GIs whose protests against the U.S. military provoked censure and threatened imprisonment. The Ramstein 2 case in Germany, which garnered massive attention, serves as one example.

The Ramstein 2 were Black Panthers as well as ex-GIs. They worked for *Voice of the Lumpen,* an underground publication created by black activists and German students who as early as 1966 had aligned with Black Power radicals. Some of these student radicals had formed a Panther Solidarity Committee in West Germany and a reading group in Frankfurt. Launched in 1970, *Voice of the Lumpen* encouraged black GIs—some 60,000 were stationed in West Germany alone—and working-class German students to challenge "U.S. militarism and racism in both Germany and abroad."[53] Just as importantly, *Voice of the Lumpen* was part of the Revolutionary People's Communications Network created by Kathleen Cleaver to disseminate news about "active liberation movements taking place throughout the world." *Voice of the Lumpen* news articles covered the struggles of the Republic of New Afrika and the murder of George Jackson. One article inveighed against "the two most repressive and brutal institutions of U.S. society: 1. The Prison System [and] 2. The U.S. Military Est."[54]

On November 19, 1970, the Ramstein 2—Lawrence Jackson and William Frederick Burrell—and two other men drove to the U.S. Air Force Base in Ramstein. They were helping to organize a Thanksgiving Day rally. Kathleen Cleaver was to be the featured speaker. They passed out leaflets and hung up posters on area military bases. On that fateful day, a German guard denied them entry to Ramstein. Then, as the story goes (and there were differing versions), shots rang out from the car, wounding the guard, Dieter Lippeck. The car fled. Police arrested Jackson of Detroit, Michigan, who was a member of the Special Forces in Vietnam from 1966 to 1967, and Burrell of Pontiac, Michigan, who had refused to serve in Vietnam. Burrell later explained why he refused to serve in Vietnam: "[I did not] want to help a government that is oppressing my own Black brothers and sisters inside the United States carry out this dirty war of extermination against the Vietnamese people."[55] In the meantime, Kathleen Cleaver was on her way to Frankfurt. When she arrived at the airport, German authorities arrested her "on the orders of the Interior Minister" Hans-Dietrich Genscher, "summarily expelled [her] from the country and order[ed] [her] to never again return."[56]

Following a public protest and a formal university invitation, however, Kathleen Cleaver did return. At the University of Frankfurt the next year on July 7, she addressed over 1,000 people at the Ramstein 2 teach-in.[57] She wore an Afro and a khaki military shirt. Behind her on the blackboard were written the following words:

Nieder mit dem US-Imperilismus
und seinen Westdeutschen Kollaborateuren!
Freiheit für die Ramstein 2!
Power to the People![58]

The translation: "Down with U.S. imperialism and its West German collaborators! Freedom for the Ramstein 2! Power to the People!"

The Ramstein 2 trial began on June 16, 1971, and ended five days after the teach-in. Burrell would be acquitted and turned over to the Panthers' International Section.[59] Sentenced to six years on an attempted pre-meditated murder, Jackson was placed in solitary confinement at Zweibrucken. In *Voice of the Lumpen,* the newly released Burrell had this to say: "The pig rulers of the military have a special brand of kangaroo justice for all brothers who try to do political work amongst black GI's. U.S. military stockades all over the world are full of black brothers who have spoken out against the system. Many brothers in the stockades were busted for acts of revolutionary violence against the military machinery."[60] While Burrell found safe haven in Algiers, the country slowly became a less hospitable place for Panther Party operations. By the summer of 1972, the number of Black Panthers in Algiers had dwindled. By the end of the next year, the International Section for all intents and purposes no longer existed.

Like Cuba and Algeria in the late 1960s, Black Power advocates deemed Sweden a friendly nation as well. A social democracy, Sweden became familiar with the black freedom struggle as early as 1964 when Dr. King won the Nobel Peace Prize. Thereafter, the country's media followed black people's liberation struggles, so much so that in Sweden, black radicals were an "important topic for our education," according to Göran Hugo Olsson. A Swedish filmmaker, Olsson would make *The Black Power Mixtape* more than four decades after the demise of Black Power. Stated Olsson: "We were a radical society at the time!"[61]

In 1967 Carmichael gave a lecture in Sweden and signed copies of *Black Power* for standing room only audiences. Swedish National Broadcasting Company reporters interviewed Carmichael's mother Mabel Carmichael in New York and even reported on his trip to Paris. From 1967 to 1976, in fact, the Swedish National Broadcasting Company reported on Black Power–era struggles throughout the world, filming in Oakland, Detroit, Harlem, and Brooklyn; in Algiers; and right in their own backyard of Stockholm. In early 1969, Bobby Seale visited Stockholm, at which time he told reporters: "Socialism is the order of the day and not Nixon's black capitalism. That's out." [62] (That would be easier said than done.) Once back in the United States, Seale was arrested with Ericka Huggins in the New Haven 14 case. On their behalf, a Sweden-based Panther Solidarity Committee staged "Free Bobby," "Free Ericka," and eventually "Free Angela" protests. Connie Matthews and Emory Douglas, among others, made trips to Scandinavia. The Swedish National Broadcasting Company also reported on the murder of Fred Hampton; the "political trials" of Panthers in New York, Oakland, and New Haven; the 1971 killing of Soledad Brother George Jackson that precipitated the Attica rebellion; and the activities of the International Section in Algiers.

At least one black political refugee, Detroit black artist and radical labor activist Glanton Dowdell, actually settled in Sweden. Born August 9, 1923,

Dowdell joined the Michigan Communist Party at 19 years of age. Seven years later, he went to prison on a second-degree murder charge for which he received a 30- to 40-year sentence. While incarcerated, he studied with the Society of Arts and Crafts in Detroit. Out on parole in 1962, he began to reestablish his life. He married, had five children, and worked as an artist and construction and factory worker. Between 1967 and 1968, Dowdell helped to establish the Federation for Self-Determination, form the Panther Party in Detroit, and organize Local 124, a black-controlled construction and trades union.[63] He also painted the Black Madonna in Rev. Cleage's Shrine of the Black Madonna.[64]

In March 1968, Dowdell was charged with trying to forge U.S. savings bonds with three others, who pled guilty. Milton Henry (who became Gaidi Obadele of the Republic of New Afrika) was Dowdell's attorney stateside. Indicted on the testimony of an undercover agent and fearing the involvement of the FBI, Dowdell left the country and arrived in Sweden sometime in early 1969. By June 1970, he had secured work and residential permits. The United States sought extradition, and shortly thereafter Dowdell secured a Swedish advocate, Hans Goran Franck, who began the process of seeking "political refugee" status. The Stockholm Committee, a Swedish group, formed to fight for his political asylum. Franck drew on the poor race relations' record of the United States. He argued that Dowdell like many black urban residents faced deplorable living conditions and political suppression.[65]

The U.S. government's attempts to extradite Dowdell were unsuccessful. He was given humanitarian status, and Sweden became his new home. He lived and died there, and at least in the immediate years after taking political flight carried on his labor activism from there as well. Dowdell joined a study group formed by the editorial board of *kommentar,* an independent socialist magazine focused on international relations. He advised Gudrun Ryman, an editorial board member, on how to find out more information about U.S. labor practices. In particular, he suggested that Ryman write to the LRBW. Ryman contacted LRBW for photos and interviews dealing "with the everyday life and struggle of workers in the US."[66] Back in the states, LRBW member John Watson, with the help of white progressives, made and distributed a documentary on the organization, "Finally Got the News," through *Newsreel* in Europe (including Sweden and Germany), Africa, and Palestine.[67] While in exile, Dowdell also established "ties with progressive European workers' organizations and student groups" to challenge the unfair labor practices of U.S. firms with branches in Europe and to "agitate around political issues and cases for example Angela Davis."[68]

European and African as well as Asian and Caribbean countries served as homes for those in exile, staging grounds, and sites of informational exchange for black American activists in the Black Power era. Such activists, however, did more than escape, live, lecture, travel, and set up political bases abroad. Like with civil rights, they inspired indigenous people's struggles. This would be the case in Australia as elsewhere. There, local activists emulated black models of resistance to power and inequality and soon indigenous Panthers would be on the prowl.

Australia: Black Power, 1968–1975

In 1968 articles on "Black Power" increasingly appeared in the pages of Australian newspapers. This represented a substantive change from the mid-1960s. While Aboriginal and U.S. black people had an earlier history of global political connections, "black" as a racial term and identity for Aboriginal peoples was still in the making. During the era of expansive Black Power politics, black as a racial identity, particularly with increasing awareness of global anti-racist liberation struggles, began to have greater resonance.

By the late 1960s, Aboriginal activists began organizing as "black people." While legislation had been passed to afford voting rights, prevent discrimination in hotels and bars, and provide equal legal access, Aboriginal people still had to mobilize to achieve their social and political rights. The Aboriginal woman poet Oodgeroo Noonucal (nee Kath Walker) penned the "Black Commandments." These commandments exposed the extent of her (and others') disappointment in government policies that failed to translate into "practical benefit" and substantive change in education and employment. Linking politics to culture in a way that prioritized identity and self-determination, the Black Commandments listed numerous "Thou shalts," including, "Thou shalt work for black liberation" and "Thou shalt think black and act black."[69]

In April 1968 Charles Perkins, who at the time headed the Foundation for Aboriginal Affairs, spoke at a lunch event for the Aboriginal Scholarship Group at Melbourne University. An Aboriginal student, Perkins told 600 students that Australia needed "an American-style black power movement," given the "depressed sociological and economic situation" and the perpetuation of "prejudice and discrimination."[70] As had numerous SNCC activists who began to demand Black Power, Perkins and Kath Walker also had come out of an earlier struggle in Australia that had put its faith in the power of legal reforms during the 1950s. The grandson of a "full-blood Arunta tribeswoman from Central America," Perkins was born in Alice Springs in the Northern Territory of Australia in 1936.[71] He went to school in Adelaide in the state of South Australia, played soccer for a couple of English teams in the late 1950s, and began to advocate for Aboriginal rights in Adelaide. In 1961 he became vice president of the Federal Council for Aboriginal Advancement (FCAA).

Founded as a predominantly white organization, an increasing number of Aboriginal people joined FCAA to advance their cause as Aboriginal people. At a meeting in Brisbane in 1961, Aboriginal women, in particular Kath Walker, Ruth Wallace, and Gladys O'Shane, led the call for human rights and the protection of Aboriginal culture, land, and organizational leadership.[72] FCAA incorporated

Torres Strait Islanders in 1964 and became FCAATSI—a national, multiracial pressure group for indigenous rights. This was the same year that news about the U.S. black liberation struggle (for instance, the protests in Birmingham, Alabama) reached university students such as Perkins. Students held sympathy demonstrations and also formed Students Actions for Aborigines (SAFA) in 1964. Challenging similar types of racial exclusion in Australia, Perkins organized a freedom ride with white students in February 1965.[73] As had happened numerous times over in the United States, white resisters in Australia responded violently.

In June 1968 just months after Perkins's lunchtime speech, Perkins adamantly issued the same warning, this time at Flinders University in Adelaide: "An outbreak of 'black power' violence could occur" before the end of the year, unless the federal government improved the opportunities and quality-of-life conditions of Aboriginals.[74] "We have taken 185 years of second-class citizenship, and we are not taking any more of it," Perkins maintained.[75]

In 1968 Australian anti-racist stances in solidarity with Black Power manifested abroad as well. During the U.S. Olympics in Mexico, Tommie Smith and John Carlos, who won the gold and bronze medals in the 200-meter race stood on the victory stand and turned to the U.S. flag. As the U.S. national anthem played, they thrust clenched black fists into the air. Smith and Carlos each wore one black glove and black socks to represent black poverty. As one telling of the story goes, the white silver medalist, 26-year-old Peter Norman, a physical education teacher and Salvation Army officer born in Melbourne, actually suggested that since Carlos forgot his gloves, the medalists should share Smith's pair. Smith wore the right glove, Carlos the left. Smith said the right glove stood for power, and the left for unity.[76] The silver medalist who wore an Olympic Project for Human Rights badge, Norman, not only stood in solidarity with Smith and Carlos, but also critiqued racism in Australia.[77]

Harry Edwards, a black college student from the U.S., had initiated the Olympic Project, which called for a boycott of the world games to protest racism wherever it existed. Spurred by the stripping of Muhammad Ali's boxing title because he refused to fight in the Vietnam War, "conscious young black athletes responded." Kwame Ture (Stokely Carmichael) recalled decades later, "They organized and called for a black boycott of the Olympics unless Ali's titles were restored and South Africa and Rhodesia [were] excluded from the games."[78] Racial apartheid and white minority rule were the orders of the day in South Africa and Rhodesia. While the games proceeded, some athletes still supported the project by wearing badges. Smith and Carlos took it one step further. Carmichael, who was watching the Olympics when it happened, remembered: "[I] was on my feet shouting. I mean shouting. I can still feel the pride and admiration that flooded every fiber of my being in that moment. Black people all over the world felt that way."[79] After the medal ceremony, the white Australian national Norman stated: "I believe that every man is born equal and should be treated that way."[80] The Olympic Committee expelled Smith and Carlos from the Olympic Village and took away their medals. Norman did not lose his medal, but Australian athletic authorities did reprimand him.

In Australia, Black Power gained even greater allure under Victoria Aborigines Advancement League (AAL) president Bob Maza and member Bruce McGuinness. Born in Queensland, Bob Maza lived in Melbourne in the late 1960s. Inspired by "the honour, integrity, and self-discipline of the old Aborigines," Maza campaigned to "create an awareness of Koorie as a race." In June 1969, he suggested that the black nationalist teachings and example of Malcolm X could enhance indigenous people's self-discovery: "I only hope that when I die I can say I'm black and it's beautiful to be black."[81] Born on the Erambie Mission in the state of New South Wales, McGuinness was of Aboriginal, Torres Strait Islander, and European descent. In 1942 he moved with his family, which included nine brothers and two sisters, to Fitzroy in Sydney. Often called a "nigger" as a child by those lighter skinned than he, McGuinness joined the youth branch of the AAL when he was 18 years old to fight for Aboriginal land rights.[82] Land rights, alongside urban services, were consistent concrete demands.

In August 1969 the AAL hosted Roosevelt Brown, a 36-year-old Caribbean Black Power activist, academic, and member of the Progressive Labour Party serving in Bermuda's House of Assembly. Just months before his visit to Melbourne, Brown had organized an international Black Power conference in Bermuda. There, activists formed the Black Beret Cadre, opened a liberation school, and held political education classes.[83] During his three-day visit, after which he planned to travel to a Black Power conference in the United States, Brown speculated about whether Aborigines struggling for rights and empowerment might end up dead like others, such as "Patrice Lumumba, Medgar Evers, the Togo leaders, Kennedy, Malcolm X, King, [and] the other Kennedy," who tried "to bring about justice for black people."[84] White Australian authorities, the mainstream media, and Aboriginal moderates responded to Black Power with "frenzied overreaction." For them, Black Power conjured up violence and dictatorships.[85] U.S. media depictions of Black Power, alongside the most radical as well as vitriolic rhetoric, had traveled abroad with zeal.

The Roosevelt Brown Affair instigated what has since been referred to as "The Great All Black Power Scare in 1969." Brown's visit and the debate over Black Power exposed the ideological and generational fault lines within the Aboriginal community. Pastor Doug Nicholls, a founder and co-director of the Victoria AAL, was particularly critical. Unaware that Brown had been invited to speak, the 63-year-old Nicholls asked him during his presentation: "Who invited you?" Nicholls then lambasted Brown, maintaining that Black Power had no place in Australia, and that "it will only harm [the Aboriginal] cause."[86] The 30-year-old Bruce McGuinness argued, however, that Black Power already existed in Australia. For him, the Aboriginal Tribal Council of Victoria, for instance, was a Black Power movement—an all-black organization that fought for self-determination for Aboriginal people. As AAL liaison officer, McGuinness focused on unity and unified action: he "declared that Black Power 'does not necessarily involve violence' but rather . . . 'in essence . . . black people are more likely to achieve freedom and justice . . . by working together as a group.'"[87] The chair of the Aboriginal Tribal Council of Victoria, Eric Onus, stated: "We should have Black Power as far as making our own policies and presenting a united front." He continued: "When the white man hears of Black Power, he shudders—just think what black people have been through all those years under white power."[88]

Aboriginal Black Power activists pushed for greater control over their fates and the policies that would shape their quality of life. At its annual meeting in August 1969, the Victoria AAL issued a statement, quoting a white French existentialist philosopher, playwright, and anti-colonial activist: "To use the words of Jean-Paul Sartre: 'Not so very long ago, the earth numbered two thousand million inhabitants: five hundred million men, and one thousand five hundred million natives.' That is white power. . . . Since the end of World War 2, many of the colored peoples who lived under white colonial rule have gained their independence and colored minorities in multi-racial nations are claiming the right to determine the course of their own affairs in contradiction to the inferior state under which they had lived. That is black power."[89]

Fanon's books, Carmichael and Hamilton's *Black Power*, Malcolm X's speeches, news of anti–Vietnam War protests, and the 1960s rebellions of youth from Paris to Chicago routed through Australia. Indigenous activists also frequented the left-wing Third World Bookshop, which carried books on U.S. black and Native American history. Aboriginal Black Power activists secured political information and music from U.S. black servicemen, as had the Sydney wharf workers in the 1920s. Black GIs stationed in Vietnam traveled to Sydney on leave. Linkages between Aboriginal Australians and black Americans seeking self-determination had deep roots extending as far back as the Garvey movement. Some of those wharf laborers later became political leaders in the Aboriginal community. According to historian John Maynard, "International black movements and ideologies" formed "the core of the political directives and rhetoric." The writings of Du Bois, Carter G. Woodson, and Garvey circulated in Australia, and an officer with the Australian Aboriginal Progressive Association (AAPA) expressed interest in *The Negro World* in correspondence with Amy Jacques Garvey. Aboriginal men even founded a UNIA chapter.[90]

Just months after Roosevelt Brown's visit in October 1969, dissension flared over the question of Black Power and the fate of interracialism in Australia. Pastor Nicholls resigned from the AAL to protest the Black Power turn of the organization. A cohort of Aboriginal Black Power advocates, which included Bob Maza and Harry Penrith, demanded that black people run the AAL Management Committee. While the white head of the committee resigned, the November election did not produce an all-black committee to the advocates' chagrin.

As in the United States, race consciousness, pride, and self-determination were enticing organizational philosophies for power-based movements in Australia. In

August 1970 five members of the Victoria AAL, at the time directed by McGuinness, who with Denis Walker (the son of Kath Walker), Maza, and Penrith formed the all-black National Tribal Council in 1970, went to the United States for a one-month study tour of race relations between "Negroes, Indians, and Whites." McGuinness, Maza, Patsy Kruger (as new president of the AAL), Jack Davis (the public relations officer of the Aborigine Advancement Council), and Solomon Bellear (a student at Sydney University) attended the Congress of African People's five-day convention in September in Atlanta, Georgia. The delegation was eager to learn "how best to start a revolution for Aboriginal rights in Australia."[91] Amiri Baraka had founded the congress in 1970. Aboriginal delegates attended sessions and reported on Aborigines' second-class status, and sought to build international support for indigenous land rights. Inspired by Baraka's National Black Theater in Harlem, Maza started one in Redfern in 1972.[92] However, overall, the conference disappointed McGuiness, according to a brief report in the *Australian* newspaper: "The Congress of African Peoples was about as much use to Australian Aboriginals as me having a hole in the head."[93] He criticized the attendees for being "incredibly parochial" and lamented, "There was virtually no awareness of our particular problems at all. . . . It just fell on deaf ears."[94]

In 1971 Aboriginal Black Power activists also formed the first Black Panther Party in Brisbane in Queensland. Just as the U.S. Black Panther Party was fracturing, Denis Walker announced the party's formation. "The Black Panthers will be the vanguard for all depressed people, and in Australia the Aboriginals are the most depressed of all," stated Walker, minister of defense, in a news article in the *Australian* announcing the party's formation. Dressed in black with a blowout Afro and fingering a cigarette, Walker projected the vintage look of Huey P. Newton. Gary Foley, Paul Coe, and other Aboriginal men served as field marshals. Exuding militancy, Denis Walker believed in black self-determination, the overthrow of the existing system, and armed self-defense. Rule 16 required all Panthers to "learn to operate and service weapons correctly" in the case of "the Aboriginal community [needing] to defend itself from police." The rules did not merely focus on weaponry, just as the party would not simply advocate violence despite a growing flair for verbal provocation. Members had to remain sober, which meant not being "drunk or loaded from narcotics or weed," and "read for at least two hours a day to keep abreast of the changing political situation."[95]

Aboriginal Black Power activists established community programs such as a newspaper, free "child-minding centre," children's breakfast program, legal service, and health clinic. Through the convincing of Coe, they launched a police patrol featuring notebooks and pencils, but no guns, to monitor police in inner-city Sydney neighborhoods. Coe, like McGuinness, had grown up on the Erambie Mission station in New South Wales. With "milk-coffee skin and thick black hair," Coe made it clear that he preferred to be called "black": "The black people have to assume their own identity." While he acknowledged the role of women and argued that he was not "running them down," Coe echoed a stance similar to that of many U.S. black male nationalists. "The time has come for the men to be strong," he told a newspaper reporter in December 1970.[96]

The community patrols eventually led to the establishment of the first Aboriginal Legal Service of New South Wales, controlled by indigenous people. Years later, Coe would argue that the legal service not only provided assistance, but also represented movement toward establishing a black nation: "I believe, and always have believed that the Aboriginal people have never ever relinquished their sovereignty of their rights . . . that we have always been and still are, a nation within in a nation—that we are a sovereign people."[97] This black nation did not emerge, at least not spatially, just as it would not in the United States, but the language of self-determination continued to undergird Aborigines' political, cultural, and economic efforts.

The 1970s featured a series of public protests. They occupied and demonstrated on federal land in order to highlight the marginalized conditions of indigenous people—just as U.S. Native Americans had in their struggles for Red Power.[98] On January 26, 1972, on Australia Day, activists established the Aboriginal Embassy. Black Power activist Roberta "Bobbi" Sykes, who formed the Black Women's Action group, served as its first secretary. They set up an Aboriginal Embassy on the front lawns of the Parliament House in Canberra. It started with four men: Billy Craigie, Tony Coorie, Michael Anderson, and Bertie Williams.[99] They set up green striped umbrellas and tents, and posted cardboard placards provocatively demanding, "land rights or bloodshed." The Aboriginal men exuded a black cultural aesthetic: clenched fists and black leather jackets and berets.[100] Scholar Jennifer Clark writes: "The Tent Embassy spoke both in the language of the international black revolution and domestic Indigenous experience."[101]

The encampment in Australia's Canberra also evoked the spirit of Native Americans' occupation of Alcatraz Island in the United States. In November 1969, U.S. Native Americans under the mantle "Indians of all Tribes" had occupied Alcatraz Island, an abandoned federal penitentiary in San Francisco Bay, to "protest genocidal policies." The occupation lasted until 1971. The Alcatraz takeover highlighted "racist exploitation" and the egregious living conditions of Native Americans on reservations. The American Indian Movement, which started in 1968 in Minneapolis to address mostly urban-based issues, became the iconic driver of Red Power struggles. While Native Americans in the United States did not relinquish the importance of land rights and sovereignty, the dismal conditions they experienced in cities such as poor housing, sanitation, healthcare, and employment opportunities also required their attention.[102]

The Canberra encampment started with 11 tents. By June (their winter), however, when nighttime temperatures dropped below freezing, only four tents remained. One diehard protestor used "wooden boxes as a bed and 11 blankets to fight off the cold."[103] The tent embassy lasted until the end of July when Parliament passed an ordinance outlawing camping on government grounds. The police acted, removing the Aboriginal Embassy on July 20. People returned. Three days later, police again removed the tents and violently clashed with protesters.[104] The media attention drew sympathizers from Brisbane. They arrived on a bus, "mostly young fellas."[105] Hedley Johnson remembered: "I was about 14, all the Brady boys, they were about my age. We all piled on the bus. It was the middle of winter; we just went down with what we had on."[106] The protesters rebuilt the embassy one more time, but fearing that additional clashes might result in fatalities, they allowed police to remove the tents for the last time without incident.[107]

Months later the only national black publication in Australia, *Identity,* published a special issue on "Black Power." Launched by Aboriginal Publications Foundation in 1971, the foundation chair was the very same Pastor Nicholls who two years prior turned away from Black Power. The issue's editor was John A. Newfong. An artist, Newfong had worked with the Victoria AAL as well as served as a spokesperson for the five-month Canberra tent embassy. Newfong compared *Identity* to international publications such as *Black Orpheus* and *Pan Africa,* as well as viewed it, at times, as Australia's *Ebony* or *Jet.* He was aware of critiques of *Ebony*—one Black Panther called it a "glossy magazine for glossy niggers"—but Newfong nevertheless believed that "the white press in America [took] its cue in Black American Affairs from 'Ebony' more than any other black publication." He hoped *Identity* would "serve a similar function [in Australia], then the Aboriginal Advancement Movement will be all the stronger for it."[108] The November 1972 special issue featured essays on black politics, labor, the "Aboriginal vote," a cultural festival, and "The Black Woman in Australia."

In 1975 another publication, *Black Power in Australia,* put Black Power as a philosophy "on trial." The book explicitly questioned Black Power's effectiveness as a liberation strategy. The book's very first paragraph read: "Black Power in Australia—a spurious American import or a genuine movement expressing the frustration and anger of black Australians? A path to violence or a viable means of uniting Australia's dispossessed?"[109] The debaters were Bobbi Sykes and Senator Neville Bonner.

A grassroots Black Power advocate, Sykes had grown up in Townsville in North Queensland. Achieving a primary level education, Sykes had labored as a dishwasher, a waitress, floor scrubber, factory worker, and briefly as an exotic dancer. In 1964, she became an organizer with OPAL—the One People for Australia League (OPAL), which was "a charitable group committed to the welfare of indigenous people."[110] Sykes brought new zeal to the organization as she worked to provide resources to families, but was expelled after helping Gurindji families in the Wave Hill Station strike in 1966 to protest poor working conditions and advocate for land rights.[111] Sykes left behind OPAL to engage in more activist campaigns for black liberation and economic justice.

Neville Bonner was born in New South Wales in 1922, the grandson of a "fully initiated member of the Brisbane Rivers Aboriginals Tribe."[112] After his mother died when he was 13, he received his only formal year of schooling before working on a banana plantation and eventually becoming a stockman. He married, had a son, and moved his family to Palm Island. In 1972, he was not only elected for the first time to the Australian Commonwealth parliament as a Senator from Queensland, but was serving his fifth term as state president of OPAL—the same organization from which Sykes was expelled for her militancy.

The Black Power debates between Bonner and Sykes in the mid-1970s speak to the complexity of Aboriginal politics and its indigenous and international roots and routes. Signaling her cultural and political attachments to U.S. black liberation politics, Sykes wore an Afro and championed Black Power as a way forward for Aboriginal people. For her, Black Power was not "blood and guts" as depicted by the media covering the "American black summer riots." Nor was it "black capitalism" where primarily a small black elite or middle class benefited. Instead it was "black action" that benefited the black masses.[113] She wrote: "Australian 'Black Power' . . . [is] the power generated by people who seek to identify their own problems and . . . strive to take action in all possible forms to solve those problems."[114] Referencing Malcolm X and the "bullet or the ballot," Sykes believed that political power and education were critical, otherwise people might be forced by "sheer desperation to consider the power of the bullet."[115]

Bonner took a Manichean view. He identified two kinds of Black Power—"good" and "bad." Good Black Power focused on race pride and besting "the white man's environment and him at his own game."[116] There was no room for overthrowing the system or transforming its structures. That was bad Black Power, and Bonner would "have no truck" with that. Wrote Bonner: the Black Power "creed of muscle and violence can only serve as fodder for biggots [sic], a balm for dosed minds."[117] He critiqued the belief "that all power comes from the barrel of a gun" as "just another example of the romantic revolutionary myth that the world has copied from America in the last decade."[118] Truth be told, there were U.S. black leftists who waged this critique as well, but the belief that Black Power was reducible to violence was itself also a myth. Some activists did believe in armed revolution, but this was far from fully accepted by all those moved by the zeitgeist of Black Power in the United States.

As far as Bonner was concerned, Aborigines had little in common with U.S. black people, and were not a part of a global black world. He criticized Sykes, saying she engaged in "contortions" to "identify 'Aborigine power' with America's 'Black Power.'" He argued, "There is a similarity between the plight of the American Negro and the Australian Aborigine: they are both clearly identifiable disadvantaged minorities in an advanced technological society, but that is just as far as the similarity extends."[119] Sykes disagreed. "The word 'black'" was "highly desirable" and Aboriginal men and women were part of an international community waging struggles against oppressive forces. This included, for some, not just white supremacy and anti-imperialism, but also patriarchy.

The same year of *Black Power in Australia*'s publication, Aboriginal women participated in the International Year of the Woman for which the Australian government committed $2 million. This did not sit well with some Aboriginal women who struggled to provide for their families. This celebration featured the Women and Politics Conference in Canberra. As part of the conference, organizers invited and paid the expenses for nine international guest speakers, one of whom was Flo Kennedy. Upon her arrival, Kennedy learned of plans underway for an Aboriginal women's demonstration. Without missing a beat, she let her hosts and the media know that she would be attending that demonstration.

Flamboyant as ever, Kennedy put on a chiffon dress and her mink, met the prime minister at the Parliament House reception, and then went to join the Aboriginal women protesters—described by the press as "youngsters with their wild Afros and their radical ideas." These protesters, who attended the conference alongside "Liberal Labor" activists and "ultra-conservatives from the Right to Life" movement, were accused of spoiling the "lovely party."[120] The next day "Mum Shirl" from the Redfern Aboriginal Medical Service, which Sykes also participated in, kept the protest alive. At an event attended by 600 middle-class conservative women, the Aboriginal women called attention to their dire living situations and vowed that they would not "be content to be the silent minority any longer, living in tents with sick children on the outskirts of country towns." Human rights, civil rights, social needs, land rights, and Black Power—all appeared on these radical Aboriginal women's agendas. A *Sydney Morning Herald* reporter quoted Aboriginal trade unionist Edith van Horn: "[I thank] black people for [not only] teaching us to fight for our rights" but also "that men are not going to give us the kind of life we want without a fight." They rallied around their own self-determination and sovereignty claims and, in doing so, they joined marginalized and dispossessed people and women of color across the world in revolt.

From Detroit to Durban, New York to Havana

These people of color revolutions in the Black Power era were inextricably linked to questions of access to resources and wealth—whether in U.S. ghettos, over indigenous land rights, for reparations, or against poverty. Some also plainly revealed the reach and operation of U.S. political and economic power at home and abroad. In May 1973 the Black Workers Organizing Committee (BWOC) issued a 25-cent publication titled "From Detroit to Durban." Threading the relationships photographically, "From Detroit to Durban" depicted African miners as the producers of South African wealth, black Zimbabweans protesting against the white-led regime in then Rhodesia, Angolans training to fight the Portuguese colonials, black GI "resistance to the war and military racism," primarily black women workers striking at the Oneita Mills in South Carolina since January 1963, and a daycare demonstration on the Tri-Borough Bridge in New York City in March 1973.[121]

Supporting the anti-apartheid struggle and seeing parallels with the exploitation of U.S. black workers, the Bay Area "collective of black workers" proclaimed: "THEIR STRUGGLE IS OUR STRUGGLE." The mechanisms of control in South

Africa registered as eerily familiar to those in United States. Black South Africans could be jailed for sitting on a white bench or even producing political graffiti (the charge was "sabotage"). The police targeted and suppressed the ANC and incarcerated its leader Nelson Mandela on Robben Island. Black South Africans could not vote, experienced high unemployment, earned "near-starvation level wages," and suffered "miserable medical care" and high infant mortality rates. This, too, in a country where already four million whites owned 87 percent of the residential land. Seventeen million African, "Colored," and "Asian" people squeezed together on the remaining 13 percent. This people-of-color majority could not depend on land as a source of income, let alone wealth. They had to work. But even then they were not hired in skilled or trade jobs, which were reserved for white Afrikaners. Joining unions or engaging in labor strikes resulted in an automatic three-year prison sentence.[122]

Similarities went beyond worker exploitation and the suppression of civil and social rights in the United States and South Africa. White supremacy and capitalism knitted together global systems of privilege and power. This included local employment and property practices, as well as international trade and investments. In South Africa, U.S. corporations helped to bankroll South African apartheid and its political regime, which held "white rule . . . as an unquestionable virtue." In fact, major U.S. corporations jockeyed for position alongside those from Britain, France, and Germany. In the midst of major black urban relocation and land dispossession campaigns, as well as aggressive subjugation of black South Africans and anti-apartheid activists, white South Africa "experienced one of the highest rates of economic growth in the world."[123]

General Motors, Ford, and Chrysler, the "Big 3" auto industries in Detroit, had plants in South Africa, and U.S. banks such as Chase Manhattan and First National invested in the country after the Sharpeville massacre of 1960. Union Carbide, Standard Oil, and International Harvester also did business with the apartheid regime. By 1973, 400 U.S. companies (including Polaroid, which made photos for black South African passbooks) had economic interests in South Africa. Race, capital, and profit were starkly intertwined. So much so that BWOC asserted: "This incessant drive for more and more profit is like a tapeworm. You can't feed it enough. It only gets bigger and wants more."[124]

These realities resonated with revolutionary nationalist and black labor activists in the United States.[125] In 1972 at one African Liberation Day event, held throughout the diaspora to rally support for liberation movements in Africa, a sprawling banner read: "No Power Can Defeat the International Black Struggle" and a sign blared: "Colgate Fights Cavities and Freedom; Fight Colgate." Across the United States, 50,000 people "rallied from coast to coast." In April 1972 black longshoremen in Burnside, Louisiana, with the support of 300 black Southern University students, protested the United States' flouting of the United Nations embargo on Rhodesia by "refus[ing] to unload chrome from Rhodesia." In August 1972 Baltimore dockworkers followed suit. Five months later, 12,000 workers in the American Metal Climax mine in Namibia went on strike, and in February 1973, 50,000 workers protested poor wages and working conditions in Durban. This was just three months before the BWOC issued its "Detroit to Durban" pamphlet.[126]

In South Africa, in the midst of black worker unrest and the banning of the ANC and the Pan-African Congress, a student-led black consciousness movement also was on the rise between 1968 and the mid-1970s. The black consciousness movement challenged white-skin privilege among white supremacists as well as white anti-apartheid activists. It supported self-determination, group power, and culture. Medical student Steve Biko led it. In 1976, Soweto students boycotted schools to protest learning Afrikaans. Biko suffered a brutal police beating. As a result of those injuries and lack of hospital treatment, Biko died.[127]

By the time the BWOC released its pamphlet, self-determined black activists, particularly those challenging racial privilege and capitalism, faced intensified repression not just abroad but in the United States as well. The case of Joanne Byron (Chesimard), who became Assata Shakur, is instructive. In the early 1970s, Assata, who believed that the deliverance of South Africa from apartheid was "the most important battle of the century for Black people," found herself facing the horror of a lifetime.[128] Assata had become a committed revolutionary, building on the heady days rife with learning from African students from Columbia University and a series of encounters that included working briefly with Native American activists at Alcatraz, conversing with a Red Guard cadre at a protest, visiting the Black Panther Party in Oakland, attending Jonathan Jackson's funeral, and learning of Angela Davis who was on the run. Her aunt and lawyer Evelyn Williams recalled: "Joey talked in terms of global parameters, Africa, and the politics needed to ensure permanent change in the United States."[129] Back from her trip to the West Coast, Assata went to the Black Panther Party office on 7th Avenue, joined, and that evening took a bus ride to Philadelphia to attend the Panther Party's Revolutionary People's Constitutional Convention on Labor Day weekend in 1970. The convention, which attracted anywhere from 6,000 to 15,000 people, sought "to guarantee the rights of the poor and oppressed."[130]

Assata counted among her best friends Moore (Dhoruba) and Tabor (Cetewayo) of the New York Panther 21. She had long conversations with them about international politics. She met Afeni Shakur, also one of the Panther 21, and Zayd Shakur, the New York party's minister of information, and helped to raise money for the New York Panther 21's defense. Over time, Assata worked in the party's medical cadre, breakfast program, and its Saturday liberation school until about 1971. After the factional split and expulsions, she decided to leave the Black Panther Party. At about the same time that Assata left the Panthers, police amplified their target against the Panthers and her. They papered New York with "Wanted" posters that charged Assata with a bank robbery. Assata went, as Angela Davis had, underground, and found comradeship and safety among the ranks of the Black

Liberation Army. Two years later Assata's running ended. On the New Jersey turnpike state troopers pulled over the car in which she and two friends Zayd Shakur and Sundiata Acoli rode. They were stopped for a traffic violation—an authorized form of harassment to apply pressure on known or suspected Black Power activists. This policing tactic anticipated another practice of racial profiling on the nation's highways—"driving while black."

That traffic stop left Assata near death. She was shot while sitting in the car. State troopers argued otherwise. "The air was like cold glass," Assata later recounted in her memoir. "Huge bubbles rose and burst. Each one felt like an explosion in my chest."[131] Troopers dragged her out of the car, and punched and kicked her, while holding a gun to her head. They then dragged her across the pavement and asked whether she was dead yet. Assata was taken to the hospital. There police beat her some more, called her "nigger bitches," interrogated her about the Black Liberation Army, and leg-cuffed her to the bed rail.[132] At the end of it all, Zayd Shakur and one of the state troopers lay dead, and Assata and Sundiata Acoli were arrested, tried, and convicted for the state trooper's death.

In April 1978, paying dearly for her commitment to black people's liberation, Assata was transported to the Federal Prison for Women in Alderson, West Virginia, where Claudia Jones had been incarcerated shortly before her deportation over two decades prior. In April 1978, Assata was incarcerated in the prison's maximum-security unit. She was the only black woman. Her fellow inmates were white supremacists, Nazi sympathizers, Manson family women, "hillbilly prisoners," and "niggah lovers." The latter included Rita Brown, a lesbian feminist who worked with the George Jackson Brigade on the West Coast. Assata served her time there in the maximum-security unit (later deemed unconstitutional), and only joined the general population when the unit was phased out. That's when she discovered: "Many of the sisters were Black and poor and from D.C., where every crime is a violation of a federal statute. They were beautiful sisters, serving outrageous sentences for minor offenses." What she witnessed was the concrete impact of disparate sentencing practices and expansion of the mass carceral state. Assata also, to her excitement, met Lolita Lebron. She admired Lebron whom she considered "one of the most respected political prisoners in the world." Lebron was "dedicated to the independence of Puerto Rico and the liberation of her people." Assata also met Mary Alice, a nun who introduced her to liberation theology.[133] When the unit finally closed, Assata went back to Clinton Correctional Facility for Women in New Jersey. She would not be there long. Shortly after returning, Assata escaped from prison. She surfaced in Cuba.

The island nation offered her safe haven and represented—as it had in the past for others—a beacon of hope. By the time Assata arrived, it had been nearly a decade since the first set of black exiles had arrived there. Cuba, which granted her political asylum, provided a concrete example of socialist revolution. The government offered its residents free healthcare and education and more affordable rents, and Cuban activists continued their struggle against racism—a chronic system of inequality and power that had to be intentionally attacked no matter the economic system.

In Cuba Assata deliberated on the lessons learned in the United States—of COINTELPRO, race and class struggles, nationalism, and internationalism. According to Assata: "Any community seriously concerned with its own freedom has to be concerned about other people's freedom as well. The victory of oppressed people anywhere in the world is a victory for Black people. Each time one of imperialism's tentacles is cut off we are closer to liberation." She believed: "The defeat of apartheid in South Africa will bring Africans all over the planet closer to liberation. Imperialism is an international system of exploitation, and, we as revolutionaries, need to be internationalists to defeat it."[134] It would take almost two decades (until the early 1990s) before legal apartheid crumbled under the weight of local revolutionary struggle and international economic and humanitarian pressure. By then, with the United States and Britain leading the way, a new global political order emerged, punctuated by the retrenchment of social welfare policies, renewed fervor of law and order, and the ascendancy of conservative political and economic agendas.

As black people struggled against white supremacy, state violence, and economic oppression in the Black Power era, they also had to contend with differing beliefs and tendencies within the black community. Indeed, the myriad calls and strategies to achieve Black Power and liberation—as much as they brought black people together to wage battle against common enemies—also challenged any notion of romantic black unity by unveiling undeniable hierarchies based on gender, class, and sexuality. These debates and the "counterrevolutionary" behaviors that they spurred were as much a part of the story of Black Power and the Black Power era as were ideological, organizational, and generational differences.

Notes

1 Gil Scott-Heron and Brian Jackson, "Third World Revolution," *Secrets.* Arista Records, 1978.
2 See Chapter 2 for more details on the kidnapping case involving Robert F. Williams, Mallory, and the Stegalls. "Charles Anderson to Mae Mallory, March 15, 1963, Folder: Correspondence 1963, Box 1, Mae Mallory Papers, Walter P. Reuther Library, Wayne State University, Detroit, Michigan.
3 The spellings in this poem appear as in the original. Charles Anderson, "Forcast Storm," 1963, Folder: Correspondence 1963, Box 1, Mae Mallory Papers.
4 Charles Anderson, "Forcast Storm," 1963.
5 Mae Mallory to Lorraine Hansberry, June 1, 1963; Mae Mallory to Richard Gibson, August 24, 1963; Mae Mallory to Mabel and Robert Williams, June 3, 1963, Folder: Correspondence 1963, Box 1, Mae Mallory Papers.
6 "Open Letter to an American Governor," *Ghanaian Times,* July 24, 1963, Folder: Monroe Defense Committee, 1962–63, Box 1, Mae Mallory Papers.
7 Davis, 29.

8 "An Open Letter to My Sister, Angela Y. Davis," November 19, 1970, History Is a Weapon website, www.historyisaweapon.com/defcon1/itcitmbaldwin.html.
9 On Thompson-Patterson, see McDuffie, *Sojourning for Freedom*, 193. On William Patterson, see Horne, *Black* Revolutionary, 204. Also see, Ransby, *Ella Baker*, 352–353.
10 Klimke, "The African American Civil Rights Struggle," 99. Also, Höhn, 135.
11 Aptheker, 29.
12 Davis, 119.
13 Joseph, *Waiting 'Til the Midnight Hour*, 104; Marable, 307–320.
14 Angela Davis, "Memories of Black Liberation," in *Claim No Easy Victories: The Legacy of Amilcar Cabral*, ed. Firoze Manji and Bill Fletcher Jr. (CODESRIA & Daraja Press, 2013), 463.
15 Forman, *The Making of Black Revolutionaries*, 406.
16 Ibid., 407–408.
17 Ibid., 483.
18 Bogues, 96.
19 Ibid., 111.
20 Prashad, 192, 330n1.
21 Forman, *The Making of Black Revolutionaries*, 484.
22 Forman, *The Making of Black Revolutionaries*, 488; Allen, 254.
23 Johanna Fernandez, "Between Social Services Reform and Revolutionary Politics: The Young Lords, Late Sixties Radicalism, and Community Organizing in New York City," in *Freedom North*, ed. Theoharis and Woodard, 259.
24 Ibid., 264–269.
25 Roberto P. Rodriguez-Morazzani, "Political Cultures of the Puerto Rican Left in the United States," in *The Puerto Rican Movement*, ed. Torres and Velázquez, 39.
26 "Young Lords Party 13-Point Program and Platform," The Sixties Project Website, www2.iath.virginia.edu/sixties/HTML_docs/Resources/Primary/Manifestos/Young_Lords_platform.html.
27 Yohuru Williams, "American Exported Black Nationalism," 14.
28 Shakur, 226.
29 Harboring a common enemy in global white supremacy and imperialism sometimes trumped nuanced understandings of country-specific politics. See, for instance, Robeson Taj Frazier, 929–953.
30 Rose C. Thevenin, " 'Boundaries of Law & Disorder': The 'Grand Design' of Eldridge Cleaver and the 'Overseas Revolution' in Cuba," in *Diasporic Africa*, ed. Gomez, 254.
31 Kathleen Neal Cleaver, "Back to Africa: The Evolution of the International Section of the Black Panther Party (1969–1972)," in *The Black Panther Party [Reconsidered]*, ed. Charles E. Jones, 216–217. On Cuba, black struggle, and cultural revolutions, see Young, 18–53.
32 Martin Schram, "Hijackers Find Cuba Unpleasant," *Sarasota Journal*, November 15, 1972; "Hijackers Prefer Death in U.S. to Cuban Life," *Pittsburgh Press*, February 3, 1978; David B. Offer, "Hijacker Talks of Cuban Jailers, US 'Neglect,'" *Milwaukee Journal*, May 20, 1978.
33 "2 Airliners Hijacked to Havana with a Total of 145 on Board," *New York Times*, January 29, 1969. Between 1961 and 1972, 218 people, of different races, had been involved in 159 hijackings, with the highest percentage landing in Cuba. The United States began seeking an international treaty to punish hijackers. Robert Lindsey, "218 Persons Involved in 159 U.S. Hijackings since 1961, F.A.A. Says," *New York Times*, November 19, 1972.
34 Reitan, 219.
35 Bloom and Martin, 350–351; Reitan, 217–218; Yohuru Williams, "American Exported Black Nationalism."
36 Reitan, 218.

37 Rose C. Thevenin, " 'Boundaries of Law & Disorder': The 'Grand Design' of Eldridge Cleaver and the 'Overseas Revolution' in Cuba," 257. Also, Reitan, 227–229.

38 Prashad, 125.

39 Joel Vinocur, "Fanon's Black Power Message Wins Posthumous Attention in Martinique," *Washington Post,* February 21, 1968; "Complete Unity, Dedicated Struggle, Total Victory, for World's Oppressed Peoples!" *Did You Know?,* March 1966, Folder: *Did You Know?* (newsletter), Box 1, Mae Mallory Papers. Under the pen name Asa Lee, Ethel A. Johnson initially wrote a column "Did You Know?" in Robert F. Williams' *The Crusader* newsletter based in Monroe, North Carolina. Starting in 1963, Johnson co-edited the newsletter *Did You Know?*, also based in Monroe.

40 Forman, *The Making of Black Revolutionaries,* 506–508.

41 Ibid., 514.

42 "Bandung to Algiers," *Did You Know?,* July 24, 1965, Folder: *Did You Know?* (newsletter), Box 1, Mae Mallory Papers.

43 Prashad, 130.

44 Ibid., 131.

45 Ibid., 132. On U.S. corporation oil deal, Bloom and Martin, 350–351; Michael L. Clemons and Charles E. Jones, "Global Solidarity: The Black Panther Party in the International Arena," in *Liberation, Imagination, and the Black Panther Party,* ed. Cleaver and Katsiaficas, 28.

46 Kathleen Cleaver, "Back to Africa: The Evolution of the International Section of the Black Panther Party (1969–1972)"; "Cleaver Arrives for Algiers Fete," *New York Times,* July 16, 1969. According to Robyn Spencer, 24 countries were represented at the cultural festival as well as six liberation movements. Black Panther Party leaders David Hilliard, Raymond "Masai" Hewitt, and Emory Douglas also attended. Robyn Spencer, "Merely One Link in the Worldwide Revolution," in *From Toussaint to Tupac,* ed. West, Martin, and Wilkins, 215–231.

47 Michael L. Clemons and Charles E. Jones, "Global Solidarity: The Black Panther Party in the International Arena," 36. On establishment of International Section, see Clyde H. Farnsworth, "Black Panthers Open Office in Algiers," *New York Times,* September 14, 1970.

48 Chris Booker, "Lumpenization," in *The Black Panther Party [Reconsidered],* ed. Charles E. Jones, 354.

49 Klimke, *The Other Alliance,* 118–120. Connie Matthews was born in Jamaica and, according to a *New York Times* article, at the time of Tabor's flight from the United States was an "Algerian citizen" with a passport and visa. Edith Evans Asbury, "Newton Denounces 2 Missing Panthers," *New York Times,* February 10, 1971.

50 Donald Cox, "The Split in the Party," *New Political Science* 21:2 (1999): 171–176.

51 James C. McKinley Jr., "A Black Panther's Mellow Exile: Farming in Africa," *New York Times,* November 23, 1997. Also, Robert M. Smith, "Chicago Official Testifies: Aide Says He Was Asked to Destroy Gun Receipts," *New York Times,* October 14, 1969; "Black Panther is Indicted on Charge of Jumping Bail," *New York Times,* August 6, 1972; James C. McKinley Jr., "A Black Panther's Mellow Exile: Farming in Africa," *New York Times,* November 23, 1997.

52 Kathleen Neal Cleaver, "Women, Power, and Revolution," in *Liberation, Imagination, and the Black Panther Party,* ed. Cleaver and Katsiaficas, 123.

53 Höhn, 133.

54 "What Is the Revolutionary Peoples Communications Network," *Voice of the Lumpen* 1 (October 1971), African-American Involvement in the Vietnam War, G.I. Publications, www.aavw.org/served/gipubs_voice_lumpen_abstract01.html.

55 "Black Political Prisoners, USA: The Ramstein II," *Sun Reporter,* September 18, 1971.

56 "Black GI Released from West German Prison to International Section Black Panther Party Algiers," *Voice of the Lumpen* 1 (October 1971).

57 Klimke, *The Other Alliance,* 124, 126.

58 Klimke, "The African American Civil Rights Struggle," 101. A hearty thanks to my colleague Ken Ledford for translating the message on the blackboard.

59 "Black GI Released from West German Prison to International Section Black Panther Party Algiers," *Voice of the Lumpen* 1 (October 1971).

60 Ibid.

61 Between 1967 and 1973, the county provided humanitarian asylum for 800 black and white anti-war American GIs (many of whom arrived by way of Germany). Scott, 123–142. On the Swedish press coverage, see Channing Kennedy, "Trove of Unseen Footage Revives History in 'The Black Power Mixtape,'" *Colorlines,* September 6, 2011.

62 *The Black Power Mixtape 1967–1975.* Directed by Göran Hugo Olsson. Story AB, Sveriges Television AB, and Louverture Films LLC, 2011. Also, Alan Maass, "The Black Power era," October 25, 2011, socialistworker.org/2011/10/25/black-power-era.

63 A. Muhammad Ahmad, "The League of Revolutionary Black Workers: A Historical Study," History Is a Weapon website, www.historyisaweapon.com/defcon1/rbwstudy.html.

64 "Ex-Detroiter held in Sweden for U.S." *Detroit News,* March 16, 1971.

65 Request for Asylum for Glanton Dowdell by attorney Hans Goran Franck, to Statens Invandraverk (State Immigration Department), n.d., Folder 25: Glanton, Box 6, Kenneth V. and Sheila M. Cockrel Papers, Walter P. Reuther Library, Wayne State University, Detroit, Michigan.

66 Letter to John from Gudrun Ryman, 19 February 1971, Folder 8, Box 3, Dan Georgakas Papers, Walter P. Reuther Library, Wayne State University, Detroit, Michigan.

67 Hamlin with Gibbs, 33–38.

68 The Black Causes Association for the International Black Appeal, Benefit Flier, "A Profile of Glanton Dowdell (at home and abroad), circa 1971, Folder 8, Box 3, Dan Georgakas Papers.

69 McGregor, 163.

70 "Black Power Warning by Perkins," *The Australian,* April 27, 1965, The Koori History Website (KHW hereafter), www.kooriweb.org/foley/indexb.html.

71 "He Fears 'Black Power,'" *The Sun,* June 15, 1968, KHW.

72 Anna Haebich, "Aboriginal Women," The Encyclopedia of Women & Leadership in Twentieth-Century Australia, www.womenaustralia.info/leaders/biogs/WLE0022b.htm.

73 Clark, " 'The Wind of Change' in Australia," 99, 103; Curthoys; Lydon, 216.

74 "He Fears 'Black Power,'" *The Sun,* June 15, 1968, KHW.

75 Ibid.

76 Edwards, 104.

77 On the version about the forgotten pair of gloves, see Reynolds, 42. For the full list of demands, see Edwards, 58–59. The campaign emerged from a workshop that Edwards led at the Los Angeles Black Youth Conference—the same one at which Forman discussed Fanon. Those who attended the boycott workshop included Tommie Smith, Lew Alcindor (Kareem Abdul Jabbar), Lee Evans, and Otis Burrell. Edwards, 50–52.

78 Carmichael with Thelwell, 708.

79 Ibid.

80 Michael Carlton, "Peter Norman: Unlikely Australian Participant in Black Athletes' Olympic Civil Rights Protest," *The Guardian,* October 5, 2006. I would also like to thank Colin Samson at the University of Essex for bringing to my attention Harry Edwards and his role in this athletic Black Power moment.

81 Kathy Lothian, "Moving Blackwards: Black Power and the Aboriginal Embassy," in *Transgressions,* ed. Macfarlane and Hannah.

82 "Bruce Hit the Headlines over 'Black Power,'" *Northcote Leader,* June 17, 1970, KHW.

83 "National Hero Profile: Roosevelt Brown," *Bernews,* April 30, 2011, http://bernews.com/2011/04/national-hero-profile-roosevelt-brown/; Edmondson, 693–716. Also, Michael L. Clemons and Charles E. Jones, "Global Solidarity: The Black Panther Party in the International Arena," 24.

84 "Black Power Leaders Angers Pastor," *The Sunraysia Daily,* August 9, 1969, KHW.
85 Gary Foley, "Black Power in Redfern, 1968–1972," October 5, 2001, KHW.
86 "Neil Mitchell, "Pastor Nicholls Hits at 'Black Power'"*The Age,* August 29, 1969, KHW.
87 Gary Foley, "Black Power in Redfern."
88 "Ian Baker and Neil Mitchell, "Yes, Black Power—but Not Violent,"*The Age,* August 30, 1969, KHW.
89 " 'Black Power' Ideas Give Aborigines New Faith in Selves," *The Tribune,* October 15, 1969, KHW.
90 Quote appears in Maynard, "In the Interests of Our People," 11. Also, Gary Foley, "Black Power in Redfern"; John Maynard, "Transcultural/Transnational Interaction and Influence in Aboriginal Australia," in *Connected Worlds,* ed. Curthoys and Lake; Clark, "The Wind of Change," 90.
91 Quote in Deborah Garland, "Patsy wants to learn how to start a thought rebellion," *Australian,* February 9, 1970; "Aborigines to Study in U.S.A.," *Northcote Leader,* August 2, 1970.
92 Kathy Lothian, "Moving Blackwards: Black Power and the Aboriginal Embassy."
93 "Native Rights Plea Ignored," *Australian,* March 18, 1970.
94 Ibid.
95 "Aboriginals Set Up Militant Black Panther Movement," *Australian,* January 19, 1972.
96 Elizabeth Riddell, "Introducing Paul Coe," *Australian,* December 23, 1970.
97 Kathy Lothian, "Moving Blackwards: Black Power and the Aboriginal Embassy."
98 Josephy et al., 1–2.
99 Lydon, 230.
100 Kathy Lothian, "Moving Blackwards: Black Power and the Aboriginal Embassy."
101 Clark, *Aborigines & Activism,* 203.
102 In 1960, 28 percent of Native Americans lived in cities. A decade later this figure had increased to 44 percent. The concerns of city dwellers were not totally dissimilar from those on reservations, for poverty was ubiquitous. Josephy et al., 7. On Alcatraz, see Paul Chaat Smith and Robert Allen Warrior.
103 Aird, 116.
104 Lydon, 230.
105 Aird, 116.
106 Ibid.
107 Kathy Lothian, "Moving Blackwards: Black Power and the Aboriginal Embassy."
108 John A. Newfong, "Editorial," *Identity,* November 1972.
109 Turner.
110 Reynolds, 64.
111 The strike lasted eight years, ending with land being handed back on August 16, 1975. Lydon, 223. Coe also participated in this strike. He was convicted of "offensive behavior, resisting arrest, and kicking a policeman." "Introducing Paul Coe" *Australian,* December 23, 1970.
112 Turner, 31.
113 Ibid., 8–9.
114 Ibid., 10.
115 Ibid., 26–27.
116 Ibid., 32.
117 Ibid., 33, 39.
118 Ibid., 52.
119 Ibid., 68.
120 Kennedy, 6–8; "Sounds of Change 'Spoiled Our Lovely Party,'" *Sydney Morning Herald,* September 4, 1975.
121 Black Workers Organizing Committee, "U.S. Investments—Who Benefits?" in *From Detroit to Durban: Black Workers' Common Struggle* (Oakland, CA: United Front Press, May 1973). Rhodesia became independent Zimbabwe in 1980.

122 Ibid.
123 Meredith, 412–413.
124 Black Workers Organizing Committee, "U.S. Investments—Who Benefits?"
125 The anti-apartheid struggle also took root in the academy by the early 1980s with calls for divestment.
126 Black Workers Organizing Committee, "U.S. Investments—Who Benefits?" On the ALSC and African Liberation Day, see Plummer, *In Search of Power,* 277–280.
127 Grady-Willis, 93–96; Meredith, 417–418.
128 Shakur, 267.
129 Evelyn A. Williams, 8.
130 Shakur, 216.
131 Ibid., 3.
132 Ibid., 8.
133 Ibid., 254–255.
134 Ibid., 267.

7

REVOLUTION FOR WHOM?

Unraveling Romantic Black Unity

> Revolutions start from the inside out and from the bottom up. They grow organically provided actions can be made conscious and organized through developing political awareness and study.
>
> —*Patricia Murphy Robinson (1966)*[1]

Consistent with a radical organizing tradition among women of color, a collective of poor black women in Mount Vernon and New Rochelle, New York, joined with black socialist feminist Patricia Murphy Robinson to pen a letter "to a North Vietnamese Sister from an Afro-American Woman." Robinson, who had helped to initiate Black Women Enraged (BWE) in the aftermath of Malcolm X's assassination, eventually left that organization, claiming that some of its members prioritized their relationships with black male nationalists and possessed middle-class myopia with regard to poor black women and children. A mother of three children, Robinson earnestly embraced "self-determination," and she credited growing up in a "patriarchal and black oriented" family with pushing her to recognize her "real class and caste position." Robinson wrote, "I am positive that there are many women like me, Mexican, Puerto Ricans, Chinese, etc. *Revolutionary* out of experience and inner need."[2] As part of her political journey Robinson read Fanon and *The Crusader,* traveled to Cuba, and kept abreast of the goings-on with Ethel Johnson, Robert F. Williams, and the Revolutionary Action Movement. Hailing from the Baltimore *Afro-American's* Murphy family, Robinson, a psychotherapist, worked at Planned Parenthood in Mount Vernon, a majority black city on the southern tip of primarily white Westchester County.[3] Through her job and community work, Robinson met low-income black women who over the years became a part of the collective, also known as "Pat Robinson and Group" or alternatively the Mount Vernon/New Rochelle Group.[4]

The women whom Robinson met lived the reality of urban inequality. Primarily domestic workers and welfare recipients, they were forced to eke out a means of survival in often cramped and squalid residences. They were also mothers who grew tired of the local schools complaining about their children and mis-educating them. Their concerns echoed decades of critiques by other rights and Black Power activists—among them Hobson in D.C., Mallory in Harlem, Black Panther Party members in Harlem and Oakland, and mothers who started parents' councils to push for school reform.

They were, in a very real sense, obsessed with education, not as a tool to achieve middle-class respectability, but as a means of empowerment. Fed up, some of the women decided to start a small "Freedom School—right in [their] kitchens where everybody gathered anyhow." It operated on Saturdays. The mothers guided the classes, as well as invited a couple Manhattan teachers (also Robinson's friends from BWE) to teach on topics such as "Negro history." On one occasion, the children provided a "raging and true indictment of the teachers in the public school. . . . Every mother *shut up* and heard." Fighting mis-education, however, did not start and end with children. Adults were mis-educated as well, and their voices muted and too often ignored. So, among the several things they did as a collective was develop the Poor Black Women's Study Papers and write letters of protest.[5]

The "Letter to a North Vietnamese Sister" that they produced was as much about internationalizing their own struggle as positioning poor black women on the spectrum of American and global oppression. The communiqué started with a history lesson. Addressed to "Dear Sister," it discussed the post-Reconstruction era, described the KKK as "frightened fascists in white hoods," and explained that black people had to work land that they "did not have the power to own." While they critiqued Back-to-Africa and integration strategies as the purview of bourgeois black people, they touted Du Bois and Robeson as "middle-class Black radicals who had analyzed the system as the enemy." Unfortunately, neither man had "the resources or followers to unite with the poor Blacks," but "like Nkrumah, they saw the opportunities socialism could offer their people."[6] Overall, the letter depicted the late 1950s and early 1960s as years of seduction—a time when "the prospects of education and integration" stymied revolution.

The letter praised Malcolm X as "a brilliant Black humanist" for daring to break away from the Nation of Islam and wrote about the new generation of U.S. radicals, born like them, in the "belly" of the "monster counter-revolutionary oppressor." This new generation believed that "unity [was] necessary to the freedom of the Black colonies or ghettoes." However, the letter continued: "We are still in the period of trying to bring the middle class and the poor Blacks together in a united front." The problem was "privilege." Without dismantling white-skin and class privilege, the letter continued, "Black United Fronts and Black Power, at this point in our history, are in reality a historical continuum of an elite group of moderate and petit-bourgeois Blacks attempting to gain power over the existing urban Black communities." If this was to happen, they predicted, then, black middle-class people would replace white leaders and, as mediators with white capitalists, would merely become "new puppet exploiters."[7]

The "Letter to a North Vietnamese Sister" also rendered an "analysis of capitalism" that paid attention to women and race. The writers clearly recognized that "the poor Black woman is the lowest in this capitalist social and economic hierarchy."[8] The Poor Black Women's Study Papers (and eventually *Lessons from the Damned*) made this point even more boldly. In "On the Position of Poor Black Women in this Country," the opening lines declared: "It is time to speak to the whole question of the position of poor Black women in this society, and in this historical period of revolution and counter-revolution."[9]

The collective's letter and study papers raised age-old and contemporary concerns. They discussed poverty, cities under siege, the Vietnam War and oppressed nations, embattled low-income black women, "male capitalistic culture," and what they deemed counter-revolutionary impulses. The critiques were strident, the wariness demonstrable. In doing so, they also opened the blinds on many Black Power windows and shone light on the interlocking nature of oppression as other black radical women had been doing for decades. As far back as Ida B. Wells-Barnett, Claudia Jones, and the Sojourners for Truth and Justice, radical black women, with varied relationships to anti-racist struggle and the politics of self-determination, had discussed how race, class, gender, and empire impacted their lives. This included Ella Baker, who queried, "Who was this [black] power for and how would it be exercised?"[10] Just like U.S. democracy would not automatically liberate black people, neither would notions of Black Power based on uncritical calls for black unity—whether in black politics, churches, workplaces, homes, families, marriages or intimate relationships, communities, or liberation organizations. Herein lay the powerful question: Revolution by and for whom?[11]

Supporting the Revolution

A letter in the *Black Panther* newspaper provocatively attempted to answer that question while simultaneously calling on black women to "Support the Revolution." "It is not necessary to carry a gun or to fight alongside [men] against the racist dogs when they go out to battle," the letter writer explained, "but it is most important to let him know that YOU are his woman, and behind him in spirit and mind." The letter concluded: "This is the most important thing to a revolutionary soldier. A woman can make her man, or break him."[12] In this privileging of patriarchal gender roles, black men were the fighters and women their supporters and emotional bedrocks. No doubt, for some, excusing women from armed conflict made the revolution more palatable, particularly for those who may have been accustomed to the patriarchal hierarchy described by Robinson. Moreover, some women were uncomfortable with the glamorized paramilitary stances of some Black Power organizations. They found it imprudent—given increased state repression—or ineffective in addressing everyday people's needs. However, other black women did abide the idea of armed revolution and wanted to receive weapons and tactical training. This was so with the Black Panther Party even as it dropped "self-defense" from its name and moved increasingly toward community programs by the early 1970s. Whether black women believed in picking up the gun or not, however, they did not necessarily view their most important role in the revolution as emotionally supporting men. Black women sought to, and did, make the revolution through their community work, as party leaders, and even in paramilitary units.

Afeni Shakur did all three. She knew about police brutality, militarism and deadly attacks, as well as materialism and poverty. For her the personal was political. She witnessed violence in her family and by white people. Her mother had suffered spousal abuse, and she knew of black and Native American people challenging the KKK in Robeson County, North Carolina. She recalled that the indigenous Lumbees "got guns and rifles and ambushed the Klan" at a rally the Klan held to support a curfew to control black and Lumbee people. While that was not the young Afeni Shakur's (nee Alice Faye Williams) "first smell of revolution," it was her "first taste of *resistance*." She was about 10 years old. "Resist. Not revolution," she said. "I didn't know shit about changing the world. I just knew there were some foul, hateful people in it that torture us for no reason, and I needed to resist that."[13]

At 11 years of age, she moved to the South Bronx with her mom and sister. They lived in a one-room apartment. Her mom worked a low-wage job in a lampshade factory.[14] In New York, she had many opportunities to defend herself from street bullies and snarky students who teased her because of her race. Her concrete realities and developing political consciousness led her to consider the need for self-defense. Like Robinson and the collective of poor black women, she was on her own journey of political transformation. She attended political rallies, hippie be-ins, and West African bembe drum ceremonies conducted in the Yoruba religion. Significantly, at one of those ceremonies, she received her new name Afeni and deity Oya, an African goddess and woman warrior who avows anger, life, death, renewal, and change. On another day, Afeni Shakur found herself on the corner of 125th Street and 7th Avenue—the same corner on which stepladder speakers railed against racism and economic injustice in the early to mid-20th century. She joined a throng of people—"mothers, hustlers, teachers, domestics, and kids, gangsters"—who listened to Bobby Seale announce the opening of a Black Panther Party office that would bring "change and order to [the black] community," help "heal the wounds of slavery and Jim Crow," and "take arms against the aggression." He ended: "They will not beat our ass anymore!"[15]

Soon thereafter, she made her way to that office and joined the local section of the national party that had started as a small all-male enclave in California and eventually grew to thousands, a majority of whom were increasingly women.[16] The local examples of Lumumba Shakur, the Harlem section leader, and the Bronx captain Sekou Odinga, as well as the "only visible female force" of Kathleen

Cleaver, also inspired her. "They were brilliant to me," said Afeni Shakur. "I wanted what they had."[17]

As a Panther, Afeni Shakur was hell-bent on "pushing for women to have more rights in the party" and preparing them for revolution, even though Lumumba, whom she admired and married (even though he already had a wife), felt otherwise. "I pushed for weapons training classes for the women," Afeni Shakur remembered. "I would lead the Political Education classes to ensure that we were learning the same thing the men were learning. . . . We were soldiers. Lumumba kept telling me women weren't qualified. 'Train them and they will be!' I argued."[18] In Vietnam, women served as fighters in the Laos Revolutionary Party—Neo Lao. Whether in Vietnam or the United States, the belief "that women should be as brave as men" directly challenged previous presumptions of "women as the weaker sex."[19] At one time, Pat Robinson and several of the women, who identified themselves as "poor-poor" in the Mount Vernon/New Rochelle collective, belonged to "a rifle club started by some nationalists." Robinson was a sharpshooter, but she left the group over class differences.[20] Fellow Panther Regina Jennings also believed that whether man or woman, one just might have "to pay a price for freedom in the tradition of Harriet Tubman, Frantz Fanon, and Malcolm X."[21]

Just six months after joining the party, Lumumba's arrest thrust Afeni Shakur into the position of section leader.[22] In this capacity, she like many other black women inside and outside the Panther party worked with neighborhood residents around bread-and-butter issues, community control of schools, housing, and healthcare. In a matter of months, another life-altering change befell her. In a police roundup, she recalled, "[I] was arrested from my sleeping bed on 117th Street" (Fred Hampton and Mark Clark in Chicago would not be so lucky). She was charged with 30 counts of conspiracy that could result in more than 350 years in prison. Police claimed that she and others, who became known as the New York Panther 21, had conspired to blow up department stores, the New York Botanical Gardens, railroad rights-of-way, and a police station. Each was held on $100,000 bail. Afeni was one of two women. The other was 20-year-old Joan Bird who taught at P.S. 175 and took night classes in nursing at Bronx Community College. Neither had a police record. The trial of the New York Panther 21 ended over two years later in May 1971 when all the defendants were found not guilty on all counts.[23] The price people were willing to pay for freedom obviously differed—as did the currency they paid with and the internal community contradictions they had to navigate.

If, as that particular *Black Panther* letter writer and Lumumba maintained, black women were not expected (or qualified) to be "soldiers," what other things might they do? Sell the organization's newspaper, collect donations for guns, perform secretarial duties, or oversee the day-to-day needs of the programs. Of course, there was nothing wrong with any of these tasks. In fact, communications, fundraising, and administrative work kept organizations and programs operating. Men, too, fulfilled some of these tasks. Still, at issue was the belief that particular kinds of work might be deemed more appropriate for women. Masculinist politics shaped presumptions about, if not always the material reality of, black women's activist labor in the Black Power era: a form of politics Margaret Wright ill tolerated.

Married and a mother of four, Wright was a member of Women Against Repression and expressed little patience for racism and sexism. She led the community-based United Parents Council, which had 50 branches in Los Angeles County. In that role, she consistently criticized white public officials and black leaders whom she deemed "bankrupt" or "opportunists."[24] In a newspaper article, she talked about how black women, in addition to being low on the employment "totem pole" *and* exploited by "Miss Ann" (white women employers), at times, were also "exploited in the Movement." "We run errands, lick stamps, mail letters, and do the door-to-door," she said. "But when it comes to the speaker's platform, it's all men up there blowing their souls, you dig?"[25]

Putting black men out front whether on the political stage or in the family, as a way to shore up black manhood, reflected masculine power politics. These tendencies existed in religious, cultural, and revolutionary nationalist organizations. In the early years of the US organization, many women members accepted the presumption that they should "submit to male leadership, without question." These women believed that their primary role was "to inspire [their] man, educate the children and participate in social development"—a stance that even had its echoes in the 1967 Black Power Conference resolutions on "Black Women and the Home." According to women in the US organization, black men needed to protect their families and communities. Their taking a back seat simply provided a solution to "the crisis in black male leadership and the family."[26]

Fights to secure self-determination based on black unity in the Black Power era did not eliminate gender hierarchies or conflict; both were a part of the activist and societal fabric. After all, heterosexual gender oppression did not belong to a specific race, culture, or class. It was democratic in that sense, and the tool kit included sexism, homophobia, patriarchy, violence, and sex (as in the carnal act). Eldridge Cleaver, who in *Soul on Ice* had written frighteningly about raping white women as a political act—one that he "perfected" on black women—later talked about women having "pussy power" during his 1968 presidential bid.[27] Within the next year, in the wake of Panther women's political sacrifices and critiques of sexism, according to scholar Tracye Matthews, Eldridge Cleaver's public commentary became more egalitarian, sensitive to women's liberation, and critical of male chauvinism—though charges of domestic abuse still followed him. This occurred before Newton's public statements of support for women's and gay liberation in August 1970, or women and gay liberationist platforms at the Panther Party's Revolutionary People's Constitutional Convention a month later. Indeed Eldridge Cleaver's wife, Kathleen Cleaver, enhanced the party's communications network, and rank-and-file Panther women, alongside women residents, administered the community programs.[28]

Like other kinds of relationships, even the most intimate were subject to sexism, power plays and abuse—something that Black female activists knew both outside and within Black Power organizations. US organization leader Maulana Karenga, for example, served four years for his role in subjecting two women to torture in May 1970. According to historian Scot Brown, Karenga thought the women were plotting to poison him. Abusing drugs and paranoid about government infiltration, Karenga's fear took a horrifying turn when he "ordered as well as participated in their beating and torture," using a "water hose, soldering iron, and caustic chemicals."[29]

Some black men expected sex as proof of women's revolutionary commitment. It could and did result in unsavory predicaments—one that women such as Jennings found themselves navigating alongside their political work. In 1968, Jennings left Philadelphia to join the Panther Party in Oakland. Only 16 years old, Jennings "knew racism and police brutality intimately." She witnessed police beating black citizens and worked in a secretarial pool with white women who did not acknowledge her presence. (As with Assata Shakur, being a woman did not automatically make for easy alliances with white women workers.) The society Jennings navigated trampled on her humanity consistently. She arrived in Oakland ready to "smash racism" and with admiration for how the Panthers "faced White America forthrightly without begging or carrying signs for equality and justice." This is why she decided to resist the unwanted advances from a male captain instead of just leaving the party.[30]

Jennings reported the incident to the Central Committee. The committee supported the captain, and told her that she was being "foolish and counterrevolutionary" by maintaining an "attitude of sexual abstinence." Some Panther men, however, did support her "against the foolishness of [the] captain. These men were also ostracized."[31] Even with black male and female Panthers pushing against retrograde gender expectations, however, such behavior remained a contested part of the party's, and era's, politics. "My captain wanted me" [sexually,] wrote Jennings, but "all I wanted was to be a soldier," and "I was determined not to leave the Party because I felt there was no other place in America where I could fully be my Black revolutionary self." At this time, the Panthers offered her the best option despite its gender contradictions. She had made commitments. "I had store owners and other Oakland people who only purchased papers from me," Jennings explained. "I assisted senior citizens with their grocery shopping, participated in political organizing, and personally instructed a group of young children in reading. . . . I could always get a good meal, and neighborhood residents consistently watched my back."[32] The captain, however, was not one of them; he transferred her to Berkeley.

In Berkeley she confronted similar "vicious sexism" and "vulgar male behavior."[33] Kathleen Cleaver was abroad, and Elaine Brown had not yet taken the reins of power. That did not happen until 1974 when Newton fled to Cuba and appointed Brown chair of the party, not that her chairwomanship could have single-handedly eliminated (and it did not) male bravado or patriarchy. That would have been a tall order in a society where patriarchy, alongside race and class, structured intimate, political, and economic relationships. In joining the party, black women had committed themselves, according to Kathleen Cleaver, to "contesting the remaining legacy of racial slavery."[34] According to Cleaver, it was in that context of fighting "legal, social, psychological, economic, and political limitations still being imposed on our human rights, and on our rights as citizens," that "we fought to remove the limitations imposed by gender, clearly aware that it could not be fought as a stand-alone issue."[35] For other black radical women, however, tackling gender oppression and its intricate relationship to racial and economic oppression stood at the center, if not the forefront, of their agendas.

Reproducing Revolution

In dealing with the everyday realities of relationships, gender roles, and sex, black women and men also confronted the controversial question of reproductive rights and quite literally, in some instances, women's role in reproducing the revolution. The Black Unity Party in Peekskill, New York, disapproved of birth control and said so in their newsletter in 1968. They argued that black women ought to have babies because that "aid[ed] the REVOLUTION in the form of NATION building."[36] Black Unity Party members had company in their beliefs. In a CORE Target City Project newsletter *Black Dispatch,* the editor pointed to the Vietnam War and family planning centers as ways "to exterminate the Black people." Norman Collins, then, told black women that their main function "in life, is to mate with the male of [their] choosing" and have children. This would result in pride, unity, and "Black Power."[37] In both cases, these black nationalist men adamantly rejected the pill, still a new technology at that time. The FDA had approved the oral contraceptive in 1960, and this put a measure of reproductive power in the hands of women—at least those who knew about, could afford, or wanted to use the pill. By 1963, over one million women used birth control pills to prevent unwanted pregnancies. Black men who wanted to reproduce revolutionaries, however, accused black women of undercutting the liberation struggle and advancing genocide.

Low-income black women in the Mount Vernon/New Rochelle collective responded to the Black Unity Party. On September 11, 1968, writing as "Black sisters," they addressed their "Dear Brothers" directly: "Poor black sisters decide for themselves whether to have a baby or not to have a baby." Black women's decisions reflected their own desires and responses to concrete circumstances. This included taking into account the lack of support from those "poor black men" who, the sisters claimed, "won't support their families, won't stick by their women—all they think about is the street, dope and liquor, women, a piece of ass, and their cars." The Black sisters argued that they no longer would countenance being exploited for sex or for what little money they had. They also shifted the terms of the genocide debate. Indeed, they argued that birth control gave them the "freedom to fight genocide of black women and children." They, then, linked it to international freedom struggles, including that of the Vietnamese, the "South American poor," and the "African poor." The letter was signed by Patricia Haden (welfare recipient), Sue Rudolph (housewife), Joyce Hoyte (domestic), Rita Van Lew (welfare recipient), Catherine Hoyt (grandmother), and Patricia Robinson (housewife and psychotherapist).[38]

One of the signers, the church-going Rita Van Lew was in her early thirties and had five children. Her husband was a maintenance worker in a hospital, but was fired after confronting a supervisor. Unable to find work, Rita applied for welfare to support the family and began organizing fellow recipients in her building. Her landlord evicted her. Just three months after forming the first welfare rights group in lower Westchester County, which spurred tension between her and her husband, they separated. All the while, for three years in fact, Rita sought training through a government program as a nurse, but was only offered training as a secretary. She still could not earn enough to make ends meet, and so, even while working, she still qualified for and received a welfare supplement.[39] Outspoken, she participated in demonstrations for increased welfare allowances and better treatment by investigators. She also argued for poor black women's right to express their sexual and emotional desires as they wished, including controlling their fertility.

Across the country, low-income black women such as Rita Van Lew struggled for power and dignity against those forces that failed to recognize their autonomy and full humanity. Laboring women like Dorothy Bolden in Atlanta formed the National Domestic Workers Union of America to unionize hard-to-unionize jobs such as maids. Bolden believed: "Women should have a voice in making decisions in their community for betterment. Because this woman in the slum is scuffling hard, and she's got a very good intelligent mind to do things."[40] Welfare recipients like Margaret "Peggy" McCarty in Baltimore and Etta Horn in D.C. struggled for welfare rights and income. They called for power—for poor people, black people, women, and different combinations of all three. They fought for literal control over their work, communities, and bodies. They questioned middle-class presumptions that viewed them and their families as inadequate or unworthy, and criticized government programs that did not sustain them or provide ample employment opportunities. They also contested negative images, such as the "matriarch stick."

It was just a word—matriarch—but it had ruthless power with not so subtle gender and class resonances. In a *For Us Women* newsletter, prepared by SNCC's NBAWADU, for instance, a column warned black women to beware a system that deviously sought "to maintain a black matriarchal family by using welfare and by using the draft. Black women need black men at home now!!"[41] While clearly an effort to challenge the draft and the inadequacy of Aid to Families with Dependent Children, critiquing welfare as a tool to maintain "matriarchal families" had its dangers. After all, matriarch was not a value-free word. Language had power and in this case it registered abnormality. Matriarch was most often deployed to malign single black mothers as emasculators, and then generalized to those black women who showed strength or challenged men. The column, in its own way, then, while critiquing the state for using war and welfare to drive black men away from their families, in the same stroke of the pen unwittingly cast aspersions on women-led families by the mere act of labeling them matriarchal. Policies such as the "man in the house" rule (which prevented low-income women from securing welfare benefits if an intimate lived under the same roof) intruded upon black women's privacy and hampered their freedom to establish heterosexual relationships. It was one of the innumerable silent ways that patriarchy challenged black female autonomy.

That is why poor black women in NWRO and local welfare rights unions fought such intrusive rules. They also demanded expansive benefits and (ultimately unsuccessfully) a guaranteed income, as well as living-wage jobs. As NWRO chair, Johnnie Tillmon demanded respect and equal opportunities for women as citizens of the nation. Low-income, subsidy-reliant women did not want to be subjugated by their men or "the Man."[42] They wanted improvements in welfare benefits, and public housing for that matter, because both provided them with a social safety net when husbands died, when relationships failed or turned violent, when jobs could not be found or jobs found could not adequately support them and their families, or even when they desired to stay home and raise their young children without men. It was less about men's manhood than women's rights, their children's needs and well-being, economic justice, and garnering power to make decisions about their lives. Theirs were struggles for self-determination and respect and dignity.

The fear of becoming "matriarchs"—well, that registered as bunk for quite a few, and as such needed to be debunked. Margaret Wright actually called it "bull," continuing: "Black men have been brainwashed into believing they've been emasculated. I tell them they're nuts. They've never been emasculated. Emasculated men don't revolt."[43] While black men had suffered political and economic exclusion, Wright reaffirmed black men's mettle and shifted the terms of the debate. Black women were not to blame—that honor belonged to "the white man who's oppressing, not [black women]." And she flipped the script yet again, arguing that black women's liberation was not about equality with "chauvinistic" men. "I don't want to be chauvinistic," Wright said. "Some women run over people in the business world, doing the same thing as men. I don't want to compete on no damned exploitative level. I don't want to exploit nobody. I don't want to be on no firing line, killing people. I want the right to be black and me."[44]

A reckoning was in order—at least according to some. Black Power simply should not reaffirm patriarchy and class oppression mediated through black male control. While black people needed power, it could not be at the expense of black women. This was all too clear to cadres of low-income black women and other black feminist activists such as Frances Beal, a critical architect of the Third World Women's Alliance (TWWA) still a couple years away.[45]

In 1966, Beal returned from France where she had met Malcolm X and become friends with Richard Wright's daughter Julie Herve. Upon her return, she began working with SNCC formally. Making sense of the "oppressive relations that existed in [her] marriage," she gained greater clarity about how her individual experience related to a broader social problem. She learned this through conversations with other women in SNCC and elsewhere. She also grew concerned that some SNCC men and male Black Power activists were paying increasing attention "to the Muslim and particularly the Nation of Islam perspective"—"talking about abortion [as] genocide."[46] As early as 1965 the Nation of Islam had "decried 'the sins of birth control' and 'the deadly pill'" in its newspaper *Muhammad Speaks*.[47] Beal believed in women's reproductive choices—whether to secure a safe abortion, to avoid sterilization abuses, or just to not have children at all. She presented a position paper on these very issues at an SNCC staff meeting in New York.[48] She also recommended the creation of "a black woman's caucus to explore the impact of sexism on the organization's constituency in addition to racism."[49] This caucus expanded into the Black Women's Liberation Committee (BWLC). As the BWLC grew and increasingly included black women beyond SNCC, the committee transformed into the Black Women's Alliance with the goal of combating racism and sexism, or what Beal coined as "double jeopardy."

Beal drafted the "Black Women's Manifesto; Double Jeopardy: To Be Black and Female" in the late 1960s.[50] A revised version appeared a year later in Robin Morgan's *Sisterhood is Powerful* and Toni Cade (Bambara)'s *The Black Woman*—the same two anthologies that also published versions of the Mount Vernon/New Rochelle collective's (or Pat Robinson and Group's) letters and statements. In 1970, the same year these volumes were published, the Black Women's Alliance also expanded into the Third World Women's Alliance. "Double Jeopardy" questioned racism among white women, sexism among black men, and capitalism and imperialism in a U.S. democracy. Beal questioned whether white women activists understood their privileges. In SNCC interracial intimacy between white women and black men had caused tensions between black men and black women, as well as white women and black women. So, too, did white feminists' privileging of gender over race.

The questions abounded. Did white women understand the complexity of black women's struggles? Did white women desire "to be equal to white men in their pernicious treatment of third world peoples?" In fact, "what assurances [had] black women that white women [would] be any less racist and exploitative if they had the power and were in a position to do so?" After all, the primarily middle-class white women's movement had failed to acknowledge "the extreme economic exploitation that most black women [were] subjected to day by day." These white women, argued Beal, could buy themselves out of "degrading and dehumanizing" housework, for instance, "usually by hiring a black maid." Most black women could not afford to hire someone to do the same. That was why "the economic and social realities of the black woman's life [were] the most crucial for us."[51] A year later, Linda LaRue, a black political science graduate student at Purdue University, asked a similar kind of question in her essay, which warned against falsely arguing that black people, low-income black women, and middle-class white women experienced "common oppression": "Is there any logical comparison between the oppressions of the black woman on welfare who has difficulty feeding her children and the discontent of the suburban mother who has the luxury to protest washing of the dishes on which her family's full meal was consumed?"[52]

There were radical white feminists, however, who did not dismiss, conflate, or overlook class and race differences. They not only pushed against the white middle-class second-wave women's movement, but took their cues from black radical feminists such as Flo Kennedy. As did some Panther women, Kennedy believed Black Power had the greatest "potential for illustrating the blatant contradictions of American democracy" and proliferating self-determination for all people, including women of all races and ethnicities.[53] Kennedy did not ignore male chauvinism or for that matter believe in racial separatism. She challenged both, according to historian Sherie M. Randolph. Such relationships, however, did not generally inform the agendas of white feminists—at least not that Beal and other black radical feminists witnessed in the late 1960s.

Beal also forthrightly challenged black men's devaluing of black women. She argued that those men who have "since the advent of black power . . . exerted a more prominent leadership role" and "their 'manhood' by telling black women to step back into a domestic, submissive role are assuming a counterrevolutionary position." She acknowledged the persecution of black men, but she argued: "Black women likewise have been abused by the system, and we must begin talking about the elimination of all kinds of oppression."[54] Giovanni's 1969 "Woman Poem" echoed this sentiment: "I wish i knew how it would feel/to be free. . . . It's having a job/they won't let you work/or no work at all/castrating me/(yes it happens to women too).[55]

As Gwen Patton explained it, "Black Power forced us to deal with ourselves." This was the case with black men's (and black women's) uncritical acceptance of a "Victorian Philosophy" that depicted male-female relations as inverted—thereby undermining the potential for black unity. Instead, Patton argued, "Black men began to look upon their women as a strange breed who were against them—trying to make them weak."[56] This occurred not only in relationships and families, but also in meetings and other encounters where male chauvinism merged with machismo and patriarchal desires.

Toni Cade, an English professor, recounted such an incident during a Summer of Support G.I. meeting. At the meeting, the black men "began the list of *things* to be sent to the off-base radical projects." What did they imagine? "Home cooked soul food, blues and jazz records, Black journals, foxy Sisters who can rap, revolutionary pamphlets." Toni Cade bristled at the "foxy sisters" statement, so she shared her feelings. There would be no apology forthcoming. Instead, she and the other equally disturbed sisters had to suffer comments from black men about "overly sensitive, salty bitches trying to disrupt [the] meeting with that feminist horseshit."

As if that were not enough, then one of the men, after a round of impromptu calisthenics, "castigated the Sisters to throw away the pill and hop to the mattresses and breed revolutionaries and mess up the man's genocidal program." That did it, at least for one black woman whom Cade described as a bit tipsy. She "tore the place up" with "gusts and sweeps of historical, hysterical documentation of mistrust and mess-up, waxing lyric over the hardships, the oatmeal, the food stamps, the diapers, the scuffling, the bloody abortions, the bungled births. She was mad as hell and getting more and more sober." Then she pointed her finger at the man and yelled: "And when's the last time you fed one of them brats you been breeding all over the city, you jive-ass so-and-so?" [57] The bluster and shenanigans of this brother not only caused a ruckus, but also starkly expressed how, for some, black liberation meant the privileging and recuperation of black manhood.

As did those black women who challenged the Black Unity Party and the black men at the GI support meeting, Cade, too, argued that black women were being "regarded as objects, commodities" and wombs for the revolution. Like Beal, Cade described such behavior as "counterrevolutionary." [58] For Cade self-determined reproduction was critical. She did not believe that the pill was a panacea for black women's liberation. It did not have *that* much power. Instead, the pill gave black women the "power" to "control" choices as they devised and waged battles against racial and economic injustices. Her sentiment echoed the stance on birth control in the "Letter to a North Vietnamese Sister." [59]

Nor did a belief in women's power to control their fertility mute the concern about genocide. However, Mississippi native, veteran civil rights activist, and black sociologist Joyce Ladner wrote in *Tomorrow's Tomorrow* (1971), which focused primarily on low-income black girls striving toward womanhood: "It is legitimate to assume that it is a question of genocide that is involved in conservative political officials' campaigns to 'peddle' pills and other contraceptives in the Black community." She continued: "But it is ludicrous to assume that Black women who have had all the children they care to have and can afford should be denied information on ways to cease giving birth." [60] Tillmon agreed. While "birth control can be perverted into a weapon against poor women," she maintained, "the word is choice." [61]

The birth control pill did not represent the entirety of reproductive rights choices. Abortion provided another option. Before 1970, only 10,000 of some one million abortions were legal, and most illegal abortions were performed on poor women who then ended up in the hospital. [62] "Botched abortions" represented the largest cause of death, especially for pregnant non-white women. [63] Race and economics had disparately influenced black women's access to doctors and reproductive services. This was true for black women when it came to free health clinics established by Black Power organizations as well. The Black Panther Party's Berkeley clinic did have a weekly women's clinic, and such services may have existed in other cities as well. Overall, however, the Panther Party had limited resources and could not provide a "breadth of treatment and services of any kind," according to Alondra Nelson. Would the Black Panther Party have welcomed a full range of reproductive services if they could have financially supported them? This is not clear either way; however, what is clear is that with regard to justice and medical services in the black community, for black women this included reproductive care too.[64]

In Washington, D.C., the Citywide Welfare Alliance fought for the expansion of access to free abortions for low-income women at the public hospital.[65] Mary Treadwell, who helped run Pride Inc. in D.C., posed a few questions on this score. She wondered how federal legislators—"overwhelmingly white and overwhelmingly male"—could oppose affording a social safety net and greater opportunities to the same women whom they denied family planning options. "While rejecting legalized abortion, these very men sit in hypocritical splendor and refuse to provide an adequate guaranteed annual income for these children born to women without financial and social access to safe abortion," stated Treadwell, continuing: "These very men refuse to fund quality, inexpensive prenatal and post-natal care to women without access to abortion . . . [and] refuse to fund quality education and training for the children of women without access to abortions." Treadwell also believed—as did Cade, Beal, and other black women activists—that "black women particularly need this personal freedom to be able to fulfill themselves sexually without fear of conception. The outside pressures of this society wreak enough havoc within the black home and the black unit. It is unspeakable that legislated, racist pressures should accompany the black woman to her bedroom and creep insidiously into the center of her bed."[66] At the Revolutionary People's Constitutional Convention, the Workshop on Self-Determination of Women agreed: "Women must have the right to decide. . . . There should be free and safe birth control, including abortion, available on demand."[67]

This was several years before *Roe v. Wade,* but in the midst of the journey toward that historic 1973 Supreme Court decision, battles raged. Black women, as key participants, shared their views. The same year as the *Roe* decision, black feminists formed the National Black Feminist Organization (NBFO). Among them was Flo Kennedy. A founding member of the National Organization of Women in 1966 and a Black Power advocate, Kennedy worked as a lawyer "to repeal New York's restrictive abortion laws."[68] She also formed the Feminist Party, which would support the presidential campaign of another Black Power advocate, abortion rights supporter, and NBFO member: Shirley Chisholm. It was one of the myriad ways that race and gender politics often merged around core issues.

Shirley Chisholm, who served in the New York State Assembly, became the first black woman elected to Congress in 1968. She defeated veteran CORE activist and Freedom Rider James Farmer, who ran as a Republican. Shortly after her election to the House of Representatives, Chisholm spoke at Howard University. Quoting Frederick Douglass, like Paul Robeson and so many others before her and since, Chisholm in her lilting voice said: "'Power concedes nothing without a struggle.' It never has, and it never will." She then turned to the topic of the day: "'Black Power.' Oh how that phrase upsets so many people. Let me give you my definition of Black Power. Black Power is no different from any other kind of power in this country." Black Power conveys black people's attempts "to control their destinies." The difference, Chisholm maintained, "[is] everybody is so hysterical and panic stricken because of the adjective that precedes the word power—'black.'" But, "people just have to get used to that word, 'Black Power.'" Then, Chisholm raised a caution—one she witnessed firsthand. She argued, "[Power] is consistently being dissipated by factionalism [and] black people will gain only as much as they can through their ability to organize independent bases of economic and political power."[69]

In August of that same year, the newly established New York–based National Association for the Repeal of Abortion Laws (NARAL) contacted Chisholm and asked her to be its national spokesperson. Chisholm, like Kennedy, organized with white feminists. Neither woman harbored romantic illusions about racial or gender unity. The range of impassioned demands (even if motivated by different realities) propelled them to respond. Initially, Chisholm only supported expanding access to therapeutic abortions, not the repeal of all abortion laws, but that changed when she witnessed the concrete impact of denying women a desperately desired procedure. Two young women she knew "had suffered permanent injuries at the hand of illegal abortionists." One became sterile; the other needed lifelong treatment for injuries suffered. This changed her mind. Chisholm, however, was still quite concerned about the political fray she knew herself to be entering—"an even more serious step than for a white politician." Having just spoken on Black Power and factionalism, she knew this to be a fracturing issue—one that conjured "a deep and angry suspicion among many blacks that even birth control clinics are a plot by the white power structure to keep down the numbers of blacks, and this opinion is even more strongly held by some in regard to legalizing abortions." Ultimately, like Flo Kennedy, however, Shirley Chisholm believed that "to label family planning and legal abortion programs 'genocide' is male rhetoric, for male ears."[70]

Instead, she and other black feminists listened to black and Puerto Rican women who suffered sterilization abuse at the hands of doctors and through state programs. They needed woman-centered, empowered approaches to reproduction, family planning, economic stability, childrearing, revolution, and desire—ones that privileged their choices and challenged male and state oppression. Members of NWRO, TWWA, and NBFO, including the soon-to-be founders of the Combahee River Collective, all supported a woman's right to control her body, as well as an end to sterilization abuse.

Throughout the late 1960s and early 1970s, greater concern emerged about the conservative gender and economic tendencies of Black Power. Pat Robinson wrote to Vilma Sanchez (the alias of Joan Jordan) as early as 1967: "There is a conscious plan afoot to control the black power movement under a Demo-liberal-labor coalition. It all depends on whether the civil rights leaders can move that far left. That's no joke! We have had a saying among us black women that *all* black men are hustlers, had to be to make it in the big city. The middle-class and 'the proletariat' are hustlers. Man, they hate to give up all that loot! Even CORE leadership wants a piece of the pie and says so."[71] On the latter score, Robinson was no doubt referencing McKissick, who became a Nixon supporter. Whether he was strategically positioning himself to access resources or not—for the Department of Housing and Urban Development did issue a $14 million bond for "Soul City" (and foreclosed on it early in 1979)—his jump to the Republican Party reeked of betrayal and opportunism. While her characterization of *all* black men as hustlers is debatable, there is no debating that the elastic concept of Black Power was being claimed on the streets, in politics, and everywhere else that power could be traded.

Hustling Black Power

The saliency and allure of Black Power were strong, and it took some quite interesting turns on the streets. Gang members, drug users, dons, and those otherwise dispossessed were drawn to it just like others. This was not necessarily a surprising or automatically terrible thing, though it would present challenges. Targeting the lumpen proletariat was part of the Black Power game plan, at least among revolutionary nationalist groups such as the Black Panther Party. The Panthers actually had success luring such men and women into the Black Power orbit, particularly with their enticing calls for self-determination, an end to poverty and police brutality, and gun-barrel politics. For instance, Bunchy Carter, a Slauson gang leader and ex-felon joined the party. Pete O'Neal left the illegal hustle of pimping, cars, and money behind to start a Panther chapter. Regina Jennings, who was addicted to drugs, traveled cross-country, detoxed, and dedicated herself to the people. Afeni Shakur, who experimented with LSD (and heroin once), became a section leader. And according to a group of researchers, focusing on black youth who supported the Panthers, the party had such relevance that it could "pull a young dude back from the traditional comfort of dope" and to "the demands of urban guerrilla life [to] offer a substitute for the desperate habitual rhythm of hustling."[72]

Anticipating and desiring involvement from the "lumpen," the Panthers established rules regarding narcotics and alcohol use, gun handling, and petty crime. Not everyone (including Newton, who abused cocaine) followed the rules, but the Panthers did publicize their expectations in an October 1968 issue of *The Black Panther*. The stated penalty for using hard drugs was expulsion. Possessing marijuana and other so-called soft drugs was forbidden "while doing party work," as was intoxication when carrying weapons. The Panthers also evoked Chairman Mao's injunction that a party member "cannot steal or take from the people, not even a needle or a piece of thread."[73] The Panthers established drug addiction programs as well, during a moment when drug treatment had not yet fully succumbed to the rhetoric and policy of punishment.

In the late 1960s and early 1970s, the war on crime, law-and-order policies, the conservative political ascendancy, and the War on Drugs, however, provided rich soil for the seeds of the mass carceral state to grow. For instance, mid-1960s anti-crime legislation, passed during Johnson's presidency, made possible Detroit's STRESS program. Standing for "Stop the Robberies, Enjoy Safe Streets," STRESS was an undercover police unit established in 1971. It quickly became known "as little more than an all-white, Detroit Police Department-sanctioned vigilante organization"—one that used "excessive force" to target crime in poor, black inner-city communities.[74] Once in office, President Nixon unabashedly deployed the "metaphor and mindset of war" with regard to narcotics.[75] In July 1969 in a special message to Congress, Nixon called for increased attention to state and federal enforcement:

> Within the last decade, the abuse of drugs has grown from essentially a local police problem into a serious national threat to the personal health and safety of millions of Americans. A . . . new urgency and concerted national policy are needed at the Federal level to begin to cope with this growing menace.[76]

The growing menace often had a familiar look and police target—black people in inner cities. The dispossessed, wretched, and damned would be in the cross-hairs even as they continued to bear the brunt of federal retrenchment of the social safety net. In the midst of a moratorium on public housing construction and attacks on welfare, the Nixon administration initiated the War on Drugs—alongside the wars on liberation struggles, radical Black Power organizations, and poor black people.

In the same year as Nixon's special message, Cetewayo Tabor asserted in a pamphlet the "revolutionary ideology of capitalism plus dope equals genocide." He, too, called for a reckoning of state power and drugs with black liberation. The political and health issue was very personal. Tabor had started using heroin at age 13. He believed: "Dope is a form of genocide in which the victim pays to be killed." The charge of genocide had a powerful emotional resonance among black people, who had for generations heard stories of, as well as witnessed, black people dying through individualized and state violence, unequal social and economic conditions, and the denial of services and opportunities. Continued Tabor: "The Plague" revealed "chemical warfare in the African-Amerikan Bantustan"—an analogy that referenced South Africa's forced removal of blacks to government-designated black residential spaces. For him, heroin was a "poisonous, lethal, white powdery substance, sold by depraved, money-crazed beasts to Black youths [. . .] desperately seeking a kick."[77] Some of those "beasts," unfortunately, looked like Tabor—even as international traffickers and governments, some U.S. ally nations, controlled major trade routes.

More addicts and addict-peddlers tromped inner-city streets, but, of course, drug dealers were there to supply them. It was black capitalism, demand and supply, but on dealers' terms. As entrepreneurs, they, too, sought to control a piece of the urban economic pie. Some of them even felt that black men should control the drug trade in black communities. They laid claim to an illegal predatory expression of Black Power if ever there was one.

The toxic combination of poverty, unemployment, and drug addiction fed crime. In 1968 Baltimore had the highest crime rate of the 10 largest U.S. cities, and ranked fifth in total number of known persons addicted to drugs. New York stood at the front of the pack (in fact, the city had half the known cases of drug addiction), followed by Chicago, Los Angeles, and Detroit.[78] Governor Nelson Rockefeller and Mayor John Lindsay of New York responded. Lindsay declared a drug menace in New York City, and Rockefeller lobbied for strict laws to control that menace. By 1973, the New York legislature established mandatory minimum sentences of 15 years to life for possessing the smallest amounts of marijuana, heroin, or cocaine. Police hit the streets, and drug addicts and petty criminals in predominantly black and brown communities increasingly landed in jails. The notorious Rockefeller drug laws helped to swell the prison population, even as "hard drug use actually increased."[79]

While the sober majority of residents did not want crime or drugs in their neighborhoods, questions did arise regarding the "draconian" Rockefeller drug laws. Tabor particularly focused on the economics of the drug trade, its impact on poor minorities, and the criminalization of addicts. While he was no fan of dope (not even countercultural drug use), he reproached Rockefeller and Lindsay for their approach to the problem. "Rockefeller and Lindsay give less than a damn about the lives of Black people," said Tabor, "and if we don't know by now how the police feel about us, then we are in *really* bad shape."[80]

Tabor also lamented the reality of black people in search of disastrous highs. Embedded within that lament was a message to stop self-medicating and wake up, or mortgage the revolution. "As long as our young Black brothers and sisters are chasing the bag, as long as they are trying to cop a fix, the rule of our oppressors is secure and our hopes for freedom are dead," said Tabor. "It is the youth who make the revolution and it is the youth who carry it out"—but not if they are anesthetized. Dope endangered the revolution.[81] James Baldwin had written something similar in 1963 in his bestselling book *The Fire Next Time:* "I remembered my buddies of years ago, in the hallways, with their wine and their whiskey and their tears; in hallways still, frozen on the needle; and my brother saying to me once, 'If Harlem didn't have so many churches and junkies, there'd be blood flowing in the streets.'"[82]

During a speech at Howard University on April 10, 1970, in which Stokely Carmichael called for black unity, he pointed out, as Tabor had, the danger of dope for the revolution. "Dope pushing must be dealt with in our community, because it is the trick of the oppressor," argued Carmichael. "Whenever consciousness arises in the community they send more dope pushers into the community. . . . We have to clean up our community and begin to organize."[83] An undated "Letter to a Black Serviceman from a Poor Black Woman" made similar arguments about dope. Articulating a familiar community view, the poor black woman wrote: "The powerful white man . . . control[s] the country by controlling all the land and the factories and the banks. They allow dope in the armed forces and country so our black brothers (poor white brothers, too) won't wake up to how they are being used." The letter linked war, military service, drugs, family problems, poverty, unemployment, and "no future" to white supremacy and capitalism. "We are all brainwashed to care just about ourselves, get what you can, by conning, hustling, jiving . . . money, never people," the writer continued, but she and others were "waking up."[84]

In 1970, the celebrated hustler and author Robert Beck Jr. talked about how he too was waking up because of newly gained "ball power." This meant swearing off his days of pimping and shooting dope, just in time for his mother who died in Los Angeles to see how he had changed. In "Letter to Papa," Beck forgave his father for childhood abuse, writing, "I understand now that the most hellish aspect of America's racism is that for generations it has warped and twisted legions of innately good black men, causing the vital vine of black family stability and strength to be poisoned."[85] Then, he shared how he had "gained [this] wonderful new ball power from the courage and daring exploits of the Black Panthers in this Eden of genocide." For Beck, "ball power" meant black men confronting white power, not making money off of the misery of the black community. The call for Black Power and the "ballsy" Black Panthers provided Beck, an old head hustler, with a potentially different vision of black life in America. In 1971 the Los Angeles-based Holloway House published his *The Naked Soul of Iceberg Slim*. Beck dedicated his book "to the heroic memory of Malcolm X, Jack Johnson, Melvin X, Jonathan Jackson; to Huey P. Newton, Bobby Seale, Ericka Huggins, George Jackson, Angela Davis; and to all street niggers and strugglers in and out of the joints."

Having been politicized by the struggles of the day, Beck wrote of trying to turn brothers away from the pimp and dope game. His book *Pimp* inspired Donald Goines to turn from pimping to writing. A Detroit native and Korean War veteran, Goines also struggled with a drug habit that he had picked up while in the military. Unlike for Beck, however, the black liberation struggle did not have the same redemptive power for Goines. In the penitentiary at the time, he felt the civil rights movement did not impact him.[86] That was politics. For him, it remained about "the hustle." According to biographer Eddie Stone in *Donald Writes No More*: "The movement that he had seen developing around him did not interest him. What did interest him was his sense of power through money." Stone further explained: "It was fine for others to sit around and talk about ideals and dreams, but Donald knew that the only way to achieve such things was through monetary gain and the power it brought with it. For him, there still was no other way."[87] However, Beck's ghetto-real story, alongside the fact that he made money legally by writing about it, did impact Goines. His writing success began with *Whoreson* and *Dopefiend*. More than a dozen other books followed.

Black gangsters who remained gangsters *and* bought into Black Power adhered to a notion of brotherhood, cultural pride, and self-determination. Some participated in Black Power organizations, but this did not necessarily mean giving up the illegal hustle. Nor did organizing the community around a political or economic agenda necessarily excite them or pay the bills. Nicky Barnes is a case in point.

Leroy "Nicky" Barnes began his drug-dealing career in the mid-1950s. He became known as the "Teflon don," the "Black Godfather," and "Mr. Untouchable." Born in Depression-era New York, Barnes dealt heroin, as well as gave gifts of food and toys to neighborhood residents. His journey toward black cultural and religious nationalism began in Green Haven Prison in Stormville, New York, in February 1966. There he buried the hatchet with Frank James, a stick-up artist in Harlem who robbed stash houses and drug dealers. James introduced him to "a crew of Black Muslims" who rejected the white, blue-eyed Jesus.[88] As one prisoner told Barnes: "If Jesus is your father, he's gotta be black!" "Attracted by that sense of well-being, a sense of black pride," Nicky Barnes became a Muslim. In the prison yard, the Black Muslim crew read from *Muhammad Speaks!* and believed that Elijah Muhammad "came into the black community to raise [them] like Lazarus from the grave of irresponsibility." He embraced Africa, cut out drug use, pork, and "calling each other motherfucker and nigger." He cut back on the amount of time he spent in prison talking with Italians, who also were in the drug game (men like Matthew "Matty" Madonna of the Lucchese crime family and Joey Gallo), because "that closeness between black and white just wasn't in vogue." Nicky Barnes even shaved his conk and went bald, culturally rejecting "that European sense of value."[89]

What Nicky Barnes did not cut out, not for a long period anyway, was drug dealing and hustling. Reconnecting with his black network once he was back on the streets, Barnes, Madonna, and Gallo engaged in drug exploits together. Initially Barnes did try to turn the corner, at least the way he tells it.

> I really meant it. Islam changed me. All those ideas on Black Power weren't just coming out of Green Haven, either. It affected people in the street. It had a real resonance in Harlem. I saw myself being a strong force in that. I wanted to be down with all the positive things going on in the neighborhood. But I had to live and pay the bills, so when Jimmy started on about Fat Jack's Broasted Chickens, my ears perked.[90]

Investing in a business, however, required cash, which Barnes did not have at the time. So he decided to make some quick money through drugs. It took him a month, and in the meantime he had "made inroads with the brothers involved in the nationalistic efforts—the Nation of Islam, the [Black] Liberation Army, and the Black Panthers." He visited the Panthers' office in Harlem, making sure to park his new Cadillac up the street. However, he could never fully commit his time, not with having to think about how his dealers handled his packages on the street.

During those times when Barnes listened to the brothers "talk about community activism and different things they were doing," he noticed that while they worked hard, they wore the same clothes and shoes. Ultimately, he realized how different he was from the Panthers: "[I] thought we'd have a more mutual groove. . . . I didn't feel that with the Panthers, or any of the guys in the Black Power thing." Barnes continued: "What could I do with them? I had a brand new Cadillac, money and a great place to live. They didn't have *anything* like that. So I naturally gravitated back to powder, seeking my own comfort level. That hustling field just drew me in more than anything else."[91] This did not sit well with his girlfriend who had taken care of his business while he was incarcerated and now wanted a different life. She wanted him to go legitimate. Nicky Barnes decided otherwise. His decision resulted in kilos of heroin, times over, hitting inner-city streets. It also landed him back in prison and eventually on a path against his so-called brothers in the business.

Black hustlers such as Barnes created black "mafias" and thereby empowered themselves through the illegal, underground economy. They, too, built black businesses. Unfortunately, they traded on people's misery and sacrificed black communities' health as they viciously muscled out competition for profit and literally provided opiates to the masses.[92] They turned away from community-based Black Power organizing, because they saw in the nitty-gritty work few immediate financial dividends. They viewed the collective struggle as incapable of providing them with an income that could fulfill their individual appetites for status and success—all that America was selling them—let alone the level of wealth needed to vie against white power. Living-wage jobs were unavailable; high-rolling employment in corporate America remained out of reach. They made their choices within a specific context, as did everyday working-class and poor people whom such black hustlers built their economy of misery upon. In this equation, black unity succumbed to individual advancement, the allure of the market, and pleasure through imbibing alcohol, cocaine, heroin, and other drugs flooding city streets. The worst (arguably) was yet to come.

Politics: A Black Male Preserve?

Drug dealers were not the only ones hustling Black Power. The 1970s marked the ascendancy of white conservatism that, with political shrewdness and intentionality, used Black Power to its own ends while also dismantling its more radical intentions. Touting economic self-help and capitalist enterprise as Black Power, the Nixon administration established the Office of Minority Business Enterprise in March 1969 even as it forwarded a strategy of economic retrenchment. In fact, Nixon's advisor on domestic affairs, who had also worked under President Johnson as the assistant secretary of labor, was none other than Daniel Patrick

Moynihan. "The time may have come when the issue of race could benefit from a period of 'benign neglect,'" Moynihan advised Nixon. "The forum has been too much taken over by hysteria, paranoids and boodlers on all sides. We may need a period in which Negro progress continues and racial rhetoric fades."[93]

Progress "for whom" remained the question. While Black Power was under assault, contested, and even unraveling, black activists and politicians continued to debate what shape Black Power should take into the early to mid-1970s—before the dusk of the movement. The National Black Political Convention in Gary, Indiana, in March 1972 represented one of those strategies. The Gary Convention and Chisholm's run for the U.S. presidency in 1972 exemplified the advancing struggle for independent black political power. Mayor Hatcher of Gary, Congressman Charles C. Diggs (Michigan), Amiri Baraka, and political scientist Ronald Walters organized the Gary Convention. Under the slogan "Unity without Uniformity," 2,700 delegates and 4,000 alternates gathered.[94] The issues varied widely. Education, poverty, welfare rights, trade unionism, foreign policy, reparations, and political representation—all were on the agenda. The Gary Convention represented an amazing gathering of people based on the call for black electoral power, self-determination, and unity. It also exposed roiling debates within Black Power and persistent differences within black America.

Here, too, unity was an aspiration, but far from an uncomplicated reality. Detroit labor activist Charles Denby (the pen name of Simon P. Owens), who believed power came "out of the mass power and reason of people organized to win and defend freedom," attended.[95] He expressed profound disappointment: "Every delegate I questioned said nothing had been done and that everything was in a state of confusion." The Michigan delegation, which was comprised of representatives from labor and elected officials, "dicker[ed] over the preamble" and eventually walked out. According to Denby: "Nobody knew where the Black Convention would go, but there were signs clearly seen by many that too many conflicting forces were pulling for their own position that did not permit the kind of unity to carry the Convention further. It simply died a stillbirth, although many thought it was headed toward the organizing of a Black Third political party."[96]

In electoral politics as in organizations, gender also shaped visions of who within the black community should be the bearers of black political power. In *From Slavery to Freedom* Evelyn Brooks Higginbotham notes, "[In] 1966 there were 97 black members of state legislatures and six members of the Congress of the United States, but no black mayors in any American city. By 1973 more than two hundred blacks sat in thirty-seven state legislatures, and blacks had already served as mayors of Cleveland, Los Angeles, Gary (Indiana), and Newark (New Jersey)."[97] Most of these black elected officials were men, and black women continued to have a difficult time breaking into the male preserve of electoral politics in the age of black political empowerment.

In 1972, Shirley Chisholm campaigned for the Democratic presidential nomination. Born to working-class West Indian immigrant parents in Brooklyn, New York,

Chisholm had spent her formative years in Barbados with her grandmother. Her mother had worked as a domestic and seamstress, her Garveyite father as a factory worker. Chisholm returned to the United States when she was 10 years old, and eventually attended Brooklyn College where she became increasingly aware of racial discrimination. After graduating Columbia University with a degree in early childhood education and excelling as a debater, she became involved in Democratic Party politics.[98] However, the growing black political establishment, which envisioned a "new black politics" led by black men, did not support her. In this way, numerous black male leaders, as aspiring politicians in the Black Power era, fostered gender politics as usual.[99]

In May and November 1971, black male elected officials had held strategy sessions to discuss the potential of running a black presidential candidate. Chisholm had not been a part of those sessions, even though her interest in the 1972 presidential race was known. A *Jet* poll only gave her a meager five percent of the potential vote. Black male politicians considered her an unlikely presidential winner (which she too admitted). Some also denigrated her as a castrator and, at a November 1971 forum on women and politics at the Black Expo in Chicago, described her as "that little black matriarch who goes around messing things up." Following her own political compass and asserting her right to run, Chisholm announced her candidacy on January 25, 1972, before some 500 people (mostly women) in Concord Baptist Church's school auditorium in Brooklyn. She did so without black male politicians' approval.[100]

Racist attacks salted the open wounds on the "Chisholm Trail." She received hate mail. A box of bumper stickers had been defaced with the words "nigger go home." Black delegates at the 1972 Gary Convention, which she did not attend, did not get behind her presidential bid either. She stood in the gap at the crossroads. Even so, Chisholm did have a dedicated multi-racial campaign team that took to Greyhound buses and hit the streets disseminating campaign literature across the nation. Her base of support included, for instance, the future black Congresswoman Barbara Lee (California), black journalist and author Paula Giddings, and black science fiction writer Octavia Butler. The Black Panther Party's Bobby Seale also endorsed Chisholm, who did not fear aligning herself with the radical activists. She supported the Black Panther Party's survival programs and asserted that people needed to ask the question: What made the Panthers necessary in the first place? A few Congressional Black Caucus members supported her campaign including Parren Mitchell from Baltimore and "half and half" John Conyers from Detroit. Conyers could not make up his mind, explained Chisholm. Ron Dellums from California stood behind Chisholm, at least until the Democratic Convention in Miami. Thinking in retrospect about the highly charged campaign in 1972, Dellums wondered aloud: "What made Shirley Chisholm frightening to you? Her womanness, her blackness, her black womanness, her progressive thoughts? Did she have the audacity to take the historical moment you were too slow to take? . . . What was it? What was the problem?"[101]

While Chisholm wrapped her arms around Black Power, black male politicians, at the end of the day, did not wrap their political arms around Chisholm. William Clay, a black congressman, publicly questioned her motives, judgment, and even her sanity. Why did she stay in a political campaign, Clay queried, when the people "rejected" her? Chisholm held her delegates with the hope of potentially leveraging concessions in the Democratic platform. When she spoke to the Black Caucus, she encouraged them to do the same: "My brothers and sisters, let me tell it to you this afternoon like it really is. The only thing that you have going, my brothers and sisters . . . [is] your one vote. Don't sell that vote out. The black people of America are watching us. Find out what these candidates who need our votes to get across to the top are going to do for us concretely, not rhetorically." This strategy of leveraging black delegate votes did not take hold. At the Democratic National Convention, most black elected officials had already promised their support to Hubert Humphrey. When Humphrey dropped out, they threw their political weight to George McGovern. Unlike Chisholm, McGovern did not support issues "important to groups on the margins" such as a $6,500 guaranteed income, women's right to abortion, or, for that matter, any other programs to explicitly advance the black community.[102] Nixon won the presidency.

It was a taxing presidential campaign that ended unsuccessfully, but Chisholm told her supporters that she was not "disillusioned" or "bitter." Until her retirement in 1983, she continued to push for the empowerment of black people. As a member of Congress for 14 years, Chisholm had helped to found independent political institutions for black people and women, including the Congressional Black Caucus and the National Women's Political Caucus.[103] And she continued to be guided by struggling for Black Power, or as she put it, "organizing the rage of black people," and "putting new hard questions and demands to white America." Chisholm maintained: "We will build a new sense of community among our people. We will foster a bond between those who have made it and those on the bottom."[104] For Chisholm, however, the notion of democracy remained a fraught concept into the 21st century—one often lauded, but not carried out. Democracy suffocated under the blanket of backstage political bargaining.

Despite some black women's dedication to power politics, it became clear that many manifestations of Black Power were not automatic allies of black women. Nor did they always attend to the concerns of poor black people—men or women. Class oppression within the black community would require explicit attention and contestation. Some black radical women who sought empowerment and transformation in the overlapping realms of, for instance, race, gender, sexuality, and class took up this work.

"The Black Power Shit"

Ongoing racial exclusion and poverty in a country that valued personal success and freedom based on property and materialism—two of the currencies of the American Dream—had led people to both individualize their problems as well as seek strategies that promoted opportunities for individual success. For some, this meant seeking access to the halls of economic and political power, not necessarily changing power dynamics. For others, this resulted in blaming each other or even self-medicating by tripping "out on smack." At least this is, in part, what the collective authors of "The Revolt of Poor Black Women" in *Lessons from the Damned* argued. They maintained that their fellow damned did not understand the systems that structured their lives. At one time, they too understood little about the role of "big capitalism, and imperialism and neo-colonialism." They wrote, "We would have laughed at those words. They were too damn big and we had never heard them in school."[105] But they had become radicalized.

When *Lessons* was published in 1973, the collective struggles for racial and economic justice at the grassroots level appeared to be declining. The recession cast an economic pall, tempering whatever optimism might have remained among black workers who desired well-paid jobs. As law-and-order politics proliferated, FBI domestic counterintelligence operations decimated black revolutionary organizations through internal sabotage and murder, and citizenry and state attacks mounted against rights and power groups that questioned the underlying logic and operation of U.S. democracy. The authors of *Lessons* witnessed the significance of the moment and moved to address it.

The authors of the essays (some written by the same women from the Mount Vernon/New Rochelle collective) lauded, dissected, and in other cases, outright dismissed Black Power. It had everything to do with the particular tendencies of Black Power prevalent at the time. In particular, they deemed petty capitalist strategies of black empowerment—both legal and illegal—as counterrevolutionary. In their quest to understand poor people's conditions and seek liberation, the Damned questioned what they called "the Black Power shit," and the race, class, and gender politics undergirding it.[106] Actually, they echoed the point in the "Letter to a North Vietnamese Sister." Revolutionary struggle would involve a clear expression of the problem devoid of trite political formulations.

Reflecting on their 1960s experiences and writing in the early 1970s, they explicitly critiqued the concept of black capitalism, arguing that it would reify hierarchies of power within the black community and broader society. They had harsh words for the black bourgeoisie and petty bourgeois strivers who uncritically accepted capitalism as the pathway to securing Black Power built on gender and class privilege. In "Wanting to Be Somebody!" the Damned wrote: "For us poor blacks, the programming about the American Dream and the Dream of Black Capitalism has kept us striving—'wanting to be somebody.'" Calling out the American Dream as a "hustle," the authors linked class privilege to militarism (the invasions of Korea and Vietnam), automation (lessening labor costs to increase profits), black unemployment and urban poverty, and finally "aid to former European colonies in Africa and Asia" that produced and protected consumer markets.[107]

For the Damned, the Black Power that ascended opened up pathways for the black petit-bourgeoisie to maintain "their blackness" while gaining power to "hustle off both the capitalist system and those poor blacks left at the bottom." The authors clearly distinguished between this Black Power and "another kind of blackness, one that spread the idea of 'Power to the People.'"[108] The former was reactionary, they believed, the latter revolutionary. Truth be told, simply spreading power to the people—however "the people" was defined—would not by itself guarantee revolution. Ultimately, how and to what ends people used the power they fought for would make the difference.

In another essay, "Black Nationalists," the Damned avowed that gaining a new consciousness that directly challenged self-hatred and black inferiority, as well as made apparent black oppression, was critically important. Black people could not stop there, however. They could not simply hate "whitey," be for the people "without doing any real hard work," or fall into the trap of desiring the trappings of the U.S. elite. They wrote: "Whenever somebody talked about blacks having *power* we would never have realized that that meant *power to rule* the rest of us blacks." The authors also critiqued cultural nationalism, which they argued relied on a romantic past of black male power: "The black nationalist stage really made us black so-called men feel like kings. After a while we would refer to ourselves as kings and our black women as queens. This automatically set them below us."[109]

Turning to history, the authors of "The Revolt of Poor Black Women" explained why they, too, would not accept black unity blindly. Alongside gender, class drove their lessons. They wrote: "Now we have to tell you. A whole lot of us very poor blacks didn't go for the Black Power shit. There were a lot of different reasons—but class difference is the one we're talking about here." The specter of black slaveholders served as a caution. The writers did not distinguish between those black slave owners who purchased relatives. Important to their analysis was exposing the existence and danger of class and status differences based on wealth and privilege. They continued: "Today we can look forward to black capitalists doing the same thing, trying to use us as wage slaves."[110] On this score they critiqued Black Power *as* black capitalism, which gained cache while failing to remedy widespread unemployment for the black masses or dismantle class hierarchy in the black community.

Assata, like the Damned, worried about black powerbrokers who seemed to forget the black masses. As a student at Manhattan Community College, she got "into heated arguments with sisters or brothers who claimed that the oppression of Black people was only a question of race." Assata disagreed. "I argued that there were Black oppressors as well as white ones," she continued. "That's why you got Blacks who support Nixon or Reagan and other conservatives. Black folks with money have always tended to support candidates who they believed would protect their financial interests. As far as I was concerned, it didn't take too much brains to figure out that Black people are oppressed because of class as well as race, because we are poor and because we are Black."[111] Class, politics, and ideology made a difference.

Members of the Black Panther Party such as Ericka Huggins, who held firm to "all power to the people" and engaged in community survival programs, operated on that premise as well. In fact, Huggins believed that the Black Panther Party's focus on poverty and organizing poor people, poor black people in particular, was really what frightened "oppressive government"—one that launched deadly counterintelligence operations. "See, they could hear all the buy black, do black, think black, be black, black on, and black power," explained Huggins, speaking of politicians. She continued: "They could hear that. . . . It was when poor niggers started talking about class struggle that they got frightened. And not just talked about it, but did something."[112]

Black Power in the garb of capitalism and inadequately funded government programs did not address the root causes of oppression. It did not alleviate poor black women's conditions, but helped the black middle class and strivers who serviced inner cities and wanted to get away from their poorer brethren; and it reified a kind of acceptable disgust. This was the argument of the poor black women's collective. They described the types of jobs poor black and Puerto Rican women held and the wages they made as laborers in an electronics factory and a tomato packing plant, and as domestics in the 1950s and 1960s. They also outlined the impact of automation, drugs, and crime. In doing so, they struggled to make sense of the oppressive impact of capitalism, and identify what they deemed the counterrevolutionary and "fascist" tendencies internal to the black community. Wrote the collective, "We wanted our children to know the power poor people had to understand things deeper than the bourgies. Now that we had some inside power, we read and scoped for ourselves just how we were being screwed by everybody—blacks included."[113] The essay continued:

> All of us have begun to learn to live beyond the rhetoric, beyond Black Power, beyond the American Dream, beyond striving for bourgieness [sic], beyond leaving our brothers and sisters who are now trapped in the slums. We know the struggle from deep down below and we know it must be hard and we know it must be long because we know it must be thorough so it can not be turned around. We are keeping on, getting up![114]

Like the poor black women's collective that penned "The Revolt of Poor Black Women," the authors of the other essays and letters in *Lessons from the Damned* agreed that Black Power, or equal opportunity to positions of power, did not automatically eliminate hierarchies of power. The dispossessed could—and would—very easily remain dispossessed and damned.

Black radical women broached in particularly poignant ways the question of how a community, nation, or people were to be defined. They exposed the miner's canaries of double, triple, and multiple interlocking oppressions. They unmasked the violence of racism, classism, patriarchy, and imperialism. They critiqued the turn to individualism and black capitalism as a pathway to black liberation. *The Black Woman, Lessons from the Damned,* and TWWA's journal *Triple Jeopardy*—all took on these liberation issues.

In April 1975 a group of black socialist lesbian feminist women, formerly of the NBFO, became the independent Combahee River Collective. The Boston-based group named the collective after a South Carolina river where Harriet Tubman waged a battle to free 750 slaves. Barbara and Beverly Smith and Demita Frazier, who believed "in collective process and a nonhierarchical distribution of power," issued their black feminist statement that not only forthrightly challenged racism, sexism and patriarchy, and imperialism, but also homophobia among men and women.[115] A year later, Michele Wallace wrote *Black Macho & the Myth of the Super-Women.* In it, Wallace critiqued patriarchy and sexism, and kicked up a flurry of debate.[116] But that debate, as well as others that exposed romantic black unity, clearly was not new in 1978. These women contributed to an ongoing dialogue, which had its roots in the quotidian, material, and political quests of those whose lives and activism contested broader claims of American democracy and freedom.

In 1982 black radical lesbian feminist Audre Lorde gave a lecture during a Malcolm X weekend celebration at Harvard University. It was published under the title "Learning from the 60s" in *Sister Outsider,* a collection of her writings. Challenging the Black Power–era myth of black unity, Lorde wrote: "A small and vocal part of the black community lost sight of the fact that unity does not mean unanimity—Black people are not some standardly digestible quantity." Characterizing the era as "vital years of awakening, of pride, and of error," Lorde explained: "The civil rights and Black power movements rekindled the possibilities for disenfranchised groups within this nation. Even though we fought common enemies, at times the lure of individual solutions made us careless of each other." She continued: "In the 60s, white america—racist and liberal alike—was more than pleased to sit back as spectator while Black militant fought Black Muslim, Black Nationalist badmouthed the nonviolent, and Black women were told that our only useful position in the Black Power movement was prone. The existence of Black lesbian and gay people was not even allowed to cross the public consciousness of Black america."[117] In the words of the black gay filmmaker Marlon Riggs, who credited radical black feminists, such acerbic and alienating "Black is, black ain't" politics limited struggles against oppressive systems of inequality and power, as well as for liberation and human dignity.

Gender, class, sexuality, economic approaches, and political agendas influenced relationships, roles, expectations, community, and black people's concrete demands vis-à-vis each other and white power elites. This would continue to be the case as the formal era of Black Power politics came to an end—the result of repression, death and fatigue, co-optation, assimilation, and the ascendance of new liberal and conservative policies. In the wake of conservative backlashes, "frontlashes,"[118] and retrenchment, this question of "revolution by and for whom" would remain important. Indeed, the answers to that question, in part, would shape who black leaders were, how leaders led, what their agendas looked like, and what visions of social change could even be imagined to empower the masses of black people in ongoing struggles against systemic and structural inequality.

Notes

1 Pat Robinson to Vilma Sanchez, December 17, 1966, Folder: 1–2, Joan Jordan Papers 1966–1972, MSS 197, Wisconsin Historical Society, Madison, Wisconsin. Vilma Sanchez is Joan Jordan's alias.
2 Pat Robinson to Vilma Sanchez, March 23, 1967, Folder: 1–2, Joan Jordan Papers 1966–1972, MSS 197.
3 Roth, 87.
4 M. Rivka Polatnick, "Poor Black Sisters Decided for Themselves," in *Black Women in America,* ed. Kim Marie Vaz (Thousand Oaks, California: Sage Publications Inc., 1995), 110–130.
5 Pat Robinson to Vilma Sanchez, December 17, 1966 and March 23, 1967. Also, "The Revolt of Poor Black Women," in *Lessons from the Damned,* 94; M. Rivka Polatnick, "Poor Black Sisters Decided for Themselves," 115.
6 Pat Robinson and Group, "Letter to a North Vietnamese Sister from an Afro-American Woman—September 1968," in *The Black Woman,* ed. Cade, 241.
7 Ibid., 243–244.
8 Ibid., 243–245.
9 Pat Robinson and Group, "On the Position of Poor Black Women in This Country," in *The Black Woman,* ed. Cade, 246, 249–250.
10 Quotes appear on the pages in this order: Ransby, *Ella Baker,* 350, 346. Ella Baker believed calls for self-determination and revolutionary rhetoric "increased confrontation," but felt that "anti-white sentiments" were "counterproductive" for the advancement of black liberation. Ransby, *Ella Baker,* 351.
11 "The Revolt of Poor Black Women," in *Lessons from the Damned,* 99.
12 It is unclear whether women or men actually wrote the letter. The "we" in the statement—"WE MUST SUPPORT OUR MEN. We are their backbone"—intimates women, but it is hard to know for sure. For other examples of what Tracye Matthews calls "prescriptive literature," see Matthews, "No One Ever Asks, What a Man's Role in the Revolution Is," in *The Black Panther Party [Reconsidered],* ed. Charles E. Jones.
13 Guy, 13–14.
14 Ibid., 31–32.
15 Ibid., 60–61.
16 Angela D. LeBlanc-Ernest, "'The Most Qualified Person to Handle the Job': Black Panther Party Women, 1966–1982," and Matthews' essay, both in *The Black Panther Party [Reconsidered],* ed. Charles E. Jones. Also Elizabeth A. Castle, "Black and Native American Women's Activism in the Black Panther Party and American Indian Movement," in *Visions and Voices,* ed. Peters and Straus, 85–99.
17 Guy, 62.
18 Ibid., 102.
19 Zinn, 482.
20 Pat Robinson to Vilma Sanchez, March 23, 1967.
21 Regina Jennings, "Why I Joined the Party: An Africana Womanist Reflection," in *The Black Panther Party [Reconsidered],* ed. Charles E. Jones, 261.
22 Ibid., 82–83.
23 Guy, 95. Also, "Free the New York Panther 21," *Black Panther,* June 7, 1969, It's About Time website, www.itsabouttimebpp.com/BPP_Newspapers/pdf/Vol_III_No7_1969.pdf; Annette T. Rubinstein and Robert Rhodes, Lili Solomon, Janet Townsend, "The

Black Panther Party and the Case of the New York 21," prepared by members of the Charter Group for a Pledge of Conscience, n.d., http://archive.lib.msu.edu/DMC/AmRad/blackpanthercase.pdf.

24 Wright also established an independent black community board of education and was affiliated with the Los Angeles–based Black Congress. "Woman Loses Plea for U.S. School Controls," *Los Angeles Times,* July 27, 1967; Jack Jones, "Parents Unit's Head Quits, Claims Threats," *Los Angeles Times,* February 4, 1969.

25 Margaret Wright, "I Want the Right to Be Black and Me," in *Black Women in White America,* ed. Lerner, 607. Also, Scot Brown, 84; Kelley, *Freedom Dreams,* 141–142.

26 Scot Brown, 56–57.

27 Eldridge Cleaver, *Soul on Ice,* 10–11.

28 "Revolutionary People's Constitutional Convention Plenary Session: Workshop on Self-Determination of Women," and "Statement of Demands to the Revolutionary People's Constitutional Convention from the Male Representatives of National Gay Liberation," Rainbow History Project, documents in author's possession. On Eldridge Cleaver, see Matthews' and LeBlanc-Ernest's essays in *The Black Panther Party [Reconsidered]*, ed. Charles E. Jones. Also Kathleen Cleaver, "Women, Power, and the Revolution" and George Katsiaficas, "Organization and Movement," in *Liberation, Imagination, and the Black Panther Party,* ed. Cleaver and Katsiaficas; Angela LeBlanc-Ernest and Ericka Huggins, "Revolutionary Women, Revolutionary Education: The Black Panther Party's Oakland Community School," in *Want to Start a Revolution?,* ed. Gore, Theoharis, and Woodard.

29 Scot Brown, 128.

30 Regina Jennings, "Why I Joined the Party," 257–265.

31 Regina Jennings, "Why I Joined the Party," 263. For a discussion of sex and power and the "psychosexual dimensions of Party life and practices," Margo V. Perkins, "Inside Our Dangerous Ranks," in *Still Lifting, Still Climbing,* ed. Springer, 93.

32 Regina Jennings, "Why I Joined the Party," 263.

33 Ibid.

34 Kathleen Cleaver, "Women, Power, and Revolution," 123. Also Matthews, "No One Ever Asks," 230–256.

35 Kathleen Cleaver, "Women, Power, and Revolution," 123.

36 "Birth Control Pills and Black Children: A Statement by the Black Unity Party," Chicago Women's Liberation Union (CWLU) Herstory Archive, http://uic.edu/orgs/cwluherstory/CWLUArchive/blackwomen.html.

37 Rhonda Y. Williams, "The Pursuit of Audacious Power," in *Neighborhood Rebels,* ed. Joseph, 229.

38 "The Sisters Reply," September 11, 1968, Digital Collections, Duke University Library, http://library.duke.edu/rubenstein/scriptorium/wlm/poor/#reply.

39 Pat Robinson to Vilma Sanchez, July 24, 1967. They were also known as the Black Women's Liberation Group. Nadasen, 217.

40 Dorothy Bolden, "Organizing Domestic Workers in Atlanta, Georgia," in *Black Women in White America,* ed. Lerner, 238.

41 *For Us Women* newsletter, Folder: National Coordinating Committee of Black Organizations against the Draft, Box 32, Social Action Vertical File c. 1960–1980, MSS 577.

42 On Tillmon, see Premilla Nadasen, "'We Do Whatever Becomes Necessary,'" in *Want to Start a Revolution?,* ed. Gore, Theoharis, and Woodard, 317–338.

43 Margaret Wright, "I Want the Right to Be Black and Me," 608.

44 Ibid.

45 Ella Baker was among those who attended the founding meetings of TWWA. Ransby, *Ella Baker,* 552.

46 Frances Beal, interview by Loretta Ross, March 18, 2005, Oakland, California, *Voices of Feminism Oral History Project.*

47 Stephen Ward, "The Third World Women's Alliance," in *The Black Power Movement,* ed. Joseph, 125.

48 Frances Beal, interview by Loretta Ross, 18 March 2005, Oakland, California. Ward, "The Third World Women's Alliance," 125.
49 Springer, *Living for the Revolution,* 47.
50 Benita Roth, "The Making of the Vanguard Center," in *Still Lifting, Still Climbing,* ed. Springer, 73; Stephen Ward, "The Third World Women's Alliance," 125.
51 Frances M. Beal, "Black Women's Manifesto; Double Jeopardy: To Be Black and Female," www.hartford-hwp.com/archives/45a/196.html. This is the original version of the pamphlet written by Beal in 1969. A revised version appeared in *Sisterhood Is Powerful* and *The Black Woman.* Also, Charlayne Hunter, "Many Blacks Wary of 'Women's Liberation' Movement in U.S.," *New York Times,* November 17, 1970.
52 Linda LaRue, "The Black Movement and Women's Liberation," in *Words of Fire,* ed. Guy-Sheftall, 164.
53 Sherie M. Randolph, "Women's Liberation or . . . Black Liberation," in *Want to Start a Revolution?,* eds. Gore, Theoharis, and Woodard, 223–247.
54 Frances Beale [*sic*], "Double Jeopardy: To Be Black and Female," in *Words of Fire,* ed. Guy-Sheftall, 147–148.
55 Nikki Giovanni, "Woman Poem," in *The Black Woman.* Margo Natalie Crawford, "Must Revolution Be a Family Affair?," in *Want to Start a Revolution?,* eds. Gore, Theoharis, and Woodard, 198.
56 Gwen Patton, "Black People and the Victorian Ethos," in *The Black Woman,* ed. Cade, 180, 182; Crawford, 185–204.
57 Toni Cade, "The Pill: Genocide or Liberation?," in *The Black Woman,* ed. Cade, 203–205. This essay originally appeared in *Onyx* in August 1969 and was reprinted in *The Black Woman.*
58 Ibid., 203.
59 Ibid., 206.
60 Ladner, 256.
61 Premilla Nadasen, "We Do Whatever Becomes Necessary," 328.
62 Zinn, 509–510; Valk, "Mother Power."
63 Shirley Chisholm, "Facing the Abortion Question," in *Black Women in White America,* ed. Lerner, 605.
64 Author's email exchange with Alondra Nelson, July 2013. I want to thank Alondra, who shared that she neither found evidence "for" nor "against" the provision of reproductive services in Black Panther Party free clinics in her research on medical care. Instead, we both agree more research needs to be done. See Nelson.
65 Nadasen, 218.
66 Valk, *Radical* Sisters, 105–106.
67 "The Workshop on Self-Determination of Women," Revolutionary People's Constitutional Convention Plenary Session, Rainbow History Project, documents in author's possession.
68 Sherie M. Randolph, "Women's Liberation or . . . Black Liberation," 223. Also, Kelley, *Freedom Dreams,* 138–139.
69 Shirley Chisholm, "Speech at Howard University," in *Say It Loud!,* ed. Ellis and Smith, 107–108.
70 Shirley Chisholm, "Facing the Abortion Question," in *Black Women in White America,* ed. Lerner, 603–604.
71 Pat Robinson to Vilma Sanchez, March 23, 1967.
72 Regina Jennings, "Why I Joined the Party"; Levine, et al., 20. Plummer, *In Search of Power,* 235.
73 United States House of Representatives, Committee on Internal Security, *Gun-Barrel Politics,* 73.
74 In the first nine months of its existence, the STRESS unit arrested 1,400 and killed 10 suspects (nine of them black). Thompson, *Whose Detroit?,* 81–82.

75 McCoy, 391.
76 Richard Nixon, "Special Message to the Congress on Control of Narcotics and Dangerous Drugs," in *The American Presidency Project,* ed. John Woolley and Gerhard Peters, www.presidency.ucsb.edu/ws/index.php?pid=2126&st=&st1=.
77 Michael Cetewayo Tabor (Political Prisoner NY 21), *Capitalism Plus Dope Equals Genocide,* pamphlet of the Black Panther Party U.S.A., 1969, Freedom Archives, http://freedomarchives.org/Documents/Finder/DOC513_scans/Michael_Cetewayo_Tabor/513.Michael.Tabor.Capitalism.Dope.Genocide.pdf.
78 Bloom and Martin, 188; "Baltimore Ranks No. 5 in Total of Dope Addicts," *Baltimore Evening Sun,* April 2, 1968.
79 Sonnie and Tracy, 133.
80 Michael Cetewayo Tabor, *Capitalism Plus Dope Equals Genocide.*
81 Ibid.
82 Baldwin, *The Fire Next Time,* 105.
83 "Carmichael Terms Unity Key to Black Liberation," *Washington Post,* April 10, 1970.
84 "Letter to a Black Serviceman from a Poor Black Woman," n.d., Folder 1–7: Literature on the Negro through Working Women, Joan Jordan Papers 1966–1972, MSS 197.
85 Beck, 45.
86 Eddie Stone, 112.
87 Ibid., 113.
88 Barnes with Folsom, 194.
89 Ibid.
90 Ibid., 204.
91 Ibid., 207.
92 Howard Kohn, "Dope Czar's Burial Lavish as His Life," *Detroit Free Press,* n.d., Folder: Drugs—Clippings, 1973, Box 169, New Detroit, Inc. Records.
93 Lawson, 144. Also, Robert E. Weems Jr., "Whatever Happened to the Business of Black Power?," and Michael West, "Whose Black Power?," both in *The Business of Black Power,* ed. Hill and Rabig, 304–306 and 283–291, respectively.
94 Franklin and Higginbotham, 581; Joseph, *Waiting 'Til the Midnight Hour,* 276.
95 Denby, 212. Regarding pen name, Dillard, 209.
96 Denby, 231, 233.
97 Franklin and Higginbotham, 580.
98 Editors' Preface to Shirley Chisholm, Speech at Howard University, in *Say It Loud!,* ed. Ellis and Smith, 102–103.
99 Harris, 7.
100 Joshua Guild, "To Make That Someday Come," in *Want to Start a Revolution?,* ed. Gore, Theoharis, and Woodard, 248–270.
101 *Chisholm '72: Unbought & Unbossed.*
102 Harris, 3–17.
103 Editors' Preface to Shirley Chisholm, Speech at Howard University, 102–103.
104 Shirley Chisholm, Speech at Howard University, 107–108.
105 Editors' Preface to Shirley Chisholm, Speech at Howard University.
106 "The Revolt of Poor Black Women," in *Lessons from the Damned,* 99.
107 "Wanting to be Somebody!," in *Lessons from the Damned,* 29.
108 Ibid., 27.
109 "Our Black Nationalist Stage," in *Lessons from the Damned,* 32.
110 "The Revolt of Poor Black Women," in *Lessons from the Damned,* 99.
111 Assata, 190. Robert Allen and Julius Hobson agreed. Allen believed capitalism was "the most successful system of exploitation in the world," and Hobson advised, "Youthful black power advocates . . . go left young men." He did not mention women. Michael West, "Whose Black Power?," 278; Allen; Julius Hobson, "Black Power: Right or Left?," in *The Black Power Revolt,* ed. Barbour.

112 Ericka Huggins, Interview by Michele Russell, April 20, 1977, Oakland, California.
113 "The Revolt of Poor Black Women," in *Lessons from the Damned,* 95.
114 Ibid., 101.
115 Barbara Smith, interview by Loretta Ross, *Voices of Feminism Oral History Project*; Combahee River Collective, "A Black Feminist Statement," in *Words of Fire,* ed. Guy-Sheftall, 232–240.
116 Wallace.
117 Lorde, 136–137. Lorde does not capitalize "america" in her essay.
118 Vesla M. Weaver coined the term "frontlash." It means "the process by which losers in a conflict become the architects of a new program, manipulating the issue space and altering the dimension of the conflict in an effort to regain their command of the agenda." Weaver, 236.

EPILOGUE

Echoes

Revolution. It's Not Neat or Pretty or Quick.

—Pat Parker (1980)[1]

In a very real sense the words of black feminist writer Pat Parker caution us about offering a tidy conclusion to the era of expansive Black Power politics. Unlike the legislative victories of the civil rights era, the legacies of Black Power must be sought in the politics of community, ongoing contests over power, and the echoes of the era.

Activists in the Black Power era were armed with visions of different worlds—some revolutionary, some not. Their commitment to struggle grew out of a fundamental belief that, in spite of the stark reality of concrete conditions, there had to exist something better. Their pursuit of this something better—what many termed liberation—took many forms including studying and theorizing, identifying and analyzing issues, mobilizing and organizing people, and developing campaigns and programs that might alter power relations. Integration was no longer the simple (if it ever was), or prevailing, solution. Legislative actions had indeed registered decisive blows against Jim Crow, opening up literal spaces and providing legal rights once denied. However, these same victories did not—in fact could not alone—eradicate entrenched privilege and power. White supremacy, patriarchy, and economic oppression, wounded but alive, began their own processes of regeneration.

Demands for self-determination and Black Power—whether the early 1900s' portents, the 1950s' articulations, or the 1960s' revolt and its many manifestations throughout the 1970s—revealed aspirations and a sense of urgency rooted in people's material conditions. This would remain so even as the Black Power era waned, for pressing societal and community problems, while addressed and at times assuaged, did not merely go away with laws, the growth of a black middle class, or black faces in high places. Grappling with the development, expressions, nuances, as well as repercussions of Black Power politics exposes the fertile imaginings and multiple attempts to enact alternative scenarios and societies, and not always just for black people. To echo Audre Lorde: "Through examining the combination of our triumphs and errors, we can examine the dangers of an incomplete vision. Not to condemn that vision but to alter it, construct templates for possible futures, and focus our rage for change upon our enemies rather than upon each other."[2]

This desire to envision different futures also unmasks the underbelly, unmet promises, and, for many, falsehoods of U.S. democracy—or what Malcolm X had called "disguised hypocrisy." It does this by contributing to our understanding of the resilience of systems of inequality and power—whether through culture, politics, and economics; through vigilantism, the police, courts, or the state; or in neighborhoods, schools, workplaces, unions, businesses, or churches. The list is long. And, that is precisely why struggles for self-determination and the legacies of the Black Power era continue to echo in the present.

Thus the warning that Richard Wright issued to Kwame Nkrumah in *Black Power* and the question that Shirley Chisholm posed to those frightened by the Black Panther Party provide echoes of past political wisdom and lessons. In 1953 Wright counseled Nkrumah to beware the "chary of other slaveries"—that is, foreign ideas and money that could lead to mortgaging the people's future. Almost a decade later in 1972, a reporter asked Chisholm whether she feared that the Panthers' endorsement of her presidential candidacy might alienate a broader voter base. She not only responded that people should get behind the Panthers, but just as importantly they must also consider the *circumstances* that birthed and made necessary a Black Panther Party. These two statements—though separated by time, place, and political context—are not disconnected. They speak to the "whys" of Black Power writ large.

Black Power was a series of responses to black subjugation, as well as a generative space for speaking truth to all kinds of power. This included confronting oppressive power relations within the black community. The searches for Black Power, the ideologies and grounded protests—as well as the contradictions that they reveal—have a history, and they will have a future whether "black" recouples with "power" or not. This question of power and how it continues to shape visions of "revolution by and for whom" in local (but not necessarily parochial) ways require our attention as scholars and activists. For as James Baldwin wrote: "Power . . . which can have no morality in itself, is yet dependent on human energy, on the wills and desires of human beings."[3]

To be clear, the era of Black Power proliferation is over, but the legacies of people, their desires, and organizing traditions linger whether we are aware of them or not. In that sense, they become a part of, as well as help create, new contexts that will give issue to their own concrete demands. The question remains: What will we remember, seek to find out, or pay attention to as we live and struggle to forge new futures based on human dignity? In attempting to respond to this question, this epilogue, in a sense, operates as an echo chamber, one that seeks to remember by "blending time"—a phrase inspired by a Ravi Coltrane CD.[4] Blending, or putting into dialogue, the echoes of past and present (without collapsing them) begs us to ruminate over the hardships, successes (even if short-lived), and shifting realities. This requires offering a few updates about some of the activists and organizations while also considering the legacies that have seeded the ground for sure enough struggles and futures.

Blending Time

Numerous Black Power–era activists faded from the limelight. Some died, and others simply grew weary of struggle. The most publicly prominent or radical Black Power organizations, including SNCC, RAM, the Black Panther Party, and the League of Revolutionary Black Workers (LRBW), fell prey to personal conflicts, ideological fracturing, aggressive state repression, and political backlashes and power realignments. CORE grew more conservative with its leaders turning toward the Republican Party.

In the wake of the conservative ascendancy in the 1970s, the Reagan revolution of the 1980s, and the maturing of neoliberalism in the 1990s, some veteran black liberationists, however, continued to struggle around issues that they believed could bring stability, power, equity, and human dignity. For instance, Marian Kramer, who organized with the Michigan Welfare Rights Organization and LRBW, has participated in anti-poverty summits across the nation. Former public housing resident-activists such as Shirley Wise continued to champion the rights of low-income people and advocate for affordable housing, safe communities, and decision-making power. Among many other grassroots activists, Don Freeman, who co-founded RAM, fights for community voice in public education, has pushed for greater access to the still overwhelmingly white trades and construction industry, and most recently called attention to what he dubbed the "Cleveland Atrocity"—the killing of two black people in a hail of 137 police bullets on November 29, 2012.[5] Republic of New Afrika (RNA) members continued to work towards the development of conduits of black political and economic self-determination. On the eve of the fiftieth anniversary of Medgar Evers's murder in Jackson, Mississippi, former RNA leader and attorney Chokwe Lumumba became mayor of that city, but died unexpectedly a year later.

Incarcerated as political prisoners, several Black Power–era activists watched the movement's ebbs from behind prison walls. Others escaped the United States. Three decades after Assata Shakur became an exile in Cuba, the FBI decided to place her on its "terrorist list"—created in the aftermath of 9/11—and doubled her $1 million bounty. "It seems to me that the attack on her reflects the logic of terrorism," remarked Angela Davis on *Democracy Now!*, continuing, "because it precisely is designed to frighten young people, especially today, who would be involved in the kind of radical activism that might lead to change."[6]

Others returned to the United States during the mid-to-late 1970s for an array of reasons, including homesickness, dismay at what they witnessed throughout the Third World, and realization that there was plenty still yet to do in the United States. Robert and Mabel Williams arrived back in the United States in 1969 and led fairly quiet existences in Michigan. Eldridge and Kathleen Cleaver and their two children returned from exile in Paris in 1975. The Cleavers eventually divorced, taking very different paths. Kathleen Cleaver became a scholar and civil rights lawyer, and Eldridge Cleaver a born-again Christian.

Huey Newton returned from Cuba in July 1977. He was acquitted of the outstanding criminal charges, but his demons remained. Succumbing to drugs, Newton was killed in August 1989 in the wee hours of the morning near a crack cocaine house. By that time, business closures and relocations, deindustrialization, automation, and other new technologies resulted in both a net exodus of blue-collar jobs from cities as well as transformed the type of work available. It was in the wake of these economic transformations that crack cocaine also appeared in cities—unfortunately, ushering in illegal work and hustles. As was the case with Newton in 1989 (actually decades before), Black Power activism did not make one immune to the problems one fought against. Newton is a testimony to that.

Drug dealing and drug use, as well, reveal not only increasingly tragic entice-ments, but also entrenched inequalities. While some black people may have been imprudently driven to drugs and crime by a desire for status and wealth, others simply sought a way to make ends meet when living-wage jobs (or just jobs) were few, poverty was stark, and possessing things represented a measure of success. Still others were in the pursuit of pleasure or self-medication. This set of com-plicated motivations alongside disparate policing and stringent federal sentencing guidelines that had roots in the 1960s and 1970s fueled the exponential increase in imprisonment of primarily black and brown nonviolent drug offenders. They became fodder for a growing prison-industrial complex, itself propelled by the War on Drugs.

Activists during the Black Power era called attention to the threat of drugs, police brutality, law-and-order politics, and the criminalization of urban black space. Inspired by battles to free political prisoners during the late 1960s and early 1970s, as well as her own experiences, Angela Davis, now a university professor, continues to challenge the prison-industrial complex—which, in a matter of two decades, turned the United States into the world's leading incarceration nation. As political scientist Vesla Weaver writes, "Fusing crime to anxiety about ghetto revolts, racial disorder—initially defined as a problem of minority disenfranchise-ment—was redefined as a crime problem, which helped shift the debate from social reform to punishment."[7] So much so, that by 2006, according to Heather A. Thompson, "more than 7.3 million Americans had become entangled in the criminal justice system" with "one in every thirty-one U.S. residents . . .

under some form of correctional supervision, such as in prison or jail, or on probation or parole."[8] And if one looks even further beyond the literal prison walls, as scholar Beth E. Richie has done when she examines the often ignored "matrix" of physical and emotional violence against black women—whether perpetrated by intimates, other community members, police, or social and economic systems—what becomes even clearer is how the United States has become a "prison nation."[9]

While renowned and everyday activists operating in the eras covered by *Concrete Demands* have increasingly faded from the public eye, the issues they fought over and for have not. The echoes reverberate. The waning of Black Power as a phase of the freedom struggle did not mean that the social, economic, and political realities that fueled ideas, demands, personal and political conflicts, and indignation had been resolved. Stagflation in the 1970s, recession in the 1980s, and a punitive welfare state under Republican and Democratic presidents in the 1980s and 1990s had made life for low-income people, black people, and particularly low-income black women and their families that much more challenging to say the least. Disinvestment and capital flight contributed to declining tax bases and populations in rustbelt cities, and this took its toll on the health and well-being of the least well-off communities. Obtaining living-wage jobs and income, adequate and affordable housing, equitably funded and quality public schools, and environmentally safe neighborhoods remained (and still remain) urgent issues.

Under Reagan the privileging of neoliberal markets, deregulation, privatization, and anti-unionism existed alongside the expansion of budgets for policing and prisons.[10] Reagan also helped further individualize and "race" inequality by, for instance, castigating "welfare queens," "strapping young bucks," and "big government"—code phrases that conjured black poor people as hustlers of social entitlements. While anti-poverty and social programs were defunded and placed under the logic of markets in the Nixon (1968–1974) and Reagan (1980–1988) eras, public housing and welfare ended "as we know it" under the Democratic presidency of Bill Clinton. Overall, as cuts in the welfare state increased and tax rates for the wealthy decreased, corporate profits and the racial, and overall, wealth gap grew.

While both the black middle class and black political representation grew throughout these decades, neither the progress of some, nor skin color alone, could serve as a panacea for black community advancement. Here the analyses of Black Power in its revolutionary and counterrevolutionary forms are also instructive. Just as Paul Robeson theorized, Bayard Rustin maintained, revolutionary nationalists insisted upon, and black radical feminists and low-income black women understood, struggling against racial and economic oppression (and their worldly partner imperialism) was absolutely necessary, but class interests, gender and patriarchy, and ideology and agenda, among other things, also mattered.

Struggles for black self-determination could, and did, fall victim to individual pursuits, macro-structural changes, and hubris. This occurred in Detroit—in the very city where waves of black radicalism consistently peeled back the layers of exclusion, exploitation, and excess. New urban agendas sought to manage black discontent, as well as capital, white, and black middle-class flight. This often meant catering to corporate and downtown growth interests that did not necessarily benefit working-class and poor urban residents. As of this writing, the state chair of the Michigan Welfare Rights Organization, Maureen Taylor, talked about technology replacing labor, the flight of population and jobs, abandoned houses and gentrification, and people struggling to pay bills. One result: the City of Detroit is shutting off water to "thousands of broke residents" a month. Issuing her concrete demand, the return of water service as a human right, Taylor argued on *Politics Nation* with Al Sharpton that while the "cost of living is going up . . . the chance of living is going down." She continued: "It's demonic."[11]

Therein lay a measure of the legacies, and even limits and lessons, of past and ongoing power struggles. Black leadership of a city, or an office, does not *a priori* translate into control of resources, capital, or power. Nor does black oversight of economic resources necessarily result in intra-racial or multi-racial cross-class agendas that advance the majority of residents. Evoking the words of Robeson, who wrote about black leadership: "A single-minded dedication to their people's welfare" requires intentional work; it does not inherently occur.[12]

This, then, raises a few more questions for consideration: Is single-minded dedication even possible? Who are the "people" whose welfare should be prioritized, and what does achieving the "welfare" of the people look like? Identity, social assumptions, and a sense of belonging—or connectedness—often impact political priorities. This alongside the pressures toward pragmatism (not always a friend of principles) reveals, and demands a grappling with, the limits of electoral politics to transform structures of privilege. The questions—who are the "people" and what is done for their "welfare"—also bring into relief the predicaments that can abound when the populace shies away from discussing the roots of economic power and inequality or from mounting strategic campaigns and sustained organizing to hold power accountable, no matter who wields it. This is certainly evident in contemporary times politically disconnected from, but with echoes of, the Black Power era.

These echoes are evident in those who continue to struggle at the grassroots. This includes people like Trevelle Harp, who has expressed a desire to build local power in East Cleveland, a majority black and economically challenged inner-ring suburb abutting wealthier communities. A complicated set of circumstances brought Harp back to the place that he left as a child. Once back, the conditions bothered him. He decided to buy a home and became an organizer with the Northeast Ohio Alliance for Hope (NOAH). He had no intimate or detailed knowledge of the history of Black Power (unlike, for instance, Maureen Taylor in Detroit, who, as a laid-off factory worker, received help and counsel from Marian Kramer of the Michigan Welfare Rights Organization). Even so, Harp believed that people needed to build power and institutions to make and sustain change.

Arguably, one of the significant challenges, which emerged with the trailing off of black liberation movements, was a decline of critical political education in an era rife with individualistic logics governing neighborhoods, politics, policy, and markets. And yet, still Harp has argued that residents must be—in the face of regional racial and economic inequities—"active participants in their own deliverance." Of course, who the participants are, whose voices are valued, with whom they align, and what their activism looks like—for what purpose and in whose interests—must be constantly assessed, just as what "deliverance" is must be imagined.

No End in Sight

The first decades of the 20th century seemed eons apart from the 21st century. The historic election of Barack Obama in 2008 took the nation and world by surprise. His appointment of Eric Holder as U.S. attorney general seemed to complete a political arc. In the shadow of these political victories emerged some eerie reminiscences. Redemption and reclamation—or the Civil War era's abandonment of black civil and voting rights on the altar of presidential politics—emerged as echoes in the 21st century. Indeed, the election of a black president has advanced the false notion of a "post-racial" society. This notion—kin to "colorblindness"—denies the need for a strident anti-racist agenda that attacks ongoing inequalities. This is so, even with the current attack on the 1965 Voting Rights Act—a hard-won legal right that, in its success, was still limited in its ability to extend substantive equality, as Black Power activists had argued. In June 2013, the U.S. Supreme Court struck down sections of the Voting Rights Act in a 5–4 decision. Offering the most egregious rationale was Justice Antonin Scalia, who called the act a "racial preferment." The black justice Clarence Thomas did not dissent. In the immediate wake of this decision, Republicans at the state level began to propose some of the most deleterious voter suppression policies since the passage of the initial act. Ignorance of history and the erasure of historical power politics, while simultaneously deploying the contemporary power shielded by the presumed "objective" authority of the bench, were among the abetting factors.

There also seems to be no end in sight when it comes to criminalizing not only urban space, but demonizing black men and women. For it was racial profiling based on appearance, and being "out of place," that resulted in the death of 17-year-old Trayvon Martin. The verdict, which set his killer free, conjured outrage, the historical spectacles of lynching and Emmett Till, and an unfair criminal justice system. In the wake of all this media attention, the case of Marissa Alexander, a black mother of three children, provides further evidence of a justice system that also founders on gender and patriarchy. A sufferer of domestic abuse, the 5'2" Alexander fired a warning shot into the ceiling to protect herself against her estranged ex-husband. She killed no one, but was sentenced to 20 years. After three years in prison, growing publicity about her case, and protests against

Florida's "Stand Your Ground" law, Alexander finally won a new trial in 2013. It remains to be seen what will happen not just to Alexander, but also the many black women who find themselves caught in what Richie has dubbed the male violence matrix.

Black women and men have sought to empower black communities and become self-determined people. They put not just their feet to the pavement, but also their backs and backsides on sidewalks, roads, dirt mounds, farms, prison cells, and school and government property. Literally. Most of the others—those who did not theorize, lecture, write, march, lie down, strike, leaflet, holler, organize, patrol, enter politics, critique economic injustice and state power, or set up alternative institutions in an attempt to contest white power—were witness bearers to the concrete demands that motivated searches for power. Whether people were aware or uninformed, whether they were moved or turned a blind eye, however, the signs of poverty and privilege punctuated all pieces of living—before, during, and today way after the seeding, coming of age, proliferation, and demise of the era of Black Power politics.

As part of a broader black freedom struggle and organizing traditions, the multiple streams of Black Power—and its many progenitors, believers, fellow travelers, and critics—compel important dialogue, as well as transformative potential. The spirited criticisms of romantic unity proved this by birthing new conversations, organizations, understandings of how power worked, and struggles that helped expose the complexity of inequality. Together these criticisms presaged the struggles ahead. And in their most radical formulations—such as triple oppression, secondary marginalization, intersectional analyses, and global dialogues—generated visions of collective freedom not yet achieved.

Despite no longer being coupled so grandly and publicly with the adjective "black," and all that meant during decades of struggle, battles over power are still prevalent and have no end in sight. For as the black science fiction writer Octavia Butler, who campaigned for Chisholm in 1972, put it in the 2004 documentary *Chisholm '72: Unbought & Unbossed*: "Power really is just a tool, and it's what you do with it that matters."[13] It seems, then, that the need for struggles to achieve empowerment for black people—beyond the individual or "worthy" black middle class, and even beyond a recuperated dependency on white good will—remains ever necessary. And it requires discussions of class and gender politics, systemic inequality, and liberation for poor people.

What might we do differently, if we could harness a more nuanced, complex, and sober understanding of history and political economy? Is it possible to create a new world that does not reproduce existing hierarchies made invisible by new faces? What would it take? What are our analyses of social change? How do we access the resources we need to do the necessary work and still, as Chisholm said, sleep well at night? Are these even the right questions? James Baldwin wrote in *No Name in the Street* in 1972: "Only poets, since they must excavate and recreate history, have ever learned anything from it."[14] As the accounts of struggles in this book hopefully make clear, much history remains to be excavated, and understood. We must strive to become Baldwin's poets, and I say, creators of social justice.

Notes

1 Pat Parker, "Revolution: It's Not Neat or Pretty or Quick," in *This Bridge Called My Back: Writings by Radical Women of Color,* ed. Cherrie Moraga and Gloria Anzaldua (New York: Kitchen Table Press, 1981, 1983), 238–242.
2 Lorde, 135.
3 Baldwin, *No Name in the Street,* 89.
4 Ravi Coltrane is the son of John and Alice Coltrane. *Blending Time* (2008).
5 The police car chase began in downtown Cleveland and ended in a school parking lot in the City of East Cleveland. All of the police officers, except one, were white.
6 *Democracy Now!* May 3, 2013. Also, Jamilah King, "Assata Shakur and a Brief History of the FBI's Most Wanted Lists," *Colorlines,* May 8, 2013.
7 Weaver, 230.
8 Thompson, "Why Mass Incarceration Matters," 703.
9 Richie.
10 Under Reagan, public housing allocations decreased 81 percent over six years. Goetz, 9.
11 *PoliticsNation* with Al Sharpton, MSNBC, June 23, 2014.
12 Robeson, 102. Italics in the original.
13 *Chisholm '72.*
14 Baldwin, *No Name in the Street,* 29.

SELECT BIBLIOGRAPHY

Primary Sources

Special Collections

Cleveland, Ohio.
    Western Reserve Historical Society.
        Carl Stokes Papers, 1956–1972. MS4370.
    Michael Schwartz Library, Cleveland State University.
        The Black Power Movement. Part 2: The Papers of Robert F. Williams. Black Studies Research Sources. Microfilms from Major Archival and Manuscript Collections. General Editors: John H. Bracey Jr. and Sharon Harley. Bethesda, MD: UPA, 2002.
        The Black Power Movement. Part 4: The League of Revolutionary Black Workers, 1965–1976. Black Studies Research Sources. Microfilms from Major Archival and Manuscript Collections. General Editors: John H. Bracey Jr. and Sharon Harley. Bethesda, MD: UPA, 2004.
        Cleveland Press Collection.

Detroit, Michigan.
    Walter P. Reuther Library, Wayne State University.
        Dan Georgakas Papers, 1958–1980. UP001041.
        Detroit Commission on Community Relations (DCCR)/Human Rights Department Records, 1940–1984. UR000267.
        Detroit Revolutionary Movements Collection, 1968–1976. LR000874.
        James and Grace Lee Boggs Papers, 1930s–1993. UP001342.
        Kenneth V. and Sheila M. Cockrel Papers, 1959–1999. UP001379.
        Mae Mallory Papers, 1961–1967. UP000955.
        New Detroit, Inc. Records, 1967–1975. UR000660.

Madison, Wisconsin.
 Wisconsin Historical Society.
  Joan Jordan Papers, 1966–1972. MSS 197.
  Peggy Terry Papers, 1937–2004. MSS 1055.
  Social Action Vertical File, c. 1960–1980. MSS 577.
  Student Nonviolent Coordinating Committee. Vine City Project (Atlanta, Georgia): Records, 1960–1967. MSS 347.
  United States Student Association Records, 1946–2007. M70–277.

New York City, New York.
 Interreligious Foundation for Community Organization (IFCO) Records, 1966–1984. Sc MG 227. Schomburg Center for Research in Black Culture, New York Public Library.

Washington, D.C.
 The Washingtoniana Collection. D.C. Public Library.
  Anti-Poverty March, 1968. Vertical Files.
  Julius W. Hobson Papers, 1960–1977.
  Politics and Government: Home Rule, 1966–1967. Vertical Files.

Oral History Collections. *Voices of Feminism Oral History Project.* Sophia Smith Collection. Smith College, Northampton, Massachusetts.
Voicing & Action Project, Social Justice Institute, Case Western Reserve University, Cleveland, Ohio.

Interviews conducted by Rhonda Y. Williams

Ahmad, Muhammad (Maxwell Stanford Jr.). Telephone interview by author. 18 November 2013.
Freeman, Donald. Interview by author. 4 May 2011, 1 May 2013, 24 October 2013. Cleveland, Ohio.
McCarty, Margaret "Peggy." Interview by author. 21 June 2003. Baltimore, Maryland.

Newspapers and Periodicals

The Age (Australia)
The Australian
Baltimore Afro-American
Baltimore Evening Sun
Baltimore Magazine
Baltimore Morning Sun
Black America
Black Panther
Black World/Negro Digest
Call & Post
Chicago Tribune
Cleveland Plain Dealer
Cleveland Press

Commentary
The Crisis
Detroit News
The Guardian
The Herald (Australia)
Identity (Australia)
The Illustrated News
Inner City Voice
Liberator
Los Angeles Times
Michigan Citizen
Milwaukee Journal
Monthly Review
New York Times
Northcote Leader (Australia)
Pittsburgh Press
Sarasota Journal
Soulbook
The Sun (Australia)
Sunraysia Daily (Australia)
The Tribune (Australia)
The Tri-State Defender
Voice of the Lumpen
Washington Daily News
Washington Post

Federal Bureau of Investigation (FBI) Files

Carmichael, Stokely (FBI-HQ 00–446080)
Du Bois, W.E.B. (File Number 100–99729)
Jones, Claudia (File Number 100–72390)
Organization for Black Power (FBI-HQ 157–3022)
Robeson, Paul (FBI-HQ 100–123040)
Wright, Richard (File Number 100–157464)

Works Consulted

Ahmad, Muhammad (Maxwell Stanford, Jr.). *We Will Return in the Whirlwind: Black Radical Organizations, 1960–1975.* Chicago: Charles H. Kerr Publishing Company, 2007.
Aird, Michael. *Brisbane Blacks.* Southport, Australia: Keeaira Press, 2001.
Alexander, Michelle. *The New Jim Crow: Mass Incarceration in the Age of Colorblindness.* New York: New Press, 2010.
Allen, Robert L. *Black Awakening in Capitalist America: An Analytical History.* 1969. Reprint, Trenton, NJ: Africa World Press, 1990.
Angelou, Maya. *All God's Children Need Traveling Shoes.* New York: Vintage, 1986.
Angelou, Maya. *The Heart of a Woman.* New York: Random House, 1981.
Aptheker, Bettina. *The Morning Breaks: The Trial of Angela Davis.* 2nd Ed. Ithaca: Cornell University Press, 1999.

Armstrong, Julie Buckner, Houston Roberson, Rhonda Y. Williams, and Susan Holt, eds. *Teaching the Civil Rights Movement: Freedom's Bittersweet Song.* New York: Routledge, 2002.

Baldwin, Davarian L. "Chicago's New Negroes: Consumer Culture and Intellectual Life Reconsidered." *American Studies* 44 (Spring/Summer 2003): 121–152.

Baldwin, James. *The Fire Next Time.* New York: Dell, 1963.

Baldwin, James. *No Name in the Street.* New York: Dell, 1972.

Baraka, Amiri, and Larry Neal, eds. *Black Fire: An Anthology of African-American Writing.* 1968. Reprint, Baltimore: Black Classic Press, 2007.

Barbour, Floyd B., ed. *The Black Power Revolt: A Collection of Essays.* Boston: F. Porter Sargent, 1968.

Barbour, Floyd B., ed. *The Black Seventies.* Boston: F. Porter Sargent, 1970.

Barnes, Leroy "Nicky," with Tom Folsom. *Mr. Untouchable: The Rise and Fall of the Black Godfather.* New York: Rugged Land, 2007.

Barry, Marion. *A Conversation with Mayor Marion Barry: Held on April 10, 1979 at the American Enterprise Institute for Public Policy Research.* Washington, D.C.: American Enterprise Institute, 1979.

Beah: A Black Woman Speaks. Directed by LisaGay Hamilton. 2003. New York: Women Make Movies.

Beck, Robert. *The Naked Soul of Iceberg Slim.* Los Angeles: Holloway House, 1971.

Bennett, Lerone, Jr. *Black Power U.S.A.: The Human Side of Reconstruction, 1867–1877.* Chicago: Johnson Publishing Company, 1967.

Berry, Mary Frances. *My Face Is Black Is True: Callie House and the Struggle for Ex-Slave Reparations.* New York: Alfred A. Knopf, 2005.

Berry, Mary Frances, and John W. Blassingame. *Long Memory: The Black Experience in America.* New York: Oxford University Press, 1982.

Biondi, Martha. *The Black Revolution on Campus.* Berkeley: University of California Press, 2012.

Birmingham, David. *Kwame Nkrumah: The Father of African Nationalism.* Revised Ed. Athens, OH: Ohio University Press, 1998.

Bloom, Joshua, and Waldo E. Martin, Jr. *Black Against Empire: The History and Politics of the Black Panther Party.* Berkeley: University of California Press, 2013.

Boggs, Grace Lee. *Living for Change: An Autobiography.* Minneapolis: University of Minnesota Press, 1998.

Boggs, James. *Racism and the Class Struggle: Further Pages from a Black Worker's Struggle.* New York: Monthly Review Press, 1970.

Bogues, Anthony. *Black Heretics, Black Prophets: Radical Political Intellectuals.* New York: Routledge, 2003.

Bracey, Christopher Alan. *Saviors or Sellouts: The Promise and Peril of Black Conservatism, from Booker T. Washington to Condoleezza Rice.* Boston: Beacon Press, 2008.

Bracey, John H., Jr., August Meier, and Elliott Rudwick, eds. *Black Nationalism in America.* Indianapolis: Bobbs-Merrill, 1970.

Bradley, Stefan M. *Harlem vs. Columbia University: Black Student Power in the Late 1960s.* Urbana: University of Illinois Press, 2009.

Breitman, George, ed. *Malcolm X Speaks: Selected Speeches and Statements.* 1965. Reprint, New York: Pathfinder, 1989.

Brooks, Maegan Parker, and Davis W. Houck, eds. *The Speeches of Fannie Lou Hamer: To Tell It Like It Is.* Jackson: University Press of Mississippi, 2011.

Brother Outsider: The Life of Bayard Rustin. Directed by Bennett Singer and Nancy Kates. 2002. San Francisco: California Newsreel.

Brown, Elaine. *A Taste of Power: A Black Woman's Story.* New York: Pantheon Books, 1992.

Brown, Elsa Barkley. "Womanist Consciousness: Maggie Lena Walker and the Independent Order of Saint Luke." *Signs* 14 (Spring 1989): 610–633.

Brown, Nikki. *Private Politics and Public Voices: Black Women's Activism from World War II to the New Deal.* Bloomington: Indiana University Press, 2006.

Brown, Scot. *Fighting for US: Maulana Karenga, the US Organization, and Black Cultural Nationalism.* New York: New York University Press, 2003.

Bush, Rod. *We Are Not What We Seem: Black Nationalism and Class Struggle in the American Century.* New York: New York University Press, 1999.

Cade, Toni, ed. *The Black Woman: An Anthology.* 1970. Reprint, New York: Washington Square Press, 2005.

Campbell, James. *Talking at the Gates: A Life of James Baldwin.* New York: Penguin, 1992.

Carmichael, Stokely (Kwame Ture), and Charles V. Hamilton. *Black Power: The Politics of Liberation in America.* 1967. Reprint, New York: Vintage, 1992.

Carmichael, Stokely, with Ekwueme Michael Thelwell. *Ready for Revolution: The Life and Struggles of Stokely Carmichael (Kwame Ture).* New York: Scribner, 2003.

Carson, Clayborne. *In Struggle: SNCC and the Black Awakening of the 1960s.* Cambridge, MA: Harvard University Press, 1981.

Carter, Steven R. "Commitment and Complexity: Lorraine Hansberry's Life in Action." *MELUS* 7 (Autumn 1980): 39–53.

Cha-Jua, Sundiata Keita, and Clarence Lang. "The 'Long Movement' as Vampire: Temporal and Spatial Fallacies in Recent Black Freedom Studies." *Journal of African American History* 92 (Spring 2007): 265–288.

Chepesiuk, Ronald. *Sixties Radicals, Then and Now: Candid Conversations with Those Who Shaped the Era.* Jefferson, NC: McFarland & Co., 1995.

Chisholm '72: Unbought & Unbossed. Directed by Shola Lynch. 2004. Beverly Hills, CA: 20th Century Fox Home Entertainment.

Clark, Jennifer. *Aborigines & Activism: Race, Aborigines and the Coming of the Sixties to Australia.* Perth, Australia: University of Western Australia Press, 2008.

Clark, Jennifer. "'The Wind of Change' in Australia: Aborigines and the International Politics of Race, 1960–1972." *International History Review* 20 (March 1998): 89–117.

Cleage, Albert B., Jr. *Black Christian Nationalism: New Directions for the Black Church.* New York: W. Morrow, 1972.

Cleaver, Eldridge. *Soul on Ice.* New York: Dell, 1968.

Cleaver, Kathleen, and George Katsiaficas, eds. *Liberation, Imagination, and the Black Panther Party: A New Look at the Panthers and Their Legacy.* New York: Routledge, 2001.

Clegg, Claude Andrew, III. *An Original Man: The Life and Times of Elijah Muhammad.* New York: St. Martin's Press, 1997.

Colburn, David R., and Jeffrey S. Adler, eds. *African-American Mayors: Race, Politics, and the American City.* Urbana: University of Illinois Press, 2001.

Collier-Thomas, Bettye. *Jesus, Jobs, and Justice: African American Women and Religion.* New York: Alfred A. Knopf, 2010.

Collier-Thomas, Bettye, and V. P. Franklin, eds. *Sisters in the Struggle: African American Women in the Civil Rights-Black Power Movements.* New York: New York University Press, 2001.

Cone, James H. *Black Theology and Black Power.* 1969. Reprint, San Francisco: Harper & Row, 1989.

Countryman, Matthew. *Up South: Civil Rights and Black Power in Philadelphia*. Philadelphia: University of Pennsylvania Press, 2006.

Craig, Maxine Leeds. *Ain't I a Beauty Queen? Black Women, Beauty, and the Politics of Race*. New York: Oxford University Press, 2002.

Crawford, Vicki L., Jacqueline Anne Rouse, and Barbara Woods, eds. *Women in the Civil Rights Movement: Trailblazers & Torchbearers, 1941–1965*. Bloomington: Indiana University Press, 1993.

Curthoys, Ann. *Freedom Ride: A Freedom Rider Remembers*. Sydney, Australia: Allen and Unwin, 2002.

Curthoys, Ann, and Marilyn Lake, eds. *Connected Worlds: History in Transnational Perspective*. Canberra: Australian National University E Press, 2005.

Damned, The. *Lessons from the Damned: Class Struggle in the Black Community*. Washington, NJ: Times Change Press, 1973.

Daniel, Pete. *Dispossession: Discrimination Against African American Farmers in the Age of Civil Rights*. Chapel Hill: University of North Carolina Press, 2013.

Davies, Carol Boyce. *Left of Karl Marx: The Political Life of Black Communist Claudia Jones*. Durham: Duke University Press, 2007.

Davis, Angela Y. *Angela Davis: An Autobiography*. New York: Random House, 1974.

Denby, Charles. *Indignant Heart: A Black Worker's Journal*. Detroit: Wayne University Press, 1989.

Dillard, Angela D. *Faith in the City: Preaching Radical Social Change in Detroit*. Ann Arbor: University of Michigan Press, 2007.

Dittmer, John. *Local People: The Struggle for Civil Rights in Mississippi*. Urbana: University of Illinois Press, 1994.

Dowd Hall, Jacquelyn. "The Long Civil Rights Movement and the Political Uses of the Past." *Journal of American History* 91 (March 2005): 1233–1263.

Duncan, Natanya. "The 'Efficient Womanhood' of the Universal Negro Improvement Association, 1919–1930." PhD dissertation, University of Florida, 2009.

Edmondson, Locksley. "The Challenges of Race: From Entrenched White Power to Rising Black Power." *International Journal* 24 (Autumn 1969): 693–716.

Edwards, Harry. *The Revolt of the Black Athlete*. New York: Free Press, 1969.

Elbaum, Max. *Revolution in the Air: Sixties Radicals Turn to Lenin, Mao and Che*. New York: Verso, 2002.

Ellis, Catherine, and Stephen Drury Smith, eds. *Say It Loud!: Great Speeches on Civil Rights and African American Identity*. New York: New Press, 2010.

Evanzz, Karl. *The Judas Factor: The Plot to Kill Malcolm X*. New York: Thunder's Mouth Press, 1992.

Eyes on the Prize 2: America's Civil Rights Movement, 1954–1985. Directed by Judith Vecchione and Harry Hampton. PBS Video 2000, copyright 1989. Alexandria, VA: Blackside Inc.

Fergus, Devin. *Liberalism, Black Power, and the Making of American Politics, 1965–1980*. Athens, GA: University of Georgia Press, 2009.

Ferguson, Karen. *Top Down: The Ford Foundation, Black Power, and the Reinvention of Racial Liberalism*. Philadelphia: University of Pennsylvania Press, 2013.

Fleming, Cynthia Griggs. *Soon We Will Not Cry: The Liberation of Ruby Doris Smith Robinson*. Lanham, MD: Rowman & Littlefield, 1998.

Foong, Yie. "Frame Up in Monroe: The Mae Mallory Story." MA thesis, Sarah Lawrence College, 2010.

Ford, Tanisha C. "SNCC Women, Denim, and the Politics of Dress," *Journal of Southern History* (August 2013): 625–658.

Forman, James. *The Making of Black Revolutionaries*. 1972. Reprint, Seattle: University of Washington Press, 1997.

Forman, James. *Sammy Younge, Jr.: The First Black College Student to Die in the Black Liberation Movement*. 1968. Reprint, Washington, D.C.: Open Hand Publishing, 1986.

Franklin, John Hope, and Evelyn Brooks Higginbotham. *From Slavery to Freedom: A History of African Americans*. 9th Ed. New York: McGraw Hill, 2010.

Frazier, Nishani. "*Harambee Nation*: Cleveland CORE, Community Organization, and the Rise of Black Power." PhD dissertation, Columbia University, 2008.

Frazier, Robeson Taj P. "Thunder in the East: China, Exiled Crusaders, and the Unevenness of Black Internationalism." *American Quarterly* 63 (December 2011): 929–953.

Fujino, Diane C. *Heartbeat of Struggle: The Revolutionary Life of Yuri Kochiyama*. Minneapolis: University of Minnesota Press, 2005.

Gaines, Kevin K. *American Africans in Ghana: Black Expatriates and the Civil Rights Era*. Chapel Hill: University of North Carolina Press, 2006.

Gallen, David, ed. *Malcolm X: The FBI File*. New York: Carroll and Graf, 1991.

Garrow, David J. *Bearing the Cross: Martin Luther King, Jr., and the Southern Christian Leadership Conference*. New York: W. Morrow, 1986.

Garvey, Amy Jacques. *Black Power in America: Marcus Garvey's Impact on Jamaica and Africa: The Power of the Human Spirit*. Kingston, Jamaica: United Printers Ltd., 1968.

Garvey, Amy Jacques. *Garvey and Garveyism*. Kingston, Jamaica: United Printers Ltd., 1963.

Geschwender, James A. *Class, Race, and Worker Insurgency: The League of Revolutionary Black Workers*. Cambridge, UK; New York: Cambridge University Press, 1977.

Giddings, Paula. *Ida: A Sword Among Lions: Ida B. Wells and the Campaign Against Lynching*. New York: Amistad, 2008.

Giddings, Paula. *When and Where I Enter: The Impact of Black Women on Race and Sex in America*. New York: W. Morrow, 1984.

Gilmore, Glenda Elizabeth. *Defying Dixie: The Radical Roots of Civil Rights, 1919–1950*. New York: W. W. Norton, 2008.

Giovanni, Nikki. *Black Feeling, Black Talk*. New York: W. Morrow, 1970.

Glaude, Eddie S., Jr., ed. *Is It Nation Time?: Contemporary Essays on Black Power and Black Nationalism*. Chicago: University of Chicago Press, 2002.

Goetz, Edward G. *New Deal Ruins: Race, Economic Justice, and Public Housing Policy*. Ithaca: Cornell University Press, 2013.

Goldberg, David, and Trevor Griffey, eds. *Black Power at Work: Community Control, Affirmative Action, and the Construction Industry*. Ithaca: Cornell University Press, 2010.

Gomez, Michael A., ed. *Diasporic Africa: A Reader*. New York: New York University Press, 2006.

Gore, Dayo F. *Radicalism at the Crossroads: African American Women Activists in the Cold War*. New York: New York University Press, 2011.

Gore, Dayo F., Jeanne Theoharis, and Komozi Woodard, eds. *Want to Start a Revolution?: Radical Women in the Black Freedom Struggle*. New York: New York University Press, 2009.

Goudsouzian, Aram. *Down to the Crossroads: Civil Rights, Black Power, and the Meredith March Against Fear*. New York: Farrar, Straus & Giroux, 2014.

Grady-Willis, Winston A. *Challenging U.S. Apartheid: Atlanta and Black Struggles for Human Rights, 1960–1977*. Durham: Duke University Press, 2006.

Greene, Christina. *Our Separate Ways: Women and the Black Freedom Movement in Durham, North Carolina.* Chapel Hill: University of North Carolina Press, 2005.

Guy, Jasmine. *Afeni Shakur: Evolution of a Revolutionary.* New York: Atria Books, 2004.

Guy-Sheftall, Beverly, ed. *Words of Fire: An Anthology of African-American Feminist Thought.* New York: New Press, 1995.

Hahn, Steven. *A Nation Under Our Feet: Black Political Struggles in the Rural South from Slavery to the Great Migration.* Cambridge, MA: Belknap Press of Harvard University Press, 2003.

Hamlin, Michael, with Michele Gibbs. *A Black Revolutionary's Life in Labor: Black Workers Power in Detroit.* Detroit: Against the Tide Books, 2013.

Hansberry, Lorraine (and Robert Nemiroff). *To Be Young, Gifted, and Black: An Informal Biography of Lorraine Hansberry.* New York: Signet, 1970.

Harold, Claudrena N. *The Rise and Fall of the Garvey Movement in the Urban South, 1918–1942.* New York: Routledge, 2007.

Harris, Frederick C. *The Price of the Ticket: Barack Obama and the Rise and Decline of Black Politics.* New York: Oxford University Press, 2012.

Hill, Lance. *The Deacons for Defense: Armed Resistance and the Civil Rights Movement.* Chapel Hill: University of North Carolina Press, 2004.

Hill, Lauren Warren, and Julia Rabig, eds. *The Business of Black Power: Community Development, Capitalism, and Corporate Responsibility in Postwar America.* Rochester, NY: University of Rochester Press, 2012.

Hill, Ruth Edmonds, ed. *The Black Women Oral History Project: from the Arthur and Elizabeth Schlesinger Library on the History of Women in America, Radcliffe College.* Westport, CT: Meckler, 1991.

Hine, Darlene Clark, and Kathleen Thompson. *A Shining Thread of Hope: The History of Black Women in America.* New York: Broadway Books, 1998.

Hirsch, Arnold. *Making the Second Ghetto: Race and Housing in Chicago 1940–1960.* Chicago: Chicago University Press, 1998.

Hogan, Wesley C. *Many Minds, One Heart: SNCC's Dream for a New America.* Chapel Hill: University of North Carolina Press, 2007.

Höhn, Maria. "The Black Panther Solidarity Committees and the *Voice of the Lumpen*." *German Studies Review* 31 (February 2008): 133–154.

Holsaert, Faith S., Martha Prescod Norman Noonan, Judy Richardson, Betty Garman Robinson, Jean Smith Young, and Dorothy M. Zellner, eds. *Hands on the Freedom Plow: Personal Accounts by Women in SNCC.* Urbana: University of Illinois Press, 2010.

hooks, bell. *Killing Rage: Ending Racism.* New York: Henry Holt, 1995.

Horne, Gerald. *Black Revolutionary: William Patterson and the Globalization of the African American Freedom Struggle.* Urbana: University of Illinois Press, 2013.

Horne, Gerald. *Race Woman: The Lives of Shirley Graham Du Bois.* New York: New York University Press, 2000.

Jackson, Thomas F. *From Civil Rights to Human Rights: Martin Luther King, Jr., and the Struggle for Economic Justice.* Philadelphia: University of Pennsylvania Press, 2007.

Jaffe, Harry S., and Tom Sherwood. *Dream City: Race, Power, and the Decline of Washington, D.C.* New York: Simon & Schuster, 1994.

James, Joy, ed. *The Angela Y. Davis Reader.* Malden, MA: Blackwell, 1998.

James, Winston. *Holding Aloft the Banner of Ethiopia: Caribbean Radicalism in Early Twentieth-Century America.* London; New York: Verso, 1998.

Jeffries, Hasan Kwame. *Bloody Lowndes: Civil Rights and Black Power in Alabama's Black Belt.* New York: New York University Press, 2009.

Jeffries, Judson L., ed. *Comrades: A Local History of the Black Panther Party*. Bloomington: Indiana University Press, 2007.

Johnson, Cedric. *Revolutionaries to Race Leaders: Black Power and the Making of African American Politics*. Minneapolis: University of Minnesota Press, 2007.

Jones, Charles E., ed. *The Black Panther Party [Reconsidered]*. Baltimore: Black Classic Press, 1998.

Jones, William P. *The March on Washington: Jobs, Freedom, and the Forgotten History of Civil Rights*. New York: W. W. Norton, 2013.

Joseph, Peniel E., ed. *The Black Power Movement: Rethinking the Civil Rights-Black Power Era*. New York: Routledge, 2006.

Joseph, Peniel E. *Dark Days, Bright Nights: From Black Power to Barack Obama*. New York: Basic Civitas Books, 2010.

Joseph, Peniel E., ed. *Neighborhood Rebels: Black Power at the Local Level*. New York: Palgrave Macmillan, 2010.

Joseph, Peniel E. *Stokely: A Life*. New York: Basic Civitas, 2014.

Joseph, Peniel E. *Waiting 'Til the Midnight Hour: A Narrative History of Black Power in America*. New York: Henry Holt, 2006.

Josephy, Alvin M., Jr., Joane Nagel, and Troy Johnson, eds. *Red Power: The American Indians' Fight for Freedom*. 2nd Ed. Lincoln, NE: University of Nebraska Press, 1999.

Keating, W. Dennis. *The Suburban Racial Dilemma: Housing and Neighborhoods*. Philadelphia: Temple University Press, 1994.

Kelley, Robin D.G. *Freedom Dreams: The Black Radical Imagination*. Boston: Beacon Press, 2002.

Kelley, Robin D.G. *Hammer and Hoe: Alabama Communists during the Great Depression*. Chapel Hill: University of North Carolina Press, 1990.

Kelley, Robin D.G. *Race Rebels: Culture, Politics, and the Black Working Class*. New York: Free Press, 1994.

Kelley, Robin D.G., and Betsy Esch, "Black Like Mao: Red China and Black Revolution." *Souls* (Fall 1999): 6–41.

Kelley, Robin D.G., and Earl Lewis, eds. *To Make Our World Anew: A History of African Americans*. New York: Oxford University Press, 2000.

Kenan, Randall, ed. *The Cross of Redemption: Uncollected Writings*. New York: Pantheon Books, 2010.

Kennedy, Flo. *Color Me Flo: My Hard Life and Good Times*. Englewood Cliffs, NJ: Prentice-Hall, 1976.

Kerby, Phil. *With Honor and Purpose*. New York: St. Martin's Press, 1998.

Klimke, Martin. "The African American Civil Rights Struggle and Germany, 1945–1989." *Bulletin of the German Historical Institute* 43 (Fall 2008): 91–106.

Klimke, Martin. *The Other Alliance: Student Protest in West Germany and the United States in the Global Sixties*. Princeton: Princeton University Press, 2010.

Kluger, Richard. *Simple Justice: The History of Brown v. Board of Education and Black America's Struggle for Equality*. New York: Alfred A. Knopf, 1975.

Kochiyama, Yuri. *Passing It On: A Memoir*. Los Angeles: UCLA Asian American Studies Center Press, 2004.

Kusmer, Kenneth L., and Joe W. Trotter, eds. *African American Urban History since World War II*. Chicago: University of Chicago Press, 2009.

Ladner, Joyce A. *Tomorrow's Tomorrow: The Black Woman*. Garden City, NY: Doubleday, 1971.

Lang, Clarence. *Grassroots at the Gateway: Class Politics and Black Freedom Struggle in St. Louis, 1936–75.* Ann Arbor: University of Michigan Press, 2009.

Lawson, Steven F. *Running for Freedom: Civil Rights and Black Politics in America since 1941.* 3rd Ed. Malden, MA: Wiley-Blackwell, 2009.

Lee, Chana Kai. *For Freedom's Sake: The Life of Fannie Lou Hamer.* Urbana: University of Illinois Press, 1999.

Lerner, Gerda, ed. *Black Women in White America: A Documentary History.* 1972. Reprint, New York: Vintage, 1992.

Lester, Julius. *Look Out Whitey! Black Power's Gon' Get Your Mama!* New York: Grove Press, 1968.

Levine, Daniel U., Norman S. Fiddmont, Robert S. Stephenson, and Charles Wilkinson. "Differences Between Black Youth Who Support the Black Panthers and the NAACP." *Journal of Negro Education* 42 (Winter 1973): 19–32.

Levy, Peter B. *Civil War on Race Street: The Civil Rights Movement in Cambridge, Maryland.* Gainesville: University Press of Florida, 2003.

Lewis, David Levering. *W.E.B. Du Bois: The Fight for Equality and the American Century, 1919–1963.* New York: Henry Holt, 2000.

Locke, Alain, ed. *New Negro.* 1925. Reprinted with an introduction by Arnold Rampersad. New York: Macmillan, 1992.

Lomax, Louis E. *When the Word is Given: A Report on Elijah Muhammad, Malcolm X, and the Black Muslim World.* Cleveland: World Publishing Company, 1963.

Lorde, Audre. *Sister Outsider: Essays and Speeches.* Freedom, CA: Crossing Press, 1984.

Lydon, Jane. *The Flash of Recognition: Photography and the Emergence of Indigenous Rights.* Sydney, Australia: NewSouth Publishing, 2012.

Lyles, Charlise. *Do I Dare Disturb the Universe?: From the Projects to Prep School.* Boston: Faber and Faber, 1994.

Macfarlane, Ingereth, and Mark Hannah, eds. *Transgressions: Critical Australian Indigenous Histories.* Canberra: Australian National University E Press and Aboriginal History, 2007.

Maeda, Daryl J. *Chains of Babylon: The Rise of Asian America.* Minneapolis: University of Minnesota Press, 2009.

Major, Reginald. *A Panther Is a Black Cat.* New York: W. Morrow, 1971.

Malcolm X, with Alex Haley. *The Autobiography of Malcolm X.* New York: Grove Press, 1965.

Mantler, Gordon K. *Power to the Poor: Black-Brown Coalition and the Fight for Economic Justice, 1960–1974.* Chapel Hill: University of North Carolina Press, 2013.

Marable, Manning. *Malcolm X: A Life of Reinvention.* New York: Viking, 2011.

Marable, Manning, and Elizabeth Kai Hinton, eds. *The New Black History: Revising the Second Reconstruction.* New York: Palgrave Macmillan, 2011.

Marable, Manning, and Leith Mullings, eds. *Let Nobody Turn Us Around: Voices of Resistance, Reform, and Renewal: An African American Anthology.* 2nd Ed. Lanham, MD: Rowman & Littlefield, 2009.

Marcus Garvey: Look for Me in the Whirlwind. Directed by Stanley Nelson. New York: Firelight Media, Inc. (American Experience-PBS), 2000.

Marqusee, Mike. *Redemption Song: Muhammad Ali and the Spirit of the Sixties.* New York: Verso, 1999.

Martin, Charles H. "Race, Gender, and Southern Justice: The Rosa Lee Ingram Case." *American Journal of Legal History* 29 (July 1985): 251–268.

Martin, Tony. *Marcus Garvey, Hero: A First Biography.* Dover, MA: Majority Press, 1983.

Mast, Robert H., ed. *Detroit Lives.* Philadelphia: Temple University Press, 1994.

Maynard, John. "'In the Interests of Our People': The Influence of Garveyism on the Rise of Australian Aboriginal Political Activism." *Aboriginal History* 29 (2005): 1–22.

McCoy, Alfred W. *The Politics of Heroin: CIA Complicity in the Global Drug Trade.* Revised Ed. Chicago: Lawrence Hill Books, 2003.

McDuffie, Erik S. "'I Wanted a Communist Philosophy, but I Wanted Us to Have a Chance to Organize Our People': The Diasporic Radicalism of Queen Mother Audley Moore and the Origins of Black Power." *African and Black Diaspora: An International Journal* 3:2 (2010): 181–195.

McDuffie, Erik S. "A 'New Freedom Movement of Negro Women': Sojourning for Truth, Justice, and Human Rights during the Early Cold War." *Radical History Review* 101 (Spring 2008): 81–106.

McDuffie, Erik S. *Sojourning for Freedom: Black Women, American Communism, and the Making of Black Left Feminism.* Durham: Duke University Press, 2011.

McDuffie, Erik S., and Komozi Woodard. "'If You're a Country That's Progressive, the Woman Is Progressive': Black Women Radicals and The Making of the Politics and Legacy of Malcolm X." *Biography* 36 (Summer 2013): 507–539.

McGregor, Russell. *Indifferent Inclusion: Aboriginal People and the Australian Nation.* Canberra, Australia: Aboriginal Studies Press, 2011.

Meier, August, ed. *Black Protest Thought in the Twentieth Century.* Indianapolis: Bobbs-Merrill, 1971.

Meredith, Martin. *The Fate of Africa: A History of Fifty Years of Independence.* New York: Public Affairs, 2005.

Meriwether, James H. *Proudly We Can Be Africans: Black Americans and Africa, 1935–1961.* Chapel Hill: University of North Carolina Press, 2002.

Michney, Todd M. "Constrained Communities: Black Cleveland's Experience with World War II Public Housing," *Journal of Social History* 40 (Summer 2007): 933–956.

Michney, Todd M. "Race, Violence, and Urban Territoriality: Cleveland's Little Italy and the 1966 Hough Uprising." *Journal of Urban History* 32 (March 2006): 404–428.

Moore, Leonard N. *Carl B. Stokes and the Rise of Black Political Power.* Urbana: University of Illinois Press, 2002.

Mullen, Bill V. *Afro-Orientalism.* Minneapolis: University of Minnesota Press, 2004.

Mullen, Bill V. "Transnational Correspondence: Robert F. Williams, Detroit, and the Bandung Era." *Works and Days* 20 (2002): 189–215.

Munro, John. "Ethiopia Stretches Forth Across the Atlantic: African American Anticolonialism during the Interwar Period." *Left History* 13:2 (Fall/Winter 2008), 37–63.

Murch, Donna. *Living for the City: Migration, Education, and the Rise of the Black Panther Party in Oakland, California.* Chapel Hill: University of North Carolina Press, 2010.

Musgrove, George Derek. *Rumor, Repression, and Racial Politics: How the Harassment of Black Elected Officials Shaped Post-Civil Rights America.* Athens, GA: University of Georgia Press, 2012.

Nadasen, Premilla. *Welfare Warriors: The Welfare Rights Movement in the United States.* New York: Routledge, 2005.

National Black Sisters' Conference. *Black Survival: Past, Present, and Future.* National Black Sisters' Conference, Pittsburgh, PA, 1970.

Nelson, Alondra. *Body and Soul: The Black Panther Party and the Fight Against Medical Discrimination.* Minneapolis: University of Minnesota Press, 2011.

Ongiri, Amy Abugo. *Spectacular Blackness: The Cultural Politics of the Black Power Movement and the Search for a Black Aesthetic.* Charlottesville: University of Virginia Press, 2010.

Orleck, Annelise. *Storming Caesars Palace: How Black Mothers Fought Their Own War on Poverty*. Boston: Beacon Press, 2005.

Orleck, Annelise, and Lisa Gayle Hazirjian, eds. *The War on Poverty: A New Grassroots History, 1964–1980*. Athens, GA: University of Georgia Press, 2011.

Palmer, Colin A. *Passageways: An Interpretive History of Black America. Volume II: 1863–1965*. Fort Worth, TX: Harcourt Brace College Publishers, 1999.

Payne, Charles M. *I've Got the Light of Freedom: The Organizing Tradition and the Mississippi Freedom Struggle*. Berkeley: University of California Press, 1995.

Payne, Charles M., and Adam Green, eds. *Time Longer than Rope: A Century of African American Activism, 1850–1950*. New York: New York University Press, 2003.

Perry, Jeffrey B., ed. *A Hubert Harrison Reader*. Middletown, CT: Wesleyan University Press, 2001.

Peters, Kurt, and Terry Straus, eds. *Visions and Voices: American Indian Activism and the Civil Rights Movement*. New York: Albatross Press, 2009.

Plummer, Brenda Gayle. *In Search of Power: African Americans in the Era of Decolonization, 1956–1974*. New York: Cambridge University Press, 2013.

Plummer, Brenda Gayle. *Rising Wind: Black Americans and U.S. Foreign Affairs, 1935–1960*. Chapel Hill: University of North Carolina Press, 1996.

Prashad, Vijay. *The Darker Nations: A People's History of the Third World*. New York: New Press, 2007.

Pulido, Laura. *Black, Brown, Yellow, and Left: Radical Activism in Los Angeles*. Berkeley: University of California Press, 2006.

Ransby, Barbara. *Ella Baker and the Black Freedom Movement: A Radical Democratic Vision*. Chapel Hill: University of North Carolina Press, 2003.

Ransby, Barbara. *Eslanda: The Large and Unconventional Life of Mrs. Paul Robeson*. New Haven, CT: Yale University Press, 2013.

Reitan, Ruth. "Cuba, the Black Panther Party and the US Black Movement in the 1960s: Issues of Security." *New Political Science* 21:2 (1999): 217–230.

Reynolds, Henry. *Why Weren't We Told?: A Personal Search for the Truth about Our History*. New York: Penguin, 2000.

Richie, Beth. *Arrested Justice: Black Women, Violence, and America's Prison Nation*. New York: New York University Press, 2012.

Robeson, Paul. *Here I Stand*. Boston: Beacon Press, 1958.

Robinson, Cedric J. *Black Marxism: The Making of the Black Radical Tradition*. 1983. Reprint, Chapel Hill: University of North Carolina Press, 2000.

Robinson, Cedric J. *Black Movements in America*. New York: Routledge, 1997.

Robinson, Lewis G. *The Making of a Man: An Autobiography*. Cleveland, OH: Green & Sons, 1970.

Rogers, Ibram H. *The Black Campus Movement: Black Students and the Racial Reconstitution of Higher Education, 1965–1972*. New York: Palgrave Macmillan, 2012.

Rojas, Fabio. *From Black Power to Black Studies: How a Radical Social Movement Became an Academic Discipline*. Baltimore: Johns Hopkins University Press, 2007.

Rolinson, Mary G. *Grassroots Garveyism: The Universal Negro Improvement Association in the Rural South, 1920–1927*. Chapel Hill: University of North Carolina Press, 2007.

Roth, Benita. *Separate Roads to Feminism: Black, Chicana, and White Feminist Movements in America's Second Wave*. Cambridge, UK; New York: Cambridge University Press, 2004.

Rowley, Hazel. *Richard Wright: The Life and Times*. New York: Henry Holt, 2001.

Ruiz, Vicki L., with Ellen Carol DuBois, eds. *Unequal Sisters: An Inclusive Reader in U.S. Women's History*. 4th Ed. New York: Routledge, 2008.

Sales, William W. *From Civil Rights to Black Liberation: Malcolm X and the Organization of Afro-American Unity*. Boston: South End Press, 1994.

Scott, Carl-Gustaf. "Swedish Sanctuary of American Deserters During the Vietnam War: A Facet of Social Democratic Domestic Politics." *Scandinavian Journal of History* 26:2 (2001): 123–142.

Self, Robert O. *American Babylon: Race and Struggle for Postwar Oakland*. Princeton: Princeton University Press, 2003.

Sellers, Cleveland, with Robert Terrell. *The River of No Return: The Autobiography of a Black Militant and the Life and Death of SNCC*. 1973. Reprint, Jackson: University Press of Mississippi, 1990.

Shakur, Assata. *Assata: An Autobiography*. Westport, CT: Lawrence Hill, 1987.

Shaw, Todd C. *Now Is the Time!: Detroit Black Politics and Grassroots Activism*. Durham: Duke University Press, 2009.

Simone, Nina, with Stephen Cleary. *I Put a Spell on You: The Autobiography of Nina Simone*. New York: Pantheon, 1991.

Singh, Nikhil Pal. *Black Is a Country: Race and the Unfinished Struggle for Democracy*. Cambridge, MA: Harvard University Press, 2005.

Slate, Nico, ed. *Black Power Beyond Borders: The Global Dimensions of the Black Power Movement*. New York: Palgrave Macmillan, 2012.

Smethurst, James Edward. *The Black Arts Movement: Literary Nationalism in the 1960s and 1970s*. Chapel Hill: University of North Carolina Press, 2005.

Smith, Jean Carney, ed. *Notable Black American Women Book II*. Detroit: Gale Research Group, 1996.

Smith, Paul Chaat, and Robert Allen Warrior. *Like a Hurricane: The Indian Movement from Alcatraz to Wounded Knee*. New York: New Press, 1996.

Sobel, Lester A., ed. *Welfare & the Poor*. New York: Facts on File, 1977.

Sonnie, Amy, and James Tracy. *Hillbilly Nationalists, Urban Race Rebels, and Black Power: Community Organizing in Radical Times*. Brooklyn, NY: Melville House, 2011.

Springer, Kimberly. *Living for the Revolution: Black Feminist Organizations, 1968–1980*. Durham: Duke University Press, 2005.

Springer, Kimberly, ed. *Still Lifting, Still Climbing: Contemporary African American Women's Activism*. New York: New York University Press, 1999.

Stokes, Carl. *Promises of Power: A Political Autobiography*. New York: Simon & Schuster, 1973.

Stone, Chuck. *Black Political Power in America*. Indianapolis: Bobbs-Merrill, 1968.

Stone, Eddie. *Donald Writes No More: A Biography of Donald Goines*. Los Angeles: Holloway House Publishing Company, 1977.

Strain, Christopher B. *Pure Fire: Self-Defense as Activism in the Civil Rights Era*. Athens, GA: University of Georgia Press, 2005.

Sugrue, Thomas J. *The Origins of the Urban Crisis: Race and Inequality in Postwar Detroit*. Princeton: Princeton University Press, 2005.

Sugrue, Thomas J. *Sweet Land of Liberty: The Forgotten Struggle for Civil Rights in the North*. New York: Random House, 2008.

Taylor, Ula Yvette. *The Veiled Garvey: The Life & Times of Amy Jacques Garvey*. Chapel Hill: University of North Carolina Press, 2002.

Theoharis, Jeanne. *The Rebellious Life of Mrs. Rosa Parks*. Boston: Beacon Press, 2013.

Theoharis, Jeanne E., and Komozi Woodard, eds. *Freedom North: Black Freedom Struggles Outside the South, 1940–1980*. New York: Palgrave Macmillan, 2003.

Theoharis, Jeanne E. and Komozi Woodard, eds. *Groundwork: Local Black Freedom Movements in America*. New York: New York University Press, 2005.

Thompson, Heather Ann. *Whose Detroit?: Politics, Labor, and Race in a Modern American City.* Ithaca: Cornell University Press, 2001.

Thompson, Heather Ann. "Why Mass Incarceration Matters: Rethinking Crisis, Decline, and Transforming in Postwar American History." *Journal of American History* 97 (December 2010): 703–734.

Torres, Andrés, and José E. Velázquez, eds. *The Puerto Rican Movement: Voices from the Diaspora.* Philadelphia: Temple University Press, 1998.

Turner, Ann, ed. *Black Power in Australia: Bobbi Sykes versus Neville T. Bonner.* South Yarra, Australia: Heinemann Educational Australia, 1975.

Tyson, Timothy B. *Radio Free Dixie: Robert F. Williams & The Roots of Black Power.* Chapel Hill: University of North Carolina Press, 1999.

Tyson, Timothy B. "Robert F. Williams, 'Black Power,' and the Roots of the African American Freedom Struggle." *Journal of American History* 85 (September 1998): 540–570.

Umoja, Akinyele Omowale. *We Will Shoot Back: Armed Resistance in the Mississippi Freedom Movement.* New York: New York University Press, 2013.

United States House of Representatives, Committee on Internal Security. *The Black Panther Party, Its Origin and Development as Reflected in Its Official Weekly Newspaper The Black Panther Black Community News Service,* 91st Congress, 2nd Session. Washington D.C.: U.S. Government Printing Office, 1970.

United States House of Representatives, Committee on Internal Security, *Gun-Barrel Politics: The Black Panther Party, 1966–1971,* 92nd Congress, 1st Session. Washington, D.C.: U.S. Government Printing Office, 1971.

Valk, Anne M. "'Mother Power': The Movement for Welfare Rights in Washington, D.C., 1962–1972." *Journal of Women's History* 11 (February 2000): 34–58.

Valk, Anne M. *Radical Sisters: Second-Wave Feminism and Black Liberation in Washington, D.C.* Urbana: University of Illinois Press, 2008.

Van DeBurg, William L., ed. *Modern Black Nationalism: From Marcus Garvey to Louis Farrakhan.* New York: New York University Press, 1997.

Van DeBurg, William L. *New Day in Babylon: The Black Power Movement and American Culture, 1965–1975.* Chicago: University of Chicago Press, 1993.

Vincent, Theodore G. *Black Power and the Garvey Movement.* Berkeley: Ramparts Press, 1971.

Von Eschen, Penny M. *Race Against Empire: Black Americans and Anticolonialism, 1937–1957.* Ithaca: Cornell University Press, 1997.

Walker, Alice, ed. *I Love Myself When I Am Laughing . . . And Then Again When I Am Looking Mean and Impressive.* Old Westbury, NY: The Feminist Press, 1979.

Walker, Margaret. *Richard Wright, Daemonic Genius: A Portrait of the Man, A Critical Look at His Work.* New York: Warner Books, 1988.

Wallace, Michele. *Black Macho and the Myth of the Superwoman.* New York: Dial Press, 1979.

Ward, Stephen M., ed. *Pages from a Black Radical's Notebook: A James Boggs Reader.* Detroit: Wayne State University Press, 2011.

Washington, James Melvin, ed. *A Testament of Hope: The Essential Writings of Martin Luther King, Jr.* San Francisco: Harper & Row, 1986.

Watkins-Owens, Irma. *Blood Relations: Caribbean Immigrants and the Harlem Community, 1900–1930.* Bloomington: Indiana University Press, 1996.

Weaver, Vesla M. "Frontlash: Race and the Development of Punitive Crime Policy." *Studies in American Political Development* 21 (Fall 2007): 230–265.

Webb, Constance. *Richard Wright: A Biography.* New York: Putnam, 1968.

Weems, Robert E., Jr., and Lewis A. Randolph. "The Ideological Origins of Richard M. Nixon's 'Black Capitalism' Initiative." *Review of Black Political Economy* 29 (Summer 2001): 49–61.

Weems, Robert E., Jr., and Lewis A. Randolph. "The National Response to Richard M. Nixon's Black Capitalism Initiative." *Journal of Black Studies* 32 (September 2001): 66–83.

Weigand, Kate. *Red Feminism: American Communism and the Making of Women's Liberation.* Baltimore: Johns Hopkins University Press, 2001.

West, Michael O., William G. Martin, and Fanon Che Wilkins, eds. *From Toussaint to Tupac: The Black International Since the Age of Revolution.* Chapel Hill: University of North Carolina Press, 2009.

Williams, Evelyn A. *Inadmissible Evidence: The Story of the African-American Trial Lawyers Who Defended the Black Liberation Army.* Lincoln, NE: iUniverse.com, 2000.

Williams, Jakobi. *From the Bullet to the Ballot: The Illinois Chapter of the Black Panther Party and Racial Coalition Politics in Chicago.* Chapel Hill: University of North Carolina Press, 2013.

Williams, Rhonda Y. *The Politics of Public Housing: Black Women's Struggles against Urban Inequality.* New York: Oxford University Press, 2004.

Williams, Rhonda Y. "We're Tired of Being Treated Like Dogs": Poor Women and Power Politics in Black Baltimore." *Black Scholar* 31 (Fall/Winter 2001): 31–41.

Williams, Robert F. *Negroes with Guns.* 1962. Reprint with an introduction by Timothy B. Tyson, Detroit: Wayne University Press, 1998.

Williams, Shannen Dee. "Black Nuns and the Struggle to Desegregate Catholic America after World War I." PhD dissertation, Rutgers University, 2013.

Williams, Yohuru. "American Exported Black Nationalism: The Student Nonviolent Coordinating Committee, the Black Panther Party, and the Worldwide Freedom Struggle, 1967–1972." *Negro History Bulletin* 60 (July/September 1997): 13–20.

Williams, Yohuru. *Black Politics/White Power: Civil Rights, Black Power, and the Black Panthers in New Haven.* Malden, MA: Blackwell, 2008.

Williams, Yohuru, and Jama Lazerow, eds. *Liberated Territory: Untold Local Perspectives on the Black Panther Party.* Durham: Duke University Press, 2008.

Woodard, Komozi. *A Nation Within a Nation: Amiri Baraka (LeRoi Jones) and Black Power Politics.* Chapel Hill: University of North Carolina Press, 1999.

Wright, Nathan, Jr. *Black Power and Urban Unrest: Creative Possibilities.* New York: Hawthorn Books, 1967.

Wright, Richard. *Black Power: Three Books from Exile: Black Power, The Color Curtain, and White Man, Listen!* New York: Harper Perennial Modern Classics, 2008.

Young, Cynthia A. *Soul Power: Culture, Radicalism, and the Making of a U.S. Third World Left.* Durham: Duke University Press, 2006.

Zinn, Howard. *A People's History of the United States.* New York: HarperPerennial, 2003.

INDEX